The History and Theory of Rhetoric

By tracing the traditional progression of rhetoric from the Greek Sophists to contemporary theorists, *The History and Theory of Rhetoric* illustrates how persuasive public discourse performs essential social functions and shapes our daily worlds. Students gain a conceptual framework for evaluating and practicing persuasive writing and speaking in a wide range of settings and in various written and visual media. This new 6th edition includes greater attention to non-Western studies, as well as contemporary developments such as the rhetoric of science, feminist rhetoric, the rhetoric of display, and comparative rhetoric. Known for its clear writing style and contemporary examples throughout, *The History and Theory of Rhetoric* emphasizes the relevance of rhetoric to today's students.

James A. Herrick is Guy Vander Jagt Professor of Communication at Hope College, USA. His publications include *Argumentation: Understanding and Shaping Arguments*, *6th edition* (2017) and *Visions of Technological Transcendence: Human Enhancement and the Rhetoric of the Future* (2017).

6th Edition

The History and Theory of Rhetoric

An Introduction

James A. Herrick

Routledge
Taylor & Francis Group

NEW YORK AND LONDON

Sixth edition published 2018
by Routledge
711 Third Avenue, New York, NY 10017

and by Routledge
2 Park Square, Milton Park, Abingdon, Oxon, OX14 4RN

Routledge is an imprint of the Taylor & Francis Group, an informa business

First published by Pearson Education, Inc. 2005
Fifth edition published by Pearson Education, Inc. 2013

Library of Congress Cataloguing in Publication Data
Names: Herrick, James A., author.
Title: The history and theory of rhetoric: an introduction / James Herrick.
Description: 6th edition. | Abingdon, Oxon ; New York : Routledge, 2018. |
Includes bibliographical references and index.
Identifiers: LCCN 2017008894| ISBN 9781138223660 (hardback) |
ISBN 9781138223677 (pbk.) | ISBN 9781315404141 (ebk.)
Subjects: LCSH: Rhetoric—History. | Rhetoric.
Classification: LCC PN183 .H47 2018 | DDC 808.009—dc23
LC record available at https://lccn.loc.gov/2017008894

ISBN: 978-1-138-22366-0 (hbk)
ISBN: 978-1-138-22367-7 (pbk)
ISBN: 978-1-315-40414-1 (ebk)

Typeset in Times New Roman PS and Futura
by Florence Production Ltd, Stoodleigh, Devon UK

Visit the companion website: www.routledge.com/cw/herrick

Contents

Preface   xii

1 An Overview of Rhetoric   1

   Re-evaluating Rhetoric 3

Rhetoric and Persuasion 4

Defining Rhetoric 6
   Rhetoric and Symbol Systems 6
   Effective Symbolic Expression 8

Rhetorical Discourse 9
   Rhetoric Is Planned 9
   Rhetoric Is Adapted to an Audience 10
   Rhetoric Reveals Human Motives 11
   Rhetoric Is Responsive 12
   Rhetoric Seeks Persuasion 13
   Rhetoric Addresses Contingent Issues 16

Social Functions of the Art of Rhetoric 17
   Rhetoric Tests Ideas 17
   Rhetoric Assists Advocacy 18
   Rhetoric Distributes Power 19
   Rhetoric Discovers Facts 20
   Rhetoric Shapes Knowledge 21
   Rhetoric Builds Community 22

Conclusion 23
   Recurrent Themes 23

Questions for Review 25

Questions for Discussion 25

Terms 30

2 The Origins and Early History of Rhetoric   33

The Rise of Rhetoric 34
   Athenian Democratic Reforms 34
   Education in Athens 36
   Courts and Assemblies in Athens 37

The Sophists 38
   The Flourishing of Athens 39
   The Sophists' Reputation 39
   What the Sophists Taught 40
   How the Sophists Taught 41
   Why the Sophists Were Controversial 42

Two Influential Sophists 45
   Gorgias 45
   Gorgias' Encomium and Rhetorical Devices 46
   Protagoras 48

Isocrates: A Master of Rhetoric 49
   Isocrates the Teacher 50
   Isocrates the Political Theorist 52

Women Writers of Ancient Greece 52
   Sayings of the Spartan Women 53
   Aspasia 54
   Sappho 54

Conclusion 55

Questions for Review 57

Questions for Discussion 57

Terms 58

3 Plato versus the Sophists: Rhetoric on Trial   63

Plato's Gorgias: Rhetoric on Trial 64
   The Debate with Gorgias*: Rhetoric's Nature and Uses 65*
   Socrates versus Polus: Rhetoric as Power 67
   Socrates versus Callicles: The Strong Survive 70
   The Outcome of the Gorgias 72
   Is Plato Fair to Rhetoric and the Sophists? 72

Rhetoric in Plato's *Phaedrus*: A True Art? 73
   Components of a Techne *of Rhetoric 75*
   Rhetoric as Soulcraft 76

Conclusion 78

Questions for Review 79

Questions for Discussion 79

Terms 80

4 Aristotle on Rhetoric 83

Defining Rhetoric 84
 Rhetoric and Dialectic 84

Dialectic and Rhetoric: Similarities and Differences 85
 Similarities 85
 Differences 85
 Rhetoric as a Techne *of Discovery 86*

The Enthymeme 88
 An Argument Constructed with the Audience 88
 A Democratic Argument 89

Three Rhetorical Settings 90
 Deliberative Oratory 90
 Epideictic Oratory 91
 Forensic Oratory 92

The Artistic Proofs 93
 Logos*: The Logic of Sound Arguments 93*
 Pathos*: The Psychology of Emotion 93*
 Ethos*: The Sociology of Good Character 95*

Topoi: Lines of Argument 96
 Special Topics 96
 Common Topics 96
 Some Common Fallacies 97

Aristotle on Style 98
 Metaphors and Other Devices 98

Conclusion 99

Questions for Review 99

Questions for Discussion 100

Terms 100

5 Rhetoric at Rome 104

Roman Society and the Place of Rhetoric 105
 Rhetoric and Political Power 105
 Rhetoric and Roman Education 108
 The Rhetorical Theory of Cicero 109
 De Inventione *109*
 Studying Invention and Memory 111
 Cicero's De Oratore *114*
 The End of Cicero's Life 118

Quintilian 118
 The Toga 119
 Rhetoric and the Good Citizen 120
 Educating the Citizen–Orator 120

Contents

Longinus: On the Sublime 122
  The Emotive Power of Language 122

Rhetoric in the Later Roman Empire 126
  The Second Sophistic 126

Conclusion 128

Questions for Review 128

Questions for Discussion 129

Terms 129

6 Rhetoric in Christian Europe   134

Rhetoric, Tension, and Fragmentation 134

Rhetoric in the Early Middle Ages 136
  St. Augustine 136
  Augustine's Rhetorical Theory 137
  De Doctrina Christiana 138
  Augustine and Rhetorical Education 139
  Martianus Capella 140
  Boethius 141

Rhetoric and Medieval Education 142
  Disputatio and Sentenniae 142
  Women and Education 142
  Rhetorical Continuity 143

Rhetorical Arts in the High Middle Ages 144
  The Art of Preaching 144
  The Art of Letter Writing 146
  Letter-Writing Skill 148
  Women and Letter Writing 150
  The Art of Poetry 152
  Marie de France 155

Conclusion 156

Questions for Review 157

Questions for Discussion 157

Terms 158

7 Rhetoric in the Renaissance   163

Italian Humanism 165
  Marks of the Umanista *165*
  Notaries 166
  Petrarch 168
  Christine de Pisan 169
  Pico dello Mirandola 171
  Lorenzo Valla 172
  Juan Luis Vives 174

Rhetoric and Renaissance Education 175
Rhetoric and Renaissance Art 177

The Turn Toward Dialectic 178
Agricola 178
Peter Ramus 179

Renaissance Rhetoric in Britain 180
Teaching Rhetoric 180
Magic, Science, and Style 181

The Late Renaissance and Conversational Rhetoric 182
Madame Madeleine de Scudéry 182

Conclusion 183

Questions for Review 183

Questions for Discussion 184

Terms 184

8 Enlightenment Rhetoric   **189**

Rhetoric's Changing Roles 190

Margaret Cavendish 190
Writing Career 191

Vico and the Rhetoric of Human Thought 191
Vico versus Descartes 192
Rhetoric and Imagination 192
Rhetoric and the Evolution of Human Thought 194
Vico on Myth: The Civilization-Shaping Force of Narrative 194
Influence 195

British Rhetoric in the Eighteenth Century 195
Rhetoric in British Education 196
The Elocutionary Movement 197

The Scottish School 198
The Belletristic Movement 199
George Campbell 202
Richard Whately Revives Classical Rhetoric 205
Maria Edgeworth 207

Conclusion 208

Questions for Review 209

Questions for Discussion 209

Terms 210

9 Contemporary Rhetoric I: Arguments, Audiences, and Advocates   **215**

Argumentation and Rational Discourse 216
Perelman and Olbrechts-Tyteca: A New Rhetoric 216

The Centrality of Audience 217
Jürgen Habermas on a Rational Society 220

The Rhetoric of Science 223
Precursors 224
A Rhetorical Approach to Science 226
The Power of Unexamined Science 226
Advocacy in the Sciences 227
Science and Communities 227
Deirdre McCloskey and the Rhetoric of Economics 228
Rhetoric in Anthropology 228
John Campbell on the Rhetoric of Charles Darwin 229

Conclusion 232

Questions for Review 233

Questions for Discussion 233

Terms 234

10 Contemporary Rhetoric II: Situation, Story, Display   **239**

Rhetoric in Context 239
Kenneth Burke and Rhetoric as Symbolic Action 240
Lloyd Bitzer and Rhetoric as Situational 247

Rhetoric and Narration 249
Changes 249
Mikhail Bakhtin and the Polyphonic Novel 250
Wayne Booth and the Rhetoric of Fiction 252
Authors as Advocates 252
Reflecting on Narrative 253
Walter Fisher on the Rhetoric of Narration 253
Ernest Bormann on Stories and Communities 255

The Rhetoric of Display 256

Digital Rhetorics 257
The Architecture of the Online Experience 257
Andrea Lundford's New Literacy 258

Conclusion 259

Questions for Review 259

Questions for Discussion 260

Terms 260

11 Contemporary Rhetoric III: Texts, Power, Alternatives   **265**

Postmodern Rhetoric 266
Questioning the "Taken for Granted" 266
Jean-Francois Lyotard and Postmodernism 267
Michel Foucault 268

Queer Theory 271
Jacques Derrida 272

Feminism and Rhetoric: Critique and Reform 275
The Loss of a Woman's Voice 276
Reconceptualizing Rhetoric 277
Constructing Gender Rhetorically 278
Rhetoric as Conquest 278
Rhetoric as Invitation 280
"Works," "Texts," and the Work of Reading 280
Feminism and the Ancient Tradition 281

Comparative Rhetoric 282
African Rhetorical Forms 282
George Kennedy on Non-European Rhetorics 283
Aztec and Egyptian Rhetorics 283
Rhetoric in Ancient China 284
"Private Speaking" 284
Chinese Sophists and the Intrigues of the Warring States 285
Jian, Shui, Pien, and the Traveling Persuaders 286
Averroes and the Aristotelian Tradition: Arabic Rhetoric in the Twelfth Century 286
Re-visioning the Greek Tradition 288

Conclusion 288

Questions for Review 289

Questions for Discussion 290

Terms 291

Glossary 297
Bibliography 307
Index 321

Preface

MY goal in the 6th edition of *The History and Theory of Rhetoric*, as in previous editions, is to provide students with an engaging and accessible survey of the history of rhetoric as it has developed in the Western world. This text also equips students with a conceptual framework for evaluating and practicing persuasive writing and speaking in a wide range of settings and in various written and visual media.

Each chapter introduces readers to influential theories of rhetoric advanced by some of history's greatest thinkers. Through encountering the rhetorical tradition, students are better prepared to understand and participate in the wide array of persuasive symbolic practices that mark our social and private lives. The principles and developments discussed here should assist students to recognize and evaluate rhetorical qualities in a wide range of texts, including the growing digital world.

NEW TO THIS EDITION

In this edition, I have paid more attention to reorganizing and rewriting several chapters for greater clarity and accessibility. I trust the writing is clear and the material, though occasionally technical, is easily comprehensible. I have also eliminated discussions of several topics that seemed no longer current. The presentation of material has been stream-lined throughout; I hope you will find the result to be a more vivid picture of the history of rhetoric.

The coverage of the rhetoric of science, the rhetorical theory of Kenneth Burke, the rhetoric of narration, comparative rhetoric, and feminist rhetorics has been expanded in the sixth edition. In recognition of our ever-changing rhetorical contexts, I have added a new discussion of materialist approaches to rhetoric, and the complex networks of influence of which humans are only one component. This new theoretical perspective expands the traditional notion of rhetorical activity as the domain strictly of human agents.

The sixth edition features a new section on Muslim rhetorical theory of the medieval period, emphasizing the crucial role played by scholars such as Ibn Rushd (Averroes) in interpreting and preserving classical rhetorical theories. I have also added material on efforts to encourage literacy in the Middle Ages, and the impact of these efforts on an audience of women rhetoricians and readers. Where new discussions are introduced, they are accompanied by questions for discussion that should help students think through the implications for their own perspectives on rhetoric.

OVERVIEW OF CHAPTERS

Here are some of the features of individual chapters. Chapter 1 presents several defining characteristics of rhetorical discourse, as well as discussing the social functions of the art of rhetoric. I have also sought to emphasize the tensions and ambiguities that always attend efforts to define rhetoric. The question of definition is rendered more nuanced and interesting with the recognition of visual rhetoric as an important aspect of human symbolic activity. With this foundation in place, the balance of the text is organized historically.

Chapter 2 considers the Sophists as early teachers, practitioners, and theorists of rhetoric. I have tried to clarify the ways in which these experimental and controversial rhetoricians shaped, not just the history of rhetoric, but also our understanding of the symbolic nature of human existence. While I do address the controversy the Greek Sophists generated, their role as thinkers who achieved considerable insight into rhetoric's nature and power is also emphasized. I have tried to reflect in this treatment that the Sophists do not all belong to a single school of thought regarding rhetoric, but vary in their approaches to and uses of the art.

Chapter 2 also addresses the historically occluded issue of women's voices in ancient Greek rhetoric. I have expanded the treatment of Greek women, and of the conception or rhetoric itself, by discussing women as poets (Sappho in particular), as a public voice in the Spartan marketplace, and Aspasia as a rhetorical innovator.

Chapter 3 considers Plato's famous—and also controversial—criticism of the Sophistic approach to rhetoric in the dialogue *Gorgias,* as well as the philosopher's musings about a possible true art of rhetoric in the dialogue *Phaedrus.* New material has been added that sheds light on Plato's insistence on an account—a *logos*—from the Sophists concerning "the nature of" their art. The question of whether Plato has left us a fair assessment of the Sophists is also considered, as is Plato's own role as rhetorical theorist.

Chapter 4 explores Aristotle's highly influential theory advanced in his *Rhetoric.* This chapter discusses in detail Aristotle's affirmative answer to the question of whether rhetoric qualifies as a *techne* or true art. The notions of the enthymeme, artistic proofs, and topics of argumentation are all reviewed. While Aristotle's interest in deliberative oratory is well-known, epideictic or ceremonial oratory is also presented as central to his rhetoric.

Chapter 5 completes the discussion of the classical period by considering Roman adaptations of Greek rhetoric to a new social setting, and striking differences between the Roman and Greek conceptions of the citizen. Recent scholarship has provided a clearer view of the theory and practice of rhetoric in Rome. Key components in the rhetorical theory of Cicero, including his famous canons of rhetoric and his concern for the preparation of the orator-leader, remain focal points of this chapter, as do Roman attention to judicial oratory and argument. The contributions of Quintilian and Longinus to rhetorical thought are explored, as is the close relationship between rhetoric and citizenship in ancient Rome.

Chapter 6 considers the theories and uses of rhetoric that characterized the era of Church dominance running approximately from the fifth through the fourteenth centuries. St. Augustine's rapprochement between the Greco-Roman rhetoric, he knew so well, and the educational needs of the Christian church are discussed. Other leading medieval rhetorical theorists such as Martianus Capella and Boethius are also covered. In addition, the chapter examines the rhetorical arts that developed in the later Middle Ages, including preaching, letter writing, and poetry. Figures that represent these rhetorical arts, such as the skilled letter writer Catherine of Siena, are introduced. Material concerning education in the Middle Ages has been augmented to emphasize the considerable effort to expand literacy in Europe during this period. The corresponding rise of a female reading public is addressed, as well as the rise of writers addressing that audience such as Marie de France.

Renaissance rhetorical theory, particularly the contributions of the Italian Humanists, remains the focus of Chapter 7 in this new edition. However, the chapter has been substantially restructured for greater clarity. The period's intense interest in classical texts and languages, and the Renaissance's fascination with rhetoric generally, are seen as forces that produced an era of extraordinary influence for rhetoric in European education, and that led to remarkable insights on the part of rhetorical theorists. New material has been added on rhetoric's role in shaping conceptions of social decorum during the period.

The entry of women into the history of rhetoric in a substantial fashion during the Renaissance is outlined, as is women's increased access to education, audiences, and the means of communication. In addition, the tension between the contemplative and active life is discussed, as is rhetoric's role in the rise of commercial European cities, and its close relationship to the Renaissance fascination with magic. The emergence of new models—particularly a conversational approach to rhetoric—is also noted, as is rhetoric's struggle with dialectic and a scientific style of writing late in the period.

Chapter 8 focuses on mid-seventeenth through early nineteenth-century rhetorical theory. The chapter discusses the intriguing Italian theorist Giambattista Vico, a writer who saw rhetoric and myth as foundational to civilization, and assigned rhetoric a central role in the emergence of human thought. A new section has been added on Vico's highly influential treatment of myth and narrative as crucial to the formation of civilization. The chapter then moves on to consider writers of the Scottish Enlightenment, including George Campbell, Lord Kames, and Hugh Blair, who turned rhetoric in a more personal direction and away from classical conceptions of oratory. English rhetorical theorists, including the elocutionist Thomas Sheridan and traditionalist Richard Whately, are also considered who revived some elements of the classical model. The chapter opens and closes with two women writers—Margaret Cavendish and Maria Edgeworth—whose rhetorical efforts stood largely outside, and as a challenge to, the mainstream of the Enlightenment rhetorical tradition.

Renewed interest in rhetoric during the second half of the twentieth and early twenty-first centuries is taken up in the remaining three chapters that conclude the book. Chapter 9 focuses on contemporary rhetorical theories developing around conceptions of argument, strategy, audience, and rational public discourse. The chapter also explores developments in efforts to illuminate the rhetoric of science. Chaim Perelman's and L. Olbrechts-Tyteca's audience and argument-based effort to discover a "new rhetoric" is discussed. Jürgen Habermas' theory of how to create a more rational society is taken up in this chapter, with attention to his prescriptions for a more equitable and rational practice of rhetoric.

Chapter 10 explores recent theories that present rhetoric as preparation for living effectively in the rapidly changing and always evolving world of symbols. An expanded discussion of Kenneth Burke's rhetorical theory explores his notion of identification in addition to his central theory of dramatism. The chapter examines Burke's famous pentad, with a new discussion of the worldviews associated with each element. Lloyd Bitzer's situational theory is also introduced here. Mikhail Bakhtin's and Wayne Booth's influential theories of the rhetoric of narration receive careful treatment as well, as do the narrative theories of Walter Fisher and Ernest Bormann.

A new section in Chapter 10 introduces the rhetoric of material objects, concepts such as circulation and generalized symmetry, and the theory of our rhetorical interaction with objects known as Actor-Network Theory (ANT). The idea of visual rhetoric or the rhetoric of display is introduced and explored as adding an important and often missing dimension to rhetorical history. Finally, this chapter considers how new digital media may affect the rhetorical experience and even call for new conceptions of rhetoric.

Chapter 11 considers several theories of symbol use and public discourse that were shaped by Continental criticism and postmodern thought. The rise of postmodernism in Europe is addressed, setting several major figures in their intellectual context. A new section takes up the precursor to postmodernism known as structuralism. Michel Foucault's insights into the close connections among discourse, power, and knowledge are discussed, as is Jacques Derrida's critique of the instability of language itself. Queer Theory, a consequence of Foucault's theoretical insights, is introduced.

Different strains of feminist thinking about rhetoric are also considered in an updated section of Chapter 11 that moves the discussion of feminism beyond early efforts to retrieve a distinctly feminine rhetorical voice. This chapter also features an updated discussion of non-Western conceptions of rhetoric, with attention to how the competitive nature of ancient Greek culture dramatically affected Western rhetoric. New material introduces the contributions of Muslim scholars to rhetorical studies during the Middle Ages, focusing on the work of the philosopher known to the west as Averroes.

The sixth edition of *The History and Theory of Rhetoric* incorporates insights from recent research into the history of rhetoric, and seeks to achieve greater integration of the material within and among chapters. I have sought to describe the intellectual and historical contexts for each theorist and school of thought, and have tried to explain the connections between periods. Increased attention has been paid in this new edition to women's contributions to rhetoric's history, while the possibility for greater continuity between classical and contemporary theorizing is also emphasized.

Each chapter in this new edition includes a list of key terms as well as questions for review and for discussion. A complete glossary of terms should also be useful for review of important concepts. The bibliography can be of assistance to students who wish to do additional reading on a particular topic or theorist. A detailed Instructor's Manual is also available from the publisher.

The centrality of symbolic activity to our social and private lives has driven the incessant human interest in symbols and their strategic use. The written record of this interest constitutes the history of rhetoric. Our reliance on rhetorical interaction for the development and maintenance of cooperative social arrangements makes the history and theory of rhetoric a crucial study for all thinking people today. Given the pluralistic nature of contemporary society and the resulting necessity of improving our means of finding working compromises through public and private discourse, the study of rhetoric is perhaps more relevant today than it ever has been.

The rational flexibility demanded by our increasing reliance on digital forms of communication provides further justification for a concentrated focus on the insights history of rhetoric. I hope that this new edition will convey to readers the historical centrality and continuing vitality of rhetoric as the art of the intentional and productive management of all types of symbols.

I would like to thank Mrs. Linda Koetje for her help in preparing the manuscript. I am also indebted to several reviewers for their insightful comments that prepared the way for this new edition. These respondents include Robert W. Barnett, University of Michigan-Flint; Ferald J. Bryan, Northern Illinois University; Catherine A. Dobris, Indiana University–Purdue University Indianapolis; Belle A. Edson, Arizona State University; Nichole Kathol, University of Kansas; and Kathleen Torrens, University of Rhode Island.

James A. Herrick
Hope College

Chapter 1

An Overview of Rhetoric

My first problem lies of course in the very word "rhetoric."
—Wayne Booth, *The Vocation of a Teacher*

THIS chapter explores the history, theories, and practices of rhetoric. But, as literary critic Wayne Booth (1921–2005) suggests in the quotation above, the term *rhetoric* poses some problems at the outset because of the various meanings it has acquired. For some people, rhetoric is synonymous with empty talk or even deception. We hear clichés like, "That's mere rhetoric" or "That's just empty rhetoric," which are used to undermine or dismiss a comment or opinion.

Meanwhile, rhetoric has once again emerged as an important topic of study, and its significance to public discussion of political, social, religious, and scientific issues is now widely recognized. Scholars and teachers express great interest in the subject; colleges and universities offer courses in rhetoric; and dozens of books are published every year with rhetoric in their titles. Clearly, rhetoric arouses mixed feelings—it is a term of derision and yet a widely studied discipline, employed as an insult and still recommended to students as a practical subject of study. What is going on here? Why all the confusion and ambiguity surrounding the term *rhetoric*?

Negative attitudes toward rhetoric are not of recent origin. In fact, one of the earliest and most influential critical discussions of rhetoric occurs in Plato's dialogue *Gorgias*, a work written in the opening decades of the fourth century BCE when rhetoric was popular in the Greek city-state of Athens. The great philosopher, as his dialogue makes clear, takes a dim view of rhetoric, at least as practiced by some teachers of the day called Sophists. The character Socrates, apparently representing Plato's own perspective, argues that the type of rhetoric being taught in Athens was simply a means by which "naturally clever" people "flatter" their unsuspecting listeners into agreeing with them and doing their bidding. Plato condemns rhetoric as "foul" and "ugly."[1] We will discuss his specific criticisms of rhetoric in Chapter 3, and note that Plato was involved in an ongoing debate about rhetoric.

Ever since Plato's *Gorgias* first appeared, rhetoric has had to struggle to redeem its tarnished public image. Rhetoric bashing continues in an almost unbroken tradition from ancient times to the present. In 1690 another respected philosopher, John Locke (1632–1704), advanced a view of rhetoric not unlike, and likely influenced by, Plato's. The below text gives a brief description of Locke's writing in his famous and highly influential book *An Essay Concerning Human Understanding*:

> If we speak of things as they are, we must allow that all the art of rhetoric, besides order and clearness; all the artificial and figurative application of words eloquence hath invented, are for nothing else but to insinuate wrong ideas, move the passions, and thereby mislead the judgment; and so indeed are perfect cheats . . .[2]

Locke does acknowledge that one aspect of rhetoric, what he calls "order and clearness," is useful. However, he rejects the study of "artificial and figurative" language as deceptive. As we will see in Chapter 7, Locke was also immersed in a debate about language when he expressed this opinion.

The nineteenth-century German philosopher Friedrich Nietzsche (1844–1900)—who had made a serious study of rhetoric—wrote, "We call an author, a book, or a style 'rhetorical' when we observe a conscious application of artistic means of speaking; it always implies a gentle reproof." A "gentle reproof" certainly reflects a more measured assessment than Locke's "full cheats." But, Nietzsche was aware of something else, something deeper and more fundamental, lurking in the realm of the rhetorical:

> [I]t is not difficult to prove that what is called "rhetorical," as a means of conscious art, had been active as a means of unconscious art in language and its development, indeed, that the *rhetorical is a further development,* guided by the clear light of the understanding, of *the artistic means which are already found in language.*

What does Nietzsche mean by the curious phrase, "*the artistic means already found in language*"? Is he, perhaps, suggesting that language itself possesses an irreducible artistic or aesthetic quality that rhetoric merely draws out? He continues:

> There is obviously no unrhetorical "naturalness" of language to which one could appeal; language itself is the result of purely rhetorical arts. The power to discover and to make operative that which works and impresses, with respect to each thing, a power which Aristotle calls rhetoric, is, at the same time, the essence of language . . .[3]

If Nietzsche is correct that nothing in the realm of language is purely "natural" and unmarked by "rhetorical arts," that rhetoric is "the essence of language," then it is certainly a matter that deserves our attention.

RE-EVALUATING RHETORIC

Opinion about rhetoric has always been divided. Recent writers have re-evaluated rhetoric, and they have sometimes arrived at surprising conclusions. Wayne Booth, whom we have already encountered, was one of the twentieth century's leading figures in literary studies. Booth affirmed that rhetoric held "entire dominion over all verbal pursuits. Logic, dialectic, grammar, philosophy, history, poetry, *all* are rhetoric."[4]

Another important twentieth-century literary scholar, Richard McKeon (1900–1985), expressed virtually the same opinion. For McKeon, rhetoric was best understood as "a universal and architectonic art."[5] Rhetoric is universal, that is, present everywhere we turn. But what about *architectonic*? By this term, McKeon meant that rhetoric organizes and gives structure to the other arts and disciplines, that it is a kind of master discipline that orders and lends structure to other disciplines. This is because rhetoric is, among other things, the study of how we organize and employ language effectively, and thus it becomes the study of how we organize our thinking on a wide range of subjects.

In apparent agreement with Booth and McKeon, Richard Lanham (b. 1936) of the University of California has called for a return to rhetorical studies as a way of preparing us to understand the impact of computers and other digital devices on how we read and write. Rather than developing a completely new theory of literacy for the computer age, Lanham argues that "we need to go back to the original Western thinking about reading and writing—the rhetorical paideia [educational program] that provided the backbone of Western education for two thousand years."[6] For Lanham, the study that originally taught the Western world and its approach to public communication can still teach us new things, like how to adapt to the emerging media of electronic communication.

Professor Andrea Lunsford (b. 1942), Director of Stanford University's Program in Writing and Rhetoric, is among a growing number of scholars who, like Lanham, have returned to rhetoric as providing guidance in understanding how the digital revolution is shaping our reading and writing habits. After analyzing thousands of students writing samples—including blogs, tweets, and classroom assignments—Lunsford and her colleagues concluded that students today expect their writing to change the world they live in. For today's students "good writing changes something. It doesn't just sit on the page. It gets up, walks off the page and changes something."[7]

Booth, McKeon, Lanham, and Lunsford find much to commend in the study that Plato condemned as "foul and ugly," and would ask us to reconsider those elements of eloquence that Locke referred to as "perfect cheats." It appears that we are at a point in our cultural history where rhetoric is re-establishing itself as an important study with insights to offer about a surprisingly broad spectrum of human communication activities.

At the same time the practice of rhetoric maintains its Jekyll and Hyde qualities, shifting without notice from helpful and constructive to deceptive and manipulative. Why does this study of the effective uses of language and other symbols prove so difficult to evaluate, eliciting as it does such sharply opposed judgments? A complete answer to this question requires some knowledge of rhetoric's long history, which is the subject of this book. But almost certainly, rhetoric's mixed reviews have a lot to do with its association with persuasion that most suspect but essential human activity. A brief digression to explore this connection between rhetoric and persuasion will be worth our while.

RHETORIC AND PERSUASION

Though there is more to the study of rhetoric than persuasion alone, rhetoric traditionally has been closely concerned with the techniques for gaining compliance. This long-standing association with persuasion has been at the heart of the conflict over whether rhetoric is a neutral tool for bringing about agreements, or an immoral activity that ends in manipulation.

Rhetoric's intimate connection with persuasion has prompted both suspicion and interest. After all, we all are leery of persuasion. Who has not had a bad experience as the object of someone else's persuasive efforts? Think of the last time you knew you were being persuaded by a telephone solicitor, a religious advocate in an airport, a high-pressure salesperson in a store, a politician, a professor, or simply by a friend or a family member. Something in you may have resisted the persuasion effort, and you may even have felt some irritation. But you may also have felt you were being drawn in by the appeal, that you were, in fact, being persuaded. If the person doing the persuading had been employing the techniques of rhetoric, you would think you had some reason to distrust both rhetoric and the people who practice it. So, most of us have developed a healthy suspicion of persuasion, and perhaps a corresponding mistrust of rhetoric.

At the same time, a moment's thought suggests that all of us seek to persuade others on a regular basis. Many professions, in fact, require a certain understating of and capacity to persuade. Persuasion can even be understood as an important part of the world of work. Economist Deirdre McCloskey (b. 1942) has written that "persuasion has become astonishingly important" to the economy. Based on the Census Bureau data, she estimated that "more than 28 million out of 115 million people in civilian employment—one quarter of the U.S. labor force—may be heavily involved in persuasion in their economic life," a finding she regards as "startling."[8] McCloskey concludes that, "economics is rediscovering the importance of words" as economists begin to understand "that persuasion is vital for the exchange of goods, services, and monies . . ."[9]

Outside the arena of work we remain perpetual persuaders in our personal relationships. Who does not make arguments, advance opinions, and seek compliance from friends? Moreover, we typically engage in these persuasive activities without thinking we are doing anything wrong. In fact, it is difficult *not* to persuade; we participate in the practice on an almost daily basis in our interactions with friends, colleagues at work, or members of our family. We may attempt to influence friends or family members to adopt our political views; we will happily argue the merits of a movie we like; we *are* that salesperson, religious advocate, or politician. It is difficult to imagine a relationship in which persuasion has no role, or an organization that does not depend to some degree on efforts to change other people's thoughts and thus to influence their actions.

Let us consider some additional examples of how universal persuasion can be. We usually think of sports as a domain of physical competition, and not of verbal battles.

Yet, even sports involve disagreements about such things as the interpretation of rules, a referee's call, or which play to execute. And, these disagreements often are settled by arguments and appeals of various kinds, that is, by persuasion. British psychologist Michael Billig (b. 1947) notes that many of the rules governing a sport result from rhetorical interactions about such issues as how much violence to allow on the field of play. He writes, "The rules of rugby and soccer were formulated in order to transform informal agreements, which had permitted all manner of aggressive play, into defined codes that restricted violence." Rhetoric, especially its argumentative aspect, was crucial to the creation of these rules of play. "Above all, the rules were formulated against a background of argument."[10] Even the rules by which athletes compete, it appears, came into being through rhetoric.

What about a technical field like medicine? If medicine is a science, should not argument and persuasion be non-existent? In fact, medical decisions are often made after a doctor advances a convincing case for or against a particular procedure in a rhetorical exchange with other doctors. And, the decision-making exchange often is not limited to technical issues such as the interpretation of medical data like the results of a blood test. To be sure, the arguments advanced will involve medical principles, but they are arguments nonetheless, they are intended to be persuasive, and they range beyond strict medical guidelines. In medical dialogue we are likely to hear ethical concerns raised, the wishes of a family considered, and even questions of cost evaluated. Moreover, the patient often has to be persuaded to take a particular medicine or follow a specified diet or allow doctors to perform a surgical procedure. As physicians argue, rival medical theories may be in conflict and rival egos may clash. Who should perform a needed corneal transplant on a famous politician? We might think that an important decision would be based on medical criteria alone. Yet, even a question like this may be resolved on the basis of arguments between two well-known physicians at competing hospitals. Clearly, the science of medicine has its rhetorical side.

Bringing the focus down to a more personal level, does romance involve persuasion? When I seek the attention of someone in whom I am romantically interested, I start to develop a case—though perhaps not an explicit and public one—about my own good qualities. When in the vicinity of the individual concerned, I may attempt to appear humorous, intelligent, and considerate. My words and actions take on a rhetorical quality as I build the case for my own attractiveness. I might be convincing, or may fail to convince, but in either event I have made choices about how to develop my appeal, so to speak. Once begun, romantic relationships go forward (or backward) on the basis of persuasive interactions on topics ranging from how serious the relationship should be to whether to attend a particular concert.

Other activities also bring us into the realm of rhetoric. Business transactions, from marketing strategies to contract negotiations, involve persuasive efforts. As McCloskey has pointed out, many people make their livings by means of their abilities as persuasive speakers. Nor is education immune from rhetorical influence. You often are aware that a professor is advocating a point of view in a lecture that ostensibly presents simple "information," or that classmates argue with one another hoping to persuade others to their point of view. As a matter of fact, you have been reading an extended persuasive case for the importance of studying rhetoric. Textbooks, it should come as little surprise, often have a persuasive agenda embedded within them.

Efforts at persuasion mark many, perhaps all, of our interpersonal activities. In fact, we even persuade *ourselves*. The internal rhetoric of "arguing with yourself" accompanies most of life's decisions, big or small. Though our experiences may leave us leery of persuasion, it is also an important component of our occupational, social, and private lives.[11]

Now, back to rhetoric. If rhetoric is in part the systematic study of persuasion, recognizing how crucial persuasion is to daily life may suggest that this art deserves our attention. To acknowledge what we might call "the pervasiveness of persuasiveness" is not to condemn persuasion or rhetoric. Rather, it is to begin to appreciate the centrality of this activity to much of life, and to recognize that human beings are rhetorical beings. At this point, it will be important to develop a more precise definition of rhetoric.

DEFINING RHETORIC

Scholars have advanced a variety of insightful definitions of our topic. Rhetoric scholar James J. Murphy has suggested "advice to others about future language use" as one way of defining rhetoric.[12] Murphy's definition implies prior study of the topic rhetoric that has resulted in a set of tested theories and reliable techniques. Classicist George Kennedy defines rhetoric more broadly as "the energy inherent in emotion and thought, transmitted through a system of signs, including language, to others to influence their decisions or actions."[13] This definition suggests that rhetoric is simply part of who we are as human beings: Every time we express emotions and thoughts to others with the goal of influence, we express a kind of energy that Kennedy calls rhetoric.

Rhetoric and Symbol Systems

Note that for Kennedy rhetoric involves "signs, including language." I would like to focus attention on this important point for a moment, and suggest that rhetoric develops in the realm of symbols of one type or another. So, what are symbols? An individual word such as *boat* is an example of a symbol. It is a general term referring to any mark, sign, sound, or gesture that communicates meaning based on social agreement. Individual symbols usually are part of a larger symbolic system, such as a language.

Language is the symbol system on which most of us rely for communicating with others on a daily basis. However, many arts and other activities also provide symbolic resources for communicating. In fact, social life depends on our ability to use a wide range of symbol systems to communicate meanings to one another, and a rhetorical dimension can be detected in many of these.

Music

Musical notation and performance constitute a symbol system, one that uses notes, key, melody, harmony, sound, and rhythm to communicate meanings. Movie soundtracks provide convenient examples of how the symbol system of music can communicate meaning. For instance, musical techniques were used to enhance audience tension in the famous theme from the movie *Jaws*, as well as in the frightening shower scene in Alfred Hitchcock's *Psycho*. The stirring music of Tchaikovsky's famous *1812 Overture* set the right triumphal note for the opening and closing scenes of the 2006 film *V for Vendetta*. More recently, British composer Steven Price intentionally broke with movie soundtrack conventions—for instance, he avoided the use of percussion—in creating his Academy Award winning soundtrack for the movie, *Gravity* (2013). Price's score perfectly conveys the risks and emptiness of space. Perhaps the rhetoric of music is so well established that we readily understand what it is "saying" to us.

Dance and Acting

Many of the movements in dance are also symbolic because they express meaning on the basis of agreements among dancers, choreographers, and audience members. For instance, three dancers in a row performing the same robotic movement may symbolize the tedium and regimentation of modern life. Similarly, gestures, postures, and facial expressions allow mime artists and actors to communicate with audiences symbolically but without employing the symbols of spoken language. There is no actual connection between pondering a question and scratching your head, and yet a theatrical scratch of the scalp means "I don't know" or "I'm thinking about it" by a kind of unstated social agreement.

Actors and impersonators such as Jim Carrey and Kristen Wiig have mastered a range of physical symbols—gestures, postures, and facial expressions—that allow them to communicate instantly with audiences, often without speaking a word.

Painting

In painting, form, line, color, and arrangement can be symbolic. A stark line of dark clouds may symbolize impending disaster, even though clouds do not typically accompany actual disasters. But, because storms and calamity are sometimes associated, and because we often fear storms, we understand the artist's intent. Norwegian painter Edvard Munch used such a technique in his 1893 painting *Shrik* (*Scream*), where a brilliant orange–red sky symbolizes terror. But, then, what does Mona Lisa's slight grin "mean." No doubt Leonardo da Vinci had something in mind in crafting that half smile, but scholars and the public alike have never come to an agreement as to his intentions.

Architecture

The lines, shapes, and materials used in architecture can also be employed symbolically to communicate meaning. The protests by veterans' groups that greeted the unveiling of the Vietnam Memorial in Washington, D.C., were responses to what some observers took to be the *meaning* of the monument, a meaning with which they did not agree.[14] Much of the monument is below ground, perhaps suggesting invisibility or even death. Is it significant that the memorial cannot be seen from Capitol Hill? The principal material used in the monument is black granite rather than the more traditional and triumphal white marble. The polished surface is covered with the names of the fifty thousand Americans who died in the war rather than with carved scenes of battle and victory. What does the Vietnam Memorial mean? One would be hard-pressed to find its meaning to be "A united America triumphs again in a foreign war." Nevertheless, each symbolic component prompts to ask deep and troubling questions about a long and tragic war.

Sports

Perhaps the symbols employed in music, dance, acting, painting, or architecture can be readily understood as rhetorical, as they carry a meaning that can be intentionally selected and refined. However, can an athletic event carry rhetorical significance? Long-distance swimmer Diana Nyad requested permission from the Cuban government to swim the 103 mile distance between Cuba and Florida. The Cuban government reluctantly granted her permission for the swim. "The Cubans don't like the implication of somebody walking out on one of their beaches and swimming away," Nyad said in a 2010 *Los Angeles Times* report.[15] The symbolism of swimming *away* from Cuba apparently was felt to reflect negatively on the Cuban political system. Nyad finally completed the swim on her fifth attempt in 2013, after 53 hours in the water. A long and, to some, rhetorical swim.

Unexpected Locations

Rhetorical elements can reveal themselves in places we might easily overlook. For example, the typeface in which this book is printed has a rhetorical dimension. Though readers are not directed to notice the statement being made by typeface, each individual font was designed to convey a particular quality, character, or tone. Most textbooks are set in a typeface that appears to readers as serious, intentional, and, of course, legible. The typeface for a wedding invitation, however, might be selected to convey elegance or romance. Certainly if the type in this book were set in a font ordinarily reserved for a wedding invitation, a reader would immediately notice this unusual choice. So, we might say that typeface is selected, like the music in a hotel elevator, in order to not be noticed.[16]

Effective Symbolic Expression

While persuasion has long been an important goal of rhetoric, we should perhaps expand the definition of rhetoric to include other goals such as achieving clarity, awakening our sense of beauty, or bringing about mutual understanding. Thus, we can define the art of rhetoric as follows: The systematic study and intentional practice of effective symbolic expression. *Effective* here will mean achieving the purposes of the symbol-user, whether that purpose is persuasion, clarity, beauty, or mutual understanding.

The art of rhetoric can render symbol use more persuasive, beautiful, memorable, forceful, thoughtful, clear, and thus generally more compelling. In all of these ways, rhetoric is the art of employing symbols effectively. Rhetorical theory is the systematic presentation of rhetoric's principles, its various social functions, and how the art achieves its goals. Messages crafted according to the principles of rhetoric will be called rhetorical discourse, or simply rhetoric. An individual practicing the art of rhetoric will occasionally be referred to as a rhetor (RAY-tor).

As we have noted, for most of its history, the art of rhetoric has focused on persuasion by employing the symbol system of language. This traditional approach to rhetoric is still important, but recently both rhetoric's goals and the symbolic resources available to those practicing the art have expanded dramatically. This development has led some scholars to write of different kinds of rhetoric, even different rhetorics. For instance, Steven Mailloux notes that "there are oral, visual, written, digital, gestural, and other kinds; and under written rhetoric, there are various genres such as autobiographies, novels, letters, editorials, and so forth . . ."[17]

Does this mean that all communication, regardless of goal or symbol system employed, is rhetoric? Some scholars make communication and rhetoric synonymous, but this seems to ignore genuine and historically important distinctions among types of communication ranging from information and reports through casual conversations to outright propaganda. I will be taking the position that rhetorical discourse is a particular type of communication possessing several identifying characteristics. What, then, are the features of rhetorical discourse that set it apart from other types of communication? The following section describes six distinguishing qualities of rhetorical *discourse* as we encounter it in writing, speaking, the arts, and other media of expression.

RHETORICAL DISCOURSE

This section considers six distinguishing characteristics of rhetorical discourse, the marks the art of rhetoric leaves on messages. Rhetorical discourse characteristically is (1) planned, (2) adapted to an audience, (3) shaped by human motives, (4) responsive to a situation, (5) persuasion-seeking, and (6) concerned with contingent issues. Not all writing or speaking that might meaningfully be termed rhetoric satisfies all of these criteria, but the criteria will serve as a starting point for identifying, understanding, and responding to rhetorical discourse. We begin by considering rhetoric's most fundamental quality.

Rhetoric Is Planned

Regardless of the goal at which it aims, rhetorical discourse involves forethought or planning. Thinking of rhetoric as planned symbol use directs our attention to the choices people make about how they will address their audiences. Issues that arise in planning a message include the following:

—Which arguments will I advance?
—Which evidence best supports my point?
—How will I order and arrange my arguments and evidence?
—What resources of language and other symbol systems are available to me, given my topic and audience?

The planned nature of rhetoric has long been recognized as one of its defining features. Some early rhetorical theorists developed elaborate systems to assist would-be orators in planning their speeches. The Roman writer Cicero, for instance, used the term *inventio* (invention) to describe the process of discovering the arguments and evidence for a persuasive case. He then provided specific methods for inventing arguments quickly and effectively. Cicero also discussed the effective ordering of arguments and appeals under the heading *dispositio* (arrangement), while he used the term *elocutio* to designate the process of finding the right linguistic style for one's message, whether elegant or conversational.

Such concerns, already extensively studied in the ancient world, reflect the planned quality that characterizes rhetorical discourse. In subsequent chapters, we will look more closely at a number of rhetorical systems designed to assist the planning of messages.

Rhetoric Is Adapted to an Audience

Concern for forethought or planning points up a second characteristic of rhetorical discourse. Rhetoric is planned with some audience in mind. *Audience* should not be understood strictly in the traditional sense of a large group of people seated in rows of chairs in a large hall. Some audiences are of this type, most are not.

When you speak to a small group of employees at work, they are your audience and you may adapt your discourse to them. The author of a letter while writing to the editor of a local newspaper also keeps the audience in mind, though the audience is not made up of people whom the author can see or know personally in most cases. Similarly, a novelist writes with particular groups of readers in mind who constitute his or her audience. A politician may address a vast and diverse national audience by means of mass media.

Typically, a rhetor must make an educated guess about the audience he or she is addressing. This imagined audience is the only one present when a message is actually being crafted, and it often guides the inventional process in important ways. The audience that hears, reads, or otherwise encounters a message may be quite similar to the imagined audience, but even highly trained writers or speakers guess wrongly at times. In demand as a speaker, Wayne Booth pointed out that even when he thought he knew his audience, he was sometimes mistaken:

> I always wrote with some kind of imaginary picture of listeners responding with smiles, scowls, or furrowed brows. Such prophecies often proved to be wildly awry: An imagined audience of thirty teachers who would have read the materials I sent them in advance turned out, in the reality faced a week or so later, to be ten teachers, along with two hundred captive freshmen reluctantly attending as part of their "reading" assignment; the audience for a "public lecture" was discovered to contain nobody from the public, only teachers.[18]

Booth's experience is not at all unusual. Nevertheless, some effort to estimate one's audience has always been, and remains, a crucial component in the rhetorical process.

Rhetorical discourse forges links between the rhetor's views and those of an audience. This means that speakers, writers, and designers must attend to an audience's values, experiences, beliefs, and aspirations. Twentieth-century rhetorical theorist Kenneth Burke used the term *identification* to refer to the bond between rhetors and their audiences, finding identification crucial to cooperation, consensus, compromise, and action. Two other rhetorical theorists have written that rhetoric involves "continuous adaptation of the speaker to [an] audience."[19]

Audiences and Attention

Our discussion of audience adaptation should not neglect the obvious concern that a speaker or writer has for keeping an audience's wandering attention. Richard Lanham has described rhetoric as "the economics of attention," that is, as a study concerned with managing the limited resource of audience attentiveness.[20] This interest in attention focuses *our* attention on a relatively new concern for students of rhetoric: Scientific studies of the brain are revealing some of the secrets of the audience and of persuasion.

Researchers at the University of Utah medical school took a major step toward understanding how we pay attention to various stimuli in our environment. Lead researcher Jeffery Anderson comments, "This study is the first of its kind to show how the brain switches attention from one feature to the next." Apparently, different parts of the brain process information from the different senses, and a "map" within the brain directs our attention to particular stimuli at any particular moment. "The research uncovers how we can shift our attention to different things with precision," says Anderson. "It's a big step in understanding how we organize information."[21] Rhetorical scholars will no doubt be interested in studying such attention maps. The issue of attention is now widely studied, with some research suggesting that our attention spans are getting shorter.[22]

Scientists are not the only ones studying attention. Brian Boyd, an expert on narrative, notes that "To hold an audience, in a world of competing demands on attention, an author needs to be an inventive intuitive psychologist."[23] Rhetorical theorists from ancient times to the present would agree—attracting and holding audience attention requires that the skillful rhetor become a student of the human mind, that is, of psychology. Attracting and holding audience attention is a central concern of the public advocate, and much of the art of rhetoric is directed to achieving this goal.

Rhetoric Reveals Human Motives

A third quality of rhetoric is closely related to the concern for the audience. Any study of rhetoric will reveal people acting symbolically in response to their motives, a term taking in commitments, goals, desires, or purposes that lead to action. Rhetors address audiences with goals in mind, and the planning and adaptation processes that mark rhetoric are governed by the desire to achieve these goals.

Motives that animate rhetorical discourse include making converts to a point of view, seeking cooperation to accomplish a task, building a consensus that enables group action, finding a compromise that breaks a stalemate, forging an agreement that makes peaceful coexistence possible, wishing to be understood, or simply having the last word on a subject. Rhetors accomplish such goals by aligning their own motives with an audience's commitments. For this reason, the history of rhetoric is replete with efforts to understand human values, to identify factors prompting audiences to action, and to grasp the symbolic resources for drawing people together.

Of course, there are good and bad motives. Imagine, for instance, a governor running for president. As you study the governor's public statements, you look for motives animating that rhetoric: Is the governor concerned to serve the public good? Does he or she hope to see justice prevail? Is fame a motive, or greed? Perhaps all of these elements enter the governor's motivation. Of course, motives may be either admitted or concealed. The same politician would likely admit to desiring the public good, but would be unlikely to admit to seeking fame, fortune, or even merely employment. Any informed critic of rhetoric must be aware that motives may be elusive or clearly evident, hidden, or openly admitted.

Rhetoric Is Responsive

The fourth quality of rhetorical discourse typically is a response either to a situation or to a previous rhetorical statement. By the same token, any statement, once advanced, is automatically an invitation for other would-be rhetors to respond. Rhetoric, then, is both "situated" and "dialogic." What does it mean for rhetoric to be situated? Simply that rhetoric is crafted in response to a set of circumstances, including a particular time, location, problem, and audience.

The situation prompting a rhetorical response may be a political controversy concerning welfare, a religious conflict over the role of women in a denomination, a debate in medical ethics over assisted suicide, the discussions about a policy that would control visitors in university dormitories, a natural disaster, or a theatrical performance in which a plea for racial harmony is advanced. Rhetoric is response-*making*.

But, rhetoric is also response-*inviting*. That is, any rhetorical expression may elicit a response from someone advocating an opposing view. Aware of this response-inviting nature of rhetoric, rhetors will imagine likely responses as they compose or "invent" their rhetorical appeals. They may find themselves coaxing their mental conception of a particular audience to respond the way they think the actual audience might. The response-*inviting* nature of rhetoric is easy to imagine when we are envisioning a setting such as a political campaign or a courtroom. But does rhetoric also invite response in less formal settings?

Think of a conversation between yourself and a friend regarding buying expensive tickets for a concert. You have given some thought to what you might say to persuade your friend to buy tickets for the concert, and you are even aware of the response your arguments will receive. Your first argument runs something like this: "Look, how often do you get to hear the Chicago Symphony live? And besides, it's only thirty bucks." You have argued from the rareness of the experience and the minimal costs involved. But your friend, ever the studied rhetor, is ready with a response: "Hey, thirty bucks is a lot of money, and I haven't paid my sister back the money she loaned me last week." Your friend has argued from the magnitude of the costs, and from a moral commitment to fulfilling prior obligations. Not to be denied your goal by such an eminently answerable argument, you respond: "But your sister has plenty of money, and thirty bucks is barely enough to buy dinner out."

And so it goes, each rhetorical statement invites a response. Maybe you persuade your friend, maybe you do not. But the rhetorical interaction will likely involve the exchange of statement and response so characteristic of rhetoric.

Rhetoric Seeks Persuasion

As we noted earlier in this chapter, the factor most often associated with rhetorical discourse has been its pursuit of persuasion. Though rhetoric often pursues other goals, such as inquiry, beauty, or clear expression, it is important to recognize the centrality of persuasion throughout rhetoric's long history. Greek writers noted more than 2,500 years ago that rhetorical discourse sought persuasion, and a late twentieth-century rhetorical theorist can still be found stating straightforwardly that "the purpose of rhetoric is persuasion."[24] It may be helpful, however, to imagine a spectrum running from texts with relatively little persuasive intent (e.g., a news report on a link between stress and childhood obesity) to texts that are strictly persuasive in nature (e.g., a candidate's campaign speech).

Rhetorical discourse often seeks to influence an audience to accept an idea, and then to act. For example, an attorney argues before a jury that the accused is guilty of a crime. The attorney seeks the jurors' acceptance of the idea that the defendant is guilty, and the resulting action of finding the defendant guilty. Or, perhaps I try to persuade a friend that a candidate should be elected mayor on the basis of the candidate's plans to improve education in the city. I want my friend to accept the idea that this candidate is the best person for the job, and to take the action of voting for my candidate. Let us shift our focus to the arts. A play reveals through the symbols of the theater the vicious nature of racism. The play's author hopes both to influence the audience's thinking about racism and to affect the audience's actions on racial matters.

How does rhetorical discourse achieve persuasion? Speaking in the most general terms, rhetoric employs various resources of symbol systems such as language. Four such resources have long been recognized as assisting the goal of persuasion: arguments, appeals, arrangement, and aesthetics.

Argument

An argument is made when a conclusion is supported by reasons. An argument is simply private reasoning made public with the goal of influencing an audience. In fact, researchers Hugo Mercier and Dan Sperber have suggested that the entire purpose of our public reasoning—of making arguments—is to demonstrate to *others* that we have support for our views. This view has been labelled as The Argumentative Hypothesis. In other words, reasoning is not principally a matter of clarifying our own thinking but of creating a rhetorical presentation of our views for an audience. "We outline an approach to reasoning," they write, "based on the idea that the primary function for which it evolved is the production and evaluation of arguments in communication."[25]

Suppose that I wish to persuade a friend of the following claim: "The coach of the women's basketball team ought to be paid the same salary as the coach of the men's team." To support this claim, I then advance the following two reasons:

> First, the coach of the women's team is an associate professor, just as is the coach of the men's team. Second, the women's coach has the same responsibilities as the men's coach: to teach two courses each semester, and to prepare her team to play a full schedule of games.

I have now made an argument, and have sought to persuade my friend through a demonstration of my reasoning. Rhetoricians have long associated argument with the public practice of rhetoric, as will become clear from subsequent chapters.

Though we typically think of arguments as occurring in traditional texts such as speeches or editorials, they are not limited to such verbal documents. For example, music critic Tom Strini has written of conductor Andreas Delfs' "uncommon grasp of Beethoven's dramatic rhetoric" and even of the conductor's ability to discover "Beethoven's grand plan" in his Ninth Symphony. Perhaps more surprising, however, is Strini's comment that Delfs' conducting allowed his audience to "follow Beethoven's arguments" in this famous symphony. Specifically, Strini takes the Ninth Symphony to be the great composer's argument in favor of democracy.[26] Was Beethoven's symphony, then, a public argument for the correctness of his political views? From a rhetorical point of view the answer to this question may be yes!

Appeals

Appeals are strategies of language that aim to elicit an emotion or engage the audience's value commitments. We are all familiar with emotional appeals such as those to pity, anger, or fear. You probably also have encountered appeals to authority, to patriotism, or to organizational loyalty.

Appeals can be difficult to distinguish from arguments, the difference often being simply one of degree. An argument is directed to reason, an appeal to something more visceral such as an emotion, a conviction or feeling of which we may not be consciously aware. For instance, an advertisement shows a young woman standing in front of an expensive new car while cradling a baby in her arms. The caption reads: "How much is your family's safety worth?" Though an argument is implied in the picture and caption, the advertisement is structured as an appeal to one's sense of responsibility. Even if reason responded, "Yes, safety is worth a great deal, but I still can't afford that car," the advertisement's appeal could perhaps still achieve its intended effect.

Arrangement

Arrangement refers to the planned ordering of a message to achieve the effect of persuasion, clarity, or beauty. A speaker makes the decision to place the strongest of his or her three arguments against animal experimentation last in a speech to a local civic organization. He or she believes that his or her strongest argument stands to have the greatest impact on his or her audience if it is the last point they hear.

Speakers and writers make many such decisions about arrangement in their messages, but the designers of a public building often make similar decisions. The Holocaust Museum in Washington, D.C., for instance, is physically arranged to make the strongest case possible against the racial hatred that resulted in the horrors of the concentration camps, and against all similar attitudes and actions. Careful planning went into decisions about which scenes visitors would encounter as they entered the museum, as they progressed through it, and as they exited. The great impact of this museum is enhanced by its careful arrangement, a concern the famous rhetorician Cicero referred to as *dispositio*.

Aesthetics

Aesthetics are elements adding form, beauty, and force to symbolic expression. Writers, speakers, composers, or other sources typically wish to present arguments and appeals in a manner that is attractive, memorable, or perhaps even shocking to the intended audience.

Abraham Lincoln's "Second Inaugural Address" is a striking example of language's aesthetic resources employed to memorable and moving effect. Consider the use of metaphor, allusion, consonance, rhythm, and rhyme in the following lines:

> Fondly do we hope, fervently do we pray, that this mighty scourge of war may speedily pass away. Yet if God wills that it continue until all the wealth piled by the bondsman's two hundred and fifty years of unrequited toil shall be sunk, and until every drop of blood drawn with the lash shall be paid by another drawn with the sword, as was said three thousand years ago, so still it must be said, that the judgments of the Lord are true and righteous altogether.[27]

Lincoln drew upon the aesthetic resources of language in a traditional way to make his speech more aesthetically appealing and thus more moving and memorable. In some cases, however, a source may decide intentionally to offend traditional aesthetic expectations to achieve greater persuasive impact. In the following passage, for example, Malcolm X answers some of the arguments of Rev. Martin Luther King, Jr. with provocative language that violates traditional conventions:

> This is a real revolution. Revolution is always based on land. Revolution is never based on begging somebody for an integrated cup of coffee. Revolutions are never based on love-your-enemy and pray-for-those-who-spitefully-use-you. And revolutions are never waged singing "We Shall Overcome." Revolutions are based on bloodshed.[28]

Malcolm X, like Abraham Lincoln, employs allusion, consonance, repetition, and other aesthetic devices to enhance his discourse and to make it more vivid, moving, and memorable. Though Malcolm X employs the aesthetic resources of language, it would not be quite accurate to say that his goal has been to make his speech more beautiful or pleasant to listen to. Rather, his goal is apparently to shock his audience out of complacency, and to get them to reject one suggested course of action and to accept a different one.

The aesthetic dimension of rhetoric has always been important to the art. In the next chapter, we will see that one of the early Sophists, Gorgias, believed that the sounds of words, when manipulated with skill, could captivate audiences. The persuasive potential in the aesthetic resources of language is a persistent theme in rhetorical history.

Arguments, appeals, arrangement, and aesthetics each remind us that rhetoric is not only persuasive but also carefully planned discourse. Over its history, the art of rhetoric has developed around the realization that various resources available in symbol systems allow skilled practitioners to achieve various desired effects, including persuasion, clarity, beauty of expression, and capturing an audience's attention.

Rhetoric Addresses Contingent Issues

In an attempt to define the study of rhetoric, the Greek philosopher Aristotle (384–322 BCE) wrote that "it is the duty of rhetoric to deal with such matters as we deliberate upon without arts or systems to guide us" and when "the subjects of our deliberation are such as seem to present us with alternative possibilities." He added, "About things that could not have been, and cannot be, other than they are, nobody who takes them to be of this nature wastes his time in delineation."[29]

Aristotle apparently thought that rhetoric comes into play when we are faced with practical questions about matters that confront everyone, and about which there are no definite and unavoidable answers. Such contingent questions require deliberation or the weighing of options, not proofs of the type mathematicians might use. Rhetoric assists that process of weighing options when the issues facing us are contingent.

To deliberate is to reason through alternatives, and Aristotle says no one does this when things cannot be "other than they are." Rhetorical theorist Thomas Farrell (1947–2006) put the point this way: "It makes no sense to deliberate over things which are going to be the case anyway or things which could never be the case."[30] So, the art of rhetoric would not address a question such as whether the sun will rise tomorrow morning, nor one such as whether France should be made the fifty-first American state. The one is an inevitable fact (it is "going to be the case anyway"), the other a virtual impossibility (it "could never be the case").

Rhetorical theorist Lloyd Bitzer (1931–2016), quoting the nineteenth-century writer Thomas De Quincey (1785–1859), has this to say about contingency: "Rhetoric deals mainly with matters which lie in that vast field 'where there is no *pro* and *con*, with the chance of right and wrong, true and false, distributed in varying proportions among them.'" Bitzer adds, "[R]hetoric applies to contingent and probable matters which are subjects of actual or possible disagreement by serious people, and which permit alternative beliefs, values, and positions."[31]

Rhetoric addresses unresolved issues that do not dictate a particular outcome, and in the process it engages our value commitments. Thus, according to Farrell, Aristotle treated "the very best audiences as a kind of extension of self, capable of weighing the merits of practical alternatives."[32] As individuals, we face many of the same kinds of issues, practical and moral questions that demand decisions or judgments. Of course, similar questions face us as members of the larger public. Is a just war possible? What subjects should be taught in our schools? How can health care be equitably distributed? When there are alternatives to be weighed and matters are neither inevitable nor impossible, we are facing contingent issues that invite the use of rhetoric.

We can shift our focus just a bit at this point and consider the practical results achieved by the art of rhetoric in democratic societies. We will see that when the art of rhetoric is taken seriously, studied carefully, and practiced well, it performs various vital social functions.

SOCIAL FUNCTIONS OF THE ART OF RHETORIC

We began this chapter by noting some unpleasant associations the art of rhetoric has carried with it through its history. But, though rhetoric can be used for wrong ends such as deception, it also plays many important social roles. Rhetoric's misuse is more likely when the art is available only to an elite, when it is poorly understood by audiences, or when it is unethically practiced. The six functions of rhetoric I will highlight are the following: (1) ideas are tested, (2) advocacy is assisted, (3) power is distributed, (4) facts are discovered, (5) knowledge is shaped, and (6) communities are built.

Rhetoric Tests Ideas

One of rhetoric's most important functions is that it allows ideas to be tested on their merits. The practice of rhetoric can provide a peaceful means for evaluating ideas publicly. To win acceptance for a concept, I have to advocate it, and effective advocacy means thinking and acting rhetorically. That is to say, advocacy calls on one's knowledge of rhetoric. Testing ideas begins as I come up with my arguments (invention) and shape them into a structured message (arrangement), and it continues as an audience responds to my presentation.

The audience is a vital element in rhetoric's capacity to test ideas. In seeking an audience's consent, we recognize that the audience members will exercise critical judgment. Some audiences test ideas carefully while others are careless about this responsibility. The better equipped an audience is to test ideas advanced for their consideration, and the more care that goes into that testing, the better check we have on the quality of ideas. This testing of ideas in public settings constitutes a distinct benefit to society. Thus, training in the art of rhetoric is just as important for audience members as it is for advocates.

The responses of both friendly critics and opponents help me strengthen my arguments and refine my ideas. Adapting to critical responses makes my case clearer, stronger, more moving, and more persuasive. The process of testing and refining ideas is tied directly to understanding and practicing the art of rhetoric.

What goes in to testing ideas rhetorically? To critically examine an idea means answering questions such as the following:

—Do I trust the rhetor advocating the idea?

—Is the idea clear or obscure?

—Are the arguments supporting the idea convincing?

—Is the evidence advanced in the idea's support recent and from reliable sources?

—Have unnecessary appeals been employed to distract attention from faulty arguments?

—Are contradictions present in the advocate's case?

Just as advocates rely on rhetorical resources, each of these questions also finds its answer in some dimension of the art of rhetoric. This means that audiences must also be rhetorically astute if the idea-testing function of the art of rhetoric is to be robust and trustworthy.

Rhetoric Assists Advocacy

Rhetoric is the method by which we advocate ideas we believe in. Rhetoric gives our private ideas a public voice, thus directing attention to them. Recall that Richard Lanham defines rhetoric as the study of "how attention is created and allocated."[33] For this reason, he speaks of rhetoric as teaching "the economics of attention."[34]

Politics comes to mind as an activity requiring advocacy; political speeches, debates, and campaign ads promote ideas and candidates. Rhetoric is employed in preparing such messages. The same is true when lobbyists make their case to legislators, when constituents write letters to their representatives, and when committees debate the merits of a proposal. Similarly in the arena of law, the art of rhetoric helps attorneys prepare their clients' cases. Courtroom pleading itself has involved rhetorical skill since courts first appeared in the ancient world, and advocates in newer legal arenas such as environmental law also turn to rhetoric.

Advocacy in less structured settings often follows the principles taught by the art as well, whether or not advocates have had the benefit of formal education in rhetoric. For instance, when you express an artistic judgment to a friend—say, that Spike Lee's films are better than those of Steven Spielberg—you advance your reasons guided by some sense—trained or intuitive—of how to present ideas effectively.

The same holds true for a media project prepared for a course on documentary production. In a twenty-minute video presenting interviews with breast cancer patients, a student builds a case for increased funding for research. The video will be shown not only to her class but also to funding agencies. Editorial decisions are made guided by principles such as the following: Which portions of the interviews will be used? Which interviews will come first and last? Will the interviewer herself play a prominent role in the video, or will she remain in the background? Such judgments are made with some sense of how an effective case is constructed in the medium of video, within a limited amount of time, and before particular audiences.

Whether in formal contexts such as a courtroom or a less structured setting such as a conversation, the art of rhetoric is crucial to effective advocacy. Rhetoric is the study of effective advocacy; it provides a voice for ideas, thus drawing attention to them. This important function of rhetoric may easily be overlooked, but any time an idea moves from private belief to public statement the art of rhetoric is employed.

Understanding the art of rhetoric enhances one's skill in advocacy. We may at times wish that some persons or groups did *not* understand rhetoric, because we disagree with their aims or find their ideas repugnant. The solution to this problem would appear to be an improved understanding of rhetoric on our part. When we disagree with a point of view, rhetoric helps us to prepare an answer, to advance a counterargument. This brings us to the third benefit of the art of rhetoric, its capacity to distribute power.

Rhetoric Distributes Power

Our discussion of rhetoric's role in advocacy raises the closely related issue of rhetoric and power. Due to its capacity for influencing decisions, rhetoric is a form of social power. When we think of rhetoric and power, certain questions come to mind:

—Who is allowed to speak in a society?
—On what topics are we permitted to speak?
—In which settings is speech allowed?
—What kind of language is it permissible to employ?
—Which media are available to which advocates, and why?

Talk Is Action

The answers these questions receive have a lot to do with the distribution of power or influence. Issues of power and its distribution have always been central to rhetorical theory. James Berlin writes, "Those who construct rhetorics . . . are first and foremost concerned with addressing the play of power in their own day."[35] Berlin is asserting, then, that even the guidelines one sets out as normative for writing and speaking are influenced by, perhaps developed in the service of, existing power structures.

When we contrast talk to action in statements like, "Let's stop talking and *do* something," we may be misleading ourselves regarding language's great power to shape our thinking and thus our actions. Rhetorical theorists have long recognized that language and power are intimately connected, and that power involves more than physical force or monetary resources. Speaking and writing are forms of action, and thus rhetoric might be understood as the study of how symbols are used effectively as a source of power. We can identify three types of power with which rhetoric is closely associated.

Personal Power

First, rhetoric contributes to *personal* power. The art provides an avenue to success and advancement by sharpening our expressive skills. Seminars in effective speaking, writing, and even in vocabulary building suggest that the relationship between personal success and language is widely acknowledged. Human resources specialist Rebecca R. Hastings has written, "To be successful, young workers need to develop a lot more than job-specific knowledge, experts say. Of the so-called soft skills needed for success in the workplace, communication skills are particularly critical."[36] Clear, effective, and persuasive expression is not simply a matter of demonstrating your sophistication; it is an important means of advancing toward the goals you have set for yourself.

Psychological Power

Second, rhetoric is a source of *psychological* power, that is, the power to shape thought. Symbols and thoughts are intricately connected; we may change the way people think simply by altering their symbolic framework through a skillfully crafted message. In addition to its capacity to affect action, rhetoric is a means by which one person alters the psychological world of another. Indeed, symbols are perhaps our only avenue into the mental world.

Advertising provides an example of rhetoric's psychological power. Through the strategic use of symbols, advertisers seek to shape our psychological frame and thus our behavior. The repeated symbolic association in advertising between a very thin body and personal attractiveness has led many individuals to become dissatisfied with their appearance. This alteration in one's psychological world can have harmful consequences when it begins to affect a behavior such as eating. For this reason, rhetoric's power to alter the mental world of an audience must be approached with great care.

Political Power

Third, rhetoric is a source of *political* power. The distribution of political influence is often a matter of who gets to speak, where they are allowed to speak, and on what subjects. As we shall see in Chapter 11, French philosopher Michel Foucault explored this intersection of rhetoric and political power in a society. He suggested that power is not a fixed, hierarchical social arrangement, but rather a fluid concept closely connected to the symbolic strategies that hold sway at any particular time. In other words, political power is, for Foucault, directly related to the practice of rhetoric.

Some groups have a greater opportunity to be heard than do others, a fact that raises a concern for the "privileging" of some perspectives or ideologies. An ideology is a system of belief, or a framework for interpreting the world.[37] An unexamined ideology may prevent its adherents from seeing things "as they are." Thus, we need to be wary of rhetoric's use to concentrate as well as to distribute power.[38] When rhetoric is employed to advocate ideas, but its capacity to test ideas is subverted, the reign of unexamined ideology becomes a real possibility.

Rhetoric Discovers Facts

Rhetoric tests ideas, assists advocacy, and distributes power. A fourth important function of rhetoric is that it helps us to discover facts and truths crucial to decision-making. Rhetoric assists this important task in at least three ways.

First, in order to prepare a case, you must locate evidence to support your ideas. This investigative process is an integral part of the art of rhetoric. Though we may have strong convictions, if we are to convince an audience to agree with us, these convictions have to be supported with evidence and arguments. Solid evidence allows better decisions on contingent matters. Second, crafting a message involves evaluating the available facts. This process of invention often suggests new ways of understanding facts and new relationships among facts. Third, the clash of arguments brings new facts to light and refines available ones.

Audiences expect advocates to be well informed. As an advocate you become a source of information crucial to decision-making. But your audience, which may include opponents, will also be evaluating the evidence you present. Some facts may be misleading, outdated, irrelevant, or not convincing. Thus, the art of rhetoric assists not just the discovery of new facts, but also an interactive process of determining which facts are actually relevant and convincing. Of course, rhetoric might also be employed to conceal facts, which reminds us again that rhetoric always raises ethical concerns. As we shall see in Chapter 2, the realization that rhetoric assists the discovery of facts is an ancient one, as is awareness that it might also obscure facts.

Rhetoric Shapes Knowledge

How do we come to agreements about what we know or value? How does a particular view of justice come to prevail in one community or culture? How does a value for equality under the law become established? How do we know that equality is better than inequality? Though the answer to any one of these questions is complex, an important connection exists between knowledge and rhetorical practices.

Rhetoric often plays a critical social role in determining what we accept as true, right, or probable. For this reason, rhetorical scholar Robert Scott referred to rhetoric as "epistemic," that is, knowledge-building.[39] What did he mean? Through rhetorical interaction, we come to accept some ideas as true and to reject others as false. Rhetoric's knowledge-building function derives from its tendency to test ideas. Once an idea has been thoroughly tested by a community, it becomes part of what is accepted as known. Of course, this acceptance as knowledge may be temporary; further rhetorical interactions may call into question what is currently accepted as known.

How Do We "Know"?

That knowledge develops rhetorically runs counter to our usual understanding of the sources of knowledge. We often think that knowledge comes through our direct experience, or through the indirect experience which we call education. Knowledge is treated as an object to be discovered in the same way as an astronomer discovers a new star: The star was always out there, and the astronomer just happened to see it. Some knowledge fits this objective description better than does other knowledge.

Perhaps rhetoric plays a limited role in establishing this sort of knowledge. But, the star's *age* is less certain than is its existence, and may require argument among scientists to determine. Rhetoric now begins to play a role in establishing knowledge, for the scientists involved in the debate will likely draw on what they know of the art to persuade their peers. They will assess their audience, craft arguments they think will be persuasive, avoid ones that are less persuasive, arrange their arguments in an effective order, and provide evidence to support their claims. And that is not the end of the process—even if the majority of scientists *do* reach agreement, these same scientists may find themselves adapting their arguments to a new audience of non-specialists, taking into consideration a new set of audience demands. The question of what we say we know will still be important. Knowledge about the universe's age has religious significance for many people. Do we know that the star's age should be taught in schools? Do we know that money should be invested in trying to launch a telescope to get a better look at the new star? Rhetorical interactions are involved in resolving these questions as well, and the way rhetoric is practiced is important to determining what finally is accepted as knowledge.

Rhetoric Builds Community

What defines a community? One answer to this question is that what people value, know, or believe in common defines a community. Some observers fear that Americans may be losing their sense of constituting a community in the face of growing pressures toward fragmentation. If this is the case, and if preserving a sense of community is a goal worth striving for, what can be done about this problem of social fragmentation?

Many of the processes by which we come to hold beliefs and values in common are rhetorical in nature. Michael J. Hogan, a scholar who has studied the relationship between rhetoric and community, writes that "rhetoric shapes the character and health of communities in countless ways . . ." Many writers who have sought to understand the ways in which communities form have concluded that "communities are largely defined, and rendered healthy or dysfunctional, by the language they use to characterize themselves and others."[40] If this is indeed the case, as Hogan and others have suggested, then it is important to explore the specific function played by rhetoric in building—or perhaps in undermining—communities.

Communities are not simply geographical entities bounded by borders or contained in particular districts of a city. Communities are made up of people who find common cause with one another, who see the world in a similar way, who have similar concerns and aspirations. Thus, a religious organization, a group of employees, and members of an ethnic group living in the same city might constitute communities. Not every aspect of such communities results from the practice of rhetoric. For example, ethnicity is not a function of discourse. But developing common values, common aspirations, and common beliefs very often is a result of what is said, by whom, and with what effect.

Consider, for example, the community that developed around the civil rights advocacy of Dr. Martin Luther King, Jr. in the 1950s and 1960s. Dr. King was a highly skillful and knowledgeable practitioner of the art of rhetoric. He, and others working with him, created a community of value and action, and much of their work was accomplished by means of effective rhetorical discourse. More specifically, Dr. King advocated certain values in a persuasive manner. Among these were equality, justice, non-violence, and peace. He also tested particular ideas in public settings—ideas like racism, which he rejected, and ideas like unity among races, which he embraced. He brought facts to light for his audiences, such as facts about the treatment of African American people.

Dr. King provided a language for talking about racial harmony. His dream of a racially unified America and his advocacy of "nonviolent resistance" inspired many in the civil rights movement who made his terminology part of their own vocabulary. Through his rhetorical efforts, King built a community of discourse that enabled people to think and act with unity. He developed an active and effective community around powerful ideas to which he gave voice rhetorically.

Often members of a community—examples might include feminists, Orthodox Jews, or animal rights activists—do not know all of the other members of their community personally. In fact, any particular member of a large and diffuse community might know only a very small fraction of the people who would say they belong to the group. How is a sense of community maintained when a community is large and geographically diffuse? Certainly, the group's symbols, metaphors, and ways of reasoning function to create a common bond that promotes a strong sense of community despite physical separation. Moreover, communities are sustained over time by the rhetorical interactions of their members with one another and with members of other groups. As Hogan writes, "[C]ommunities are living creatures, nurtured and nourished by rhetorical discourse."[41]

This section has discussed six functions performed by the practice of rhetoric: (1) testing ideas, (2) assisting advocacy, (3) distributing power, (4) discovering facts, (5) shaping knowledge, and (6) building community. These functions are closely related to major themes in the history of rhetoric and provide connections among subsequent chapters. The next section sets out some of these themes in greater detail.

CONCLUSION

We began this chapter by considering some common meanings of the term *rhetoric*, such as empty talk, beautiful language, or persuasion. Whereas these meanings frequently are associated with the term, rhetoric was defined as the study or practice of effective symbolic expression, we noted that rhetoric refers to a type of discourse marked by several characteristics that include being planned, adapted to an audience, and responsive to a set of circumstances. We have also considered some of the rhetoric's social functions such as testing ideas, assisting advocacy, and building communities.

Recurrent Themes

Several important issues arise when we begin to think seriously about the art of rhetoric and its various uses. We will return to these themes as we consider the ways in which the art of rhetoric has developed over the past 2,500 years. The following issues will be revisited throughout this text:

Rhetoric and Power

As we have seen, rhetoric bears an important relationship to power in a society. The art of rhetoric itself brings a measure of power, and rhetorical practices play an important role in both distributing and concentrating power. Every culture makes decisions about who may speak, before which audiences, and on which topics. Altering these limitations will often mean violating such established norms, whether through the practice of rhetoric, rhetorical education, or both. If a segment of a society lacks the knowledge of rhetoric, or is denied the ability to practice rhetoric, does this mean that their access to power is correspondingly diminished? We will examine this question at several junctures in the history of rhetoric.

Rhetoric and Truth

Rhetoric discovers facts relevant to decision-making. Moreover, rhetoric helps to shape what we say we know or believe. What, then, is rhetoric's relationship to truth? Does rhetoric discover truth? Or, does rhetoric simply provide one the means of communicating truth discovered by other approaches, for instance, the scientific method? As we explore the history of rhetoric, we will uncover various answers to these questions. If truth is transcendent, rhetoric's role in its discovery or creation may be minimal. In fact, rhetoric might even be a threat to truth. If, on the other hand, truth is a matter of social agreements, rhetoric plays a major role in establishing what is true.

Rhetoric and Ethics

Persuasion is central to rhetoric. This means that rhetoric always raises moral or ethical questions. If persuasion is always wrong, then rhetoric shares this moral condemnation. If persuasion is acceptable, it is important to ask about ethical obligations of a speaker, writer, or artist. What are the moral restraints within which rhetoric ought to be practiced? Few people would want to live in a society in which rhetoric is practiced without any regard for ethical responsibility on the part of advocates.

Rhetoric and the Audience

The question of ethics is inseparable from the question of a rhetor's potential influence on an audience. Because rhetoric is a form of power, and ethical considerations attend rhetoric. How does rhetoric alter an audience's ways of thinking or prompt action on their part? Moreover, if audiences have some control over the quality of rhetoric, are we morally obliged to educate audiences about rhetoric? As we explore the history of rhetoric, the audience will often be a central concern.

Rhetoric and Society

Our discussion in this chapter has also raised the larger issue of rhetoric's role in developing and maintaining communities and societies. We have considered rhetoric's specific social functions. We depend on rhetoric to forge the compromises and achieve the cooperation needed to live and work together. Such functions are crucial to flourishing democracies. As we survey the history of rhetoric we will want to pay attention to the ways in which rhetoric shapes the values that provide societies a corporate identity and a common direction. How is it that the skillful practice of rhetoric benefits a society, not just practically but morally as well?

These themes and questions will attend our discussion of rhetoric's history. The different answers to our questions suggested by a wide range of writers, and the reasons for their answers, make the history of rhetoric a rich and intriguing source of insight into the development of human thought, relationships, and culture. In Chapter 2, we will encounter most of these themes as we begin our study of rhetoric's long and rich history by looking at its controversial origins and early development in ancient Greece.

QUESTIONS FOR REVIEW

1. How are the following terms defined in the chapter?

   rhetoric
   the art of rhetoric
   rhetorical discourse
   rhetor
   symbol
   rhetorical theory
   the Argumentative Hypothesis

2. What are the marks or characteristics of rhetorical discourse discussed in this chapter?
3. Which specific resources of language are discussed under the heading "Rhetoric Is Planned"?
4. What social functions of the art of rhetoric are discussed in this chapter?
5. Which three types of power are enhanced by an understanding of the art of rhetoric?
6. Given the definition and description of rhetoric advanced in this chapter, what might historian of rhetoric George Kennedy mean by saying that the yellow pages of the phone book are more rhetorical than the white pages? (*Classical Rhetoric and Its Christian and Secular Tradition*, p. 4.)
7. What is meant by the statement that rhetoric addresses contingent issues?

QUESTIONS FOR DISCUSSION

1. The following artifacts, Abraham Lincoln's "Second Inaugural Address" and Emily Dickinson's poem "Success Is Counted Sweetest," were written at about the same time, and each is written with reference to the Civil War. The two pieces are often held to represent two different types of discourse: Lincoln's address is categorized as rhetoric, while Dickinson's work fits best into the category of poetry. Thinking back on the characteristics of rhetorical discourse discussed in this chapter, what case could be made, if any, for distinguishing Lincoln's work from Dickinson's? Do they belong to different literary categories? Refer back to the resources of language— argument, appeal, arrangement, and artistic devices—in thinking about these two pieces. Does each employ all four resources?

Second Inaugural Address

Abraham Lincoln

Fellow-countrymen: At this second appearing to take the oath of the presidential office, there is less occasion for an extended address than there was at first. Then a statement, somewhat in detail, of a course to be pursued seemed very fitting and proper. Now, at the expiration of 4 years, during which public declarations have been constantly called forth on every point and phase of the great contest which still absorbs the attention and engrosses the energies of the nation, little that is new could be presented.

The progress of our arms, upon which all else chiefly depends, is as well known to the public as to myself, and it is, I trust, reasonably satisfactory and encouraging to all. With high hope for the future, no prediction in regard to it is ventured.

On the occasion corresponding to 4 years ago, all thoughts were anxiously directed to an impending civil war. All dreaded it, all sought to avoid it. While the inaugural address was being delivered from this place, devoted altogether to saving the Union without war, insurgent agents were in the city seeking to destroy it with war seeking to dissolve the Union and divide the effects by negotiation. Both parties deprecated war, but one of them would make war rather than let it perish, and the war came. One-eighth of the whole population were colored slaves, not distributed generally over the Union, but localized in the Southern part of it. These slaves constituted a peculiar and powerful interest. All knew that this interest was somehow the cause of the war. To strengthen, perpetuate, and extend this interest was the object for which the insurgents would rend the Union by war, while the government claimed no right to do more than to restrict the territorial enlargement of it.

Neither party expected for the war nor the magnitude or the duration which it has already attained. Neither anticipated that the cause of the conflict might cease when, or even before the conflict itself should cease. Each looked for an easier triumph, and a result less fundamental and astounding. Both read the same Bible and pray to the same God, and each invokes His aid against the other. It may seem strange that any men should dare to ask a just God's assistance in wringing their bread from the sweat of other men's faces, but let us judge not that we be not judged. The prayer of both could not be answered. That of neither has been answered fully. The Almighty has His own purposes. Woe unto the world because of offenses, for it must needs be that offenses come, but woe to that man by whom the offence cometh. If we shall suppose that American slavery is one of those offenses which, in the providence of God, must needs come, but which having continued through His appointed time, He now wills to remove, and that He gives to both North and South this terrible war as the woe due to those by whom the offence came, shall we discern there any departure from those divine attributes which the believers in a living God always ascribe to Him? Fondly do we hope, fervently do we pray, that this mighty scourge of war may speedily pass away. Yet if God wills that it continue until all the wealth piled by the bondsman's two 250 years of unrequited toil shall be sunk, and until every drop of blood drawn with the lash shall be paid by another drawn with the sword, as was said 3,000 years ago, so still it must be said, that the judgments of the Lord are true and righteous altogether.

    With malice toward none, with charity for all, with firmness in the right as God gives us to see the right, let us finish the work we are in, to bind up the nation's wounds, to care for him who shall have borne the battle, and for his widow and his orphans, to do all which may achieve and cherish a just and a lasting peace among ourselves and with all nations.[42]

"Success Is Counted Sweetest"
Emily Dickinson

Success is counted sweetest
By those who ne'er succeed.
To comprehend a nectar
Requires sorest need.
Not one of all the purple host
Who took the flag to-day
Can tell the definition,
So clear, of victory,
As he, defeated, dying,
On whose forbidden ear
The distant strains of triumph Break, agonized, and clear.[43]

2. If rhetoric accomplishes the benefits and performs the functions discussed in this chapter, it might follow that rhetorical training should be a central component in education. Has training in rhetoric or some related discipline been part of your educational experience? Should education focus more on the skills that make up the art of rhetoric?

3. Is rhetoric pervasive in private and social life, as the chapter suggests? In what realms of life, if any, does rhetoric appear to have little or no part to play? Where is its influence greatest, in your estimation? Where is it present, but hidden?

4. Steven Mailloux has written that there are "oral, visual, written, digital, gestural" rhetorics. Which other types of rhetoric would you add to this list? What special types or genres would you include under the types you have added?

5. Respond to the claim that rhetoric is important to the process of building community. Has it been your experience, when people come together to form a community, that ways of speaking and reasoning in common are an important part of that process? Could a greater understanding of the art of rhetoric enhance this process of building a community?

6. Some people have criticized rhetoric for being manipulative. Do you believe that rhetoric is, by its very nature, manipulative? If not, what ethical guidelines might be important for constraining the practice of rhetoric so that it does not become a tool for manipulation?

7. The following speech was delivered by Civil Rights activist Mrs. Fannie Lou Hamer on August 22, 1964 to the Credentials Committee of the Democratic National

Convention in Atlantic City, New Jersey. Though she lacked formal rhetorical training, the speech stands as a powerful example of morally informed oratory. Drawing on this chapter's discussion of the social functions of argument, write a one page analysis of how Mrs. Hamer's testimony before the committee illustrates any two of those functions.

Mr. Chairman, and to the Credentials Committee, my name is Mrs. Fannie Lou Hamer, and I live at 626 East Lafayette Street, Ruleville, Mississippi, Sunflower County, the home of Senator James O. Eastland and Senator Stennis.

It was the 31st of August in 1962 that eighteen of us traveled twenty-six miles to the county courthouse in Indianola to try to register to become first-class citizens. We was met in Indianola by policemen, Highway Patrolmen, and they only allowed two of us in to take the literacy test at the time. After we had taken this test and started back to Ruleville, we was held up by the City Police and the State Highway Patrolmen and carried back to Indianola where the bus driver was charged that day with driving a bus the wrong color.

After we paid the fine among us, we continued on to Ruleville, and Reverend Jeff Sunny carried me four miles in the rural area where I had worked as a timekeeper and sharecropper for eighteen years. I was met there by my children, who told me the plantation owner was angry because I had gone down—tried to register.

After they told me, my husband came, and said the plantation owner was raising Cain because I had tried to register. And before he quit talking the plantation owner came and said, "Fannie Lou, do you know—did Pap tell you what I said?"

And I said, "Yes, sir." He said, "Well I mean that." Said, "If you don't go down and withdraw your registration, you will have to leave." Said, "Then if you go down and withdraw," said, "you still might have to go because we're not ready for that in Mississippi." And I addressed him and told him and said, "I didn't try to register for you. I tried to register for myself."

I had to leave that same night. On the 10th of September 1962, sixteen bullets were fired into the home of Mr. and Mrs. Robert Tucker for me. That same night two girls were shot in Ruleville, Mississippi. Also, Mr. Joe McDonald's house was shot in.

And June the 9th, 1963, I had attended a voter registration workshop; was returning back to Mississippi. Ten of us was traveling by the Continental Trailway bus. When we got to Winona, Mississippi, which is Montgomery County, four of the people got off to use the washroom, and two of the people—to use the restaurant— two of the people wanted to use the washroom.

The four people that had gone in to use the restaurant was ordered out. During this time I was on the bus. But when I looked through the window and saw they had rushed out I got off of the bus to see what had happened. And one of the ladies said, "It was a State Highway Patrolman and a Chief of Police ordered us out." I got back on the bus and one of the persons had used the washroom got back on the bus, too.

As soon as I was seated on the bus, I saw when they began to get the five people in a highway patrolman's car. I stepped off of the bus to see what was happening and somebody screamed from the car that the five workers was in and said, "Get that one there." And when I went to get in the car, when the man told me I was under arrest, he kicked me.

I was carried to the county jail and put in the booking room. They left some of the people in the booking room and began to place us in cells. I was placed in a cell with a young woman called Miss Ivesta Simpson. After I was placed in the cell I began to hear sounds of licks and screams. I could hear the sounds of licks and horrible screams. And I could hear somebody say, "Can you say, 'yes, sir,' nigger? Can you say 'yes, sir'?"

And they would say other horrible names. She would say, "Yes, I can say 'yes, sir.'" "So, well, say it." She said, "I don't know you well enough." They beat her, I don't know how long. And after a while she began to pray, and asked God to have mercy on those people.

And it wasn't too long before three white men came to my cell. One of these men was a State Highway Patrolman and he asked me where I was from. And I told him Ruleville. He said, "We are going to check this." And they left my cell and it wasn't too long before they came back. He said, "You are from Ruleville all right," and he used a curse word. And he said, "We're going to make you wish you was dead."

I was carried out of that cell into another cell where they had two Negro prisoners. The State Highway Patrolmen ordered the first Negro to take the blackjack. The first Negro prisoner ordered me, by orders from the State Highway Patrolman, for me to lay down on a bunk bed on my face. And I laid on my face, the first Negro began to beat me.

And I was beat by the first Negro until he was exhausted. I was holding my hands behind me at that time on my left side, because I suffered from polio when I was six years old. After the first Negro had beat until he was exhausted, the State Highway Patrolman ordered the second Negro to take the blackjack.

The second Negro began to beat and I began to work my feet, and the State Highway Patrolman ordered the first Negro who had beat to sit on my feet—to keep me from working my feet. I began to scream and one white man got up and began to beat me in my head and tell me to hush.

One white man—my dress had worked up high—he walked over and pulled my dress—I pulled my dress down and he pulled my dress back up. I was in jail when Medgar Evers was murdered.

All of this is on account of we want to register, to become first-class citizens. And if the Freedom Democratic Party is not seated now, I question America. Is this America, the land of the free and the home of the brave, where we have to sleep with our telephones off of the hooks because our lives be threatened daily, because we want to live as decent human beings, in America?

Thank you.[44]

TERMS

Aesthetics Study of the persuasive potential in the form, beauty, or force of symbolic expression.

Appeals Symbolic methods that aim either to elicit an emotion or to engage the audience's loyalties or commitments.

Argument Discourse characterized by reasons advanced to support a conclusion. Reasoning made public with the goal of influencing an audience.

Arrangement The planned ordering of a message to achieve the greatest persuasive effect.

Dispositio Arrangement; Cicero's term for the effective ordering of arguments and appeals.

Elocutio Style; Cicero's term to designate the concern for finding the appropriate language or style for a message.

Ideology A system of belief, or a framework for interpreting the world.

Inventio **(invention)** Cicero's term describing the process of coming up with the arguments and appeals that would make up the substance of a persuasive case.

Motives Commitments, goals, desires, or purposes when they lead to action.

Rhetor Anyone engaged in preparing or presenting rhetorical discourse.

Rhetoric, Art of The study and practice of effective symbolic expression.

Rhetoric, Type of discourse Goal-oriented discourse that seeks, by means of the resources of symbols, to adapt ideas to an audience.

Rhetorical discourse Discourse crafted according to the principles of the art of rhetoric.

Rhetorical theory The systematic presentation of rhetoric's principles, descriptions of its various functions, and explanations of how rhetoric achieves its goals.

Symbol Any mark, sign, sound, or gesture that represents something based on social agreement.

NOTES

1   Plato, *Gorgias*, 463; trans. W. C. Helmbold (Indianapolis, IN: Bobbs-Merrill, 1952), 23–24.

2   John Locke, *An Essay Concerning Human Understanding* (1690; rpt. Oxford: Clarendon Press, 1894), 146.

3   Sander Gilman, Carole Blair, and David Parent, eds./trans. *Friedrich Nietzsche on Rhetoric and Language* (New York: Oxford University Press, 1989), 21. (Emphasis in original.)

4   Wayne Booth, *The Vocation of a Teacher* (Chicago, IL: University of Chicago Press, 1988), xiv–xv.

5   Richard McKeon, *Rhetoric: Essays in Invention and Discovery*, ed. Mark Backman (Woodbridge, CT: Ox Bow Press, 1987), 108.

6   Richard Lanham, *The Electronic Word: Democracy, Technology, and the Arts* (Chicago, IL: University of Chicago Press, 1993), 51.

7   Stanford News Service, "The New Literacy: Study Finds Richness and Complexity in Students' Writing" (October 12, 2009). http://news.stanford.edu/pr/2009/pr-lunsford-writing-101209.html. Accessed May 2, 2011.

8   Deirdre N. McCloskey, "The Neglected Economics of Talk," *Planning for Higher Education* 22 (Summer 1994): 11–16, p. 14.

9   McCloskey, 15.

10   Michael Billig, *Arguing and Thinking: A Rhetorical Approach to Social Psychology* (1989; Cambridge: Cambridge University Press, 1996), 57.

11   For a scholarly yet entertaining look at the ways we go about persuading one another in every-day life, see: Robert Cialdini's insightful book, *Influence: The Psychology of Persuasion* (1984; New York: William Morrow, 1993).

12   Jane Donawerth, ed. *Rhetorical Theory by Women before 1900* (Lanham, MD: Rowman & Littlefield, 2002), xiv.

13   George Kennedy, translator's introduction to *Aristotle on Rhetoric: A Theory of Civic Discourse* (Oxford: Oxford University Press, 1991), 7.

14   Carole Blair has written an intriguing essay on the rhetoric of the Vietnam Memorial, which appears in the book *Critical Questions* (New York: St. Martin's Press, 1994). Barry Brummett considers the rhetoric of a wide variety of cultural artifacts in *Rhetoric in Popular Culture* (New York: St. Martin's Press, 1994).

15   "Ocean swimmer Diana Nyad, 60, Preparing for Cuba-to-Florida Swim," *Los Angeles Times* (July 27, 2010).

16   If you would be interested in seeing an extended treatment of this question of the rhetoric of typeface, watch the movie *Helvetica*, a documentary devoted entirely to the history and interpretation of the titular typeface.

17   Steven Mailloux, "One Size Doesn't Fit All: The Contingent Universality of Rhetoric," in *Sizing Up Rhetoric*, ed. David Zarefsky and Elizabeth Benacka (Long Grove, IL: Waveland Press, 2008), 7–19, p. 9.

18   Booth, xiv.

19   Chaim Perelman and Lucy Olbrechts-Tyteca, *The New Rhetoric: A Treatise on Argumentation*, trans. John Wilkinson and Purcell Weaver (Notre Dame: University of Notre Dame Press, 1969), 23–24.

20   Richard Lanham, *The Economics of Attention: Style and Substance in the Age of Information* (Chicago, IL: University of Chicago Press, 2007).

21   "Utah researchers discover how brain is wired for attention," KurzweilAI.net (November 2, 2010), www.kurzweilai.net (accessed November 2, 2010). The original study appeared November 1, 2010 in online edition of the *Proceedings of the National Academy of Sciences*, www.pnas.org/

22   Leon Watson, "Humans have shorter attention span than goldfish, thanks to smartphones," *The Telegraph* (May 15, 2015), www.telegraph.co.uk/science/2016/03/12/humans-have-shorter-attention-span-than-goldfish-thanks-to-smart/ (accessed August 31, 2016)

23   Brian Boyd, *On the Origin of Stories* (Cambridge, MA: Harvard University Press, 2009), 232.

24   Joseph Wenzel, "Three Perspectives on Argument," in *Perspectives on Argumentation: Essays in Honor of Wayne Brockriede*, ed. Robert Trapp and Janice Schuetz (Prospect Heights, IL: Waveland, 1990), 13.

25   Hugo Mercier, Dan Sperber, "How do Humans Reason? Arguments for an Argumentative Theory", *Behavioral and Brain Sciences* (2011) 34, 57–111, p. 58.

26   Tom Strini, "A Taut Take on Beethoven's Ninth," *The Milwaukee Journal Sentinel* (May 13, 2006).

27   Abraham Lincoln, "Second Inaugural Address," in *The World's Great Speeches*, ed. Lewis Copeland (New York: Dover Publications, 1958), 316–317.

28 George Breitman, ed. *Malcolm X Speaks* (New York: Grove Press, 1966), 50. Quoted in: Robert L. Scott, "Justifying Violence: The Rhetoric of Militant Black Power," in *The Rhetoric of Black Power*, ed. Robert L. Scott and Wayne Brockriede (New York: Harper and Row, 1969), 132.

29 Aristotle, *Rhetoric*, trans. W. Rhys Roberts (New York: Modern Library, 1954), 27.

30 Thomas Farrell, *Norms of Rhetorical Culture* (New Haven, CT: Yale University Press, 1993), 77.

31 Lloyd Bitzer, "Political Rhetoric," in *Landmark Essays on Contemporary Rhetoric*, ed. Thomas Farrell (Mahwah, NJ: Hermagoras Press), 1–22, p. 7.

32 Farrell, 79.

33 Lanham, *The Electronic Word*, 227.

34 Richard Lanham, "The Economics of Attention," *Michigan Quarterly Review* 36 (Spring 1997): 270.

35 On the relationship of rhetoric and power, see: James A. Berlin, "Revisionary Histories of Rhetoric: Politics, Power, and Plurality," in *Writing Histories of Rhetoric*, ed. Victor Vitanza (Carbondale, IL: Southern Illinois University Press, 1994), 112–127.

36 Rebecca R., Hastings, "Communication Skills Key for Young Workers", Society for Human Resource Management (March 8, 2012), www.shrm.org/resourcesandtools/hr-topics/employee-relations/pages/communicationskillskey.aspx (accessed September 1, 2016).

37 See: Michael Billig, *Ideology and Opinion* (London: Sage, 1991).

38 Billig, *Ideology*, 5.

39 One of the earliest explorations of this issue is found in: Robert L. Scott, "On Viewing Rhetoric as Epistemic," *Central States Speech Journal* 18 (February 1967): 9–16. See also: Lloyd F. Bitzer, "Rhetoric and Public Knowledge," in *Rhetoric, Philosophy, and Literature: An Exploration* (West Lafayette, IN: Purdue University Press, 1978), 67–93.

40 See: *Rhetoric and Community: Studies in Unity and Fragmentation*, ed. Michael J. Hogan (Columbia, SC: University of South Carolina Press, 1998), introduction, xv.

41 Hogan, 292.

42 Lincoln, 316–317.

43 Emily Dickinson, "Success Is Counted Sweetest." Reprinted by permission of the publishers and the Trustees of Amherst College from *The Poems of Emily Dickinson*, ed. Thomas H. Johnson (Cambridge, MA: The Belknap Press of Harvard University, copyright © 1951, 1955, 1979 by the President and Fellows of Harvard College).

44 Used with permission of the Fannie Lou Hamer Memorial Garden and Museum Foundation, Charles McLaurin, President of the Board.

Chapter 2

The Origins and Early History of Rhetoric

I say to them that if they are to excel in oratory . . . they must, first of all, have a natural aptitude for that which they have elected to do; secondly, they must submit to training and master the knowledge of their particular subject . . . and, finally, they must become versed and practiced in the use and application of their art.

—Isocrates

THE history of rhetoric does not have a precise beginning point any more than the history of dance or painting. When human beings recognized in movement the capacity, not just for mobility, but also for expression, dance began. When pigments were employed to tell a story by producing images on a wall, painting began. When people found in symbols the capacity, not merely for communicating meaning, but also for accomplishing their goals, rhetoric began. Thus, though rhetoric's origin as the planned use of language to achieve goals cannot be known, its systematic presentation within a particular cultural tradition can be located historically.

The history of rhetoric in the Western tradition begins, as do several other histories of arts or disciplines, with that ancient cluster of highly inventive societies, the Greek city-states of the eighth through the third centuries BCE. Rhetoric scholar Richard Leo Enos points out that theories about the power of language were already implicit in the writings of Homer in the ninth century. In Homeric writing, Enos finds three functions of language: the "heuristic, eristic, and protreptic."[1]

Briefly, the heuristic function is a capacity for discovery, whether of facts, insights, or even of "self-awareness."[2] The eristic function of language draws our attention to "the inherent power of the language itself."[3] The eristic function identifies language's capacity to captivate, to motivate, or even to injure. Finally, the protreptic function of discourse expresses language's ability to "'turn' or direct human thought . . ."[4] That is, words afforded human agents the possibility for persuading others to think as they thought. These instrumental functions of language were recognized centuries before they became the foundation for a systematic study of rhetoric.

In addition to these functions of language, anyone dependent upon words for their livelihood also recognized their dependence upon audiences. Certainly, concern for holding an audience's attention, a topic introduced in Chapter 1, pre-dates the formal study of rhetoric. *Peitho*, the goddess of persuasion, appeared in the Athenian pantheon and literature long before itinerant rhetoricians arrived in Athens. Literary scholar Brian Boyd writes, "Greek bards reciting or singing about their gods and heroes already belonged to a system of competing for attention." Bards had to be innovators and inventors, wordsmiths willing to vary the pace, length, and manner of telling their stories to compete with other existing stories or to make a familiar story stand out as if being told for the first time.

Boyd suggests that Homer himself experimented with rhetorical strategies such as the method of compression, or shortening the time in which critical actions took place in the war between Athens and Troy. "As in the Iliad, Homer again in the Odyssey prefers the intensity of compression to the slackness of mere sequence."[5] So, the resources of language were widely recognized and experimented with centuries before formal rhetorical studies appeared and took hold in the Greek city-states of the fifth century BCE. What conditions prepared the way for a more organized approach to rhetoric?

THE RISE OF RHETORIC

The origins of rhetoric may be traced to a Greek city on the island of Sicily in the fifth century BCE, and to a shadowy figure known as Empedocles (490–430). This poet, magician, physician, and orator was also legendary for his speaking ability, which he apparently employed to oppose powerful rulers of his time. The studies Empedocles was known for—poetry, magic, medicine, and oratory—reflect an ancient understanding of words and their power which strikes modern readers as strange. The reasons for these connections will be explored in this and the following chapter.

Rhetoric as a systematic discipline also originated in Sicily, in the city of Syracuse around 467 BCE. The tyrant named Hieron had died, and disputes arose over which families were due land that he had seized. An orator named Corax offered training in judicial argument to citizens defending their claims in court. Corax also apparently played a role in directing Syracuse toward democratic reforms.[6]

Corax's approach to teaching public speaking was quickly adopted by others and was carried to Athens and other Greek city-states by professional teachers and practitioners of rhetoric known as Sophists. Many Sophists were attracted to the flourishing city of Athens, where they wrote speeches and provided courses in rhetoric for anyone able to pay their high fees. Athens' relatively open atmosphere and emerging democratic political system proved fertile ground for rhetoric's growth.

Athenian Democratic Reforms

Why did the Sophists find such a ready market for their rhetorical services at this particular time? Rhetoric's popularity in Greece had much to do with dramatic changes affecting several city-states, particularly Athens, in the sixth and fifth centuries.

As historian of rhetoric John Poulakos writes, "when the Sophists appeared on the horizon of the Hellenic city-states, they found themselves in the midst of an enormous cultural change: from aristocracy to democracy."

The statesman Solon (638–559 BCE) had implemented major political reforms in Athens, and leaders such as Cleisthenes (566–493), Ephialtes (d. 461), and Pericles (495–429 BCE) fostered dramatic democratic changes—free male citizens of Athens would be allowed to rule the *polis*. Around 507 BCE Cleisthenes dubbed the new form of government *demokratia*, rule by the people. Poulakos notes that these changes in the Greek political system "created the need for a new kind of education, an education consistent with the new politics of limited democracy."[7] The middle class grew in power as "family name, class origin, or property size" no longer dictated who could be involved in the courts and legislative assemblies.[8] Whereas aristocratic families with great wealth could still afford "to buy the training necessary for leadership in the Assembly, Council and courts," the new system "guaranteed a broader distribution of power across different backgrounds, occupations, and economic statuses than ever before."[9]

Athenian democracy was a remarkable political innovation. "For the first time in the recorded history of a complex society," writes Josiah Ober, "*all* native freeborn males, irrespective of their ability, were political equals, with equal rights to debate and to determine state policy."[10] Important to this innovation was a rising conception of the citizen as an individual member of the society possessing right, a notion completely unknown in many other parts of the world at this time. While Athenian women (50,000–60,000), slaves (150,000–250,000), and metics (*metoikoi*) or resident foreigners (15,000) were conspicuously excluded from power, cracks were beginning to appear in the wall separating ruling aristocratic elites and the general public. The distinction between the mass of ordinary citizens and the aristocracy in ancient Athens involved, among other things, the ability to make a persuasive speech. Thus, the Sophists' offer to teach rhetoric to anyone regardless of class appeared to many a means of gaining entrance to previously inaccessible arenas of power.

The Polis and Politics

As a larger number of men entered politics, the key factor in personal success and public influence was no longer class but speaking skill. Every male citizen enjoyed the right of *isegoria*, a guarantee of the opportunity to speak freely in public assemblies. Democratic reforms "completed a process of democratization . . . allowing for, even requiring, Athenian males to develop the ability to listen, understand, and speak about deliberative and judicial affairs of the city."[11] Moreover, courts, the legislative assembly, and the numerous festivals and funerals that were central to life in the Greek city-states all depended on the capacity of citizens to speak before an audience.

The *polis* or independent city-states, more than anything else, defined what it meant to be Greek. The ancient Greeks, according to historian H. D. F. Kitto, had an

> addiction to the independent polis—it was the polis, to the Greek mind, which marked the difference between the Greek and the barbarian: it was the polis which enabled him to live the full, intelligent and responsible life which he wished to live.[12]

The word *polis* strongly implied the presence of citizens, and Greeks were more likely to refer to Athenians and Spartans than to Athens and Sparta. Thus, the term brought to mind a group of citizens rather than a physical city. With democratic reforms, the political life of the *polis* came to be managed by citizens engaged in oratory and debate. Tyrants may have ruled other nations by "torture and the lash: the Greeks took their decisions by persuading and debate."[13] Under such circumstances, the need for rhetorical training was apparent to everyone. Apparent, perhaps, but not available to everyone. The effect of Athenian democratic reforms on women will be considered later in this chapter.

Education in Athens

The Sophists, then, offered Greek citizens education in the arts of discourse, especially training in inventing arguments and presenting them in a persuasive manner to a large audience. Newly enfranchised citizens created a market for something not previously available in Greece, that is, education in the effective speech.[14]

In most of ancient Greece, education was divided into those studies that provided moral strength to the soul—mainly music and literature—and gymnastics that strengthened the body. Higher education in our contemporary sense, that is, advanced studies intended to sharpen the intellect, was virtually unknown. Boys began their schooling at around age seven, and typically had a music teacher, a writing and reading instructor (who also taught them numbers), and an athletic trainer. Because "the Athenian democracy functioned on the assumption that all male citizens were literate," most free males received this basic education. Education was focused on developing useful skills and cultivating traditional Greek values.[15]

For this reason, classicist Jacqueline de Romilly (1913–2010) writes that the Sophists introduced a "great novelty" into Athenian life by offering education to anyone who could afford it. Formal education was rather simple, and limited in its availability to a small portion of the populace. "There was nothing that even remotely resembled what we call further education in Athens" prior to the Sophists, she writes.[16]

Training in Rhetoric

Sophists like Hippias, Protagoras, and Gorgias

> proudly advertised [their] ability to teach a young man "the proper care of his personal affairs, so that he may best manage his own household, and also of the State's affairs, so as to become a real power in the city, both as a speaker and man of action."[17]

Such advertising proved irresistible to many, and the Sophists grew in both wealth and influence. The new education offered by the Sophists did not train one in a particular craft like masonry. Rather, rhetorical education promised mastery of the skills of language necessary to participate in political life and succeed in financial ventures. The Sophists' education in rhetoric, then, opened a doorway to success and influence for many Greek citizens. Rhetoric took hold as a major aspect of culture and education, a position it maintained for much of subsequent Western history.[18]

The ability to speak persuasively had previously been viewed as a natural talent, or even as a gift from the gods. Actual training in rhetoric, however, gradually became the very foundation of Greek education, and was the principal sign of an educated and influential person. "The influence of the spoken word in fifth- or fourth-century Athens was extremely strong," writes H. D. Rankin, "and can hardly be overemphasized."[19]

Susan Jarratt and Rory Ong suggest that this was true in part because the Greeks assumed that "human deliberation and action are responsible for human destinies and can be shaped by thought and speech."[20] This assumption marks a profound change in thought, for it indicates that the Greek public gradually rejected the belief that destiny was shaped by the gods, and accepted in its place a new concept: the destiny of the individual and of the *polis* is formed by human rationality and persuasive speech. Moreover, to the Greek mind speech was not simply a means of expression, but a force— an instrument of change.

Richard Enos notes that "ancient Greeks considered rhetoric to be a discipline, accepted it as part of their education and, particularly in those cities that were governed by democracies, saw it as practical for the workings of their communities."[21] Ironically, this art of rhetoric, so important to Greek civic life and education, was brought to Athens and other cities by foreign teachers known as Sophists. The activities, beliefs, and reputations of these intriguing rhetoricians deserve a closer look. But first, a brief description of how trials were conducted in ancient Athens will help us appreciate why personal skill in oratory was so crucial to an Athenian.

Courts and Assemblies in Athens

The Athenian court was called the *Dikasteria* (*dikast*: judge or juror); in many ways it was unlike what we think of as a court today. An Athenian trial—an open-air event— consisted of two speeches: one of prosecution, the other of defense. Citizens spoke for themselves. The jury of from 200 to more than 1,500 members (male citizens over 30) did not deliberate but simply voted. Jurors were paid for their services, and the trial was concluded in a day. Testimonial evidence had to be filed with the court—really just a group of ordinary citizens—preceding the trial, and was read aloud to the gathered citizen-jury. The time allowed for the all-important speeches was determined by the seriousness of the case being heard. The presiding official's role was more that of a master of ceremonies, timekeeper, and sergeant-at-arms than a legal expert. Indeed, Athenian courts boasted no trained legal experts at all. There were no attorneys in the modern sense of the term, nor even a highly developed legal code. A citizen had to speak for himself, and the trial was largely a rhetorical contest.[22] The citizen jurors were apparently "reasonably competent to evaluate the arguments of both sides fairly and sensibly," this according to classical scholar Michael Gagarin. He adds, "We can see that orators constructed their arguments with careful attention to details, and we should grant the jurors a reasonable degree of intelligence in assessing these arguments."[23]

Beginning around 430, speechwriters or *logographers* like the Sophist Antiphon (479–411 BCE) could be hired to write a judicial speech, albeit for a hefty fee. Interpretation of what laws there were was less significant than was the individual citizen's capacity to present a persuasive speech before a large audience. Skill in speaking was thus paramount in Athenian courts, for the most persuasive public speaker carried the day. This casual court system opened a wide field to Sophists.

The Athenian Assembly (*ekklesia*), a body composed of citizens older than 18, made decisions about laws and foreign policy. With perhaps 40,000 eligible to attend, and meeting perhaps forty times each year, around 6,000 citizens attended any given meeting. The Assembly listened to speeches on a wide range of topics, including whether to build a new port, go to war, or exile an unfaithful citizen. Topics often were handed down to the Assembly by the *boule*, a representative body of 500 citizens (fifty from each of Athens' ten tribes chosen by lot), that met daily and actually supervised the city.

While the *boule*, like the Assembly, was made up of men, it appears that a woman's voice was powerfully present as well. The Greeks were pious people who consulted oracles for divine guidance. The oracle spoke through a *Pythia*, a woman considered to be in intimate contact with the gods. The Pythia's often cryptic advice was brought up in the *boule* as it debated policy. Moreover, not just the Athenians consulted the oracle at Delphi—the site was available to citizens from other city-states as well. Lynda Walsh writes of this period in Greek history:

> The fact remains that the collected pronouncements of the Pythia are the only texts remaining to us, other than Sappho's, that are known to be authored by a woman. Of course, they survive because they were inscribed by the Pythia's attending male prophetes and catalogued and expounded upon by male exegetes and chresmologoi in assemblies and courts of law all over the Greek world. So, the Delphic oracle remains problematically polyvocal—as it should be.

The individual citizen had an unusually important role in the *ekklesia*: "Any citizen who could gain and hold the attention of his fellows in the Assembly had a right to advise them on national policy." Of course, gaining and holding the attention of this several thousand-member body in an open-air arena involved considerable rhetorical skill.[24]

THE SOPHISTS

Rhetoric as a systematic study, then, was developed by a group of orators, educators, writers, and advocates called Sophists, a name derived from the Greek word *sophos*, meaning wise or skilled.[25] Central to their course of study was rhetoric, the art or *techne* of *logos*, a complex term that could mean an argument, a reason, an account, or simply a word. The title *Sophistes* (pl. *Sophistae*) carried with it something of the modern meaning of professor—an authority, an expert, a teacher.

A Sophist specializing in speechwriting was called a *logographos*. Others were teachers who ran schools in which public speaking was taught along with other subjects. A third group were professional orators who gave speeches for a fee, whether for entertainment or in a court or legislature. Of course, any particular Sophist might provide all three services—speechwriter, teacher, and professional speaker. Sophists earned a reputation for "extravagant displays of language" and for astonishing audiences with their "brilliant styles . . . colorful appearances and flamboyant personalities."[26] They were also known for their highly developed memories.

Many of the Sophists became both wealthy and famous in Greece, while at the same time they were despised by some advocates of traditional Greek social values for reasons we will consider shortly. But first we will explore how and what the Sophists taught their students.

The Sophists developed a distinctive style of teaching that proved highly successful. At the same time, they were controversial from the moment they appeared in Greece. Recent scholarship presents the Sophists as important intellectual figures who have received a somewhat unreservedly negative press.[27] Sophists were active in Athens and other Greek city-states from about the middle of the fifth century BCE until the end of the fourth century. Though there never were many Sophists active in Greece at any given time, they exercised influence on the development of rhetoric and even the course of Western culture vastly out of proportion with their numbers.[28] Important Sophists include Gorgias, Protagoras, Polus, Hippias, and Theodorus.

The Flourishing of Athens

Athens and other city-states were experiencing something of a renaissance at the time the Sophists appeared on the scene. Regarding the remarkable intellectual flourishing that characterized this era in ancient Greece, and that shaped subsequent European culture, Michael Gagarin writes: "The second half of the fifth century was a period of intellectual innovation throughout the Greek world, nowhere more so than in Athens. Poets, philosophers, medical writers and practitioners, religious reformers, historians, and others introduced new ways of thinking." He adds that "philosophy and oratory in particular thrived as Athens solidified its position as the intellectual and cultural capital of Greece."[29]

In fact, comparatively speaking, the study and practice of rhetoric had a greater influence on Athenian culture of the day than did now famous philosophers such as Plato. Gagarin notes that:

> Plato's influence on fourth-century Athenian culture was relatively slight, whereas oratory was central to the lives of most Athenian citizens, who regularly attended meetings of the courts or the Assembly in some capacity, even if they did not actively engage in legal or political affairs.

The philosophically minded Plato, his teacher Socrates, and his band of unusual followers occupied something of a fringe position in Athens, while skilled public speakers were famous and admired. The *polis* of Athens in particular "afforded more opportunities to speak in public than did other Greek cities."[30]

The Sophists' Reputation

There has been much disagreement over the interests, character, and contributions of the Sophists. Though controversial even in their own day, recent scholarship has done much to dismantle their traditional treatment as merely itinerant speechwriters or rhetorically gifted con artists. They are now often commended for their surprising insights into the power of words, the nature of symbols, and the important social role of persuasion.

The Sophists were social iconoclasts who questioned the foundational assumptions of Greek society. "Sophists loved to experiment with arguments," writes Gagarin, "and to challenge 'traditional ways of thinking,' and the more shocking the challenge, the better."[31] Sophists employed paradoxes to shock their audiences, and also to provoke debate and inquiry.[32]

To the average Athenian, some of the leading Sophists appeared to be eccentrics wrapped up in unproductive intellectual pursuits, sometimes flamboyant in dress and personal manner, and often followed by an entourage of their students. In his famous play *Clouds*, Aristophanes mocks the Sophists as endlessly debating ludicrous questions. The great playwright treats Socrates himself as a Sophist, though the philosopher neither presented speeches nor taught rhetoric.

What the Sophists Taught

The Sophists were, as we have noted, teachers of the art of verbal persuasion—rhetoric.[33] However, Sophists claimed to teach more than just speechmaking. Some professed to instruct their students in *areté*, a Greek term meaning virtue, excellence, and a capacity for success. *Areté* was associated with military virtues like courage but also suggested the qualities that marked of "a natural leader."[34] *Areté* was traditionally associated with the aristocracy, who were considered to be equipped by a superior nature to lead. Around the time the Sophists were active in Athens the concept of *areté* was coming to be associated with persuasive skills in public settings. This shift in meaning marked the end of a long period of nearly continuous war, and was a nuance of definition the Sophists eagerly encouraged. Because of its association with military and political activities Greeks doubted that *areté* could be taught moral excellence and courage were gifts of birth or the results of a careful Athenian upbringing. Such leaderly qualities certainly were not to be purchased from a professional teacher, and especially not from a foreigner who had not grown up in the *polis*.

The Greek term *demos*, often translated "the people," carried a meaning that is closer to "the masses." An elite group called the *gnorimoi* held a higher social status than did members of the ordinary *demos*. Nevertheless, a large number of daily decisions were left to the determination of this larger group. Among the qualities thought to distinguish the members of the elite were noble birth, wealth, education (*paideia*), and, of course, *areté*. Thus, for the Sophists to claim that they could teach a member of the *demos* the quality of *areté* was viewed not simply as questionable, but as socially disruptive and a threat to the ruling elite of Athens. Education was itself a means of entering a higher social class, and so the Sophists represented a considerable threat to established Athenian order.[35]

Sophistry was more than the study of persuasive speaking, as important as this was. Because the Sophists taught rhetoric, careful management of one's resources, and some aspects of leadership, it is not surprising that many young men in ancient Greece saw sophistic education as the key to personal success.

But it was principally their command of persuasive discourse that brought the Sophists both fame and controversy. Sophists asserted that their costly courses of instruction would teach control of audiences through speech. In Plato's dialogue *Gorgias*, the famous Sophist after whom the dialogue is named asserts that his art is the study of "the greatest good and the source, not only of personal freedom for individuals, but also of mastery over others in one's country." Specifically, Gorgias defines rhetoric as "the ability to persuade with words judges in the courts, senators in the Senate, assemblymen in the Assembly, and men in any other meeting which convenes for the public interest" (452). Poulakos underlines the practical nature of sophistical education by writing that it "concerned itself with rhetorical empowerment for specific, especially political and legal, purposes."[36] By what means, then, did the Sophists teach such a powerful art?

How the Sophists Taught

Learning to be an orator meant the training of a student's ability through instruction and hard study. Rhetorical competence "is gained in three ways, through *physis*, natural ability, through *technē*, theoretical instruction, or through *askēsis* or *meletē*, practice."[37]

Sophists taught by the method of dialectic (*dialektike*), or inventing arguments for and against a proposition. This exercise taught students to argue either side of a case, and the Sophist Protagoras famously boasted he would teach his students to "make the worse case appear the better." In the dialectical method, speeches and arguments started from statements termed *endoxa*, or premises that were widely believed or taken to be highly probable. An argument might develop from a premise such as, "It is better to possess much virtue than much money." One student would create an argument based on this widely accepted claim. Another student would then challenge the argument on the basis of other widely accepted notions, and by exploring the opposite points from those advanced. Thus, in dialectic, argument met counterargument in a series of exchanges that, it was believed, would yield skill in debate as well as a better view of the truth. Because of their developed ability to argue either side of a case, the Sophists' students were powerful contestants in the popular debating contests of the day, and also highly successful advocates.

Dissoi Logoi

The dialectical method was employed in part because the Sophists accepted the notion of *dissoi logoi*, or contradictory arguments. That is, Sophists believed that strong arguments could be produced for or against any claim. We will explore this idea of *dissoi logoi* in more detail shortly when we consider the famous Sophist, Protagoras.

Closely related to the idea of *dissoi logoi* is the Greek notion of *kairos*, a term meaning a favorable situation or opportune moment. *Kairos* refers originally to passing through a momentary opening before it closes, as a weaver passes a thread through the loom at just the right moment. Under the doctrine of *kairos*, the truth depended on a careful consideration of all factors surrounding an event, including time, opportunity, and circumstances. *Kairos* was also related to decorum or a concern for the words appropriate to the situation, the issue being debated, and the audience. Finally, because of the momentary nature of *kairos*, to achieve this quality in speech was a demonstration of one's quickness and skill with words.[38]

Facts were debatable, and could be ascertained only by allowing the clash of arguments to occur. The search for truth about a crime, for example, involved considering opposite points of view. Arguments were advanced about the time or place where the crime occurred and the circumstances prompting the act. Truth was discovered, or perhaps created, in the decision finally reached by a jury hearing the clash of antithetical claims and arguments.[39]

Sophistic methods helped students to analyze cases, to think on their feet, to ask probing questions, to speak eloquently, and to pose counterarguments. Sophists also compelled their students to memorize speeches, either famous ones or model speeches composed by the teacher. Students would also compose their own speeches based on these models. This method was known as *epideixis*, a word describing a speech prepared for a formal occasion.

Susan Jarratt and Rory Ong provide the following glimpse of a group of students learning to write speeches under the guidance of a Sophist.

> Speeches were generated out of common materials arranged with some spontaneity for the occasion and purpose at hand. To prepare for performance, small seminar-type groups of students working with an accomplished rhetorician would listen to and memorize speeches composed by their teacher and would practice composing and delivering speeches among themselves.

Students practiced "the production of the whole monologues," as well as doing "closer work with topoi," or frequently used types of arguments. Finally, as already noted, Sophists involved their students in "generating arguments on contradictory propositions or *dissoi logoi*." Thus, "rhetorical training created a critical climate within which to question, analyze, and imagine differences in group thought and action."[40]

Why the Sophists Were Controversial

Many Athenians doubted the high-flown claims, doubted that the Sophists really understood justice, doubted that they could teach *areté* or virtue. Those who were unimpressed with feats of verbal and mental agility saw the Sophists as merely opportunistic charlatans ready to prey on the unsuspecting and introduce into the public mind a debased understanding of truth. Plutarch wrote of the Sophists as men with "political shrewdness and practical sagacity." Plato called them simply "masters of the art of making clever speeches," and Xenophon reduced them to the level of "masters of fraud."

But, other assessments have been rendered more recently. One expert on ancient Greece, H. D. Rankin, has written that the Sophists "released their pupils from the inner need to conform with the traditional rules of the city-states so that they were freer in themselves to be active in their pursuit of success without remorse or conscience."[41] This freedom to pursue one's own goals ruthlessly, unrestrained by conventional mores, while exciting to the Sophists' pupils, caused alarm among the more traditional members of Athenian society.

Many Athenians greeted the Sophists and their art of rhetoric with great suspicion. Their ability to persuade with clever arguments, and their willingness to teach others to do the same, led some to see the Sophists as a dangerous element in Athens. Plato, who lived in the generation following the arrival of the first Sophists, encouraged such suspicion with his dialogues *Gorgias*, *Sophist*, and *Protagoras*.[42] Aristotle (384–322 BCE), Plato's student, commented on their empty arguments in *On Sophistical Refutations*.[43]

Sophists were so controversial in Athens and other city-states that their schools of rhetoric were regarded "as a public nuisance and worse."[44] Plato imagines a debate over the Sophists and what they taught in *Gorgias*. As we will see in the next chapter, Plato condemned rhetoric as "a knack of flattering with words," a criticism the art has never lived down. On the other hand, subsequent Western culture has come closer to following the Sophists' argumentative model as presented by Protagoras and Gorgias than the truth-seeking philosophy suggested by Plato.

What factors contributed to the popular feeling that the Sophists were "overpaid parasites"?[45] First, though it does not strike modern readers as a problem, the Sophists taught for pay. Some of the more famous Sophists, such as Hippias, Protagoras, and Gorgias, charged substantial fees for their services and became extremely wealthy. Being paid for teaching, and especially for teaching a student simply to speak persuasively, struck some Athenians as unethical and subversive. Exacting pay for instruction in something other than a trade like stonemasonry or shipbuilding was simply not done, and the practice seemed to encourage less than noble ideas about both education and work.

Andrew Ford notes that the Athenian bias against teaching for pay also stemmed from "an aristocratic feeling that . . . the professional teacher," that is, one accepting payment for teaching, "offered his services on the basis of who could pay and therefore would not base his associations on higher considerations such as character and personal loyalty."[46] In other words, aristocratic families sought to maintain exclusive access to education for their own children, and the Sophists threatened this system. Nevertheless, the fees charged by famous Sophists for a course in rhetoric remained out of the reach of most ordinary working Athenians.

Second, controversy surrounded the Sophists because most of them were foreigners, itinerants who traveled from city to city looking for work as teachers, entertainers, and speechwriters. People have perhaps always been suspicious of the rootless individual, the wanderer, and the foreigner. Sophistry was considered an exotic import to Athens, and all but a few of the leading Sophists were from outside of Athens.

The fact that they were from outside of the Hellenistic world and their habit of travel created a third concern. The Sophists had, as the saying goes, been around, and in their travels they noted that people believe rather different things in different places. Their cultural relativism contributed directly to Greek suspicion of these professional speechwriters and teachers of rhetoric.

Several leading Sophists had developed a view of truth as relative to places and cultures. As Jarratt notes, the Sophists "were skeptical about a divine source of know-ledge or value . . ."[47] They knew not only what the Athenians believed but also what the Spartans, Corinthians, and North Africans believed. More importantly, they knew that beliefs varied from place to place. The further one traveled from Athens, the more customs and beliefs varied. In some regions of the known world, for instance, it was the custom to burn the dead, or even to eat them, whereas in other locations such acts were capital crimes. Marriage customs, judicial procedures, and social relationships all varied dramatically from one locale to another.

Who could know, then, what was true in any absolute sense? A fourth source of controversy had to do with this uncertainty surrounding truth. According to Sophists like Gorgias and Protagoras, truth was not to be found in transcendent sources such as the gods. Rather, a momentary and practical truth emerged from a clash of arguments. Poulakos affirms that the Sophists believed "the world could always be recreated linguistically." Reality itself is a linguistic construction rather than an objective fact.[48] If truth and reality depend on who can speak the most persuasively, what becomes of justice, virtue, and social order? James Murphy and Richard Katula write that "knowledge was subjective and everything is precisely what the individual believes it to be." This meant that "each of us, not necessarily human beings in the collective, decides what something means to us."[49] Such a radical view of truth—and a rhetoric based on it—threatened Athenians steeped in Homeric virtues and traditional Greek piety.

Their relativism may help to explain another novelty introduced by Sophists into courtroom pleading: the use of the argument from probability or *eikos*. Athenian advocates and juries favored cases based on observable facts such as eye-witness testimony. Sophists such as Antiphon, however, successfully reasoned from what was likely or unlikely. For instance, a large and strong man is engaged in a fight with a small man. Who assaulted whom? The small man, employing *eikos*, argues that it is unlikely that he would pick a fight with such a large and strong man, a fight he was sure to lose. The large man, also arguing from *eikos*, reasons that it is unlikely that he would dare to pick a fight with the small man. After all, most people would condemn him for such a cowardly act.[50]

Finally, the Sophists were controversial because they built a view of justice on the notion of social agreement or *nomos*. Sophists advocated *nomos* as the source of law in opposition to other sources such as *thesmos*, or law derived from the authority of kings—*physis*, or natural law— and transcendent Platonic *logos*.[51] The Sophists' belief in *nomos* was closely related to their rejection of transcendent truth and objective reality. Public law and public morality are matters of social agreements and local practice, not the dictates of a God or a king. This view of truth, some thought, undermined the moral foundations of Greek society.

Some historians attribute the Sophists' negative image to their enemies' portrayals of them. Ancient sources suggest that at least some of the Sophists were respectable public figures, expert politicians, and diplomats. Janet Sutton has written that

> Many of the ancients . . . paint a brilliant picture of Protagoras, Lysias, Antiphon, Gorgias, and Thrasymacus as ambassadors and statesmen, as superb stylists of poetic expression and orators of civic discourse, and as practical educators and intimates of political leaders.[52]

Thus, any portrayal of the Sophists must be shaped, as they would have approved, by contradictory claims.

TWO INFLUENTIAL SOPHISTS

Regardless of the controversy surrounding the Sophists, the art of rhetoric had caught on in the Greek-speaking world of the fifth and fourth centuries. Sophists fomented a revolution in thought that even today influences ideas about education, politics, and rhetoric. The lives of individual Sophists illuminate their ideas in ways that a general survey cannot. This section offers a closer look at two of the most influential Sophists.

Gorgias

One of the greatest early teachers and practitioners of the art of rhetoric was Gorgias of Leontini, who is reputed to have lived from 485 to 380 BCE, more than one hundred years.[53] Gorgias was originally sent to Athens as an ambassador and had a tremendously successful career as a diplomat, teacher, skeptical philosopher, and speaker. Unlike other prominent Sophists, Gorgias did not claim to be able to teach *areté*. He was famous, among other things, for his three-part formulation of skeptical philosophy:

1. Nothing exists.
2. If anything did exist, we could not know it.
3. If we could know that something existed, we would not be able to communicate it to anyone else.

Gorgias emphasized the persuasive power of speech—*logos*—and his ideas about rhetoric's irresistible force gained him followers and critics throughout Greece. He is reputed to have studied rhetoric under Empedocles, whom Aristotle credited with having invented the art. Enos calls Gorgias "one of the most innovative theorists in Greek rhetoric."[54] Gorgias was active at about the same time as the most famous of all of the early Sophists, Protagoras (485–411), the subject of the following section.

Gorgias boasted of being able to persuade anyone of anything, and his powers of persuasion were legendary. He persuaded the Athenians to build a gold statue of him at Delphi, an honor unheard of for a foreigner, though some sources suggest that he paid for this statue. If the latter is the case, it illustrates the great wealth Gorgias accumulated as a Sophist. Gorgias was intrigued by the almost magical power persuasive words can exercise over the human mind.[55] His philosophy of language and knowledge suggested that the only reality we can experience "lies in the human psyche, and its malleability and susceptibility" to linguistic manipulation.[56] Rhetorical scholar Bruce Gronbeck holds that for Gorgias, persuasion (*peitho*) was "an art of deception, which works through the medium of language to massage the psyche."[57]

Rhetoric as Magic

George Kennedy suggests that Gorgias considered a rhetor to be "a *psychagogos*, like a poet, a leader of souls through a kind of incantation."[58] The comparison to poetry may confuse modern readers until we recognize that Athenians considered poetry to be persuasive and public rather than innocuous and private. Moreover, poetry was closely connected in Greek thought with religion, ritual, and the supernatural. It is true that poetry was for the Athenians "public discourse" and thus "primarily something to be performed in social or civic spaces . . ."[59] But, it is also the case that poetry was thought to have supernatural origins and to be capable of moving the soul.

Effective rhetoric had a hypnotic effect on audiences captured by the orator's verbal spell. Jacqueline de Romilly, in her book, *Magic and Rhetoric in Ancient Greece*, confirms this view when she connects Gorgias with early practitioners of magical incantations, such as Empedocles and Pythagoras.[60] Gorgias explored the power of *logos* to gain control over an audience's emotions. De Romilly refers to Gorgias as "a theoretician of the magic spell of words."[61] *Logos* was thought to have a power over the mind similar to that of some drugs.

Rhetoric was for Gorgias' verbal magic capable of exerting what one of his great critics, Plato, called an "almost supernatural" influence on audiences. The emotions were central to Gorgias' conception of employing words to direct the will of an audience. "The masters of rhetoric," writes de Romilly, sought "to sway the emotions of the audience." This was the power of rhetoric, a magical word-force similar to incantations or poetry.[62] Jane Tompkins has noted in this regard that "the equation of language with power, characteristic of Greek at least from the time of Gorgias the rhetorician, explains the enormous energies devoted to the study of rhetoric in the ancient world."[63]

Gorgias' *Encomium* and Rhetorical Devices

Gorgias was interested in the sounds of words, sounds which "when manipulated with skill, could captivate audiences."[64] If words do not represent an external reality, then perhaps their importance is as a means of creating a reality within human thought. Gorgias' experiments with sound (a reminder that he was principally a speaker rather than a writer) led to a florid, rhyming style that strikes modern readers as extravagant and even bombastic. This hypnotic style adapted poetic devices to rhetoric, poetry itself being seen as a means of working magic.[65]

An example from a translation of Gorgias' *Encomium on Helen* reflects something of the effect Gorgias sought to achieve with sounds, as well as revealing Gorgias' association of rhetoric with magic and poetry:

> All poetry I ordain and proclaim to composition in meter, the listeners of which are affected by passionate trepidation and compassionate perturbation and likewise tearful lamentation . . . Inspired incantations are provocative of charm and revocative of harm.[66]

Gorgias probably intended this famous speech to demonstrate that the skilled rhetorician can prove even the most unlikely proposition. He reveals his skill by arguing the provocative thesis that Helen cannot be blamed for deserting Menelaus and following Paris to Troy. As George Kennedy summarizes, Gorgias enumerated four possible reasons

[handwritten margin note: Rhetoric was "magical" bc it used emotions & persuasion poetically to make changes in society.]

for Helen's action: "it was the will of the gods; she was taken by force; she was seduced by words; or she was overcome by love."[67] According to de Romilly, Gorgias argues that Helen "could not have resisted the power of *logos*," or persuasive words, which constitute a type of witchcraft or magic.[68]

As poetry was considered to be of divine origin in the ancient world, the relationship between beautiful words and supernatural power was a more natural one for Gorgias than it is for modern readers.[69] Words worked their magic by arousing emotions such as fear, pity, and longing.[70] Classical scholar G. M. A. Grube notes that Gorgias was especially fond of such rhetorical devices as:

> over-bold metaphors, *allegoria* or to say one thing and mean another, *hypallage* or the use of one word for another, *catachresis* or to use words by analogy, repetition of words, resumption of an argument, *parisosis* or the use of balanced clauses, *apostrophe* or addressing some person or divinity, and antithesis.[71]

Here is the opening of Gorgias' *Encomium*. Even in this single paragraph, we can see the famous Sophist employing a variety of rhetorical devices:

> What is becoming to a city is manpower, to a body beauty, to a soul wisdom, to an action virtue, to a speech truth, and the opposites of these are unbecoming. Man and woman and speech and deed and city and object should be honored with praise if praiseworthy and incur blame if unworthy, for it is an equal error and mistake to blame the praisable and to praise the blamable. It is the duty of one and the same man both to speak the needful rightly and to refute the unrightfully spoken. Thus it is right to refute those who rebuke Helen, a woman about whom the testimony of inspired poets has become univocal and unanimous as has the ill omen of her name, which has become a reminder of misfortunes.[72]

"Style, linguistic ornament, and the sounds of spoken words have remained important aspects of rhetoric throughout its history." Shakespeare is probably the greatest master of the rhetorical figures in the English language. Contemporary orators such as John F. Kennedy also have revealed their knowledge of some of the ancient rhetorical figures. Kennedy, for example, employed *antimetabole*—the transposing of word order in parallel clauses—in a now famous line from his 1960 inaugural address:

> *Ask not what your country can do for you,*
> *rather ask what you can do for your country.*

A similar form of reversing, called *chiasmus*, takes its name from Greek letter X or *chi*. *Chiasmus* involves simply switching the order of elements in adjacent clauses, forming an X in the sentence. Thus, the statement of Jesus:

> Many who are first shall be last, and the last shall be first.

Here is an example of the same device in Shakespeare's play, *Macbeth*:

> Fair is foul, and foul is fair.

Such devices can be memorable and effective when well used, which is precisely why they were of interest to the Sophists. Speech was worthless if not effective, and the very idea of truth itself was closely tied to memory, to what could be recalled and envisioned.[73] If trite, used to excess or otherwise awkwardly employed, rhetorical devices can hinder a speech's impact by distracting the audience.

Gorgias was particularly fond of *antithesis*, a device still quite commonly used. *Antithesis*, as the name implies, involves placing opposed ideas near one another. Thus, a speaker might claim:

> My opponent proposes a war that would bring us dishonor; I advocate a peace that will bring us honor.

Here the notions of war and peace are opposed, as are the concepts of dishonor and honor. Gorgias employed this device widely in his own speaking.

Gorgias' interest in antithesis extended beyond his concern for style. Like some of the other Sophists, he held that "two antithetical statements can be made on each subject," and that truth emerged from a clash of fundamentally opposed positions.[74] The idea that truth is a product of the clash of views was, as we have seen, closely related to the concept of *kairos*, the belief that truth is momentary and relative to circumstances. This view also reflects the Sophists' commitment to *aporia,* the effort to place a claim in doubt. Once clouded in doubt, the orator's goal was to demonstrate that one resolution of the issue was more likely than another.

Protagoras

Protagoras is the figure most widely associated with the sophistic movement. Whereas Gorgias was a great practitioner of rhetoric and a famous stylist, Protagoras was more important to developing a comprehensive philosophy of rhetorical practices. He was from Abdera in the north of Greece, and probably arrived in Athens around 450 BCE, more than 20 years before Gorgias. Active in Athens for nearly 40 years until his death or banishment around 410 BCE, he traveled widely. His reputation was such that "wherever he went rich and clever young men flocked to hear him."[75] Perhaps these clever young men were drawn to Protagoras' claim that he would teach them *areté*.

Protagoras is perhaps "the first person to charge for lectures," and is considered the first of the Greek Sophists.[76] His most famous maxim is that "man is the measure of all things; of things that are not, that they are not; of things that are, that they are."[77] What he meant by this claim, in true sophistic fashion, has been the subject of much debate. He probably intended the relativistic claim that people make determinations about what is or is not true, and that there is no absolute to which we can appeal to settle questions of truth. Protagoras' claim thus also embodies the concept of *kairos*—decisions are made best by people who can balance circumstance, evidence, and the need for action. Protagoras affirmed that the existence of a god or gods was virtually unknowable given the difficulty of the subject and the shortness of human life.

In the fashion of the itinerant, Protagoras taught in Sicily, Athens, and several other Greek cities. His reputation as a scholar and teacher was widespread, and recent scholarship attributes to him a number of significant intellectual accomplishments. A trusted advisor to the famed Athenian leader Pericles, he is said to have made "important contributions to rhetoric, epistemology, the critical study of religion, the study of social origins, dialectic, and literary criticism."[78] Protagoras is also the first person to systematize eristic argument, or what amounted to contrived disputes with no particular goal other than victory, sometimes achieved using clever argumentative tricks.

Protagoras taught a practical approach to reasoning about political as well as personal questions. He would train students to manage an estate, become an influential citizen, or succeed in politics. He held that contradictory arguments are possible on any issue; every *logos* or argument can be met with an *antilogos* or counterargument. More to Protagoras' point, the resolution of important matters *requires* this clash of arguments. He developed a critical method rooted in *dissoi logoi*, contradictory claims. Indeed, the method of critical questioning usually associated with Socrates was apparently derived from the sophistic practice of generating contradictory propositions.[79]

For Protagoras, an argument prevails only when "it has been tested by and had withstood the attacks of the opposing side(s)." Even to understand a statement requires considering the statement and its opposite.[80] Protagoras' critical method was not simply an approach to rhetoric, but an approach to life. As John Poulakos writes, "Protagoras' notion of *dissoi logoi* provides a worldview with rhetoric at its center." Of value to the student was the fact that "this worldview demands of the human subject a multiple awareness, an awareness at once cognizant of its own position and of those positions opposing it."[81]

ISOCRATES: A MASTER OF RHETORIC

Isocrates (436–338 BCE) is a major figure associated with the flourishing of rhetoric in Athens during the fifth and fourth centuries. Ten years older than Plato, Isocrates was a contemporary and in some respects a rival of the great philosopher. Both men came from privileged backgrounds, both may have studied philosophy under Socrates, and both claimed him as their model.[82] It is likely that as a young man Isocrates also studied under Gorgias and perhaps Corax's famous student Tisias. Isocrates, however, never achieved fame as a public speaker. Though he possessed considerable gifts as a writer, his speaking voice was not strong enough to hold the attention of a large public audience. Thus, Isocrates turned his attention to education and writing, excelling in both arenas. Isocrates brought political rhetoric to its highest point of development. He was among the *apragmones*, the "quiet ones" who avoided the public stage and made a rhetorical impact by writing rather than speaking.

Unlike Gorgias and Protagoras, Isocrates was a native Athenian. Whereas many Sophists were itinerants and thus cosmopolitan in their outlook, Isocrates was a devoted pan-Hellenist. He actively promoted the unity of Greece, the pre-eminence of Greek culture, and the expansion of Greek influence. In some of his writings, notably his essay *Against the Sophists*, Isocrates was sharply critical of the Sophists. He attacked the leading Sophists as unscrupulous teachers who charged high fees to instruct their students in happiness, justice, and virtue—qualities that no one could promise to teach. At the same time he rejected the philosophical idealism of figures such as Plato. Michael C. Leff has noted that "while Isocrates rejected Plato's belief in absolute, abstract, and objective truth, he was equally opposed to the extreme relativism associated with Gorgias and other Sophists."[83]

Isocrates worked for a time as a highly paid *logographos* or speechwriter, often writing for the courtroom. He staunchly advocated the fair conduct of trials, including letting the accused have an equal chance to respond in court to accusers.[84] An ardent proponent of skillfully crafted words—"the work of brave and imaginative souls"— around 390 he founded the first of the rhetorical schools in Athens. Andrew Ford writes, "For nearly half a century Isocrates was the most famous, influential, and successful teacher of politically ambitious young men in Greece. He also became one of the wealthiest teachers of his day."

Ford helps us to understand just how much money Isocrates could command for his four-year course of study. "The fee for his course was 1,000 drachmas, at a time when a day laborer was paid about 1 drachma a day."[85] If we consider what someone making minimum wage today might bring home in a day, and multiply that sum by one thousand, we get a relative idea of the cost of a course from a famous Sophist. So expensive was rhetorical education under Isocrates that even the young Demosthenes—the man who would become Athens' most famous orator could not afford the tuition; he had to study with someone of lesser reputation.

Isocrates the Teacher

Isocrates' interest in rhetoric was a consequence of his concern for preparing effective leaders and advancing Greek culture. Rhetoric was not principally a set of rules to guide speechmaking, but a means of advancing a culture and propagating political ideas. To become a rhetorician, one capable of building the *polis*, "demands self-restraint, breadth of knowledge, and a cultivated sense of the common good, and as a result, it must reflect and manifest virtues intimately connected with moral character."[86] We catch a glimpse of Isocrates' deeply traditional and utterly Athenian educational curriculum in this summary by Leff.

We might see his rhetorical theory, thus, as social or political in nature. Some scholars believe that Isocrates sought to develop a new rhetorical form through his writing; his *logos politikos*—political treatises—would resemble neither the idle speculations of the philosophers nor the showy courtroom oratory of the Sophists. He sought a civic rhetoric— a practical art of political discourse that advanced the cause of Greece and its foundational institution, the *polis*.[87]

Isocrates attracted talented students, many of whom became famous and influential statesmen and orators. His greatness as a teacher was unsurpassed, and his highly refined pedagogical approaches became models for later educators. The curriculum in Isocrates' school was rigidly structured and scrupulously pragmatic. Students studied and memorized model speeches their teacher had written, usually reflecting his views on contemporary political issues. This approach allowed Isocrates to teach rhetoric and political theory at the same time. Two of his more famous model speeches are the *Panegyricus* (c. 380) and the *Plataeicus* (c. 373). In the former, he wrote that Athens "gave honor to skill in words, which is the desire and envy of all."[88]

Though he claimed to teach rhetoric, Isocrates did not claim to teach *areté*.[89] "Let no one suppose," he wrote, "that I claim that just living can be taught; for I hold that there does not exist an art of the kind which can implant sobriety and justice in depraved natures."[90] For the Sophists to claim that they could morally improve their students— could instill in them *areté*—was simply absurd. Isocrates did, however, advocate high moral standards in his own followers and in the citizenry generally. He upbraided the Athenians for heeding the corrupt rhetoric of politicians who promised them what they wanted, but who did not care about the health of their souls or the city's good. Isocrates, like Gorgias, compared rhetoric to medicine, an analogy that Plato also parodied in his dialogue *Gorgias*.[91]

Isocrates' plain and direct style of rhetoric avoided sophistic excesses and prepared the students to address serious questions. His teaching "introduced two new requirements to rhetorical education—the thematic and the pragmatic." Poulakos explains that "the thematic asked that rhetoric concentrate on significant matters while the pragmatic demanded that it make a positive contribution to the life of the audience."[92] The essence of rhetoric was sound arguments presented in "words both rhythmic and musical."[93] Isocrates' instrumental approach to language influenced later orators such as Demosthenes and Cicero.

The practical, nationalistic, and moral education Isocrates offered to students was founded on natural talent, extensive practice, and the principles of rhetoric. Where natural talent was lacking, there was little even a good teacher could do to compensate for its absence. Where talent was present, it could be developed through rigorous instruction and continuous practice—provided high moral character was also present. This concern for the orator's character set Isocrates apart from the Sophists, whose rhetorical instruction was audience-centered.

Isocrates' tendency to write out his speeches and to circulate them in this form marks a shift in Greek rhetoric from a predominantly spoken medium to one emphasizing written discourse.[94] It also suggests the sort of reputation Isocrates hoped to cultivate as a teacher of rhetoric. "Isocrates wanted to be thought of finally not as a teacher of orators, but as the teacher of the nation, as a serious and weighty commentator on the affairs of Greece."[95] Though his chosen medium of expression was the written word, his principles of composition were still largely drawn from the realm of oratory.

Isocrates the Political Theorist

What was it that Isocrates hoped to teach Greece? He devoted considerable time to working out his political ideas in written speeches that he then circulated, recognizing that the reach of a written document greatly exceeded that of even a great speech. These documents are considered among the earliest political tracts, and include *Symmachicus* and *Areopagiticus*.

Rhetoric played a central role in Isocrates' theory of civilization. Human beings possess an instinct for persuasion, the key to the cooperative activity essential to forming a society. In *Antidosis* (c. 353), Isocrates argues that:

> there has been implanted in us the power to persuade each other and to make clear whatever we desire, not only have we escaped the life of wild beasts, but we have come together and founded cities and made laws and invented arts; and, generally speaking, there is no institution devised by man which the power of speech has not helped us to establish.[96]

The art of rhetoric should not be limited to producing the shoddy and florid speeches delivered in Athenian courts and assemblies. Rather, rhetoric should advance Greek institutions and Greek unity. Richard Enos writes, "Isocrates was committed to the notion of a united Greece and believed that rhetoric was a tool that empowered his educational system to promote such an ideal in a number of different areas."[97]

As a pan-Hellenist, Isocrates urged the Greek city-states to stop fighting one another and to unite against their common foes. Despite the warnings of Isocrates and others, including Demosthenes, Philip of Macedon put an end to all efforts toward pan-Hellenism by his crushing defeat of the Greek armies at Chaeronea in 338 BCE. Following this defeat, rhetorical theory and practice went into a period of decline. A new political regime that squelched democracy, and thus rhetoric, was now in place. Rhetoric remained an important art, but the center of its practice moved east into Asia Minor. The so-called "Asian School of rhetoric" emerged with a heavy emphasis on style and ornamentation, and considerably less attention to content than was shown by the great orators of Athens.

WOMEN WRITERS OF ANCIENT GREECE

Women were not recognized as full citizens in ancient Greece, and were prohibited from a variety of occupations and public events. In Athens, even aristocratic women were seldom seen in public, and their "activities, movements, education, marriage, and rights as citizens and property holders were extremely circumscribed." Most Greek women "were confined within the house at all times, except on occasions of religious festivals."[98] Because of Athens' impact on later European cultural development, this practice may have influenced subsequent attitudes in the Western world.

Sayings of the Spartan Women

The situation was somewhat different for women in the *polis* of Sparta, where men were often absent because of military obligations. Here women were daily out in public, ran the household, received the same basic education as men (all the education Spartans deemed necessary for any citizen), participated in sports competitions with men, could inherit a portion of their father's estate, and were allowed to (and often did) own property.

Public speaking was still largely restricted, even to Spartan women, though they could and did make provocative and politically loaded statements—often to men—in the marketplace and other public spaces. This notable exception to the usual rules regarding women and public speech seems to have been allowed so as to enforce important public mores such as the need for courage in battle.

Many such statements—often pointedly humorous—became legendary, and were written down much later by the biographer Plutarch (46–120 CE) in a work known as *Sayings of the Spartan Women*. For example, a Spartan man was telling his own sister about the brave death of her son in a recent battle. She said to him, "While I am glad to hear he died thus, it's too bad that you were left behind when you might have accompanied him on such a glorious journey." Other Greeks of the day were stunned by the public presence and degree of free expression enjoyed by Spartan women.

Nevertheless, the fact remains: Greek women were, regardless of location, barred from making public speeches. In the rhetorical arena, as in others, women's treatment in ancient Greece stemmed directly from men's fear of women equipped with rhetorical skill. The Greek writer Democritus, for example, "asserts that women should not be allowed to practice argument because men detest being ruled by women. In asserting this, he describes a detestable—and not fictional—practice." Historian of rhetoric C. Jan Swearingen writes that an edict entitled "On Pleading," which dates from the sixth century BCE,

> repeats the terms of Democritus' proscription: "It is prohibited to women to plead on behalf of others. And indeed there is reason for the prohibition: lest women mix themselves up in other people's cases, going against the chastity that befits their gender."[99]

As democratic reforms took hold in Athens, the place of women did not improve appreciably. Still denied citizenship, women "did not participate in any formal public functions."[100] The very reforms that opened the way to broader political participation sometimes worked *against* women's participation. "It remains a remarkable feature of Greek history," writes Ellen Wood, "that the position of women seems to have declined as the democracy evolved."[101] The larger number of men now involved in politics made it even more difficult for women to find a place in public life. Only in rural regions and in some less democratic city-states such as Sparta did the place of women improve slightly during the fifth and fourth centuries.

Aspasia

Harsh attitudes toward women in the ancient world make the story of Aspasia, a female rhetorician of the fifth century BCE, particularly intriguing. As Susan Jarratt and Rory Ong write, "Aspasia left no written remains. She is known through a handful of references, the most substantial of which are several paragraphs of narratives in Plutarch's life of Pericles and an oration attributed to her in Plato's dialogue *Menexenus*." In response to the assertion by some historians that Aspasia was a legendary figure, they write, "allusions to her by four of Socrates' pupils help to confirm Plutarch's assertion that Aspasia was indeed a real person, a teacher of rhetoric who shared her knowledge and political skill with Pericles."[102]

Aspasia (c. 470–c. 400 BCE) apparently hailed from Miletus, a Greek colony along the coast of modern-day Turkey. The great Greek general and orator Pericles lived with Aspasia "as a beloved and constant companion."[103] They are reputed to have had one son. The Greek term for such an educated female companion was *hetaera* or courtesan, and certain exceptions were made for these women as regards education, appearing in public and even delivering speeches.

Aspasia's knowledge of politics was without equal, as was her ability as a speechwriter, conversationalist, and teacher of rhetoric. She is reputed to have "taught the art of rhetoric to many, including Socrates, and may have invented the so-called Socratic method."[104] It has been argued that Aspasia wrote Pericles' famous "Funeral Oration," one of the most powerful rhetorical performances of antiquity. Plato notes in his dialogue *Menexenus* that when Socrates was asked whether he could meet the challenge of giving a speech at a public funeral for men who have died in battle, he replied with a reference to Aspasia:

> That I should be able to speak is no great wonder, Menexenus, considering that I have an excellent mistress in the art of rhetoric—she who has made so many good speakers, and one who was the best among all the Hellenes—Pericles, the son of Xanthippus.[105]

Aspasia's story underlines both the great rhetorical skill of a remarkable woman, as well as the stringent limits placed on Greek women in the domain of rhetoric. As evidence of the barriers Greek women faced, Cheryl Glenn writes, "Aspasia seems to have been the only woman in classical Greece to have distinguished herself in the public domain."[106]

Sappho

It was noted earlier in the chapter that some rhetoricians of the ancient world functioned principally as writers rather than as orators. Isocrates is a prominent example. It was also noted that women often were prevented from developing their rhetorical skills. Again, there were noteworthy exceptions such as Aspasia.

Another exception to this rule is Sappho (620–570 BCE), an early sixth-century writer and poet who hailed from the island of Lesbos. Relatively little is known about her, though fragments of some of her poems survive. Lesbos is located in the northern Aegean Sea, east of the Greek mainland and not far from the western coast of present-day Turkey. In ancient times the island was part of Greece, and had a reputation for honoring women. Sappho's accomplishment is, nevertheless, astonishing—she remains one of the few woman artists of the ancient Greek period of whom we have any record. Despite the fact that she wrote in a dialect not widely understood by other Greeks, Sappho became famous throughout Greece for her lyric poetry; she is mentioned favorably by the philosopher Plato and the statesman Solon. Sappho traveled widely, played the lyre and wrote lyrics to be accompanied by the instrument.

Sappho's deeply personal poetry was so esteemed at home and abroad that statues were built in her honor and apparently coins even issued bearing her likeness. She came from an aristocratic family which was exiled from the island on more than one occasion. She addressed controversial topics in her poems, including romantic love between women and the crimes of politicians. The intensity of longing that characterizes her poems is evident in this brief verse entitled *Please*:

> Come back to me, Gongyla, here tonight,
> You, my rose, with your Lydian lyre.
> There hovers forever around you delight:
> A beauty desired.
> Even your garment plunders my eyes.
> I am enchanted: I who once
> Complained to the Cyprus-born goddess,
> Whom I now beseech
> Never to let this lose me grace
> But rather bring you back to me:
> Amongst all mortal women the one
> I most wish to see.[107]

CONCLUSION

Friedrich Nietzsche noted that "the *need* of men for forensic eloquence must have given rise to the evolution of the liberal art" of rhetoric. Nietzsche also recognized that rhetoric taught various habits crucial to democracy.

> [O]ne must be accustomed to tolerating the most unusual opinions and points of view and even to taking a certain pleasure in their counterplay; one must be just as willing to listen as to speak; and as a listener one must be able more or less to appreciate the art being applied."[108]

Rhetoric and democracy exist together, each requiring the other in order to flourish. The Sophists of ancient Greece played a role in developing the art of rhetoric, and thus in developing democracy.

The number of Sophists in Greece was never large, nor were the Sophists a significant factor in Greek society for very long. The major Sophists were active in Athens between about 450 and 380, only about 70 years. Nevertheless, these provocative and innovative rhetoricians had a surprising influence on Greek life and thought. De Romilly writes that "the teaching of both rhetoric and philosophy was marked forever by the ideas that the Sophists introduced and the debates that they initiated."[109] Why, we may ask, is this the case?

First, the Sophists emphasized the centrality of persuasive discourse to civilized, democratic societies. Their thinking on this matter was both insightful and provocative. Second, their appreciation for the power of language set a trajectory for subsequent intellectual development in the Western world. The Sophists' theoretical explorations remain important to discussions of language's role in social life. Third, the Sophist's view of law as conventional and truth as relative influenced later political and philosophical thought. Finally, the Sophists placed training in rhetoric at the center of education, which constituted an innovation that would continue to have influence for centuries.

Several strikingly modern factors mark the Sophists' approach to rhetoric and education, and some of their insights into politics, language, and rhetoric are only now being fully appreciated. Scholars are reassessing the contributions of this remarkable group of teachers, theorists, and practitioners of rhetoric.

It is also important to note, however, that the Sophists bring us face to face with several unavoidable ethical concerns. Rhetoric is a source of power, and power can be used for good or ill. Some of the leading Sophists were notorious for disregarding conventional Greek ideas about the moral uses of language. They also ignored conventions governing who could be educated in argument. Sophists like Protagoras insisted that a persuasive case can be made on either side of an issue, not just on the side favored by prevailing moral assumptions. Questions about the power of language, who should have access to such power, and how that power ought to be used became a permanent feature of rhetoric's history. The long debate over rhetoric, power, and ethics, raised by the Sophists, attracted the attention of the greatest philosophical mind in Athens. His assault on the Sophists' view of rhetoric is the subject of the next chapter.

This chapter has also taken note of the fact that women were restricted from making public speeches in ancient Greek city-states. This does not mean that, despite restrictions, there were no noteworthy female writers or rhetorically gifted women. The poet Sappho was widely known for her linguistic gifts in a generation preceding the rise of the Sophists. Later, in the era of democratic reforms in Athens, the *hetaera* Aspasia had a reputation as a skilled rhetorician, debater, and teacher of rhetoric. It is suggested that some of Athens' leading public figures, including Pericles and Socrates, learned techniques of reasoning and persuasion from her. Moreover, the freedom of Spartan women to speak in the marketplace reminds us that the strategic use of language is not limited to official proceedings or formal settings.

QUESTIONS FOR REVIEW

1. What beliefs, practices, and personal qualities characterized the Sophists?
2. What educational revolution did the Sophists introduce into Athenian society? Why were these teachers of rhetoric controversial in Athens?
3. What was the Sophists' view of truth?
4. Why was the concept of a clash of views important to the Sophists?
5. What was the right of *isegoria*?
6. Why, in your own words, was the study of rhetoric important to the citizens of ancient Athens?
7. What threat did the Sophists pose to traditional Greek society?
8. What claims did the Sophists make about their teaching?
9. What did Gorgias see as the relationship between rhetoric and magic?
10. What goal did Isocrates seek through his emphasis on pan-Hellenism?
11. Who was Aspasia?

QUESTIONS FOR DISCUSSION

1. What members of contemporary society, in your estimation, most resemble the Sophists?
2. After reading about the Sophists, do you think they deserve the bad reputation they had with many of their contemporaries?
3. In what ways, if any, does U.S. society appear to be sophistic in orientation?
4. Could the teaching and practice of rhetoric in our own society elicit the same controversy it did in ancient Greece? Why or why not?
5. Assuming that rhetoric is not currently a central educational concern, where do citizens today learn to reason and to speak persuasively?
6. What, if anything, might be gained by a consistent program of rhetorical studies in schools today? Is there anything to be gained by *not* teaching people to reason and speak persuasively and effectively? Which group, if any, realizes an advantage from the absence of rhetorical training?
7. What, if anything, is the relationship between truth and argument? Persuasion and ethics?
8. The Sophists built a view of justice on conventional agreements or *nomos*. Other possible sources of law or justice included the authority of kings (*thesmos*), natural law (*physis*), and certain truth derived from philosophical argumentation (Platonic *logos*). What, in your opinion, ought to be the basis of a view of justice?
9. Do you agree with Gorgias about the great potential in language for the control of the minds of others? What, if any, are the risks associated with great eloquence? How should the public be educated so as to have a defense against the great rhetorical skill possessed by some speakers and writers?
10. What effects on the subsequent history of Western culture may have resulted from the exclusion of women from rhetorical theory and practice in ancient Greece?

11. The chapter discusses the fact that women were barred from public speaking venues in ancient Greece. We have also considered that, despite this prohibition, women such as Aspasia, Sappho, the Pythia at the Oracle at Delphi, and Spartan women contributed through speech and writing to ancient Greek culture. How does the expression of women's voices differ from that of men in these ancient cultures? What might we learn from this about efforts to prevent groups or individuals from speaking in public?

TERMS

Aporia Placing a claim in doubt by developing arguments on both sides of the issue.

Areté Virtue; an ability to manage one's personal affairs in an intelligent manner, and to succeed in public life. Human excellence, natural leadership ability.

Askēsis or melet ē (Greek) Practice.

Boule Representative body of 500 Athenian citizens that met daily to supervise the city.

Chiasmus Rhetorical device that takes its name from the reversing of elements in parallel clauses, forming an X (*chi*) in the sentence.

Demos (Greek) The people.

Dialektike Dialectic, the method of investigating philosophical issues by the give and take of argument. A method of teaching that involved training students to argue either side of a case.

Dikasteria The Athenian court.

Dissoi logoi Contradictory arguments.

Eikos Arguing from probability.

Ekklesia The ruling Athenian Assembly.

Endoxa The probable premises from which dialectic began. Premises that were widely believed.

Epideixis A speech prepared for a formal occasion.

Eristic Discourse's power to express, to captivate, to argue, or to injure.

Gnorimoi An elite group enjoying higher social status in Athens than members of the *demos*.

Hataera Educated female courtesan.

Heuristic Discourse's capacity for discovery, whether of facts, insights, or even of self-awareness.

Isegoria The right of all free male citizens to speak in public settings and assemblies.

Kairos Rhetoric's search for relative truth rather than absolute certainty; a consideration of opposite points of view, as well as attention to such factors as time and circumstances. An opportune moment or situation. Also, a sense of decorum regarding public speech.

Logographos A professional speechwriter.

Logos Word; argument. Also, a transcendent source of truth for Plato.

Metoikoi In ancient Athens, a resident foreigner.

Nomos Social custom or convention; rule by agreement among the citizens.

Paideia (Greek) A course of study.

Peitho Greek goddess of persuasion.

Physis The law or rule of nature under which the strong dominate the weak.

Polis In ancient Greece, an independent city-state.

Protreptic The possibility for persuading others to think as they think, to act as they wish them to act.

Psychagogos A poet, a leader of souls through a kind of incantation.

Pythia Woman considered to be in intimate contact with the gods.

Sophistes (plural: *Sophistae*) An authority, an expert, a teacher. A teacher of rhetoric.

Techne A practical art, a science, or a systematic study.

Thesmos Law derived from the authority of kings.

NOTES

1 Richard Leo Enos, *Greek Rhetoric before Aristotle* (Prospect Heights, IL: Waveland, 1993), 4.

2 Enos, 5.

3 Enos, 6.

4 Enos, 7–8.

5 Brian Boyd, *On the Origin of Stories: Evolution, Cognition, and Fiction* (Cambridge, MA: Harvard University Press, 2009), 234.

6 Jane Sutton, "The Marginalization of Sophistical Rhetoric and the Loss of History," in *Rethinking the History of Rhetoric*, ed. Takis Poulakos (Boulder, CO: Westview, 1993), 87.

7 John Poulakos, "Terms for Sophistical Rhetoric," in *Rethinking the History of Rhetoric: Multidisciplinary Essays on the History of Rhetoric*, ed. Takis Poulakos (Boulder, CO: Westview, 1993), 53–74, p. 56.

8 Poulakos, 57.

9 Susan Jarratt and Rory Ong, "Aspasia: Rhetoric, Gender, and Colonial Ideology," in *Reclaiming Rhetorica: Women in the Rhetorical Tradition*, ed. Andrea A. Lunsford (Pittsburgh, PA: University of Pittsburgh Press, 1995), 14.

10 Josiah Ober, *Mass and Elite in Ancient Athens: Rhetoric, Ideology, and the Power of the People* (Princeton, NJ: Princeton University Press, 1989), 7.

11 Jarratt and Ong, 14.

12 Humphrey Davy Findley Kitto, *The Greeks* (1951; Baltimore, MD: Penguin Books, 1968), 120.

13 *Kitto*, 115.

14 John Poulakos, *Sophistical Rhetoric in Classical Greece* (Columbia, SC: University of South Carolina Press, 1994), 16–17.

15 Maurice Balme and Gilbert Lawall, *Athenaze: An Introduction to Ancient Greek*, Book II (New York: Oxford University Press, 1991), 105–106.

16 Jacqueline de Romilly, *The Great Sophists in Periclean Athens*, trans. Janet Lloyd (Oxford: Clarendon Press, 1992), 30.

17 William Keith Chambers Guthrie, *The Sophists* (Cambridge: Cambridge University Press, 1971), 20.

18 John Poulakos, "Toward a Sophistic Definition of Rhetoric," *Philosophy and Rhetoric* 16 (1983): 35–48; see: Ober.

19 H. D. Rankin, *Sophists, Socratics and Cynics* (London: Croom Helm, 1983), 15. Other helpful discussions of this period in Greek thought, and of the Sophists, include: Harold Barrett, *The Sophists: Rehtoric, Democracy & Plato's Idea of Sophistry* (Novato, CA: Chandler and Sharp, 1987); G. B. Kerferd, *The Sophistic Movement* (New York and Cambridge: Cambridge University Press, 1981); John Sallis, *Being and Logos: Reading the Platonic Dialogues* (Atlantic Highlands, NJ: Humanities Press, 1986).

20 Jarratt and Ong, 12.

21 Enos, ix.

22 See: Michael Gagarin, "Telling Stories in Athenian Law," *Transactions of the American Philological Association* 133 (2003): 2, 197–207.

23 Michael Gagarin, *The Murder of Herodes: A Study of Antiphon 5* (New York: Verlag Peter Lang, 1989), 14.

24 Ober, 7–8.

25 On the meaning of *Sophist*, see: Edward Schiappa, *Protagoras and Logos: A Study in Greek Philosophy and Rhetoric* (Columbia, SC: University of South Carolina Press, 1991), Chap. 1.

26 Poulakos, "Terms," 58.

27 See, for example: Susan C. Jarratt, *Rereading the Sophists: Classical Rhetoric Refigured* (Carbondale, IL: Southern Illinois University Press, 1991).

28 See: Guthrie.

29 Michael Gagarin, *Antiphon the Athenian: Oratory, Law and Justice in the Age of the Sophists* (Austin, TX: University of Texas Press, 2002), 1.

30 Gagarin, *Antiphon*, 5, 6.

31 Gagarin, *Antiphon*, 16–17.

32 Gagarin, *Antiphon*, 18.

33 See: Mario Untersteiner, *The Sophists* (Oxford: Oxford University Press, 1954).

34 Guthrie, 25. Rankin writes that *areté* "combines the factors both of high moral virtue and worldly success" (13).

35 Ober, 11.

36 Poulakos, "Terms," 57.

37 Friedrich Nietzsche, *Friedrich Nietzsche on Rhetoric and Language*, ed. trans. S. Gilman, C. Blair, and D. Parent (New York: Oxford University Press, 1989), 19.

38 See the discussion of *kairos* in Ekaterina V. Haskins, *Logos and Power in Isocrates and Aristotle* (Columbia: University of South Carolina Press, 2004), 66–70.

39 Dale Sullivan, "*Kairos* and the Rhetoric of Belief," *Quarterly Journal of Speech* 78 (August 1992): 320.

40 Jarratt and Ong, 16.

41 Rankin, 14.

42 See: Schiappa, Chap. 1.

43 See: Glen Warren Bowersock, *Greek Sophists in the Roman Empire* (Oxford: Clarendon Press, 1969).

44 Andrew Ford, "The Price of Art in Isocrates: Formalism and the Escape from Politics," in *Rethinking the History of Rhetoric*, ed. Takis Poulakos (Boulder, CO: Westview, 1992), 37.

45 Ford, 37.

46 Ford, 37.

47 Jarratt, xx.

48 Poulakos, *Sophistical Rhetoric*, 25.

49 Richard A. Katula and James J. Murphy (eds), *A Synoptic History of Classical Rhetoric* (Davis, CA: Hermagoras Press, 1995), 28.

50　See Gagarin, *Murder*, 47.

51　Jarratt, 42.

52　Sutton, 87.

53　On Gorgias' philosophy of *logos*, see: Charles P. Segal, "Gorgias and the Psychology of the *Logos*," *Harvard Studies in Classical Philology* 66 (1962): 99–155.

54　Enos, 72.

55　See: John O. Ward, "Magic and Rhetoric from Antiquity to the Renaissance: Some Ruminations," *Rhetorica* 6 (Winter 1988): 1, 57–118, especially p. 58.

56　Segal, 110. Quoted in Bruce E. Gronbeck, "Gorgias on Rhetoric and Poetic: A Rehabilitation," *Southern Speech Communication Journal* 38 (Fall 1972): 1, 27–38.

57　Gronbeck, 33.

58　George Kennedy, *Classical Rhetoric and Its Christian and Secular Tradition from Ancient to Modern Times*, 2nd ed. (Chapel Hill, NC: University of North Carolina Press, 1999), 35.

59　Jeffrey Walker, *Rhetoric and Poetics in Antiquity* (Oxford: Oxford University Press, 2000), 154.

60　Jacqueline de Romilly, *Magic and Rhetoric in Ancient Greece* (Cambridge, MA: Harvard University Press, 1975).

61　de Romilly, *Magic*, 16.

62　de Romilly, *Magic*, 6.

63　Jane P. Tompkins, "The Reader in History: The Changing Shape of Literary Response," in *Reader-Response Criticism: From Formalism to Post-Structuralism*, ed. Jane P. Tompkins (Baltimore, MD: Johns Hopkins University Press, 1980), 203–204.

64　G. M. A. Grube, *The Greek and Roman Critics* (Toronto: University of Toronto Press, 1965), 16.

65　Kennedy, 64.

66　Gorgias, *Encomium on Helen* 9 and 10, trans. LaRue VanHook, *Classical Weekly* 6 (1913): 122–123. Quoted in Gronbeck, 34.

67　Kennedy, 35.

68　de Romilly, *Magic*, 3.

69　de Romilly, *Magic*, 4.

70　de Romilly, *Magic*, 5.

71　Grube, 16.

72　Rosamond Kent Sprague, ed. *The Older Sophists* (Columbia, SC: University of South Carolina Press, 1972), 50.

73　For a discussion of the relationship between truth and memory, see Haskins, 12–15.

74　Kennedy, 66.

75　Balme and Lawall, 106.

76　Billig, 40. Billig cites Philostratus, *Lives of the Sophists*, trans. W. C. Wright (London: Loeb Classical Library, 1965); Rankin, 30, ff.

77　Plato, *Theaetetus*, 151e–152a.

78　Rankin, 32.

79　Jarratt and Ong, 15.

80　Poulakos, "Terms," 58–59.

81　Poulakos, "Terms," 60.

82　de Romilly, *Great Sophists*, viii.

83　Michael C. Leff, "What Is Rhetoric?," *Rethinking Rhetorical Theory, Criticism, and Pedagogy: The Living Art of Michael C. Leff*, ed. A. de Velasco, J. A. Campbell, and D. Henry (East Lansing MI: Michigan State University Press, 2016), 471–481, p. 479.

84 Brian Vickers, *In Defense of Rhetoric* (Oxford: Clarendon Press, 1988), 155.
85 Ford, "The Price of Art in Isocrates," 37.
86 Michael C. Leff, "Tradition and Agency in Humanistic Rhetoric," *Rethinking Rhetorical Theory, Criticism, and Pedagogy: The Living Art of Michael C. Leff*, ed. A. de Velasco, J. A. Campbell, and D. Henry (East Lansing MI: Michigan State University Press, 2016), 7–24, p. 15.
87 See Haskins, 19. Also, Takis Poulakos, *Speaking for the Polis: Isocrates' Rhetorical Education* (Columbia, SC: University of South Carolina Press, 1997).
88 Quoted in Sowerby, 108.
89 Vickers, 150.
90 The quote is from *Against the Sophists*. Quoted in Vickers, 150.
91 Vickers, 154.
92 Poulakos, *Sophistical Rhetoric*, 134.
93 Walker, 175.
94 On the importance of writing as an intellectual activity at this time, see: Kathleen E. Welch, *The Contemporary Reception of Classical Rhetoric: Appropriations of Ancient Discourse* (Hillsdale, NJ: Lawrence Erlbaum, 1990), 16–17.
95 Ford, 38.
96 *Antidosis*, 254. Quoted in Vickers, 156.
97 Enos, 114.
98 Jarratt and Ong, 13.
99 C. Jan Swearingen, "A Lover's Discourse: Diotima, Logos, and Desire," in *Reclaiming Rhetorica: Women in the Rhetorical Tradition*, ed. Andrea Lunsford (Pittsburgh, PA: University of Pittsburgh Press, 1995), 25–26.
100 Jarratt and Ong, 14.
101 Ellen Meiksins Wood, *Peasant–Citizen and Slave: The Foundations of Athenian Democracy* (London: Verso, 1988), 115. Quoted in Jarratt and Ong, 13.
102 Jarratt and Ong, 10.
103 Jarratt and Ong, 12.
104 Jarratt and Ong, 13.
105 Jarratt and Ong, 15. The Menesemus in *The Dialogues of Plato*, trans. B. Jowett (New York: Random House, 1937), *Menexenus*, p. 235.
106 Cheryl Glenn, "Locating Aspasia on the Rhetorical Map," in *Listening to Their Voices: The Rhetorical Activities of Historical Women*, ed. Molly Meijer Wertheimer (Columbia, SC: University of South Carolina Press, 1997), 19–41, p. 21.
107 Sappho, "Please,"—Trans. Paul Roche, *Isle of Lesbos*, www.sappho.com/poetry/sappho. html#not%20one%20word (accessed September 30, 2016).
108 Nietzsche, *Friedrich Nietzsche on Rhetoric and Language*, 3.
109 de Romilly, *Great Sophists*, 4.

Chapter 3

Plato versus the Sophists: Rhetoric on Trial

Your way, Callicles, has no value whatever.

—Socrates in Plato's *Gorgias* (527e)

As noted in Chapter 2, the Sophists were controversial in Greece for several decades. One of their chief critics was the great philosopher Plato (427–347 BCE), who attacked sophistic rhetoric in his dialogue *Gorgias,* while later suggesting a true art of rhetoric in *Phaedrus.*[1] Sophists and their philosophy are also mentioned in Plato's *Sophist* and *Protagoras*, as well as other places in his dialogues.[2] Whereas Plato's 30-year-long attack on rhetoric has been called "idiosyncratic and extreme," Plato's views set up the long rivalry between rhetoric and philosophy.[3] The two studies have been at odds through much of Western history.[4]

Plato in *Gorgias* anticipated the major issues that have attended rhetoric—its association with power, the potential for manipulating audiences, whether rhetoric requires actual knowledge of a subject, and rhetoric's relationship to truth. The dialogue has thus been viewed as a valuable treatment of the Sophists in particular and rhetoric in general. It should also be borne in mind that because Plato is arguing against the Sophists in *Gorgias*, his own ability as a rhetorician is on display. Historian of rhetoric George Kennedy calls Plato "a consummate rhetorician," adding "no dialogue of Plato is untouched by rhetoric."[5]

A towering philosophical genius, Plato's withering criticism of the Sophists in *Gorgias* shaped subsequent attitudes toward them and toward rhetoric. However, as will be shown, even *Gorgias* may point the way to what Plato considered the "right" uses of rhetoric. We will take a close look at his treatment of sophistry in *Gorgias* first, and then turn to Plato's thoughts about the potentially beneficial use of rhetoric in the later dialogue *Phaedrus.*[6]

It should be noted that Plato had reservations about democracy, largely due to his misgivings about the changeable *demos*, a term referring to the general public or perhaps more accurately to the masses. Himself a member of the Athenian upper-class, Plato

*he approved
of it when it
meant leading
people but not if
you made $ off it.*

believed that leadership should be limited to a small elite—his "philosopher kings." He maintained an interest in rhetoric, though he deeply mistrusted the art due to its great power to control audiences. Such power could be used by a tyrant to control a city, or by a philosopher to draw people to the truth. Those who made their living by a knack for persuasive speaking were ever suspect to Plato; at the same time, rhetoric might be employed by someone with true knowledge to bring about order and justice in the *polis*.

PLATO'S *GORGIAS*: RHETORIC ON TRIAL

In *Gorgias*, the protagonist Socrates—modeled on Plato's teacher and representing Plato's own views—debates three Sophists about rhetoric, politics, and justice.[7] *Gorgias*, an early dialogue written around 387 BCE, mixes elements from actual debates with imagined conversations reflecting the positions of Socrates, Plato, Gorgias, Polus, and Callicles.

Though Plato aims his arguments at Sophists in particular, he builds a case against anyone making their living by persuading audiences, especially politicians. All wielders of persuasive words Plato refers to collectively as *rhetores*, and it is clear that he has little respect for them. As Vickers points out, "Plato crudely lumped all politicians and rhetors together as flatterers and corrupters of the people."[8]

Plato was not alone in his suspicion of professional persuaders. Demosthenes, himself a famous orator, "discussed the 'damnable and god-hated rhetores' who sold public honors as if they were nothing." Josiah Ober notes that "in *On the Crown* (18.242) Demosthenes caps a tirade of insults against Aeschines with a claim that his opponent was a counterfeit (*parasemos*) rhetor, whose cleverness was useless to the polis." He adds, "This last suggests that the genuine rhetor might be expected to use his abilities for the good of the polis."[9] The Sophists were the most prominent and controversial rhetoricians in Athens, and thus a convenient target for Plato's attack. Athenian politicians—the very people who had put Socrates to death—also come in for condemnation as many arguments in *Gorgias* are directed against them as well. Thus, Kennedy calls the *Gorgias* "a criticism of all rhetoric and all rhetoricians."[10]

In *Gorgias*, Plato raises a series of pointed questions about rhetoric, many of which are as important today as they were in ancient Greece. What is the essential nature of rhetoric? Does rhetoric by its nature tend to mislead? What happens to a society when law and justice rest on mere persuasion, without the rational foundation of true understanding (*logos*)? The dialogue transpires before a small audience of Sophists and other guests gathered in a private home for a dinner party. The drama of *Gorgias* develops first around Socrates' dialogues with the famed Sophist Gorgias, then with a young Sophist named Polus, and finally with the villainous Callicles, a more mature Sophist in whose home the play is set.

Plato criticized the Sophists on a number of grounds, including their "taking money," "making exaggerated pedagogical claims," and "boastfulness."[11] His general contention is, however, that the Sophists' practice of rhetoric does not embody an adequate conception of justice, and is thus dangerous to the *polis*.[12] The Sophists sought only persuasion about justice by manipulating public opinion (*doxa*); true justice is founded on knowledge (*episteme*) and secures the well-being of the individual and of the city-state.[13]

Another important issue is at play in *Gorgias*. Plato viewed with suspicion advanced education based solely on the ability to pay. Sophistic training in rhetoric threatened the traditional aristocratic system he represented. At the same time, the kind of self-improvement Sophists claimed to offer was in keeping with Athenian belief in honing one's natural abilities. This conflict of values created serious tensions in Athens, tensions that animate the pages of *Gorgias*.

The Debate with *Gorgias*: Rhetoric's Nature and Uses

As *Gorgias* opens, Socrates states that he wants to ask the famous Sophist about "the power of his art, and what it is he professes to teach" (447).[14] More to the point, Socrates wants to know, "With what class of objects is rhetoric concerned?" This question reflects Plato's conviction that any true art or discipline, any *techne*, involves knowledge of some class of objects just as medicine involves knowledge of the human body. Leading Sophists had claimed they taught a techne, so Socrates's question is not off the mark. The practitioner of a *techne* ought to be able to give an account (*logos*, here meaning rational explanation) of that art, that is, explain in clear and logical terms how it achieves its goals. In the absence of such a theoretical foundation there can be no *techne*; any practitioner of a true art should be capable of presenting such a theory.

More importantly, however, is Plato's conviction that *logos* itself possesses a kind of transformative power capable of rendering a practice virtuous. Thus, the absence of a distinct *logos*, the absence, that is, of a rational explanation, relegates a practice to a low-level activity that does not reflect virtue. And, of course, the Sophists claimed to be able to teach *areté*: virtue. Philosopher Jessica Moss has argued that *logos* for Plato was a force capable of transforming practices by imbuing them with true virtue. The sheer force of *logos*, that is, transforms "inferior epistemic states like experience into techné, epistémé, or other forms of wisdom ..." This transformative force is precisely "an explanatory account" that brings to the surface that which "underlies the facts available to the proto-virtuous, or to the layman," and grants it the status of a virtue.[15] This kind of explanation of rhetoric, this transforming *logos*, is what Socrates seeks from Gorgias and his associates, and does not find. Janet Atwill finds *techne* to be a *dunamis* or force that functions more as a dynamic process than as an end point. It is for many Greek thinkers of the period "a distinct model of knowledge."[16] So, Socrates has something quite specific and quite weighty in mind as he questions Gorgias.

This ostensibly innocuous question about rhetoric's subject matter should be an easy one for a great master of rhetoric to answer. If weaving is concerned with fabrics, and music with composing songs, with what is rhetoric concerned? Gorgias responds initially, and perhaps glibly (surrounded, as he is, by a friendly audience), that he instructs in rhetoric (*rhetorike*), an art concerned "with words." This is the earliest recorded use of the Greek term *rhetorike*, which has led rhetoric scholar Edward Schiappa to conclude that Plato coined the term.[17]

Socrates is not satisfied with the answer that rhetoric is concerned with words, suggesting that this does not differentiate it from other arts (*technae*) which also achieve their ends using words. Socrates then takes a different tack, asking Gorgias what good result rhetoric produces (451). True arts regularly achieved desirable or useful outcomes or *erga* (singular: *ergon*). The art of piloting a boat, for example, regularly, though not always, gets passengers and cargo to the correct destination. The true practitioner of a skill or art is one who is guided by such knowledge of goals or outcomes—*erga*.

Again, Gorgias' answer is more eloquent than substantive. Rhetoric, he asserts, produces "the greatest good and [is] the source, not only of personal freedom for individuals but also of mastery over others in one's own country." Socrates is not satisfied with this apparently evasive answer; he challenges Gorgias again. A command of persuasive words to achieve personal power and render one a person of influence in the city does not constitute a true art.

In his second attempt to answer Socrates' question, Gorgias narrows the scope of rhetoric to *persuasive* words. But, is this a sufficient definition of the domain of a *techne*? Socrates thinks not. All teaching, regardless of subject matter, involves a kind of persuasion about the subject under study. All teachers seek to gain adherence to their teachings. Do not all arts, in the final analysis, involve persuasion? Gorgias agrees they do, and that the field of rhetoric has not yet been defined. Throughout the opening passages of the dialogue, Gorgias willingly accepts Socrates' questioning as he scrutinizes the subject of rhetoric.

Gorgias finally affirms that "the sort of persuasion I mean, Socrates, is the kind used in the law courts and other public gatherings, as I said, just a moment ago, and it deals with justice and injustice" (454). Socrates grants that Gorgias may now be in the realm of an art, one which Socrates calls justice. However, the philosopher insists there is an important distinction to be made between "true knowledge" (*episteme*) and "mere belief" (*pistis*) or "mere opinion" (*doxa*) about justice. Socrates contends that Gorgias deals only in beliefs and opinions about justice, and not in true knowledge. Why is this?

According to Plato, the discipline of justice, like any art or *techne*, takes a long time to understand. As noted, a *techne* produced an *ergon* or useful outcome. *Technai* (pl.) included such arts as medicine or navigation, but there was also an art of government that produced functional cities, and of generalship that produced military victory. Practices requiring study but that simply resulted in objects, sculpting and pottery are examples, were categorized as productive arts or *poieses*. The Sophists wished their art of rhetoric to be recognized as a *techne*.

Understanding any complex topic is achieved only through long study, and a rhetor could not instruct a jury about a difficult subject such as justice in the short time allotted to a speech during a trial. The Sophists must, therefore, appeal to popular beliefs and opinions about justice. Gorgias agrees that what rhetoricians do in the law courts is to produce beliefs (*pisteis*) about justice, and not real knowledge (*episteme*). Socrates counters with this important summary statement on rhetoric as practiced by the Sophists: "So rhetoric, it seems, effects a persuasion which can produce belief about justice and injustice, but cannot give instruction about them." Gorgias answers, perhaps surprisingly, "Yes." Socrates is now ready to advance one of his condemnations of Sophistic rhetoric:

The rhetorician, then, is not a teacher of law courts and other public gatherings as to what is right or wrong, but merely a creator of beliefs; for evidently he could never instruct so large a gathering in so short a time (455).

Teaching about justice requires true knowledge of the subject, and such profound knowledge comes only with diligent study. This is a far cry from creating "mere belief" about justice in a jury in a speech of an hour or two. That a skillful rhetorician might lead people think they understand justice is apparent; that rhetoric teaches justice is highly unlikely. Plato argues it is dangerous to create momentary beliefs about justice in the absence of true knowledge. A person in such a state of mind may commit injustices, and a society so deceived might do the same. Later Socrates adds that this dependence on mere belief rather than on true knowledge is why rhetoric works best before a large audience, that is, "among the ignorant" (459). Before a knowledgeable audience the rhetorician will not be able to persuade by simply creating unfounded beliefs.

Plato's greatest concern about the Sophists is that they profess to teach about justice without any understanding of justice, a dangerous undertaking. In the course of his conversation with Gorgias, Socrates makes the striking assertion that one who truly understands justice could never choose to do injustice. This is because to understand justice is to love it, and at the same time to hate injustice.

Socrates versus Polus: Rhetoric as Power

Gorgias does not risk further embarrassment at the hands of the old philosopher; his young student Polus, whose name means colt, is not so wise. Plato bases this character on another Sophist who had written a treatise claiming that rhetoric was a true art, a *techne*.[18] Polus comes bravely but carelessly to his master's defense, angrily denouncing Socrates' implication that Gorgias does not understand justice. The philosopher has been "downright rude"; how dare Socrates be so arrogant as to suggest such a thing about the greatest Sophist in Athens? Socrates asks Polus to calm down and make his argument—though not a long speech—in defense of rhetoric.

For Polus, rhetoric is "the noblest of the arts" (448c). He represents the many Athenians infatuated with the Sophists' teaching, the generation of young men who viewed rhetoric as a path to fame and wealth. Nobility, status, and power attracted Polus to rhetoric, much as a life of prestige and influence in law, the military, or politics might attract a young person today.

Rhetoricians like Gorgias exercise "the greatest power in the country," power to "act like tyrants and put to death any one they please and confiscate property and banish any one they've a mind to" (466b–c). As Polus reveals, speechmaking and power were closely related in Athens. Ober writes that "direct public communication was the primary locus of whatever power, authority, or influence the Athenian rhetor might hope to exercise."[19] This was precisely Plato's concern: Rhetoric attracted practitioners by its power to manipulate and coerce. Adele Spitzer has noted that "Polus is concerned to conquer . . . [and] power must be unbridled force if Polus is its example."[20]

Rhetoric as Knack

In the interaction between Socrates and Polus, Plato develops a famous set of comparisons among true and false arts. When Polus asks what kind of thing Socrates thinks rhetoric is, the philosopher responds that he finds it to be a "foul" and an "ugly" one. He compares rhetoric to a knack achieved by experience and repeated practice (*empeiria kai tribe*) like the ability some people have of cooking pleasing foods or concocting folk remedies that make one feel better. Such pursuits involve no real knowledge of medicine or of restoring health; thus, their practitioners cannot provide a theory to explain what they do. This and similar activities are not true arts, but rather examples of "flattery" (*kolakeia*) because they "aim at pleasure without consideration of what is best" (465).

Rhetoric's Relationship to Other Arts and Knacks

Socrates deploys a series of analogies in his interaction with Polus in order to give his own account of what rhetoric is. He describes both true and sham arts, each addressing the health of either the body or the soul. The true arts (*technae*) are those that bring genuine health to the body and to the soul. Imitations or counterfeits of each true art flatter people into thinking they are healthy when in fact they are not. Real health is a state of well-being in which a person possesses mental and physical powers and directs these toward good ends. Health is an ideal state pursued through arts that demand discipline and thus may involve pain.

Socrates discusses four arts of health, two for the body and two for the soul—an art of maintenance and an art of restoration for each. The art that maintains physical health Socrates labels as gymnastic or physical education; its practitioner is named as the physical trainer or coach. Medicine is the art that restores lost physical health and its practitioner is the physician. So, gymnastic practice maintains the body's health, and medicine restores the body's health when it is lost. The trainer practices the former *techne*, the physician the latter.

Turning to arts associated with the soul, the art that maintains the health in the soul Socrates labels as legislation or lawmaking. What did Plato mean by this? He apparently viewed the job of a legislator as developing laws that help people act properly, and not go wrong morally. Thus, a good legislator assists members of the polis to maintain a healthy soul. Such a lawmaker must possess a sound knowledge of virtue and vice, and how to ensure that virtue is pursued and vice avoided. In this way the health of the soul is maintained.

When the individual goes wrong, however, there is an art to assist the soul's restoration to health. Socrates labels that art as justice, and its practitioner is the judge who metes out penalties to help bring the soul warped through crime or immorality back into line, that is, back to health. It is crucial, then, that a judge understands justice, that is, can give an account of justice and how it is achieved.

THE ARTS OF HEALTH

	Body	Soul
Maintain	Gymnastic	Legislation
Restore	Medicine	Justice

We have overviewed the four true arts of health in the body and soul which Socrates sets out in his interaction with Polus in Plato's dialogue, *Gorgias*. The boxed diagram helps us to apprehend this first set of health-related arts.

Socrates also sought to expose counterfeits or "shams" of each of these true arts, false practices that created the impression of well-being or health. These sham arts or knacks flatter members of the *polis* into thinking they are healthy when they are not. So, what were the imitation arts that Socrates opposes to his four true arts of health?

The imitation of the *techne* of gymnastic Socrates calls the knack of makeup. This sham art involved the use of colorings for the face and hair, beautiful clothing, and other artificial aids to help an aging man look younger and healthier than he actually was. Only the appearance of health is achieved by the makeup artist; no real knowledge of health is required of the cosmetologist.

The imitation of medicine is for Socrates "cookery," a reference to preparing pleasing foods that make one feel satisfied, or perhaps concocting folk remedies for various ailments. Plato apparently has in mind the chicken soup approach to medicine. Some people possess a knack—gained through experience and practice—for preparing foods that make one feel temporarily healthier, but which achieve their effect with no knowledge of the body, its ailments, or cures. Again, medical knowledge is not required of the cook or the folk healer, only a knack for making a suitable dish, soup, or drink that creates the impression that health has been restored. However, the cook cannot provide an account of how his or her concoctions work. So, in Socrates' analogies makeup parallels gymnastic and cookery parallels medicine.

The imitation of legislation Socrates calls sophistic—making long speeches in the legislature to influence legislation to benefit oneself or one's constituents. Why is this the sham art of legislation? When a Sophist uses rhetoric to affect the form of laws, he is not concerned to discover what is likely to ensure the moral goodness of the people, but rather to pass laws that will protect his own interests or those of his employers. Such laws benefit no one because they do not assist one in living a just life. Rather, they deceive one into thinking that he or she is living justly, when the opposite may be the case.

Finally, Socrates affirms that the counterfeit of the *techne* of justice is rhetoric itself. Justice, recall, aims at restoring health to a soul that has been made sick through unjust or immoral activity. Courtroom rhetoric as practiced by the Sophists is not concerned to restore the health of an infirm soul, but rather to mislead judges and juries. Because they lack knowledge of justice but are skilled in creating beliefs about justice, Sophists may lead their audiences to commit injustices. Socrates is of the opinion that to be the victim of injustice is not the worst condition in which you might find yourself; committing an injustice is worse.

THE SHAM ARTS OF HEALTH

	Body	*Soul*
Maintain	Makeup	Sophistic
Restore	Cookery	Rhetoric

Socrates attempts to show Polus that power and honor belong not only to the tyrant, but also to the wise and just individual. He brings Polus to accept a conclusion that seems absurd, "That to do wrong and not to be brought to justice is the first and greatest of all evils." Thus, rhetoric ought to be employed to bring oneself and one's friends to justice. This is consistent with Plato's view of justice as an art, a *techne*, that restores health to the soul:

> Crime must not be concealed, but be brought to light so that the criminal may pay the penalty and grow well again. A man must force himself and his friends to grit the teeth without flinching and ignore the pain (480c–d).

The art Polus loved because it brought power ought to be valued for its power to bring justice.

Socrates versus Callicles: The Strong Survive

Socrates' third interaction concerning rhetoric in *Gorgias* is with the notorious Sophist Callicles, a hardened defender of "natural justice," the strong dominating the weak in human society as in nature. "This I conceive to be justice according to nature: he who is better and more intelligent should rule and have the advantage over baser men" (490). Callicles despises the very foundation of democracy in the *polis*—law based on convention (*nomos*), rules rooted in social agreements. The weak craft such "unnatural" regulations in an effort to control the strong. "The manufacturers of laws and conventions are the weak, the majority, in fact" (483).

Callicles contends that the strong person should pursue desire without reservation. This unbridled pursuit of desire is the "beautiful and just" life, according to Callicles:

> What is beautiful and just by nature I shall now explain to you without reserve. A man who is going to live a full life must allow his desires to become as mighty as may be and never repress them. When his passions have come to full maturity, he must be able to serve them through his courage and intelligence and gratify every fleeting desire as it comes into his heart (492–493).

Disdainful of Socrates' lofty arguments about the just life, Callicles redefines morality as following desire (*hedone*) rather than virtue (*areté*). In the process, he turns traditional Athenian morality on its head.

Socrates counters this revolutionary argument by affirming that Callicles is not free, but is a slave to both his own desires and those of his audience, the masses (*demos*). The fact of his enslavement is evident any time Callicles steps before the Athenian assembly to make a speech. "If you are making a speech in the Assembly," Socrates remarks, "and the Athenian Demos disagrees, you change and say what it desires" (481d–e). Callicles serves his desires and his audiences; despite his cleverness and rhetorical skill he cannot resist the pull of these forces.

Callicles is not his own master, according to Socrates, but is driven by his lust for power and pleasure. Socrates tempts his sophistic opponent with a true love—philosophy—in contrast to Callicles' fickle love, the Athenian *demos*. We can see that Socrates has adapted his own argument—his rhetoric—to his audience, that is, to Callicles. Having identified Callicles as someone who loves power and pleasure, Socrates constructs arguments that promise those things will come to Callicles if he will lead a life devoted to justice. Callicles is not convinced. He argues that strong people like himself are sometimes successfully "charmed" and "enslaved" by the weak. He rejects Socrates' life of justice-seeking, which Callicles sees as simply the product of convention (*nomos*). Callicles makes an eloquent, even beautiful, defense of his philosophy of greed and power:

> [W]e mold the nature of the best and strongest among us, raising them from infancy by the incantations of a charmed voice, as men do lion cubs; we enslave them by repeating again and again that equality is morality and only this is beautiful and just. Yet I fancy that if a man appears of capacity sufficient to shake off and break through and escape from all these conventions, he will trample under foot our ordinances and charms and spells, all this mass of unnatural legislation; our slave will stand forth revealed as our master and the light of natural justice will shine forth (483d–484a)!

In his famous work *Republic*, Plato himself deployed a similar metaphor to commend the training of children by their mothers and nurses. By nature wild and unruly, children are only transformed into productive and loyal citizens by the careful repetition of Greek values. Education is thus a persuasive enterprise, an exercise in rhetorical magic. As one expert writes of Plato's view, stories encapsulating Greek values were to be "poured into nurslings along with the milk" by mothers and nurses. Plato says this constant repetition of values works "like incantations" or spells (*epoidai*).[21] Spells were thought to have medicinal effects, even working to induce labor in a pregnant woman. Thus, a child's exposure to moral enchantments began even before birth.

Socrates is not shaken by Callicles' dismissal of his arguments. He continues to advocate for a just life guided by philosophy—the love of wisdom—and leading to true health and happiness. Rhetoric ought to be employed to persuade others to live justly as well:

> [T]his is the best way to spend one's days: to live and die in the pursuit of justice and the other virtues. Let us follow it, then, and urge others to do the same and to abandon the way in which you put your confidence and your exhortations; for your way, Callicles, has no value whatever (527e).

Callicles is impossible to persuade; having practiced an unjust rhetoric for so long, he is convinced of its truth. Philosophy is an occupation for weak men content to spend their time with "lisping boys." Callicles' goal is the raw power that rhetoric brings him.

He manifests the very danger Socrates warned Polus and Gorgias against: leading an unjust life and hating wisdom, he thinks he is living justly.

The Outcome of the *Gorgias*

The dialogue *Gorgias* presents Plato's criticism of sophistic rhetoric as merely a knack for creating persuasive speeches that lack any foundation in justice. Practicing such debased rhetoric is dangerous as it leads to an unjust society. Educating young people to do the same is reprehensible and corrupts the *polis*.

Does Socrates win this debate? None of the major contestants—Gorgias, Polus, Callicles—is clearly convinced by Socrates' arguments about rhetoric and philosophy. The outcome of the interaction with Callicles is particularly uncertain, and this conclusion may suggest that Plato held serious reservations about reversing the direction of an unjust life. Notice that Socrates himself acts as a rhetorician in this dialogue, and that even his great skill in argument is not enough to change Callicles' mind. Nevertheless, Plato's *Gorgias* hints that there exists a true art of rhetoric with justice as its goal.

Is Plato Fair to Rhetoric and the Sophists?

After reading *Gorgias* during a visit to Athens, the great Roman orator Cicero commented: "What most surprised me about Plato in that work was that it seemed to me that as he was in the process of ridiculing rhetors he himself appeared to be the foremost rhetor."[22] Other readers have made similar observations.

Historian of rhetoric Brian Vickers thinks that Plato stacks the deck against the Sophists in Gorgias.[23] Vickers notes that though Socrates says he rejects the rhetorical way of arguing from probability (*eikos*), witnesses, beliefs, and even ridicule, he engages in these tactics when they serve his ends. Similarly, Richard Leo Enos writes that Plato's case in *Gorgias* should be viewed as "rhetorical argument of the kind associated with sophistic rhetoric."[24] Thus, a profound irony resides at the heart of *Gorgias*.

Plato might also unfairly represent the Sophists, portraying them as worse offenders against justice than they actually were. Callicles, for instance, may be an extreme example rather than a typical Sophist. Then again, Plato likely had a hidden agenda in the dialogue, as the real-life Callicles apparently encouraged the trial leading to the death of Socrates, Plato's beloved teacher. Enos finds the portrayal of Gorgias himself so exaggerated as to be unrecognizable. "The biased characterization of Gorgias of Leontini in Plato's famous dialogue," writes Enos, "was a gross misrepresentation . . ."[25]

Plato contends that rhetoric deceives audiences into thinking they are discovering truth when they are dabbling in opinions, that they are rendering justice when they are committing injustice, that they are healthy when they are desperately sick. Rhetoric dupes even its most astute practitioners into thinking they wield real power when they are, in fact, slaves to public opinion. But, if these are the points he wishes to prove, why does Plato endanger his case by engaging in sophistic tactics to refute the Sophists? Why does he deploy rhetoric against rhetoric? There is perhaps no satisfactory answer to this question, unless Plato wished to exhibit his own mastery of rhetoric in building his case against the rhetoricians.

The condemnation of rhetoric as trafficking in opinion and pandering to audiences has dogged the art ever since Plato wrote *Gorgias*. Here we encounter one of the themes of rhetoric's history mentioned in Chapter 1—the art's relationship to truth. The Sophists held that rhetoric created a truth useful for the moment (*kairos*), crafting it out of *doxa* or the opinions of the people. Socrates will have no part of this sort of temporary truth. But, is such truth essential to a democracy? Truth to the philosopher is transcendent and absolute, and not to be had by persuading an uninformed audience. Plato's argument against rhetoric extends to any aspect of democracy (rule by the *demos*) that seeks truth by weighing opposed arguments from probability and public opinion.

Another, and related, concern of *Gorgias* is the rhetor's relationship to an audience. Sophists, according to Socrates, are willing to tell their audiences whatever they wish to hear. Socrates asserts that in this way the audience ends up controlling the rhetor. Seeking to manipulate their audiences, the equation often is reversed for rhetors. Truth is ignored while the audience is flattered. Truth, for Socrates, exists independently of audiences. To make truth a matter of persuading audiences is dangerous, for audiences are easily deceived by a clever speaker who says what they want to hear.

Rhetoric's relationship to power is also a concern in the Gorgias. The Sophists want the power that persuasion brings them—control over an audience gained by flattery. For Socrates, power is self-control grounded in true knowledge, and its goal is justice. This latter version of power is not something sophistic rhetoric can deliver. In the next section we will consider Plato's other great statement on rhetoric, the *Phaedrus*, in which rhetoric takes on a different quality, and may even achieve the status of a *techne*, or genuine and useful art.[26]

RHETORIC IN PLATO'S *PHAEDRUS*: A TRUE ART?

In a second dialogue addressing rhetoric, this one titled *Phaedrus*, Plato hints at a true art of rhetoric. This would not be the same art practiced by the Sophists and criticized in *Gorgias*. In fact, this Platonic art of rhetoric may not have been practiced by anyone in Athens, with the possible exception of Plato himself. Distinguished classical scholar Jacqueline de Romilly (1913–2010) writes, "in the *Phaedrus*, Plato was to recognize another kind of rhetoric," which she terms "a science of dialectics." She adds,

> the contrast [to *Gorgias*] constituted by [*Phaedrus*] emphasizes the inadequacies of the rhetoric of the Sophists; but it certainly does nothing to diminish the force of Plato's first reaction as expressed in the *Gorgias*, where, in the name of morality, he wanted to reject rhetoric utterly.[27]

In *Phaedrus* Plato suggests a rhetoric used for the good of the individual and of the society, but he does not retract his earlier criticism of sophistic rhetoric.

Phaedrus is not devoted strictly to discussing rhetoric; the dialogue also offers some of Plato's views on love, immortality, the soul, and poetry. However, rhetoric is given a prominent place. Much of the dialogue consists of speeches, one of which is considered among the greatest accomplishments of Greek speech writing. Plato argues that a true art of speech aims at an ordered society through a study of the different kinds of human souls, and how strategic language influences these different types. Of particular significance to Plato's thinking about rhetoric is the interaction of the themes of love and rhetoric in *Phaedrus*.

Phaedrus presents a conversation between Socrates and the title character, Phaedrus, a young student of the Sophist Lysias. Phaedrus is "an immature youth intoxicated with rhetoric."[28] He loves speeches, and is taken with the beauty of words at the command of great orators. It is also clear that Socrates finds this young man attractive, physically as well as intellectually. Thus, the themes of erotic love and of rhetoric arise as natural consequences of the interests of both parties. So inspired is Socrates by his attraction to Phaedrus that he actually claims he is capable of making a speech for the occasion—the only time Socrates ever makes such a claim.

The early portion of the dialogue develops around three speeches. Phaedrus reads the first of these to Socrates, noting that Lysias wrote it himself (231–234). The theme of this speech is love; Phaedrus considers it a brilliant piece of work, "marvelously eloquent, especially in its use of language."[29] But it proves a rambling and sophomoric affair of no merit whatever. The speech argues that it is better to be a "nonlover" than a true lover. That is, to care nothing for a lover is better than actually to care for him.

Socrates is unimpressed and promises a better speech on the same topic. Socrates' speech is better organized and argued than is the speech of Lysias. Socrates feigns embarrassment at speaking on such an impious theme, but he wishes to demonstrate the ineptitude of the earlier speech. Socrates makes a second speech that addresses several themes. Love is described as "divine madness," akin to the poet's trance. Socrates also discusses the human soul, its immortality, and its various types. Here the famous myth of the charioteer illustrates the relationships among the three parts of the soul. Before exploring this myth and its relationship to rhetoric, it will be helpful to overview Plato's theory of mind or soul.

The Complexity of the Soul

As is evident from his *Republic* and other dialogues, Plato believed the soul (*psyche*) was complex, consisting of three parts. Each of these parts pursues its own interests and is engaged in a struggle with the other two parts for control of an individual's thoughts and actions.[30]

Plato distinguished the soul's three parts by the characteristic loves of each. One part loves wisdom; the philosopher's soul is governed by this part. The second part loves nobility and honor, and people of a military cast of mind are controlled by this part of the soul. The third is the appetite or desire loving part. People controlled by this part spend their lives pursuing pleasure, never knowing peace of mind or self-control. This three-part theory of the soul complements Plato's view of justice as reviewed in our discussion of *Gorgias,* where Socrates, Polus, and Callicles may represent souls controlled by these different loves—Socrates by a love of wisdom, Polus by a love of nobility, and Callicles by a love of desire.

The Myth of the Charioteer

Plato's theory of the soul is our key to understanding the myth of the charioteer. In his second speech Socrates states that the soul "is like the composite union of powers in a team of winged horses and their charioteer" (246a). In the myth, he "divided every soul into three parts, two of which had the form of horses, the third that of a charioteer" (253). The wisdom-loving part is portrayed as the charioteer himself as he tries to control two powerful horses. "One of them is noble and handsome and of good breeding," says Socrates of one horse, "while the other is the very opposite, so that our charioteer necessarily has a difficult and troublesome task."

The "noble and handsome" horse is easily controlled; the charioteer speaks and this horse responds to his "word of command alone." This horse is the lover of honor; it represents the nobility-loving part of the human soul and the person controlled by this part. The nobility-lover is, or ought to be, under the lover of wisdom's control. The other horse is wild, strong, ugly, and unheeding of the driver's commands. This unruly horse will "hardly heed whip or spur," and represents the appetite-loving part of the soul. This horse, left to its own devices, will take control of the chariot and its driver with disastrous results.

The wise charioteer knows the different kinds of horses under his command, and understands how to control each. When the horses are properly controlled the soul enjoys peace and happiness:

> If, then, the better part of the intelligence wins the victory and guides them to an orderly and philosophic way of life, their life on earth will be happy and harmonious since they have attained discipline and self-control: They have subdued the source of evil in the soul and set free the source of goodness (256).

The myth of the charioteer is charged with sexual imagery, and illustrates Socrates' understanding of erotic love more specifically than his view of rhetoric. However, Phaedrus and Socrates' conversation, following the myth of the charioteer, is about speech writing, speech making, and a true art of rhetoric. There is, then, some connection between love and rhetoric in *Phaedrus* that makes the myth relevant to each concern. What is that connection?

Components of a *Techne* of Rhetoric

Phaedrus provides an answer to the question of which studies would make up a true art of rhetoric. Certainly such an art involves knowledge of justice and the other virtues. Socrates notes that "when an orator who knows nothing about good or evil undertakes to persuade a city in the same state of ignorance," the results are dangerous. Therefore, a lover of wisdom wishing to use rhetoric well must study truth. "I bring no compulsion to learn the art of speech on anyone who is ignorant of the truth," says Socrates. And truth comes via the arduous study of philosophy.

Socrates defines rhetoric as "an art of influencing the soul [*techne psychagogia*] through words [*logoi*]" (261). Plato chooses the same word, *psychagogia*, that Gorgias himself used to describe his version of rhetoric. *Psychagogia* means to lead the soul, and Plato's use of the Sophists' own term may suggest that he aims to provide the rational account of the art of rhetoric that Gorgias failed to provide in the dialogue that bears his name.

Plato's rhetoric is the art of leading the soul toward truth through words and arguments (*logoi*). Thus, foundational to a *techne* of rhetoric are knowledge of truth and knowledge of the soul. Plato confirms this point in writing that anyone "who addresses words to another in a scientific manner" must be equipped to "accurately describe the nature of the object" to which the speech is addressed. "And this," adds Socrates, "I suppose, will be the soul" (270). Socrates sets about sketching the outline of this knowledge:

> Since it is in fact the function of speech to influence souls, a man who is going to be a speaker must know how many types of souls there are. Let us, then, state that they are of this or that number and of this or that sort, so that individuals also will be of this or that type (271).

Guided by an understanding of different psychological types, a rhetorician "must discover the kind of speech that matches each type of nature" (277b). Orators ought to be skilled psychologists, soul-knowers. And, since Socrates' *techne* of speech also relies on a knowledge of *logoi*, rhetors must master a repertoire of arguments persuasive to each type of soul. De Romilly writes that Plato's *techne* of rhetoric is built on "a thorough classification of the different kinds of *logoi* and of the different kinds of souls."[31] Similarly, G. M. A. Grube notes that "the speaker must learn the parts of the soul, their number, and the nature of each. He must then classify the different kinds of argument, when each is appropriate and why, thus relating his technique to his psychology."[32] *Phaedrus*, then, contends that the ability to adapt arguments to different types of people is central to an art or *techne* of rhetoric.[33] The speaker "must discover the kind of speech that matches each type of nature."

Rhetoric as Soulcraft

How, then, does one compose a speech guided by this true art of speech? And what is the goal of speechmaking? Socrates describes a process by which a rhetor would

> arrange and adorn each speech in such a way as to present complicated and unstable souls with complex speeches, speeches exactly attuned to every changing mood of the complicated soul—while the simple soul must be presented with simple speech (277).

Only when one has gained a thorough knowledge of souls and of *logoi* "will it be possible to produce speech in a scientific way, in so far as its nature permits such treatment, either for purposes of instruction or of persuasion" (277b). Toward what end is such an art practiced?

Rhetoric, Harmony, and Justice

The goal of Plato's art of rhetoric is to establish health-giving order in the individual and in the *polis*. Such health occurs when the wisdom-loving part of the soul persuades the other two parts voluntarily to submit to its control. Similarly, wisdom-loving people in the city-state would persuade other kinds of individuals to submit to their control. The goal of the *techne* of rhetoric, then, is voluntary submission of the lower parts to the wisdom-lover, a submission producing harmony and justice in the soul as well as in the *polis*.[34]

Phaedrus also takes up the topic of love; where does love enter the rhetorical picture? The wisdom-lover's art of rhetoric is guided by a thorough understanding of the loves of the other two parts of the soul. Plato scholar Jon Moline provides the key: "[T]he wisdom-loving part . . . must learn what each part loves and must construct discourses which are effective owing to their promising each part what it loves."[35] Moline adds that "the business of the wisdom-loving part is to guide the other parts by persuasion, to transplant into alien parts its own opinions." This is why the wisdom-lover must know souls, for "it is not likely to succeed in doing this unless it recognizes the number and nature of those alien parts."[36] Once the wisdom-lover has this knowledge, it can design arguments to bring these "alien parts" under its control.

A wisdom-lover's rhetoric is guided by a thorough understanding of the loves of the other two parts. Grube explains that the "method a rhetorician must learn" is to discern "the different kinds of love existing."[37] The goal of rhetoric, then, is the voluntary submission of the lower parts to the wisdom-lover.

In sum, Plato's psycho/sociological rhetoric employs persuasion toward "the good ordering of our lives which is called virtue," and this "depends on the right ordering of the two lower parts so that they obey reason, in the same way as good government depends on the lower orders obeying the wise rulers."[38] Plato's *techne* of rhetoric, then, involves two related studies:

1. a psychological study of the human soul, focused on its three different types or parts and the loves of each; and
2. a logical study of arguments (*logoi*) directed to each type of soul.

The ultimate goal of this *techne* of rhetoric is harmony, virtue, health, or, to use a favorite term of Plato's, justice.

Rhetoric's Relationship to Truth

Plato's discussion of rhetoric raises the question of whether rhetoric discovers truth or simply propagates it. Opinion is divided on this question. Susan Jarratt suggests that Plato's rhetoric does not discover truth; this is the role of philosophy employing dialectic.[39]

Thus, rhetoric has only an advocacy role, while the more philosophically rigorous art of dialectic reveals the truth. Patricia Bizzell and Bruce Herzberg take a different view. They argue that rhetoric is a means of "attaining truth" in *Phaedrus*; Socrates is "working out the truth in his own mind by talking to Phaedrus about it and correcting the less experienced thinker's misconceptions."[40]

Plato's art of rhetoric is one tool philosophers employ to bring about justice in the individual and in the *polis*. Rhetoric assists the recognition of truth, which certainly is not discovered through political speechmaking of the sophistic sort. It can also be employed to propagate a correct understanding of justice. Dialectic—rigorous, critical questioning—is a component of justice-seeking rhetoric; Plato's conversations in *Gorgias* are an example. His treatment of rhetoric as soul-craft in *Phaedrus* may be an answer to Isocrates' tendency to make rhetoric a tool in the service of politics. But Isocrates' pan-Hellenism does not embody an adequate view of truth, politics, or rhetoric for Plato.[41]

From Speaking to Writing

Finally, the debate between Plato and the Sophists marks the beginning of a gradual but monumental shift from speaking as the principal form of verbal communication to writing. The Sophists, as we have seen, were largely known for their speaking ability, and rhetoric developed as a spoken art. Figures such as Isocrates and Plato, however, recorded and disseminated their ideas in written form.

As the Western world shifted from an oral culture of education and government to a written one, corresponding changes were taking place in the structure of human thought. Oral cultures such as ancient Greece require techniques for keeping track of information without writing it down. They develop easily remembered forms such as the story or the poem, and they also create figures of speech such as the various rhetorical devices. Father Walter J. Ong, among others, explored this question of the shift from oral to written culture, and we will be considering more of his thought on this important issue in the subsequent chapters.[42]

CONCLUSION

Plato recognized the great power of persuasive language, particularly when employed by a trained practitioner of rhetoric. But he also saw a great danger in this power. The Sophists represented for him that danger manifested in Athenian society. The power of rhetoric in the service of personal motives, and appealing to an ignorant public concerning an issue as sensitive as justice, would lead a society to ruin. In *Gorgias*, he attempts to reveal the problems inherent in the practice of rhetoric when it is not joined to a love of wisdom and a true knowledge of justice. Plato is also asking his readers to consider what constitutes "the good life." Is it personal power in the service of pleasure and mastery over other people, or is it perhaps the practice of virtue and the pursuit of wisdom? Rhetoric can serve either goal, and it is up to the individual practitioner to decide on the proper uses of the art.

Can there actually be a true art of rhetoric, one founded on a love of wisdom and a knowledge of justice? Perhaps, as Plato suggests in *Phaedrus*, there can be such an art. It would consist of a thorough knowledge of the different types of human souls, as well as a thorough knowledge of how to make arguments that would appeal to each type of soul. Moreover, the true rhetorician would understand truth and justice. The goal of this art would be to order society properly so that a healthy *polis* would result.

In *Gorgias* and *Phaedrus* Plato presents us with two pictures of rhetoric—one corrupt and one virtuous. His view of the corrupt uses of rhetoric may be exaggerated, and his view of a good rhetoric utopian. Nevertheless, Plato anticipated many of the important themes that have colored the history of rhetoric, including its connection to power, its relationship to conceptions of truth, and its potential for shaping a society. The ethical questions raised by the rhetor's relationship to his or her audience are also considered in these dialogues, as is the question of the proper content of rhetoric as a discipline. Thus, Plato's *Gorgias* and *Phaedrus* still reward the study of anyone interested in better understanding the art of rhetoric and its many implications for free societies.

QUESTIONS FOR REVIEW

1. What were Plato's main objections in *Gorgias* to rhetoric as practiced by the Sophists?
2. Why is Plato concerned about the difference between mere belief and true knowledge, particularly concerning the issues of justice?
3. What criteria must a pursuit satisfy in order to be considered a techne by Plato?
4. Plato argues in *Gorgias* that rhetoric is a sham art. He also discusses a number of true arts. What is the true art to which rhetoric corresponds? What does Plato apparently mean by this comparison?
5. What are the various types of souls Plato discusses in *Phaedrus*?
6. What is the specific role assigned to a true art of rhetoric by Plato in *Phaedrus*?

QUESTIONS FOR DISCUSSION

1. Do you agree with Socrates that rhetoric works better informed? Does the quality of an audience best "among the ignorant"? Can the quality of an audience govern the qualities of rhetoric it is likely to hear?
2. Based on your reading of this chapter and Chapter 2, has Plato been fair to the Sophists? Does he have a good argument against them?
3. Does Plato make a convincing case in *Phaedrus* that there may be a true and just art of rhetoric? When he calls it an art, or techne, of "leading the soul" through words, is he suggesting a role for rhetoric that cannot be defended as ethical? That is, is his rhetoric any different from that of the Sophists?
4. Plato suggests in *Gorgias* that certain arts, such as justice and medicine, are essential to society. Others, such as the Sophist's brand of rhetoric, are imitations of these essential arts. If you had the opportunity to set up a society's system of government,

what role, if any, would the study of rhetoric play in it? Would you place any restrictions on the practice of this art?

5. Respond to Plato's suggestion in *Gorgias* that the absence of a transforming logos for rhetoric leaves the art in a state lower than a virtuous *techne*. Does the presence of a systematic explanation of a practice or undertaking render it morally improved?

6. Do you think that Plato has a point when he suggests in *Phaedrus* that there are different types of human souls dominated by the different things they love? Is his brand of psychology too simple, or does he perhaps have an insight?

TERMS

Demos The people; ordinary citizens or masses.

Dialectic Rigorous, critical questioning.

Doxa A belief or opinion. Also, "mere opinion."

Empeiria A knack; a skill learned by experience.

Epoidai Spells or incantations.

Episteme True knowledge.

Ergon The goal or outcome of a true art.

Hedone Pleasure.

Kolakeia Flattery. Promising people what they want without regard for what is best for them.

Logos (pl. *logoi*) An account, a clear and logical explanation of a true art or *techne*. Word. Argument. Transforming explanation.

Parasemos Counterfeit.

Pistis Mere belief.

Polis The city-state, particularly the people making up the state.

Psychagogia The art of influencing the soul.

Psyche Mind or soul.

Rhetores Rhetors or orators. Those making their living and wielding power by means of persuasive words.

Techne A true art or discipline. A scientific or systematic pursuit capable of a full account and arriving regularly at a good product or outcome.

Tribe A knack; an ability acquired through practice.

NOTES

1 To view the complete text of any of Plato's dialogues, visit www.persues.tufts.edu. For a discussion of Plato's *Phaedrus* as rhetoric, see: Jane V. Curran, "The Rhetorical Technique of Plato's *Phaedrus*," *Philosophy and Rhetoric* 19 (1986): 66–72. There are many excellent sources on Plato, his philosophy, and his thought on specific topics. Such works that take up issues discussed in this chapter include: I. M. Crombie, *An Examination of Plato's Doctrines*, v. I (London: Routledge and Kegan Paul, 1961); Michael Despland, *The Education of Desire:*

Plato and the Philosophy of Religion (Toronto: University of Toronto Press, 1985); and R. M. Hare, *Plato* (Oxford: Oxford University Press, 1982).

2 On these dialogues, see, for example: Plato's *Sophist*, trans. William S. Cobb (Savage, MD: Rowman and Littlefield, 1990); Plato, *Protagoras*, trans. Christopher Charles Whiston Taylor (Oxford: Clarendon Press, 1991); and B. A. F. Hubbard and E. S. Karnofsky, *Plato's Protagoras: A Socratic Commentary* (Chicago: University of Chicago Press, 1982).

3 Brian Vickers, *In Defense of Rhetoric* (Oxford: Oxford University Press, 1988), 148.

4 For a detailed discussion of this question, see: Vickers, Chapter 3, "Territorial Disputes: Philosophy versus Rhetoric," 148–213.

5 George Kennedy, *Classical Rhetoric and Its Christian and Secular Tradition*, 2nd ed. (Chapel Hill: University of North Carolina Press, 1999), 54.

6 A good introduction to these dialogues and their relationship to one another is: Seth Benardete, *The Rhetoric of Morality and Philosophy: Plato's Gorgias and Phaedrus* (Chicago: University of Chicago Press, 1991). Also helpful: Adele Spitzer, "The Self-Reference of the *Gorgias*," *Philosophy and Rhetoric* 8 (1975): 1–22.

7 All passages are from *Gorgias*, trans. W. C. Helmbold (Indianapolis, IN: Bobbs-Merrill, 1952). Other translations include: Plato, *Gorgias*, trans. T. Irwin (Oxford: Clarendon Press, 1979). For a detailed introduction to and commentary on *Gorgias*, see: George Kimball Plochmann and Franklin E. Robinson, *A Friendly Companion to Plato's Gorgias* (Carbondale, IL: Southern Illinois University Press, 1988).

8 Vickers, 153.

9 Josiah Ober, *Mass and Elite in Democratic Athens* (Princeton, NJ: Princeton University Press, 1989), 105.

10 George Kennedy, *The Art of Persuasion in Greece* (Princeton, NJ: Princeton University Press, 1963), 185.

11 Bruce Gronbeck, "Gorgias on Rhetoric and Poetic: A Rehabilitation," *Southern Speech Communication Journal* 38 (Fall 1972): 35.

12 For discussions of Plato's theory of art as it relates to rhetoric, see: Hans-George Gadamer, *The Idea of the Good in Platonic–Aristotelian Philosophy* (New Haven, CT: Yale University Press, 1986), 46–49, 78–80; and Rupert C. Lodge, *Plato's Theory of Art* (1953; New York: Russell and Russell, 1975), Chaps. III and IV.

13 Crombie suggests that rhetoric's product would be "spiritual order," evidenced in "justice and self-restraint," and that these are "the qualities that the scientific orator would aim to produce in his hearers" (197).

14 On the themes treated in Gorgias, see: Edwin Black, "Plato's View of Rhetoric," *Quarterly Journal of Speech* 44 (December 1958): 361–374.

15 Jessica Moss, "Right Reason in Plato and Aristotle: On the Meaning of *Logos*," *Phronesis* 59(3) (2014): 181–230, p. 188.

16 Janet M. Atwill, *Rhetoric Reclaimed: Aristotle and the Liberal Arts Tradition* (Ithaca NY: Cornell University Press, 1998), 6.

17 Edward Schiappa, "Did Plato Coin *Rhetorike*?" *American Journal of Philology* 111 (1990): 457–470. See also, Kennedy, *Classical Rhetoric*, 59.

18 Vickers, 97.

19 Ober, 107.

20 Spitzer, 10.

21 Marcel Detienne, *The Creation of Mythology*, trans. Margaret Cook (Chicago: University of Chicago Press, 1986), 85.

<table>
<tr><td>Plato versus
the Sophists:
Rhetoric on
Trial</td><td>22</td><td>Cicero, De Oratore, 1. 11. 47. Quoted in Enos, 91.</td></tr>
</table>

Plato versus the Sophists: Rhetoric on Trial

22   Cicero, *De Oratore*, 1. 11. 47. Quoted in Enos, 91.
23   Vickers, 113–120.
24   Richard Leo Enos, *Greek Rhetoric before Aristotle* (Prospect Heights, IL: Waveland, 1993), 92.
25   Enos, 72.
26   Some scholars have argued that as Plato criticizes rhetoric in *Gorgias*, he also employs the art. See, for example: Jan Swearingen, *Rhetoric and Irony* (Oxford: Oxford University Press, 1991).
27   Jacqueline de Romilly, *The Great Sophists in Periclean Athens*, trans. Janet Lloyd (Oxford: Clarendon Press, 1992), 71.
28   John Poulakos, *Sophistical Rhetoric in Classical Greece* (Columbia: University of South Carolina Press, 1995), 79.
29   Plato, *Phaedrus*, trans. W. C. Helmbold and W. G. Rabinowitz (Indianapolis, IN: Liberal Arts Press, 1956), 12. All passages from *Phaedrus* are taken from this edition unless otherwise indicated.
30   This view may remind you of Freud's id, ego, and superego, and, while there are some similarities in the two theories, the analogy is not exact.
31   Jacqueline de Romilly, *Magic and Rhetoric in Ancient Greece* (Cambridge, MA: Harvard University Press, 1975), 51.
32   George Maximilian Antony Grube, *Plato's Thought* (1935; rpt. Boston: Beacon Press, 1958), 214–215.
33   T. Benson and Michael H. Prosser, *Readings in Classical Rhetoric* (Boston: Allyn and Bacon, 1969), 22.
34   Regarding the relationship between the harmony of the individual and the harmony of the state, Moline explains that on Plato's view:
     [T]he individual is wise in the same way, and in the same part of himself, as the city. . . And the part which makes the individual brave is the same as that which makes the city brave, and in the same manner, and everything which makes for virtue is the same in both. . . The city was just because each of the three classes in it was fulfilling its own task.
     Jon Moline, *Plato's Theory of Understanding* (Madison: University of Wisconsin Press, 1981), 55.
35   Moline, 65.
36   Moline, 65.
37   Grube, 212.
38   Hare, 54.
39   Susan Jarratt, *Rereading the Sophists: Classical Rhetoric Refigured* (Carbondale, IL: Southern Illinois University Press, 1991), xvi.
40   Patricia Bizzell and Bruce Herzberg, *The Rhetorical Tradition: Readings from Classical Times to the Present* (Boston: St. Martin's Press, 1990), 28.
41   de Romilly, *Magic*, 58.
42   See: Walter J. Ong, *Orality and Literacy: The Technologizing of the Word*, 2nd ed. (New York: Routledge, 2002).

Chapter 4

Aristotle on Rhetoric

Rhetoric is the faculty (dunamis) of observing in any given case the available means of persuasion.

—Aristotle, *Rhetoric*

ONE major contributor to the development of Western thinking about rhetoric is the great Greek philosopher Aristotle (384–322 BCE). A native of the city of Stagira in northern Greece, Aristotle came to Athens in 367 as a young man. Rhetoric was already a well-established discipline in Athens, Gorgias having arrived in the city-state 60 years earlier. The famed Sophist had died 13 years earlier.

Aristotle's early education "probably included the usual study of language, poetry, music, and geometry, as well as athletic training in the gymnasium." George Kennedy notes that Aristotle also "learned something about medicine from his father," who was court physician to King Amyntas of Macedon.[1] Entering Plato's Academy—an association of intellectuals interested in philosophy and astronomy—at about the age of 17, he joined an intellectual circle that "included some of the most eminent philosophers and scientists of the age."[2] Aristotle maintained his association with the Academy for 20 years. The chief rival to Plato's school in Athens was that established by Isocrates, whose ideas about rhetoric we considered in Chapter 2.[3] Forbes Hill notes that "Aristotle began his career as an orthodox Platonist who carried forward a running battle with the Sophists."[4] That battle would certainly have included issues regarding rhetoric.

Aristotle took an interest in the art of rhetoric being practiced in Athens, at first adopting Plato's skeptical attitudes toward the topic. Later, however, he turned his attention to a systematic study of the art. Aristotle was inclined toward science; a prolific writer and a universal genius, he possessed limitless curiosity and intellectual energy. It is estimated that he wrote as many as 550 books and a total of more than 6,000 pages in modern print.[5] Only about one third of his works survive, and among them is his highly influential *Rhetoric*.[6]

Aristotle began teaching rhetoric around 350, "while still a member of [Plato's] Academy." His course "seems to have been open to the general public—offered in the afternoon as a kind of extension division of the Academy and accompanied by practical exercises in speaking."[7] In *Rhetoric*, Aristotle sets out a systematic approach to the subject for the benefit of his more advanced students and in an effort to legitimate the study of rhetoric in his school, the Lyceum. Avoiding the moralizing tone of his teacher of 20 years, Aristotle's approach to rhetoric was pragmatic and scientific.

Much of Aristotle's theory of rhetoric is a response to Plato's criticisms, and to inadequate sophistic works on rhetoric. Sophistic treatises, according to Aristotle, "deal mainly with non-essentials" and focus on courtroom speaking. Aristotle agreed with Plato that the Sophists had not presented a true *techne* of rhetoric (1354a). There was more to be said, and the topic was more important to civic life than others had realized.

Aristotle's system of rhetoric is perhaps the most influential ever advanced, and still offers valuable insights into many aspects of public and private discourse. Seeking to improve on the shallow text-book treatments circulating in Athens, Aristotle seems also to be addressing Plato's charges that rhetoric was not a *techne* or true art. Many claims in Aristotle's *Rhetoric* stand "in direct contradiction to some part of the *Gorgias*."[8] One of those claims opens *Rhetoric*.[9]

DEFINING RHETORIC

Aristotle's *Rhetoric* confronts us with several perplexing questions, and scholars are not in agreement about how to interpret the book.[10] Some of this uncertainty stems from the fact that early manuscripts of *Rhetoric* derive from student notes. In addition, scholars believe that portions of *Rhetoric*, perhaps an entire additional book (on humor?), have been lost. With these cautions in mind we will explore Aristotle's sophisticated theory of persuasive speaking and its role in a democratic society.

Rhetoric is divided into three sections or books. Book I defines the domain of rhetoric, and describes the three types of oratory. Book II discusses rhetorical proofs derived from character and emotion, and Book III deals with matters of style and arrangement.

Rhetoric and Dialectic

Aristotle opens his treatise on rhetoric with the assertion that "rhetoric is the counterpart of dialectic" (1354), the latter art being discussed in another of Aristotle's books, the *Topics*. The term *counterpart* is a translation of the Greek word *antistrophos*, and it is the same term used in Plato's *Gorgias* when Socrates asserts that rhetoric is the "counterpart of cookery" (465). By stating that rhetoric is the counterpart to the *techne* of dialectic, Aristotle may be answering his teacher's claim that rhetoric is a mere analogy to the knack of cooking. Aristotle is convinced that there is more to rhetoric than that.

Dialectic was a method of debating issues of general interest, starting from widely accepted ideas or *endoxa*. Aristotle writes in the *Topics* that he is seeking "a method from which we shall be able to syllogise about every proposed problem on the basis of generally accepted opinions"[11] Dialectic resolved foundational questions in philosophy, and could also be employed to reason through practical issues.[12] By allowing critical examination of both sides of a question, dialectic tested old ideas and discovered new ones.[13]

Both rhetoric and dialectic begin with *endoxa*, that is, both involve reasoning from commonly held opinions. However, rhetoric employs sources of support that dialectic avoids—proofs from the speaker's character and from emotions aroused in an audience. Moreover, rhetoric is a public art for resolving issues in politics and justice before large audience.[14] Thus, the typical form of rhetoric is the public speech, while dialectic involves briefly stated questions and similarly brief answers. Rhetoric's audience lacks formal training in logic, while dialectic addresses a small group of trained advocates. Finally, rhetoric usually resolves specific issues such as, "Is Cleanthes guilty of robbing Chaerophon?" Dialectic, on the other hand, addresses general questions such as one debated in *Gorgias*: "Is it better to suffer injustice, or to commit injustice?"

Thus, rhetoric and dialectic, discussed in *Rhetoric* and *Topics* respectively, represent two complementary arts of reasoning from widely accepted opinions to probable conclusions on a range of topics. By calling rhetoric the "counterpart of dialectic," Aristotle may have hoped to distinguish rhetoric from sophistry on the one hand and philosophical inquiry on the other. And, though rhetoric is concerned with matters of style, it is not itself the study of beautiful and moving language, a topic Aristotle addresses in his *Poetics*. Rhetoric is something other than sophistry, dialectic, or poetry. What, then, distinguishes this art from other closely related uses of language?

DIALECTIC AND RHETORIC: SIMILARITIES AND DIFFERENCES

Similarities

—Each deals with questions that concern everyone.
—Each deals with questions that do not belong to a specific science or art.
—Each can reason on either side of a case.
—Each starts with *endoxa* or common opinions.

Differences

	Dialectic	Rhetoric
Purpose:	Testing an argument	Defending an idea or self
Practitioner:	Experts in reasoning	Ordinary citizens
Method:	Question and answer	Speech
Issue:	General questions	Specific questions
Audience:	Small audience	Large audience
Argument:	Syllogism	Enthymeme
Proofs:	Arguments	Arguments, character, and emotion

Rhetoric as a *Techne* of Discovery

At the beginning of Book I Chapter 2 of *Rhetoric*, Aristotle advances a second definition of rhetoric—and it has become the most famous definition of rhetoric ever formulated as well as the most influential. "Rhetoric," he writes, "is the faculty (*dunamis:* capacity, power) of observing in any given case the available means of persuasion (*to endekhomenon pithanon*)" (1355b). Notice that in making this claim Aristotle aligns rhetoric with inventional (creative) rather than practical (oratorical) considerations. His art of rhetoric is a process rather than a product. Aristotle presents rhetoric as the study of *discovering* persuasive arguments and appeals, not as advice about making persuasive and impressive speeches. The Sophists taught their students to memorize model speeches and to debate in order to learn persuasion by imitation and constant practice. Aristotle taught his students the investigative, rational ability to discover what is persuasive in any setting. Has he described a *techne*? A *techne* must address concerns not addressed by other arts. Aristotle affirms that rhetoric's domain—discovering the "available means of persuasion" —is not "a function of any other art." Rhetoric's goals are not ones accomplished by other *technae*, including dialectic, logic, or poetry. "Every other art," he explains:

> can instructor persuade about its own particular subject matter; for instance, medicine about what is healthy and unhealthy, geometry about properties of magnitudes, arithmetic about numbers, and the same is true of the other arts and sciences (1355b).

Like other arts, rhetoric has its own subject matter: the means of persuasion. Aristotle seems concerned to answer Plato's charge in *Gorgias* that rhetoric has no identifiable study of its own.

Aristotle also notes that no art achieves its goals in every case. Medicine proves this point: It only helps us to become as healthy as we can be under the circumstances, but it by no means guarantees health in every instance. Similarly, rhetoric's "function is not simply to succeed in persuading but rather to discover the means of coming as near such success as the circumstances of each particular case allow" (1355b). Aristotle contends that rhetoric is an art, and that it can thus be studied systematically. He shows some hesitancy, however, to declare that rhetoric and dialectic parallel other *technai*, for each is a mental capacity rather than a physical ability, and each shows itself in the form of speech rather than in a material outcome. Moreover, neither deals explicitly with a discrete set of facts as do other arts such as medicine. Thus, rhetoric and dialectic are arts, but of a distinct type: arts of investigation and expression (1359b). The particular function (*ergon*) of rhetoric is to guide our reasoning when a decision among various options must be made, when there are no specific arts to instruct us—such as medicine or generalship—and when facing an audience not trained in rigorous reasoning. (1357a)

Why Rhetoric Is Useful

In addition to addressing a distinct set of concerns, a *techne* produced social utility; for instance, the art of government produced stability and peace in the city-state. Aristotle suggests four reasons why the art of rhetoric is useful to the *polis*.

First, rhetoric is socially useful because of its relationship to truth. Aristotle writes:

> Things that are true and things that are just have a natural tendency to prevail over their opposites, so that if the decisions of judges [audience members] are not what they ought to be, the defeat must be due to the speakers themselves, and they must be blamed accordingly (1355a).

Aristotle appears to believe that if all other things were equal, true and just ideas would prevail on their own. This claim is rooted in his view of truth as arising from the natural world (*physis*) and thus as either observable or clear to reason.[15] But, clearly, all other things often are not equal and we cannot depend on true and just notions prevailing in the give-and-take of public debate. Thus, even true and just ideas require the advocacy of capable speakers and writers.

The philosopher's second reason for rhetoric's social usefulness derives from the nature of audiences. "Before some audiences," Aristotle writes, "not even the possession of the exactest knowledge will make it easy for what we say to produce conviction." Why is this? Aristotle's answer is that "there are people whom one cannot instruct" (1355a). Is this a harsh condemnation of the general public's reasoning capacity, or is it simply an observation about the nature of some members of some audiences?

Experience confirms that it is difficult to persuade some audiences with a simple presentation of "the facts." What does rhetoric instruct us to do in such a circumstance? Aristotle's answer is to reason from points accepted by nearly everyone. "Here, then," writes Aristotle, "we must use, as our modes of persuasion and argument, notions possessed by everybody . . . when dealing with the way to handle a popular audience." Aristotle is not advocating verbal trickery or specious arguments, nor is he urging his students to water down the content of their messages. Rather, he is suggesting that rhetoric, by its very nature, makes connections between the point being argued and beliefs already held by listeners. This is perhaps the most important dimension of audience adaptation— welding our case to others' experiences, values, and beliefs. Rhetoric offers instruction in this skill, according to Aristotle, and it is a highly valuable skill in any democracy.

Aristotle's third reason for rhetoric's usefulness reminds us of the Sophists' two-sided approach to rhetoric: "We must be able to employ persuasion," he writes, "on opposite sides of a question . . . in order that we may see clearly what the facts are, and that if another [advocate] argues unfairly we on our part may be able to confute him" (1355a). As was noted in Chapter 2, sophistic instruction in rhetoric involved practice in arguing opposite sides of an issue. This was valuable training for the two reasons Aristotle mentions: It helped one to see all of the facts in the case (to discover all of the "available means of persuasion"), and it taught one to answer any argument with a well-framed counterargument. Aristotle is certainly not suggesting that we are obliged to actually present both sides of a case to our audience. Rather, he is stating a practical fact: Rhetoric teaches one to think out the pros and cons of any issue, and this is a useful skill. This habit of thought provides arguments for a case and helps us in refuting an opponent's case.

The fourth and last reason Aristotle presents for the rhetoric's usefulness involves an analogy to self-defense. It's absurd, he contends, that citizens should be taught to defend themselves with their hands and feet, and yet be unable to "defend [themselves] with speech and reason." Aristotle argues that "the use of rational speech is more distinctive of a human being than the use of his limbs." To the objection that people who know rhetoric can use this ability to "do great harm," Aristotle responds with apparent indignation that "*that* is a charge which may be made in common against all things except virtue, and above all against the things that are most useful, as strength, health, generalship." The most useful things are also the most dangerous, and rhetoric is very useful.

Aristotle presents rhetoric as a practical art, a *techne* he can recommend to his students as beneficial. Beyond its personal utility, understanding rhetoric benefits the *polis*: It allows defense of true and just ideas, weak arguments to be refuted, and those wrongly accused to make their case. Moreover, rhetoric encourages critical examination of a wide range of political issues on which judgments must be rendered. Rhetoric also assists one to communicate clearly and persuasively to the large, public audiences that make important decisions in the *polis*. Finally, rhetoric provides the citizen with a valuable resource for self-defense.

THE ENTHYMEME

Central to Aristotle's treatment of rhetoric is a type of argument or an approach to reasoning that Aristotle famously termed the *enthymeme*. There has been much debate as to what Aristotle intended by this concept.

Early in *Rhetoric*, Aristotle calls the enthymeme (*enthymema*) "a sort of syllogism," that is, a rhetorical syllogism (1354). A syllogism is a deductive argument that moves from a general premise (the major premise), through a particular application of that premise (the minor premise), to a specific conclusion. Aristotle's own famous example is often still used to illustrate syllogistic reasoning: All men are mortal, and Socrates is a man, so Socrates is mortal.

This is a syllogism, but what makes a syllogism an enthymeme, that is, a *rhetorical* syllogism? Aristotle contrasts the enthymeme with another type of argument he terms the *paradeigma*, or example. This is an inductive argument that moves from a particular instance or small number of instances to a probable generalization.[16] He summarizes by writing that "the *paradeigma* [example] is an induction, the *enthymema* a syllogism," or deduction (1356).

This initial definition of the enthymeme as a rhetorical deduction or syllogism is, however, too narrow to represent the complete concept as Aristotle develops it throughout the *Rhetoric*. For instance, he suggests at some points in his treatise that the substance of *all* rhetoric is the enthymeme. We need to pursue this concept further to gain an accurate understanding of what Aristotle has in mind.

An Argument Constructed with the Audience

It is clear that Aristotle held rhetoric to be constructed of arguments and appeals involving beliefs shared by the speaker and audience.[17] The Greek term *enthymema* literally means something like "grasped internally," the root term *thymos* referring to the visceral or emotional self that makes us human. Thus, for an argument to be enthymematic meant not simply that it connected with the audience's convictions, but that the argument also engaged their emotions or deeply held beliefs. The enthymeme was thus a "heartfelt" argument in which the audience sensed in the rhetor's language and delivery a passionate commitment to the position being staked out. Emotion and reason were not separated in Greek thought, but were viewed as aspects of the same crucially important undertaking— arriving at rational judgments through public deliberation.[18]

So readily apparent was the agreement on a foundational belief shared by audience and speaker that this mutually accepted belief need not be explicitly stated in the speech itself. Such an unstated reason is, literally, "grasped internally" by both audience and orator. Thus, the enthymeme was constructed or completed by rhetor and audience at the same moment. Rhetorical theorist Lloyd Bitzer noted that the enthymeme's "successful construction is accomplished through the joint efforts of speaker and audience, and this is its essential character."[19]

For example, suppose I were to argue: "Our football team must be good, for even our rivals praise us." It is not necessary for me to state the obvious missing premise: "One does not praise one's rivals unless they are exceptionally accomplished." The emotional aspect of the enthymeme comes clear if I argue in a judicial setting, "Watson and Jones should receive the same sentence, for their crimes were the same." It is understood and accepted by the audience that my unstated claim is: "Similar crimes should receive similar sentences." Such a commitment is not merely accepted by audience members, but passionately endorsed. For Aristotle, all rhetoric was characterized by such enthymematic exchanges, by transactions between the speaker and the audience involving agreements rooted in deeply held or "heartfelt" convictions.

A Democratic Argument

There is another aspect of the enthymeme to consider as we conclude our introduction to Aristotle's rhetoric. Recall that Chapter 1 suggested that rhetoric is useful when reasoning about contingent matters, issues about which absolute certainty is not possible. Aristotle adds that rhetoric is employed when arguing before an audience of the general public, and not a group of highly trained experts. Finally, we can note that rhetoric is the type of discourse that characterizes debate in a democratic society where issues are resolved by a free exchange of views among members of the public.

We can conclude that to argue rhetorically is to argue with a keen awareness of public values; successful rhetoric connects with what that audience believes. By its very nature rhetoric is a communal or democratic approach to resolving issues. Recognizing this fact, Aristotle placed the enthymeme at the very center of his rhetorical theory, understanding rhetoric as the art of public discourse in democratic societies. Enthymemes have a leveling and unifying effect as arguments that obligate rhetors to regard the beliefs, values, and experiences of their audiences. The people themselves cannot be ignored in the practice of rhetoric; by making the enthymeme central to his theory of rhetoric Aristotle underlines this fact.

THREE RHETORICAL SETTINGS

Aristotle recognized that a systematic study of oratory must take into account various kinds of speeches, their settings and audiences, and the issues each type of speech addresses. He divided oratory into three categories reflecting the different settings in which speeches occur, the corresponding purpose or goal (*telos*) of a speech, and the varying roles audiences play. These divisions are discussed in Book I of the *Rhetoric*, Chapters 4–15.[20]

First, Aristotle discussed deliberative oratory presented in the legislature as laws were being debated. These speeches addressed the use of resources and solutions to problems facing the *polis*. An audience member for a deliberative speech is a judge or decision-maker (*krites*) whose focus is the future good of the *polis*. He labeled this first type of rhetoric *symbouleutikon*, a *symboulos* being an advisor who offered counsel on practical matters. Orators sometimes chose this term to describe their role in the city-state.

Second, Aristotle addressed ceremonial speeches of the type given at funerals or following a military victory. Aristotle employed the term *epideiktikon* to describe such speeches, from which the term *epideictic oratory* is derived. Epideictic speeches praised citizens for a great accomplishment, publicly condemned someone for a vicious action, or eulogized the deceased. The audience member for such speeches is a *theoron*, spectator, who observes the speaker's presentation or display.

Third, Aristotle explored courtroom pleading (*dikanikon*), also called forensic oratory.[21] Courtroom speeches usually involved accusation and defense of an individual accused of a crime. There were no formally trained judges in Athenian courts, nor were there any trained attorneys or other officials. The courts were run largely by ordinary citizens, and the laws often were not clearly set out. Each audience member for such a judicial speech is thus a judge (*krites*) rendering a judgment about a past event. In fact, citizen members of a jury would have to decide if a particular law applied to the case being heard, and how to interpret that law if deemed pertinent. It's no wonder that things could get out of hand in an Athenian court.

Jane Sutton has argued that Aristotle's preference for the first of these three types of speeches—deliberative or legislative oratory—is itself a statement against the Sophists and their preference for the third type—judicial oratory.[22] Aristotle spends more time discussing deliberative oratory than the other two types, and is relatively less concerned with judicial pleading, which he may have believed brought out the worst qualities in speakers.

Deliberative Oratory

As we have already noted, Sophists were known principally for their courtroom pleading, a kind of rhetoric that depended largely on one's ability to sway a jury and to win a favorable judgment in a short time. Judicial rhetoric often emphasized emotional appeals and appeals to personal character. Indeed, these appeals could at times become rather ridiculous displays. Aristotle apparently considered the oratory taking place in legislative assemblies to be both more substantial and, because it affected the entire *polis*, of benefit to a larger number of people. He thus found such political speaking a better model for his analysis of rhetoric than was judicial speaking.[23] Aristotle writes that "in political oratory there is less inducement to talk about nonessentials. Political oratory is less given to unscrupulous practices than forensic, because it treats wider issues" (1354b).[24]

Deliberative oratory, discussed in Chapters 4 through 8 of Book I, addresses questions of the best or most advantageous (*sympheron*) course of action for the city-state. Thus, deliberative rhetoric involved weighing evidence for and against a policy or plan. It was oriented toward the future and influenced judgments about what *should* be done. Deliberative oratory's guiding principle was *eudaimonia*, which meant well-being, happiness, or flourishing.[25] The goal of deliberative speaking was to establish policies and pursue actions that contributed to the well-being of the Athenian *polis*. A deliberative speaker must therefore understand matters of law, politics, economics, trade, and warfare, and also grasp the qualities of civic life that contribute to the general good.

The type of reasoning common to deliberative oratory occurs in many kinds of decision-making. Deliberative reasoning addresses questions of the wise use of time, money, and other resources. Thus, if you are trying to decide what type of car to buy, or whether to even buy a car, you are engaged in what Aristotle would call deliberative reasoning. By the same token, if a school board is trying to decide whether to adopt a year-round format rather than the traditional "summer off" format, the board is engaging in deliberative reasoning and will be hearing deliberative oratory.

In sum, deliberative oratory is concerned with actions, is future oriented, and deals with questions of the best uses of resources. Deliberative orators need to know what their audience envisions as a good future, what they consider to be in their best interests, and what they think of as wasteful. The deliberative orator should also grasp such issues as the available resources, the time involved in completing a course of action, and how to overcome obstacles standing in the way of pursuing a plan.

Epideictic Oratory

The second type of speaking that Aristotle identifies in Chapter 9 of Book I is ceremonial or epideictic oratory. Epideictic oratory (*epideiktikon*) characterized public ceremonies such as funerals or events commemorating war heroes. It dealt with issues of praise (*epainos*) and blame (*psogos*), seeking as its goal to demonstrate what is honorable (*kalon*). We noted in Chapter 2 the Sophists' use of *epideixis* or speeches of display as a means of practicing and demonstrating their skills. Aristotle recognized the importance of ceremonial speaking as a way, not of training speakers or entertaining audiences, but of reinforcing public values. The epideictic orator did this by praising a person deserving of honor, or blaming someone for a notorious action. If deliberative oratory dealt with questions of expedience, ceremonial oratory addressed virtue and vice.

Classics scholar Jeffrey Walker argues that epideictic was more important in ancient Greece than experts have tended to recognize. The goal of the epideictic speech was not merely to entertain, but also to encourage audience members to "form opinions, or even to revise their existing beliefs and attitudes on a given topic." Much public speaking and writing in Athens was not directed toward making policy decisions or rendering a judgment about guilt or innocence. Rather, "contemplation" of ideas by the audience was the specific purpose of epideictic discourse.

An *epideixis* is literally a "showing forth," the presentation or "demonstration" of the virtue of an idea, a practice, or an action. Epideictic orators employ amplification (*auxesis*) of an action to illuminate its beauty and greatness for all to see. Epideictic's goal was thus contemplative rather than pragmatic; it prompted the audience to think, to reflect, or to embrace a new idea. Isocrates stands as a good example of a writer who pursued such goals. Walker concludes that "'epideictic' appears as that which shapes and cultivates the basic codes of value and belief by which a society or culture lives," a crucial social role indeed.[26]

Any time that we offer reasons why someone has done a good or courageous thing we are reasoning epideictically: we describe a virtue, and we show how a particular individual has exhibited it. Has an athlete exhibited good sportsmanship under great pressure? Perhaps a sports writer writes an editorial praising her. At the same time, if a political columnist authored a piece condemning a politician for corruption, the journalist's writing would be epideictic. Martin Luther King's famous "I Have a Dream" speech is another example of epideictic oratory, one in which King upholds the values of justice, harmony, and peace. Epideictic oratory elevates virtuous people for emulation and emphasizes certain values that are deemed important to the well-being of the citizenry.

Forensic Oratory

Forensic or judicial speaking, discussed in Chapters 10 through 15 of *Rhetoric,* Book I, differs in several respects from deliberative and epideictic. Judicial speaking's main concern is deciding questions of justice (*dikaion*). "In the law courts," writes Aristotle, "there is either accusation (*kategoria*) or defense (*apologia*)" rather than argumentation about the wise use of resources.[27] Moreover, when a lawyer makes a case in court, the focus is not on the future, but rather on questions of past fact such as "What was done?" and "Who did it?" Other judicial questions included the seriousness of the offense and appropriate punishment.

Forensic oratory reconstructs the past. Thus, forensic speakers must be skilled in convincing a jury that the available evidence supports a particular hypothesis. The judicial advocate must be a careful observer of human character so as to be able to argue effectively that a defendant either was or was not capable of committing the crime in question. This pleader should, in addition, have a strong grasp of what the citizens think is just, and so must be familiar with public values about justice.

Any time we seek to determine what occurred and whether it was right or wrong, we are reasoning along forensic lines. In such instances we reason from available evidence to a plausible hypothesis, and we engage our beliefs about justice. If I argue that a new banking law was passed because of lobbying pressure, and that the law is unfair to the poor, I am reasoning forensically. I might support my claims with evidence about the amount of money the banking industry spent on lobbying, and additional evidence that shows that the new law makes it more difficult for poor people to borrow money. In the process of making my argument, I also try to forge connections with widely held values about equality of opportunity. Questions of what is right or just come up frequently outside of the formal courtroom setting, but the reasoning employed to argue these questions is similar. Evidence is sifted to support an evaluation of a past action, a standard of justice is applied, and the action is judged to be either just or unjust.

THE ARTISTIC PROOFS

If rhetoric is an art, as Aristotle has argued, then what does the art of rhetoric teach, and what does a student of rhetoric study?[28] This would have been Plato's question to Aristotle, as it was Socrates' question to Gorgias. In Book I, Chapter 2, Aristotle gives his initial answer to that question, identifying three technical or artistic proofs (*entechnoi pisteis*) that make up the *techne* of rhetoric. He also identifies several inartistic proofs (*atechnoi pisteis*), things such as documents or "testimony obtained under torture." Such elements may be useful in arguing, but are not part of the proper study of rhetoric.

The three artistic proofs—proofs taught by the art of rhetoric—are (1) *logos* or arguments and logical reasoning, (2) *pathos* or the names and causes of various emotions, and (3) *ethos* or human character and goodness. We can take a closer look at each of these proofs characteristic of rhetoric as Aristotle conceived the art.

Logos: The Logic of Sound Arguments

The first of the artistic proofs, *logos*, Aristotle begins to discuss in Book I, Chapter 2. *Logos* (pl. *logoi*), an important Greek term we have already encountered, had many nuances of meaning. It meant simply a word, or it could refer in a plural sense to the words of a document or speech. It also carried the sense of a thought expressed in words, a discourse, an argument, or an entire case. *Logos* could also suggest intellect or rationality generally; a capacity for *logos* was the distinctly human characteristic that separated us from other animals. Thus, John Randall writes that to act in accordance with *logos* was "to act intelligently."[29]

Greeks of the fourth century BCE did not make a sharp distinction between thinking and speaking; one activity was intimately associated with the other.[30] Words typically implied oral expression. Silent reading, for example, was unknown. Written words were also spoken words, and *logos* implied both thought and speech.[31]

In *Rhetoric*, Aristotle uses *logos* to refer to proofs available in the words, arguments, or logic of a speech. *Logos* was the study of inference making or reasoning, a study closely related to formal logic. However, in *Rhetoric* he was more concerned with the ways people actually reason about public issues than with the logic of the dialectician. *Logos* was the study of the arguments employed in practical decision-making, and in particular of the enthymeme.

Pathos: The Psychology of Emotion

Though he was critical of speakers who manipulated the emotions of their audiences, Aristotle nevertheless thought a study of emotion essential to a systematic treatment of rhetoric. *Pathos* for Aristotle was "putting the audience in the right frame of mind" (1358a) to make a good decision. He discusses this type of proof in detail in Book II, Chapters 1 through 11.

The term *pathos* is often used to refer to emotional appeals that give persuasive messages of their power to move an audience to action. However, Aristotle's interest in emotion has to do specifically with emotion's ability to affect the judgment of audiences. Jonathan Barnes writes that "the orator wants to persuade, or in other words to affect judgment—and stimulation of the emotions is therefore relevant to him only insofar as the emotions do affect judgment."[32] Having "suggest[ed] a connection between emotion and judgment," writes Larry Arnhart, this connection "becomes the underlying theme of [Aristotle's] subsequent discussion of the passions," that is, of emotions.[33]

A knowledgeable speaker can engage the strong beliefs and feelings that both influence the reasoning of audience members and move them to action. Aristotle suggests that the orator has a moral concern for *correct* judgment, not simply a pragmatic or sophistic concern for winning a debate. The difference between a good orator and a Sophist lay in the differing motives of each. The good orator serves the city-state by assisting good decision-making; the Sophist wins cases and collects a fee. The study of *pathos*, then, is the study of the psychology of emotion, governed by a moral concern for discovering and acting on the truth.

Aristotle examines the emotions we all experience, such as anger, fear, shame, and pity. In his typically systematic way, he defines the different emotions and their opposites. Thus, for example, indignation is said to be nearly the opposite of pity. Aristotle discusses the reasons we experience each emotion, and his treatment of the various emotions is extensive and detailed. For instance, anger is "an impulse, accompanied by pain, to a conspicuous revenge for a conspicuous slight directed without justification towards what concerns oneself or towards what concern's one's friends" (1378a). He proceeds to note that "there are three different kinds of slighting—contempt, spite, and insolence." Each of these three causes of feeling slighted is then discussed.

"Fear," writes Aristotle, "may be defined as a pain or disturbance due to a mental picture of some destructive or painful evil in the future" (1382). Fear appeals, he notes, often derive from three fears common to most of us. First, there is the fear of death or physical harm, either to us or loved ones. Second, we fear loss of health, wealth, or security as in the loss of occupation. Third, we know the fear of deprivation of rights or freedoms. Pity appeals usually involve suggesting or stating that someone or something helpless is being harmed, and these appeals are intensified if the harm is being done carelessly or intentionally by another. Thus, children and defenseless animals are often the sources of pity appeals.

Emotions, then, are not irrational impediments to decision-making. Rather, they are rational responses to certain kinds of circumstances and arguments. W. W. Fortenbaugh, an expert on Aristotle's theory of emotion, writes, "Aristotle's analysis of emotion made clear the relationship of emotion to reasoned argument."[34] The great philosopher "showed that emotional response is intelligent behavior open to reasoned persuasion."[35] Emotional appeals need not be irrational and irrelevant elements of persuasive discourse, and should certainly not be used to manipulate an audience. *Pathos* is properly part of a carefully reasoned case; for every instance in which a decision must be reached there are legitimate emotions that one ought to experience. Aristotle's view may be a response to that of "rhetoricians like Thrasymachus and Gorgias [who] spoke of emotional appeals as charms and enchantments."[36] Fortenbaugh adds that "it was Aristotle's contribution to offer a very different view of emotion, so that emotional appeal would no longer be viewed as an extra-rational enchantment."[37]

Aristotle's treatment of *pathos* is far from a "how to" of arousing different emotions. It is, rather, a detailed psychology of emotion intended to help the student of rhetoric to *understand* human emotional response toward the goal of adjusting an audience's emotional state to fit the nature and seriousness of the particular issue being argued.

Ethos: The Sociology of Good Character

Aristotle discusses the artistic proof he terms *ethos* in Book II, Chapters 12 through 17, where he acknowledges the persuasive potential of the speaker's character or personal credibility. It is Aristotle's opinion that this proof should develop from what the speaker says in the course of a speech, and not be imported on the basis of prior reputation with the audience (1356). He apparently has in mind that an audience makes a judgment about character based on a speech's content and rational structure—reflections of the speaker's trustworthiness—not on delivery or other performative qualities.

Aristotle breaks down good character into its three constituent parts. In order to establish *ethos*, the speaker must "exhibit *phronesis* (intelligence, good sense), *arete* (virtue), and *eunoia* (goodwill)."[38] As with *pathos*, Aristotle seeks to rehabilitate the study of character from what he took to be the abuses of earlier teachers of rhetoric. He may have particularly in view the courtroom pleaders, descendants of the Sophists, whose exaggerated use of both *pathos* and *ethos* had given rhetoric a bad name.

An effective rhetor must understand what the community believes makes a person believable. As Aristotle's study of *pathos* is a psychology of emotion, his treatment of *ethos* is a sociology of character. It is not a sophistic guide to establishing one's credibility with an audience, but a careful study of what Athenians consider to be the qualities of a trustworthy individual. Aristotle discusses the character traits typical of young, middle-aged, and elderly people (1388–1390). He also examines the character qualities associated with wealth, power, and "good birth" (1390–1391).

Aristotle held that of the three artistic proofs—*logos*, *pathos*, and *ethos*—this last one, *ethos*, was potentially the most persuasive. When people are convinced that a speaker is knowledgeable, trustworthy, and has their best interests at heart, they will be very likely to accept as true what that speaker has to say.

In sum, Aristotle saw the art of rhetoric as combining a logical study (*logos*), a psychological study (*pathos*), and a sociological study (*ethos*). *Logos*, *pathos*, and *ethos* provide the rhetor with sources of proof, that is, of persuasive possibilities. A skilled rhetor has "the faculty of discovering" such proofs or "means of persuasion." Moreover, this faculty is adaptable to "any given situation." Once these proofs have been discovered, they can be employed in a carefully achieved persuasive balance. The goal of all reputable rhetorical activity should be the improvement of life in the *polis*.

TOPOI: LINES OF ARGUMENT

Each of the artistic proofs—*logos*, *pathos*, and *ethos*—might be employed in any of the three rhetorical settings described by Aristotle: the deliberative, the epideictic, and the forensic. But it is also true that certain kinds of proof and lines of argument were used more often in one setting than in the others. The Greek term *topos*, often translated topic (pl. *topoi*), literally means "place" and came to refer to a type of argument.[39] Aristotle describes two distinct kinds of *topoi* in *Rhetoric*.

Special Topics

Focusing attention on the arguments employed in the three oratorical settings, Aristotle wrote about what he called the *eidei topoi* or special topics. These were lines of argument especially important to one of his three rhetorical settings or question.

Deliberative oratory was of particular interest to Aristotle, and he spends a good deal of time in Book I, Chapters 4 through 8, discussing the arguments and knowledge that a deliberative orator must command, including "finances, war and peace, national defense, imports and exports, and the framing of laws" (1359b).[40] Aristotle also examines the constituents of human happiness (*eudaimonia*), and of what people consider to be the good life. Any argument or bit of information that could prove a course of action useful or useless, expedient or inexpedient, wise or foolish, or contributing to happiness was an argument of special use to the deliberative orator.

The epideictic orator's special topics, on the other hand, had to do with human virtue and vice, and with being able to prove someone to be praiseworthy or blameworthy. Thus, arguments and information that assisted an orator in demonstrating that an individual possessed a virtue or, conversely, that they were vicious, might be among the special arguments of the epideictic orator.

Similarly, the judicial orator must understand the causes of wrongdoing, the desires that drive people to do wrong, and the qualities of character that lead one to commit crimes. Moreover, the deliberative orator needed a thorough grasp of arguments regarding what was best for the citizen and the *polis*.

Common Topics

Arguments and strategies useful in any of the three rhetorical settings Aristotle called *koinoi topoi* or common topics. These are sometimes also referred to as universal lines of argument. In Book II, Chapter 23, Aristotle listed twenty-eight such common topics. This list includes a wide range of arguments and strategies that might be employed in all sorts of debate and speaking contexts. There does not seem to be any particular order or system to these topics, and the assorted suggestions are sometimes surprising.

A consideration of opposites appears in Aristotle's brief catalogue of universal lines of argument. Thus, someone argues that because peace has brought economic woes, war is needed to bring prosperity. Or, one might reason from correlative ideas, so that if someone *gave* you a gift, you must have *received* the gift. Also included in the twenty-eight lines are strategies such as turning the tables—using the same charge against your opponent that he has used against you. A few linguistic devices are also included such as considering the nuances of a crucial word in order to derive the desired conclusion. For example, a pleader might reason: "You have said that you benefited from the action of which you accuse my client. If you *benefited* from his action, it must have been a *beneficial* action, and beneficial actions cannot be prosecuted." Wordplay? Perhaps, but also a means of habituating an advocate to thinking about words themselves as a source of rhetorical strategies.

The common topics also include lines of argument such as reasoning deductively from general to particular, or enumeratively by division of possibilities. Such division arguments proceed like this: "There are only three causes of such a disaster, A, B, and C. A and B are not even suspected in this case, so the cause must have been C."

The twenty-eight *koinoi topoi* are not an exhaustive but rather a suggestive list of the kinds of arguments, strategies, and language considerations that might be used in any of Aristotle's three rhetorical settings. The combination of the special and universal lines of argument constituted much of what went into the study of *logos*. There has been considerable discussion of what Aristotle intended by his lists of topics, both universal and special. It is often assumed that they were to be guides to inventing or discovering arguments.[41]

Other understandings of the topics are also worth considering, however. William Grimaldi, for example, has argued that Aristotle may have intended the topics as suggesting a method of thinking productively about a range of problems that face individuals and societies.[42] Thomas Conley has suggested that the topics were means of "justifying" claims already arrived at.[43] Yet, a third scholar, Donovan Ochs, has argued that the topics of Aristotle are not intended as a system of inventing arguments at all, but rather should be understood as the primary elements of enthymemes.[44]

Some Common Fallacies

In addition to understanding good arguments, a rhetor must be aware of the various forms of fallacious reasoning. Toward the end of Book II, Aristotle catalogued nine types of enthymemes that seem serious or reasonable, but on closer examination are not. These are, to his thinking, fallacies. Aristotle discusses such tactics as misleading wordplay, the fallacy of reasoning from part to whole, and even the use of indignant language such as, "Why, it's just plain rude to make such claims!"

Aristotle also notes that an opponent might make what appears to be a sound argument by reasoning from a single atypical instance to a generalization. Thus, I might argue that because the famed scientist Carl Sagan was a highly paid academic, all academics are well paid. He also notes causal fallacies such as the *post hoc* fallacy. This fallacy suggests that because one event followed another, the former caused the latter. Thus, someone might reason: "The recession hit after the invasion of Iraq, so military actions cause economic troubles." One can also reason deceptively by omitting relevant facts. Thus, one might argue that, because a politician failed to sign the health care reform bill, she opposes health care reform. What is not mentioned is that the politician in question was preparing to introduce her own health care reform bill.

ARISTOTLE ON STYLE

Book III of Aristotle's *Rhetoric* discusses the issues of the delivery, style, and arrangement of speeches. Aristotle says that he considers the matter of delivery to be "unworthy" of systematic discussion but, because it is part of rhetoric it must be discussed. He admits that delivery can be important to how an audience receives a speech, for "the way in which a thing is said does affect its intelligibility" (1404a). Nevertheless, really effective delivery is hard to teach because "dramatic ability is a natural gift." If interested, one can seek out a teacher of diction to help with delivery, but it is hardly the proper study of a *techne*.

The style of a speech, its linguistic manner, should be appropriate to the occasion; above all, a speaker must be clear. "Clearness is secured," writes Aristotle, "by using words (nouns and verbs alike) that are current and ordinary" (1404b). Thus, a speaker must have a good ear for everyday spoken language. The effective orator should not use so many artistic devices in speaking that the speech takes on an artificial feeling, for "naturalness is persuasive." Aristotle's advice on style is reaction against the highly stylized speaking of the Sophists, and perhaps even the polished written style of Isocrates.

Metaphors and Other Devices

Aristotle advises his readers on the use of metaphors, writing that "metaphor . . . gives style clearness, charm, and distinction as nothing else can." Good metaphorical comparisons "must be fitting, which means that they must fairly correspond to the thing signified . . ." The "inappropriateness" of a bad metaphor "will be conspicuous" because the "want of harmony between two things is emphasized by their being placed side by side." Thus, great care must be devoted to the construction of apt comparisons.

Aristotle offers practical advice on employing metaphors as implicit arguments. For instance, if you wish to compliment an action or person, "you must take your metaphor from something better in the same line; if to disparage, from something worse" (1405a). Thus, if I wished to elevate or compliment a homeless person's request for money in a prose piece, I might compare it to an act of prayer. If I wished to disparage the act, I might compare it to theft.

Though he offers advice on composing metaphors, real skill with this device is beyond the scope of an art; metaphor "is not a thing [that] can be taught . . ." (1405a). Aristotle goes on to discuss a wide range of stylistic devices such as simile, rhythm, and antithesis. Those of his students who wish to study the qualities that bring beauty to language in greater detail Aristotle refers to his book *Poetics*.

As was discussed in Chapter 2, some of the Sophists, most notably Gorgias, maintained a strong interest in the aesthetic aspects of rhetoric, particularly the sounds of spoken language. But, Gorgias seems to have been interested in auditory aesthetics only for its ability to captivate an audience. Aristotle, on the other hand, is developing an art that will improve political discourse in the *polis*, and good style can hold an audience's attention and render a speech more memorable.

CONCLUSION

Aristotle set out to present a systematic treatment of the art of rhetoric, and, by most accounts he succeeded. His discussion of rhetoric remains one of the most complete and insightful ever penned, and certainly the most influential. Nevertheless, some scholars have noted that Aristotle's rhetorical theory has been of greater interest to historians of rhetoric than to practicing orators, and more influential in subsequent historical periods than it was in his own day.

Rhetoric was, for Aristotle, "the faculty of discovering the available means of persuasion in any setting." Like the art of dialectic it was not limited to one class of subjects, reasoned to probable conclusions, and could be deployed to develop arguments on either side of an issue. Like the art of poetry, rhetoric was concerned for the beauty of language. But rhetoric was unique in its capacity to adapt messages to large audiences made up of people who lacked special training in reasoning. Moreover, rhetoric addressed questions of public significance that engaged the community's most important values, such as those regarding happiness, virtue, and justice.

Aristotle held that a successful rhetorician must understand arguments. It was also necessary, however, to possess a thorough understanding of emotion and of good character. The rhetorician must also apprehend a range of substantive issues associated with the particular kind of oratory being practiced. And, it helped if an orator possessed some natural dramatic ability, and had a good grasp of the aesthetic dimension of language. Thus, to be a truly accomplished speaker was a demanding occupation indeed.

The major themes of Greek rhetoric continued to play an important role in the thinking of rhetorical theorists for several centuries. In fact, Greek rhetorical theory—particularly Aristotle's treatment of the subject—still provides the foundation for much instruction in both speaking and writing. In the next chapter we will see how the tradition of Greek rhetoric was translated into the cultural context of another great civilization.

QUESTIONS FOR REVIEW

1. How is Aristotle's view of rhetoric different from Plato's?
2. Aristotle called rhetoric the counterpart (*antistrophos*) of dialectic. In what ways are the two arts similar, and how are they different?
3. What does Aristotle mean by "artistic proofs" (*entechnoi pisteis*)?
4. What are the three types of artistic proofs Aristotle identifies, and with what is each concerned?
5. What is an enthymeme?
6. What role does Jeffrey Walker find that epideictic discourse played in ancient Greece?

QUESTIONS FOR DISCUSSION

1. Describe the courses someone might take in a modern university in order to learn the components of the art of rhetoric as Aristotle presents that art in the *Rhetoric*.
2. Many Greeks of Aristotle's day believed that good character was a more reliable form of proof than was physical evidence. The reasoning behind this preference, apparently, was that it is much easier to fake physical evidence than it is good character. What do you think of this view of the relative reliability of physical evidence, which Aristotle treats as an inartistic proof about which he has little to say, and good character, which he makes perhaps the most important and persuasive of the three artistic proofs?
3. What is your response to Aristotle's argument that studying rhetoric is useful for (a) defending the truth, (b) adapting complicated ideas to a large and untrained audience, (c) thinking through both sides of a case, and (d) self-defense? Are these still good reasons for studying the subject, or have things changed too much since Aristotle's day for these reasons still to hold? Is there any use of rhetoric that should be added to Aristotle's list?

TERMS

Apologia Defense; one type of pleading common to forensic oratory, the other being accusation.

Areté Virtue; a component of *ethos*.

Artistic proofs (*entechnoi pisteis*) Proofs taught specifically by the art of rhetoric—*logos*, *pathos*, and *ethos*.

Auxesis Amplification.

Common topics (*koinoi topoi*) Arguments and strategies useful in any rhetorical setting.

Contingent matters Matters where decisions must be based on probabilities, because absolute certainty is not possible.

Deliberative oratory (*symbouleutikon*) Speaking in legislative assemblies.

Dialectic A method of reasoning from common opinions, directed by established principles of reasoning to probable conclusions. A logical method of debating issues of general interest, starting from widely accepted propositions.

Dikanikon Courtroom or forensic oratory.

Dunamis Faculty, power, ability, or capacity.

Eidei topoi The special topics of Aristotle, appropriate to special rhetorical settings such as the courtroom.

Enthymeme (*enthymema*) A rhetorical syllogism or a rhetorical argument based on a premise shared by speaker and audience.

Epainos Praise; one of two functions of epideictic oratory, the other being blame.

Epideictic oratory (**epideixis**) Speaking characteristic of public ceremonies.

Ergon Function, specifically the function of an art of *techne*.

Ethos The study of human character; one of the three artistic proofs; The persuasive potential of the speaker's character and personal credibility.

Eudaimonia Human well-being or happiness; goal of deliberative oratory.

Eunoia Goodwill; a component of *ethos*.

Forensic oratory (*dikanikon*) Courtroom speaking.

Inartistic proofs (*Atechnoi pisteis*) Proofs not belonging to the art of rhetoric.

Kalon Honorable.

Kategoria Accusation; one of the two functions of forensic oratory, the other being defense.

Koinoi Topoi Common topics; arguments useful in various settings.

Krites A judge, an audience member.

Logos The study of arguments; one of the three artistic proofs.

Paradeigma Argument from an example or examples to a probable generalization; the inductive argument that complements the deductive enthymeme.

Pathos The study of the psychology of emotion; one of the three artistic proofs.

Phronesis Intelligence, good sense; a component of *ethos*.

Psogos Blame; one of two functions of epideictic oratory, the other being praise.

Syllogism A deductive argument moving from a general premise, through a specific application of that premise, to a specific and necessary conclusion.

Symboulos An advisor; someone offering wise counsel on practical matters.

Sympheron Advantageous course of action and actions.

Theoron A spectator or observer. An audience member for an epideictic speech.

Thymos The passions or inner self.

Topos Line of argument.

NOTES

1 George Kennedy, trans. *Aristotle on Rhetoric: A Theory of Civic Discourse* (New York: Oxford University Press, 1991), introduction, p. 3. To view the complete text of Aristotle's *Rhetoric* visit www.perseus.tufts.edu.

2 Jonathan Barnes, (ed.), The *Cambridge Companion to Aristotle* (Cambridge, UK: Cambridge University Press, 1995), 4. On Aristotle's life and his relationship with Plato, see: Geoffrey Ernest Richard Lloyd, *Aristotle: The Growth and Structure of His Thought* (Cambridge, UK: Cambridge University Press, 1968), Chaps. 1–3.

3 Barnes, 4.

4 Forbes I. Hill, "The Rhetoric of Aristotle," in *A Synoptic History of Classical Rhetoric*, (ed.) James J. Murphy (Davis, CA: Hermagoras Press, 1983), 19.

5 Barnes, 8.

6 Kennedy's translation, cited above, is helpful. Other widely used translations of the *Rhetoric* include those by Lane Cooper (New York: Appleton-Century-Crofts, 1932); and W. Rhys Roberts (New York: Modern Library, 1954).

7 Kennedy, 5.

8 Hill, 24.

9 Unless otherwise indicated, all quotations from *Rhetoric* are from: Aristotle, *Rhetoric*, trans. W. Rhys Roberts (New York: Modern Library, 1954).

10 Kathleen Welch quotes Ellen Quandahl to the effect that "The *Rhetoric* is Difficult to Read, Full of Discrepancies, Gaps, Repetitions," in *The Contemporary Reception of Classical Rhetoric: Appropriations of Ancient Discourse* (Hillsdale, NJ: Lawrence Erlbaum, 1990), 22; Quandahl, "Aristotle's Rhetoric: Reinterpreting Invention," *Rhetoric Review* 4 (January 1986): 128.

11 Kennedy, appendix I, 289–290.

12 See: Larry Arnhart, *Aristotle on Political Reasoning* (DeKalb: Northern Illinois University Press, 1981), 18–19.

13 Arnhart, 19.

14 Arnhart, 39.

15 Kennedy, 34, note 24.

16 See: Gerard A. Hauser, "The Example in Aristotle's *Rhetoric*: Bifurcation or Contradiction?" Philosophy and Rhetoric 1 (1968): 78–90.

17 On Aristotle's theory of the enthymeme, see: Lloyd Bitzer, "Aristotle's Enthymeme Revisited," *Quarterly Journal of Speech* 45 (1959): 399–408.

18 See: Jeffrey Walker, *Rhetoric and Poetics in Antiquity* (Oxford: Oxford University Press, 2000), 175.

19 Bitzer, 408.

20 For a detailed discussion of Aristotle's divisions of speeches, see: Ekaterina V. Haskins, *Logos and Power in Isocrates and Aristotle* (Columbia: University of South Carolina Press, 2004), 58 ff.

21 The Kennedy translation of Aristotle's *Rhetoric* has been very helpful in preparing this section.

22 Jane Sutton, "The Marginalization of Sophistical Rhetoric and the Loss of History," in *Rethinking the History of Rhetoric*, ed. Takis Poulakos (Boulder, CO: Westview 1993), 75–90.

23 Sutton, 84.

24 Quoted in Sutton, 84.

25 On Aristotle's thinking about happiness, see: Anthony Kenny, *Aristotle on the Perfect Life* (Oxford: Clarendon Press, 1992).

26 Walker, 9.

27 Kennedy trans., Bk. 1, Chap. 3, sect. 3 (Emphasis added).

28 For a detailed answer to the question of rhetoric's subject matter, see Fr. William Grimaldi's "The Role of the *PISTEIS* in Aristotle's Methodology," appendix to *Aristotle, Rhetoric I: A Commentary* (New York: Fordham University Press, 1980), 349–356.

29 John H. Randall, Jr., *Aristotle* (New York: Columbia University Press, 1960), 253.

30 On the difference between ancient and modern understandings of the relationship of thought and expression, see: Welch, 15 ff.

31 See, for example: George Maximilian Antony Grube, translator's introduction to Longinus, *On the Sublime* (Indianapolis, IN: Library of Liberal Arts, 1957), x.

32 Barnes, 267.

33 Arnhart, 37. See also: David Charles, *Aristotle's Philosophy of Action* (Ithaca, NY: Cornell University Press, 1984), 176–188.

34 William W. Fortenbaugh, *Aristotle on Emotion* (New York: Barnes and Noble, 1975), 17.

35 Fortenbaugh, 17.

36 Fortenbaugh, 17.

37 Fortenbaugh, 18.

38 James M. May, *Trials of Character: The Eloquence of Ciceronian Ethos* (Chapel Hill: University of North Carolina Press, 1988), 2.

39 On *topoi* and Roman *loci*. see: Michael Leff, "The Topics of Argumentative Invention in Latin Rhetorical Theory from Cicero to Boethius," *Rhetorica* 1 (Spring 1983): 23–44.

40 Kennedy translation.

41 See, for instance, Leff.

42 On this view, see: Fr. William M. A. Grimaldi, "The Aristotelian Topics," *Traditio* 14 (1958): 1–16.

43 Thomas M. Conley, " 'Logical Hylomorphism' and Aristotle's *Koinoi Topoi*," *Central States Speech Journal* 29 (Summer 1978): 92–97.

44 Donovan J. Ochs, "Aristotle's Concept of Formal Topics," *Speech Monographs* 36 (1969): 419–425.

Chapter 5

Rhetoric at Rome

[R]hetoric formed the pedagogical and political bedrock of a common imperial culture stretching from Spain to Syria and from southern Britain to north Africa.[1]
—Joy Connolly

"RHETORIC," writes classicist Manfred Fuhrmann, "like all subjects of instruction in the ancient world, was created by the Greeks; the Romans dutifully adopted both its forms and its subject-matter, which had acquired their ultimate outlines in the Hellenistic period."[2] At the same time, as another expert points out,

> the Romans . . . had a complex and tortured relationship with Hellenic culture. The intelligentsia was simultaneously entranced by it and wary of it, had a passion for Greek language, literature, art and learning, but also a passion to appropriate and control it.[3]

Despite this tension between Greek and Roman culture, Greek-based rhetorical studies resided solidly at the center of a liberal education in Rome for several reasons. First, rhetoric was a means of achieving personal success in politics. Second, rhetoric provided a method for conducting political debates, undertaking trials, and addressing the citizenry on important topics. Third, the study of rhetoric developed the verbal skills that signaled refinement, wisdom, and accomplishment. Finally, rhetoric allowed the ruling class and the masses in Rome to negotiate a governmental arrangement founded on a collaboration of unequals. In order to play a significant role in Roman society, it was virtually a requirement that one be skilled in rhetoric. Thus, rhetorical education was vitally important to the Romans.

Rhetoricians such as Cicero (106–43 BCE), the greatest orator and rhetorical theorist of Rome; and Quintilian (35–100 CE), Rome's most famous and successful teacher of rhetoric, wrote extensive treatises on and developed elaborate methods of teaching rhetoric. So successful were these writers that Europeans employed their methods of teaching rhetoric right up until the time of the American Revolution. Never in human history has a subject and an approach to teaching that subject achieved such educational dominance as did rhetoric and the Roman methods of teaching the art. This chapter explores the aspects of Roman society that made rhetoric so important, the Roman practice of rhetoric, and Roman methods to teaching rhetoric. We will devote considerable time to examining the rhetorical thought of the most influential Roman orator and rhetorical theorist, Cicero.

ROMAN SOCIETY AND THE PLACE OF RHETORIC

When we speak of Rome or the Roman world, we are really talking about a society that existed in various political forms over a very long period of time, at least the 700 years from approximately 300 BCE to about 400 CE. During this time much of the Mediterranean world was dominated by one culture with its capital at the city of Rome in Italy. We must also talk about Rome under two quite different systems of government, one a limited democracy called the Roman Republic and the other a monarchy, or tyranny, called the Roman Empire.

Rhetoric and Political Power

At the time of its founding as a sovereign political entity, Rome was a republic governed by elected executives, a senate, and popular assemblies. This is not to suggest, however, that Rome was a popular democracy in the modern Western or even in the ancient Athenian sense. In order to vote or wield power, one had to own land or be a member of some important group such as the military or a powerful family.

As the Roman Republic grew, incorporating diverse people often living at great distances from Rome, shared methods of communication studied under the discipline of rhetoric became crucial to governing and maintaining unity. Rhetoric also played a fundamental role in shaping daily political and social life. With its disciplining of speech, cultivating of reason, and capacity to bring about cooperative action, rhetoric was an important source of support for Roman civilization, and perhaps the source of all civilizations. Cicero writes in *De Inventione*, "There was a time when men wandered around in the fields in the manner of beasts, and sustained life on wild food; they did nothing by the reason of the mind, but by bodily strength" (1.2). Joy Connolly comments that rhetoric and civilization arrive together for Cicero when

> [A] *magnus vir*, a great man, becomes aware of man's potential and he compels and gathers the men scattered in the fields in one place (*unum in locum*) by means of reason and speech. Eloquence is thus the original transporter of men; it collected them in the first political society. Without its power, politics is literally unimaginable . . .[4]

Rulers and Ruled

Rome was a patriarchy, and power in the Roman Republic usually belonged to men fortunate enough to belong to a *gens* or clan. These highly influential family groups—never more than twenty or so in number—were so powerful that it was difficult for an outsider to achieve political prominence. This is not to say that it was impossible, for Cicero, one of the most important politicians in Rome, was not from a politically influential family. He was considered a "new man" in Roman politics, a political outsider with sufficient intellect and rhetorical talent to become influential without family connections.

Roman thinking about political power was bound up with assumptions about character, and character was believed to be related to the system of *gens*. "Character was an extraordinarily important element in the social and political milieu of Republican Rome," writes one authority, "and exerted a considerable amount of influence on native Roman oratory." Character was considered to be a more or less fixed quality that "demands or determines" a person's actions.[5] In fact, so fixed was character that it was believed to run in families, and a well-known ancestor might be invoked in a public speech to provide the speaker needed courage or wisdom. Thus, oratory and personal character were inseparable concepts to the Romans.

Romans placed less value in the opinion of the individual citizen than in the collective response of the citizenry, the *res publica*. Perhaps for this reason there was no equivalent of Athenian *isegoria* in Rome, no guaranteed right of the citizen to address a legislative body. Joy Connolly writes that

> Athens compensated for inequalities of wealth and birth by establishing legal and political equality among free men. Regardless of status, all citizens voted, served on juries, and could (if they wished) speak in the assembly.

In Rome, inequality was the bedrock of the political system."[6] Roman juries, for instance, typically were made up of only wealthy citizens. In Rome, most public speeches were delivered by elected officials, signifying that a great gap existed between the rulers and the ruled. Nevertheless, politicians were expected to address gatherings of citizens— *contio*—in the Forum, and the response of such groups was important to shaping policies. Speakers actively sought audience approval, and sought to align themselves with audience interests. The belief that one's ancestors passed along their noble character extended in some degree to the Roman citizenry generally, a matter of which speakers liked to remind their audiences.

Roman laws also provided something of an equalizing force between rulers and ruled. The Romans held a high view of their law, and it stood above even the powerful individual. As the Roman historian Livy wrote, "The power of the laws (is) greater than that of men."[7] Law and religion were the forces that bound Roman to Roman.

Rhetoric and Roman Government

The most important governing body in the Republic was the Senate, which had power over both domestic and foreign policy. The Senate was made up of men who were supposed to possess political wisdom; the Latin word *senatus* means a council of elders.

The Senate—an advice-giving rather than a legislative body—consisted of about 300 noblemen, but after 81 BCE it sometimes had as many as 600 members. These wealthy and powerful advisors occupied their positions for life as long as they met certain financial qualifications. Most senators had held other political offices either in Rome or in one of its colonies.

The Republic operated on the basis of a complex system of checks and balances among representative assemblies of common people, assemblies of ruling elites, and powerful individuals. In this elaborate structure, it was possible for one group, or even an individual, virtually to stop the progress of government by objecting to a policy. Persuasive speaking in the Senate and other bodies was crucial to forging the agreements and alliances essential to Roman government and expansion during this period. "The practice of oratory," writes Harold Gotoff, was "the stock in trade of the professional politician" during the period of the Roman Republic. Thus, proficiency in speaking was vital to political success.

A senator like Cicero "put his competence and authority on the line every time he performed" by making a speech.[8] Rhetoric reigned not only in the Senate but also in the courtroom and in the public forum, where many important issues were discussed.

> The orator could not afford to pander in facts or trifle in words; he had to be a man of true wisdom and eloquence. For on his speech hung the fate of an accused, the reputation of an opponent, indeed the tenor of a society, the strength of its resolve, the focus of its worship, the direction of its future.[9]

The Republic's Decline

Through military might and participative government, the Romans were able to consolidate their rule of the Italian peninsula, and, by about 200 BCE, to extend their influence to other areas of the Mediterranean world. Through a long series of wars occurring between about 240 and 140 BCE, Roman armies conquered much of what was then the known world. Rhetoric and the cooperative policymaking it allowed was as important as military might to the success of the Republic.

But success did not come without crises. By 130 BCE Rome was a rich and powerful empire, but one made up of many competing forces. Tensions between the landed rich and working poor became acute, and the government grew more and more to depend on a powerful army to maintain control of an increasingly unhappy populace. As the Senate became more ruthless in wielding power, certain generals decided to take control of the situation in Rome themselves.

This development, which began around 100 BCE, led eventually to the creation of the Roman Empire, with Rome transformed into a virtual monarchy. Combining their forces, the two powerful generals, Pompey and Crassus, took total control of Rome in 70 BCE. Under the rule of the Consuls, the Senate continued to function as a policymaking body. It was during this period that the most important Roman orator, Cicero, was prominent in the Senate. Rhetorical prowess was still a crucial element in achieving and holding power, as well as in the conduct of government in Rome.[10] No one better illustrates this fact than does Cicero, whose views on rhetoric we will consider.[11]

Rhetoric and Roman Education

To be educated in the Roman Republic was to be immersed in Greek language and culture. Rhetoric occupied the very center of such instruction. Indeed, as classicist G. M. A. Grube points out, rhetoric "remained, through Greco-Roman times, the essential content of higher education."[12] Another scholar, Calvin Troup, expresses a similar judgment in writing that "rhetoric was *the* system of education in the Roman Empire."[13]

Rome's rhetorically centered educational system differed from modern educational approaches in important ways. As our own educational methods depend heavily on written texts, it would be easy to assume that ancient Greek or Roman education was transmitted in a similar fashion; such was not the case. Education developed principally in the medium of oral expression. The spoken word was crucial to education just as it was to politics. Thus, eloquence, or skill with the spoken word, was the key to social influence and political success. The primarily oral culture of the day also meant that training the memory was much more important than it is in a culture based on written texts. Where written texts are relatively rare, memory becomes essential.

Greece was ever-present in a Roman school; all subjects were taught in the Greek language, and rhetorical instruction followed Greek rhetorical theories. Roman treatises on rhetoric were based on earlier Greek *technai*, or textbooks.

Educating a male Roman youth from a privileged family involved "years of instruction in rhetoric" that "proceeded according to a strictly methodical system." Both rhetoricians and philosophers provided education in rhetoric.[14] Indeed, skilled rhetoric teachers were among a rising class of experts in Rome that included professional teachers in new fields of study such as history, law, mathematics, and astrology. On a few occasions teaching rhetoric was banned, likely because politicians feared the rhetoricians' growing influence.

Rhetorical education emphasized speaking skill and ingenuity in debate. Memorizing and delivering great speeches from the past was also stressed. One type of memorized speech, the *controversia*, was a mock judicial speech presented by the advanced student of rhetoric. This kind of practice allowed the aspiring orator to demonstrate his potential as a courtroom pleader. The *suasoria* was a more elementary exercise, a practice speech for the younger student of rhetoric. A typical *suasoria* exercise involved offering advice to an important public figure.

Roman rhetorical training also emphasized style and diction, making the aesthetics of language central to effective speech. The Roman writer Longinus, whom we will consider later in the chapter, explored sounds and rhythms in his treatise on rhetoric, leading one scholar to note his interest in "the music of language."[15] More was in view in rhetorical training, however, than simply producing effective speakers. Romans were always aware of political realities and the practical demands of maintaining an empire. Thus, Joy Connolly has written that "[t]he demanding blend of bodily and mental skills involved in rhetorical training" was itself "designed to reflect the values of the Roman governing class and reinforce its traditional dominance."[16]

Was there, then, a strategic goal to even the training a young orator endured, a rhetoric of Roman rhetorical education? Apparently so, and for good reason: The practice of a common rhetoric, rooted in Roman values, was as crucial to the Roman Empire's expansion and maintenance as was the Latin language and the famed Roman roads.

The Rhetorical Theory of Cicero

Marcus Tullius Cicero was born on the third of January, 106, and died in December of 43 BCE. More is known about Cicero than about any other figure in Roman history, one scholar noting, "no one else in antiquity is as well known . . . with Julius Caesar and the emperor Julian far behind."[17] Throughout his long political career he demonstrated "an unfailing willingness to talk about himself, both publicly and in confidential letters."[18] Fifty-eight of Cicero's one hundred and six major public addresses survive. Moreover, copies exist of more than eight hundred letters by Cicero to others, and of one hundred letters of others to him. Also surviving are at least six books on rhetoric, and parts of seven on philosophy.

Cicero was the greatest speaker and one of the most prolific writers of his day, a philosopher and politician with an unparalleled master of argument with an astonishing understanding of his Roman audiences.[19] "Every rhetorical stance, every anecdote, every argument, every inflection of a speech, and the manner in which each of these is presented," writes one expert on Cicero, "is calculated to control and direct the attitude of a defined audience in a particular situation."[20] A virtuoso performer in the public oratorical arena, brilliant eloquence marked Cicero's career as a politician and lawyer. Cicero "embodied an age in which to be educated meant to command the skills of eloquence."[21]

De Inventione

As noted earlier, Romans adhered closely to Greek methods of rhetorical education, a fact reflected in such well-known Roman treatises as Cicero's *De Inventione* and the anonymous *Rhetorica ad Herennium*.[22] Both works were written at about the same time, around 85 BCE. The former was Cicero's youthful effort to adapt Greek rhetorical theory to Roman purposes, and this section explores his approach.

The latter, *Rhetorica ad Herennium*, has been called "our first complete Hellenistic rhetoric," that is, an essentially Greek rhetorical treatise written in Latin, for Romans by a Roman.[23] Throughout its long history of use, this popular treatise was translated into several vernacular languages and was often used alongside Cicero's *De Inventione* to introduce students to rhetoric. Teaching academic subjects such as rhetoric in Latin, which *Rhetorica ad Herennium* and *De Inventione* allowed, was considered a suspect activity by Rome's upper classes who had been educated in Greek. A Latin-based approach to rhetoric instruction broadened the audience and the influence of rhetoric; rhetoric no longer belonged solely to the ruling class.

Both *De Inventione* and *Rhetorica ad Herennium* were enormously popular in the Roman world. Brian Vickers writes that they were "the two most popular rhetoric-books of antiquity, and perhaps the two most disseminated books of any kind."[24] These treatises emphasize judicial argument, thus expressing a preference for the sophistic tradition over the legislatively focused Aristotelian tradition.

De Inventione (87 BCE), Cicero's first book on rhetoric, was written when he was about 19 years old. A collection of notes and musings on the art of oratory, *De Inventione* provides a glimpse of how rhetoric was taught to young men like Cicero in the late Roman Republic.[25] It is not, however, a mature work on the nature or practice of rhetoric. One scholar calls it "severely technical," and Cicero himself later commented that *De Inventione* was "inchoate and rough."[26] This work seems to draw on Greek Stoic approaches to logic and discourse. Cicero's efforts in bringing Greek philosophy and rhetorical theory to a Roman audience were both unique and significant. He was skilled at "creating the Latin terms capable of expressing the meaning of the Greek ones."[27]

De Inventione sounds the major theme of Cicero's rhetorical career—the union of wisdom and eloquence. He writes: "I have been led by reason itself to hold this opinion first and foremost, that wisdom without eloquence does too little for the good of states, but that eloquence without wisdom is generally highly disadvantageous and is never helpful."[28] Wisdom was the virtue that Romans admired perhaps above all others. But the Roman conception of wisdom differed from the Plato's contemplative "lover of wisdom." Wisdom to a Roman was largely practical in nature, and guided in making sound decisions in public and private.

On Cicero's model, then, the rhetorician studied philosophy, ethics, and other disciplines important to good government. There is always a practical bent to Cicero's interest in rhetoric and wisdom. Rhetoric is *the* civilizing force that makes human social life possible. By skill in rhetoric we overcome our human tendencies toward violence and the rule of the strongest, a theme reminiscent of Plato's debate with Callicles in *Gorgias*. But rhetoric's great power is useful only when tempered by great wisdom. "For from eloquence," Cicero writes, "the state receives many benefits, provided only it is accompanied by wisdom, the guide of all human affairs."[29]

The Canons of Rhetoric

In *De Inventione*, Cicero advances his best-remembered contribution to the history of rhetoric, the five canons of oratory. He admits, however, that these divisions are not new with him: "The parts of [rhetoric], as most authorities have stated, are Invention, Arrangement, Expression, Memory, and Delivery."[30] Cicero's canons provide a useful means of dividing the work of the orator into units, each of which suggests a course of study.

The canons of rhetoric accomplished more, however, than teaching one how to divide up a speech. They also imposed an order on talk, and thus on thought that preceded it. Rhetoric in this way played a crucial role in defining what was considered rational. In addition, the canons and their associated systems of invention disciplined the life of the aspiring orator. Thus, Connolly writes that "the practice of rhetoric, with its insistence on rigid discipline and careful expression, actually shaped the moral self for Cicero."[31]

The first of the canons is invention (*inventio*), which Cicero described as "the discovery of valid or seemingly valid arguments." In the following sections we will examine methods that were employed for teaching the skill of developing appropriate and effective arguments. Much of Roman rhetorical training was focused on invention, and most of *De Inventione* is devoted to this one concern.

The second canon is arrangement (*dispositio*) or "the distribution of arguments thus discovered in the proper order." In addition to discovering materials for a speech, the orator must know how to order those materials—especially arguments—effectively.

The third canon, expression (*elocutio*), focused on "the fitting of the proper language to the invented material." Rhetors needed a command of language sufficient to allow them to convey their arguments in striking and persuasive phrases. Great language captures and holds an audience's attention, a fact that Cicero both notes and demonstrates in this passage from his book, *Brutus*, where he employs to great effect a device called *asyndeton* or the elimination of conjunctions. Note how he reverses the device in the passage's last sentence, employing *polysyndeton* or the inclusion of extra conjunctions:

> The listening multitude is delighted, and it is led by the oration: it is drowned, so to speak in pleasure. Do you disagree? It rejoices, it grieves, it laughs, it weeps, it approves, it hates, it disdains, it envies, it is brought to pity, shame, regret, it grows angry, it is amazed; it hopes, it fears; these things happen as the minds of those who are present are skillfully managed by words and thoughts and delivery (188).[32]

Cicero's fourth canon may strike modern readers, accustomed to writing everything down, as less central to rhetoric than the first three. He writes, "memory [*memoria*] is the firm mental grasp of matter and words" of a speech. We have already noted the centrality of memory to an oral culture. Because orators delivered long and complex arguments without written notes, a trained memory was essential. Because an actual public speech might go on for several hours, delivered from memory, students were required to memorize long practice speeches.

Finally, "delivery (*pronuntiatio*) is the control of voice and body in a manner suitable to the dignity of the subject matter and the style."[33] A speech in a Roman courtroom or in the Senate was a performance, and the skilled orator needed the presence, poise, power, and grace of an actor. Orators practiced movement, gesture, posture, facial expression, and vocal tone and volume. Accounts of Roman orators slapping their thighs, stamping their feet, and even ripping open their togas to reveal war wounds suggests that delivery in Rome was quite a different matter from the "talking-head" approach to speaking characteristic of contemporary politicians.

Studying Invention and Memory

Roman orators—many of whom were trained as what we would not call attorneys—had an extraordinary interest in judicial argument, a consequence of their equally intense interest in law. The Roman legal code was vastly more complex than that used by the Athenians. In fact, the Romans invented and refined the concept of jurisprudence—the science or philosophy of law. This feat was accomplished by applying the Greek notion of *techne* to the study of law. Mastering the Roman legal code—which in its final form represented a thousand years of development like mastering rhetoric—required years of rigorous study. Such a master of the law was termed a jurist, and their advice was valued by politicians and private parties alike.

Invention—the discovery of arguments—received much attention in training judicial orators. Training the memory to retain a lengthy judicial argument was also a central concern. Various methods of teaching invention and memory thus emerged.

Stasis Systems

In Book I of *De Inventione*, Cicero discusses a method for thinking through a judicial case that involved anticipating likely points of conflict or *stasis*.[34] For example, in legal disputes issues of fact involved questions such as, what occurred? and when did it occur? An issue of fact might become a point of clash between two sides arguing the case, a point at which agreements would stop and arguments be advanced.

Other points of *stasis* in legal argumentation were also likely. For instance, once issues of fact had been argued, issues of definition would emerge. Cicero writes, "the controversy about a definition arises when there is agreement as to the fact and the question is by what word that which has been done is to be called."[35] Definitional questions include, how shall we classify this act? or, more specifically, was this a case of murder? Issues of definition might be followed by arguments about an issue of quality, which addressed the act's severity. Was the killing committed in a moment of great passion? Was it carefully planned ahead of time for personal gain?

Finally, issues of procedure could produce moments of *stasis* if either side wished to raise an objection to how the case was being pursued. Cicero writes that questions will arise "as to who ought to bring the action or against whom, or in what manner or before what court or under what law or at what time, and in general where there is some argument about changing or invalidating the form of procedure."[36] Cicero further subdivides each of these four points of *stasis*—fact, definition, quality, and procedure—into additional issues that might arise under each heading.

Students studying a *stasis* system learned to think through a legal case by following the points at which disagreements were likely to arise. Points of *stasis* divided a complex case into its component questions. *Stasis* also allowed an orator to anticipate counterarguments, and to identify the strengths and weaknesses of a case before its public presentation. Arguments relevant to each question in a *stasis* system were rehearsed until they became integrated into the student's pattern of thinking.

It would be easy to assume that training in a system such as *stasis* was preparation for the courtroom speaker only. But, as Joy Connolly points out, such rhetorical education provided basic instruction in what today might be termed critical thinking, important preparation for participation in a civic life. She writes:

> As it trains the speaker to investigate the causes of civic dispute: as a matter of fact (what happened?), circumstance (under what conditions are criminal acts justified?), legal interpretation (what are the limits of written law?), and correct application of the law (what courts may sit in judgment, and which men may speak in public, and about what, and when?), it teaches the basics of civic education: how to evaluate evidence, the conflict of laws, and what influences fellow citizens (2.28).[37]

By developing rational methods for investigating important questions faced by any society, the Romans were creating the basic components of democratic processes.

Loci: From Memory to Invention

Whereas a *stasis* system provided a means of anticipating the direction a case might take, *loci* systems offered advocates a supply of potential arguments by cataloging and organizing the most common ones. We encountered a similar approach to invention in our discussion of Aristotle's *topoi* in Chapter 4.[38]

Loci or "location systems" began as memory devices and evolved into inventional methods. The earliest location system of memory is attributed to the Greek poet, Simonides (556–468 BCE), who was reputed to have developed his memory abilities by associating items to be remembered with images and locations in a well-known public building. Because Roman orators spoke from memory, often for a long time, training the memory was crucial. Location systems were found to be particularly effective. A rhetor would associate an argument in a speech with a place in a familiar building, putting each argument, literally, in its place. Recalling the arguments, then, involved a mental stroll through the building, retrieving arguments along the way. By such means, orators accomplished amazing feats of memory, reciting complex speeches of 2 or 3 hours in length without the aid of written notes.

Loci systems gradually developed into methods for discovering persuasive arguments. From places in which to locate an argument for later recall, the *loci* often referred to by the Greek term *topoi* (places), anglicized as topics—became categories of arguments, general types that could be explored in developing a case. As such, topical systems assisted education in invention as well as memory.

Learning these foundational categories also trained the prospective orator to reason through a case as preparation for presenting it in public. More sophisticated topical schemes suggested possibilities for investigating a complex rhetorical problem. One scholar notes that the system presented in Cicero's later work, *Topica*, "is considerably less mechanical" than the system presented in the earlier *De Inventione*."[39] *Loci* were not, then, an orator's artificial gimmick for quickly discovering an argument, but rather tended to stimulate and discipline natural thought processes.[40] Like *stasis* systems, topical systems cultivated a set of rhetorical habits that would come to the rhetor's aid in a wide range of circumstances, from preparing a speech to answering an unexpected challenge during a trial.

Attributes of Person and Act

Most Roman topical systems were oriented to courtroom speaking. Judicial arguments often were arranged under two headings discussed in Cicero's *De Inventione*: the attributes of the accused person and the attributes of the act in question.[41]

First, in a culture elevating personal character, questions surrounding the accused person's reputation were bound to arise. Cicero writes, "we hold the following to be the attributes of the person: name, nature, manner of life, fortune, habit, feeling, interests, purposes, achievements, accidents, speeches made."[42] Thus, a Roman lawyer might consider issues that modern readers would find irrelevant to deciding a case, such as where an individual was born, or even the manner in which he or she was reared. Historian of rhetoric Michael Leff notes that Cicero's list of eleven personal attributes "is not exhaustive (later authorities list more than twenty divisions), nor is there any apparent attempt to rationalize the items in this inventory into a coherent structure."[43] These *loci* of the person simply suggested possible arguments of accusation or defense.

Second, questions surrounding the alleged act would have to be argued. Issues of past fact are still vital to judicial pleading. Cicero's list of attributes of the act is longer and more detailed than is that concerning the person.[44] Divisions include:

1.   Topics coherent with the act itself, which would include issues such as motive and summary statements representing the nature of the act;
2.   Topics involved in the performance of the act, which would focus attention on considerations of time, place, and occasion;
3.   Adjuncts of the act or topics of relation in which the act in question is compared to, contrasted with, or somehow brought into relation with another act;
4.   Consequences, which were topics based on things that follow from the performance of the act, which meant principally public reactions to the act.[45]

Loci of the person and the act were a common feature of Roman rhetorical treatises and remained important to rhetorical education for centuries.

Cicero's *De Oratore*

Following a long and distinguished political career, Cicero was banished in 58 BCE for alleged illegalities in his fight with Catiline, a senator who attempted to overthrow the Republic and whose plot Cicero revealed. A year later, the emperor Pompey allowed Cicero to return to Rome. While no longer important to the political scene, Cicero remained popular with the citizenry.[46] In 55 BCE, Cicero retired to his country estate to write. One of the books from this period of leisure, *De Oratore*, was probably published that same year. This mature work on rhetoric was a response to Plato's criticisms of the art in *Gorgias*. *De Oratore* is composed as a dialogue, but does not resemble the contentious dialogues of Plato.[47] Here the participants—Crassus, Antonius, Rufus, and Cotta—interact to contribute insights about rhetoric, not to refute one another.

Union of Wisdom and Eloquence

As already noted, the union of wisdom and eloquence is a persistent Ciceronian theme. "I hold that eloquence is dependent upon the trained skill of highly educated men," he writes.[48] Like other Roman rhetoricians, Cicero sought to prepare the diligent student to take the role of the complete orator. Cicero was above all a politician and his *perfectus orator* was a political leader manifesting the values of the state each time he spoke. Even the rhetorician's study of philosophy should serve the political welfare of Rome. Cicero invested this ideal of the rhetorician-leader with dignity and erudition: "In the orator we must demand the subtlety of a logician, the thoughts of the philosopher, adiction almost poetic, a lawyer's memory, a tragedian's voice, and the bearing of the most consummate actor." Not often does such a person emerge. "No rarer thing than a finished orator," Cicero concludes, "can be found among the sons of men."[49]

Because this concern for eloquence as preparation for political leadership has been largely lost, it can be difficult to understand the issue's importance to Cicero. Oratory was essential to Roman government, justice, and civic life generally. Thus, preparing an individual to be a wise and responsible speaker was a pressing matter. Nor was a goal as limited as merely maintaining audience attention Cicero's primary rhetorical concern; he viewed eloquence as nothing less than civilization's foundation. "In every free nation, and most of all in communities which have attained the enjoyment of peace and tranquility, this one art has always flourished above the rest and ever reigned supreme."[50] Cicero identified eloquence as "the key connection between civic virtue and individual virtue," thus envisioning a dynamic interaction of the speaker's virtue, that of the state, and that of the citizen.[51]

For Cicero, character was not evident in the words of a speech, as Aristotle suggested in making *ethos* a study within rhetoric. Rather, in keeping with Roman thinking, virtuous character was an inherent trait of an individual that gradually revealed itself through decisions and actions over the course of a lifetime. For Cicero, character was composed of dignity (*dignitas*), worthy achievements (*res gestae*), and a solid reputation (*existimatio*).

Cicero blamed Plato for dividing wisdom and eloquence in his attack on the Sophists in *Gorgias*. The figure Socrates in that dialogue "separated the science of wise thinking from that of eloquent speaking." Moreover,

> this is the source from which has sprung the undoubtedly absurd and unprofitable and reprehensible severance between the tongue and the brain, leading us to have one set of professors to teach us to think and another to teach us to speak.[52]

Cicero sought to reunite "the tongue and the brain," and thus to produce great speakers who also were great thinkers.

The Audience's Centrality

The audience is also a central concern in Cicero's rhetorical theory. Though a great intellect himself, Cicero recognized that rhetoric required the orator to consider ordinary citizens, the *res publica*. Roman political life transpired in public. Thus, the orator could not stand aloof from the concerns of the populace, and was in this way different from the practitioners of other arts. Cicero writes,

> Whereas in all other arts that is most excellent which is farthest removed from the understanding and mental capacity of the untrained, in oratory the very cardinal sin is to depart from the language of everyday life, and the usage approved by the sense of the community [*sensus communis*].[53]

Rhetoric must reflect the Roman public's values and hold the audience's attention by a vigorous presentation that bordered on the theatrical. Arguments, ornaments, and appeals must be accessible and pleasing to the ordinary listener. Plato, recall, criticized rhetoric's pandering to "ignorant" audiences of untrained citizens. Cicero, however, viewed the ordinary audience as an important fact rather than a fatal flaw. The citizens of Rome were Rome itself; they were to be consulted, not condemned.

The Orator's Qualities

Cicero's complete orator must understand law, politics, domestic and foreign economics, military affairs, and international issues such as trade. The orator should also appreciate poetry and the other arts. Knowing philosophy was essential, and Cicero was himself a philosopher of note. Moreover, the orator must strive for "a distinctive style" in both language and delivery, arranging and presenting words and arguments to the most forceful effect.

> Like Aristotle, Cicero made emotions as part of an orator's study. All the mental emotions with which nature has endowed the human race, are to be intimately understood, because it is in calming or kindling the feelings of the audience that the full power and science of oratory are to be brought into play.[54]

Book II of *De Oratore* discusses emotions at length, and explains how orators arouse powerful feelings in their audiences.[55] The great orator not only elicits emotions appropriate to the issue at hand, but *experiences* those same emotions. Cicero writes that

> it is impossible for the listener to feel indignation, hatred or ill-will, to be terrified of anything, or reduced to tears of compassion, unless all those emotions which the advocate would inspire in the arbitrator, are visibly stamped or rather branded on the advocate himself.[56]

In other works such as *Brutus* and *Orator*, Cicero assigns three functions to oratory: to teach (*docere*), to delight (*delectare*), and to persuade (*movere*). Persuasion was concerned with moving the audience's emotions.

Finally, an orator must possess wit, culture and charm, and the stage presence and vocal control of an actor. Is there anything the orator *doesn't* need to know? Apparently not; real orators are hard to find because very few people can master so many arts. "Indeed, in my opinion, no man can be an orator complete in all points of merit, who has not attained a knowledge of all important subjects and arts."[57] The orator's calling is such a high one, his role so important, that any amount of study is warranted to attain this office. The health and welfare of the entire nation depend on orators, "the safety of countless individuals and of the entire state."[58]

Cicero on Humor

Among Cicero's most distinctive contributions to the history of rhetoric is his treatment of humor in oratory. The dilemma of humor for the orator is discovered in two observations. First, there is "great and frequent utility" in humor. However, second, it is an "absolute impossibility" to learn wit by studying it.[59] Cicero sought to provide orators some guidance on this difficult topic.

First and foremost, it is vital to maintain dignity in the use of humor, which means respecting the audience's sensibilities. "Regard ought to be paid to personages, topics and occasions, so that the jest should not detract from dignity."[60]

This cardinal rule—respect for one's audience—must be followed if humor's benefits are to be realized. And, clearly, humor affords the orator several advantages. It "wins goodwill for its author," and audiences admire a speaker quick-witted enough to "repel or deliver an attack." Humor also reveals the rhetor to be a person of "finish, accomplishment and taste." But, "best of all [humor] relieves dullness" in a speech.

In spite of these advantages, there are "limits within which things laughable are to be handled by the orator," an issue requiring "most careful consideration." Some things one simply ought not to make fun of, including "outstanding wickedness, such as involves crime, [and] outstanding wretchedness," that is, human suffering. He writes, "the public would have the villainous hurt by a weapon rather more formidable than ridicule; while they dislike mockery of the wretched." Under no circumstances should the rhetor "inconsiderately speak ill of the well-beloved."[61] Cicero adds that the orator must not "let his jesting become buffoonery or mere mimicking"; an orator runs the risk of looking foolish if joking becomes excessive.

Cicero identified various sources of humor, including wit (*facetiae*), amusing stories, and mimicking someone well known.[62] Wit "is awakened by something pointed in a phrase or reflection." Cicero considered puns and wordplay as legitimate sources of rhetorical humor. "Regard then to occasions [and] control and restraint . . . will distinguish an orator from a buffoon," he cautions.[63] The most difficult aspect of humor in rhetoric is when to use it, and when to refrain.

Cicero notes repeatedly that "there is no source of laughing-matters [*ioci: jokes*] from which austere and serious thoughts are not also to be derived."[64] Thus, orators must ensure that they know what is worthy of humor, and know their audience's sensibilities. Nothing is more disastrous for a rhetor than to make light of a topic the audience considers a serious matter: "All is not witty that is laughable."[65]

Cicero warns that mimicry of persons (*imitatio*) should be avoided or used sparingly; the risks of looking foolish are just too great. Grimacing is also beneath the dignity of a true orator, as is obscenity.[66] Certain types of humor reveal sophistication but are not likely to get a laugh. For example, amusing ambiguities—multiple meanings—can be a sign of scholarship, but does not raise big laughs. Here is one of Cicero's examples:

> The notorious Titius, who was devoted to ball-play and also under suspicion of mutilating the holy statues by night: when his associates missed him, as he had not come to the Playing Fields, Vespa Terentius apologized for his absence on the plea, "He has broken an arm."[67]

Particularly effective humor occurs when "a word snatched from an antagonist is used to hurl a shaft at the assailant himself, as was done by Catulus against Philipus."

Philipus, during a particularly heated debate, demanded of Catulus (whose name means young dog), "What are you barking at?" To which Catulus replied coldly, "I see a thief."

Laughs can also be raised by juxtaposing words that are similar in spelling, or using a portion of a well-known verse at just the right place in a speech, or an old expression where its meaning is taken in an unexpected way. Taking a term literally when it is meant figuratively, or figuratively when meant literally, are also possibilities for humor based on words.[68] In the former category Cicero includes the humorous response of Lucius Nascia when asked by Cato the censor, "On your conscience, are you satisfied that you are a married man?" "Married for certain," returned Nascia, "but verily not to my entire satisfaction!"[69]

For the accomplished orator, humor demonstrates mental agility while at the same time attracts and holds audience interest. However, Cicero cautions the would-be wit at every turn that humor runs the dual risk of offending the audience and making the orator look foolish.

The End of Cicero's Life

Cicero's life ended abruptly as the result of his enmity with Julius Caesar. Tensions developed between the ruling Consuls and powerful members of the Senate such as Cicero. With the rise of the general Julius Caesar, Rome was on the brink of civil war. Several powerful senators opposed Caesar. In 49 BCE, Caesar returned from Gaul and invaded his own country, seizing ultimate control of the entire Roman Empire and taking the title Perpetual Dictator. Roman courts were closed and Cicero was forced into retirement.

But, this colorful and controversial orator was not to die in peace. After Caesar's murder in 44 BCE, Cicero was ordered to be killed by the powerful general Mark Antony. Cicero fled but was captured and killed; his head and hands were cut off and hung in the forum over the podium, a grim reminder to any other potential opponents of how eloquence employed against the emperor would be dealt with.

Cicero's influence on subsequent rhetorical thought and practice was unparalleled. As we shall see in the next chapter, he was the source of virtually all of the rhetorical theory of the Middle Ages. For Cicero, the truly skilled orator had a very high calling—to provide moral as well as political leadership to the state. Rhetoric was a power that went beyond Aristotle's faculty of discovering available means of persuasion. Cicero was interested in rhetoric's capacity to "move the minds and bend the wills of hearers."[70] But he was also convinced of the potential for one person, equipped with sufficient natural ability and willing to expend enough effort, to shape the course of a civilization through the power of speech.

QUINTILIAN

Just as Isocrates was the most famous and successful teacher of rhetoric in ancient Athens, the Roman whose method of rhetorical education achieved the highest degree of sophistication was Marcus Fabius Quintilianus (35–100 CE). So renowned was Quintilian for his contributions to education of Roman youth that the Roman poet Martial wrote of him:

> Quintilian, premier guide of wayward youth,
> Quintilian, glory of the Roman toga![71]

Many of Quintilian's students went on to great achievements, spread his fame, and advocated his ideas on education. Among his more famous students were the historian Tacitus and the statesman Pliny the Younger.

Born in Spain, Quintilian studied rhetoric in Rome following a mentor named Domitius Afer. He became famous first as a judicial advocate, and later as a teacher of rhetoric.[72] His multivolume work *Institutes of Oratory* is a twenty-volume cradle-to-grave guide to the orator's education.[73] Quintilian's approach to rhetoric closely follows that of his favorite rhetorician—Cicero. Training a great speaker begins virtually at birth; Quintilian cautions parents that even a child's nurses should speak proper Latin. "Be particular concerning your child's earliest training," he urges. The Roman preoccupation with character is evident here as well, as is a growing interest in good Latin grammar as a mark of a great speaker. Nannies must "be of good character and speak correctly." Nor are the parents themselves exempt: "Both parents should be as highly educated as possible, mothers included." Even the child's friends "ought to be carefully chosen."[74] Clearly, a great deal is at stake in developing a great orator.

The Toga

For Quintilian, even the famed Roman toga had to be worn properly by the respectable orator. It wasn't just appearance that concerned him, but effective gesturing during a speech. As one authority writes,

> The *sinus* or arm-sling should not be too high or too low. The *balteus* or belt should not be too tight or too loose. The fold should be thrown over the shoulder, but not cover the throat, otherwise the dress will be tight and lose the dignity lent by a broad chest (11.3.140–1).

Despite its close association with the rulers of Rome, the toga itself was copied in several respects from Greek attire.

The toga was not an easy item to wear with grace, and it could become uncomfortable in the heat of a long speech. A. Wallace-Hadrill writes, "The reader [of Quintilian's *Institutes*] becomes increasingly conscious of the sheer awkwardness of the garment, the difficulty of speaking in public with a minimum of animation without throwing the clothing into disarray . . ." Of course, the skilled speaker was also aware that the toga could be used as something of a stage prop, and propriety dwindled as the speech lengthened. As you move into the body of the speech "you can let the fold slip off the shoulder, and pull the *toga* away from your throat and upper chest as the argument hots up . . . by the end of the speech, almost anything goes, sweat, disordered clothing, the *toga* loose and falling off all round" (11.3.144–6).[75]

Rhetoric and the Good Citizen

Quintilian defined rhetoric as the art of *vir bonus, dicendi peritus*, the good citizen skilled in speaking. In addition to experience and skill, this formulation implies a moral function for rhetoric. "Mere persuasion" was of no interest to Quintilian. Rather, he cast the orator in the role of a good citizen intent on employing rhetorical powers for the benefit of Rome. The true orator must be a conservative citizen and an honorable person, one who adds to virtue natural gifts that have been honed through practice and careful instruction.

An individual of questionable character cannot counterfeit morally good eloquence through rhetorical training. However, studying rhetoric further develops the character of a good person. The preface to his *Institutes of Oratory* states,

> My aim, then, is the education of the perfect orator. The first essential for such a one is that he should be a good man, and consequently we demand of him not merely the possession of exceptional gifts of speech, but of all the excellences of character as well.[76]

Can the power of rhetoric be limited to morally good individuals? Should rhetoric be used to promote a particular vision of a moral society? By restricting rhetorical education to a select few who possess admirable traits and a particular political outlook, Quintilian gave us his answer to this question. Educational rationing does not, of course, resolve the issue.

Educating the Citizen–Orator

Studying rhetoric under Quintilian meant a great deal of hard work for the handpicked student. But, then, one was fortunate to be studying under the great master. "Eloquent speeches," he wrote, "are not the result of momentary inspirations, but the products of research, analysis, practice, and application."[77] Quintilian's system of rhetorical education was worked out in great detail. The *Institutes of Oratory* reveal the strong influence of Cicero's rhetorical theory as presented in *De Oratore*, and also incorporate elements from Greek rhetoricians like Hermagoras of Temnos.

Indefinite and Definite Questions

Rhetoric, for Quintilian, addressed two kinds of questions: indefinite and definite. An indefinite question was discussed without specific reference to persons, time, place, or other particular limitation; indefinite questions are speculative. Examples would include theological questions such as, Is the universe governed by providence? and more mundane issues such as, Should one enter politics?

Definite questions include issues concerning specific individuals, facts, places, and times. Thus, the questions, Should Cato marry? and Is Crassus guilty of theft? were definite questions. Aristotle had limited rhetoric to this second type of question, assigning indefinite questions to dialectic. Quintilian broadened the scope of rhetoric by assigning it both factual (definite) and speculative (indefinite) issues.

Bases

Quintilian also discussed the bases, or the specific issues addressed in resolving a judicial case. The bases are closely related to points of *stasis* in a debate. Quintilian identified three bases which he termed existence, definition, and quality. Existence was a question of what had occurred, a question, that is, of fact. The basis of definition involved categorizing an event. Finally, the basis of quality concerned the severity of the act once it had been defined.

Proof

Quintilian found proof to derive from four sources. First, sense perceptions are admissible as evidence. Thus, eyewitness testimony is a strong form of evidence or proof. Second, things about which there is general agreement, similar to the Greek concept of *endoxa*, were admissible as evidence. Thus, a proof might be derived from the observation that people will perform desperate acts when they are in desperate circumstances. Third, proof can be drawn from the laws and common agreements. Thus, a proof might be based on a statute or a contract. Finally, what both parties to a dispute have admitted may be a source of proof.

Loci

In his *Institutes of Oratory*, Quintilian described a *loci* system much like Cicero's. However, rather than seeing the *loci* as devices for discovering arguments Quintilian exploited their potential as a teaching tool. His *loci* were not to be memorized for quick recall, but rather were practiced in order to develop habits of thought.

Michael Leff points out that Quintilian, ever the dedicated teacher, found that the "authentic function" of *loci* was to "help promote the argumentative skills of the student, to foster the development of natural talents and to sharpen insight into cases that arise in the public arena."[78] The goal of training in various types of arguments was to create intellectual habits that would assist the would-be orator in any setting where quick thinking was imperative. This facility required "constant practice" with arguments. As Quintilian writes:

> [J]ust as the hands of the musician, even though his eyes be turned elsewhere produce bass, treble, and intermediate notes by force of habit, so the thought of [an] orator should suffer no delay owing to the variety and number of possible arguments, but that the latter should present themselves uncalled, and just as letters and syllables require no thought on the part of a writer, so arguments should spontaneously follow the thought of the orator.[79]

Topical systems following those of Cicero and Quintilian continued to appear between 200 and 500 CE, remaining a key feature of rhetorical training. Variations on a central theme were endless. In one popular system, *loci* of the act were arranged according to spatial and temporal considerations such as what preceded the act (*ante rem*), what occurred in the act itself (*in re*), what circumstances surrounded the act (*circa rem*), and what events followed the act (*post rem*).

The Parts of a Judicial Speech

Quintilian taught his students to think of judicial speeches—the type with which he was most concerned—as divided into five parts, an approach common to other Roman rhetorics such as Cicero's *De Inventione* and the anonymous *Rhetorica ad Herennium*.

The first part, the *exordium*, was an introduction designed to dispose the audience to listen to the speech. The second part, the *narratio*, was a statement of the facts essential to understanding the case, and intended to reveal the essential nature of the subject about which they were to render a decision.

The third part of the judicial speech was the proof or *confirmatio*, which was a section designed to offer evidences in support of claims advanced during the *narratio*. Fourth came the *confutatio*, or the refutation, in which counterarguments were answered. Finally the *peroratio* or conclusion was presented, a section in which the orator demonstrated again the full strength of the case presented.[80]

Quintilian's highly refined and technical approach to teaching rhetoric proved remarkably successful. His students went on to become some of the most influential and famous citizens of Rome, and they frequently credited Quintilian's rigorous education in rhetoric with their success.

LONGINUS: ON THE SUBLIME

On the Sublime is a famous Roman rhetorical treatise that emphasizes the principles of good writing.[81] Many scholars have seen this work as an early application of rhetorical theory to literary criticism, that is, to the discussion of how great writing is achieved, and how it in turn achieves its ends. Brian Vickers, for example, calls *On the Sublime* "the outstanding union of rhetoric and literary criticism."[82] Grube refers to this work as "certainly the most delightful of all the critical works of classical antiquity."[83]

The Emotive Power of Language

The author of *On the Sublime* is particularly concerned with the emotive power of language. Its authorship is uncertain though it has traditionally been attributed to Longinus (c. 213–273 CE), and I will, mainly for convenience and because his name is still conventionally attached to it, treat him as the actual author of this important work. Estimates about the date of authorship of *On the Sublime* range from the first to the third centuries. Though the details of authorship and dating are uncertain, the author's insights into the means by which the principles of rhetoric can guide effective expression are seldom doubted.

Language, Style, and Power

If Aristotle's interest in argument was perpetuated in Rome by Cicero, then Gorgias' interest in the sheer power of language and the effects of rhetorical style was advanced

TEACHING ARGUMENT AT ROME

Cicero's Five Canons of Oratory

1. Invention
2. Arrangement
3. Expression
4. Memory
5. Delivery

The Stasis System: Cicero, De Inventione

1. Issues of fact
2. Issues of definition
3. Issues of quality
4. Issues of procedure

The Topical Systems, Cicero, and Others

1. Attributes of the person: name, nature, manner of life, fortune, habit, feelings, interests, purposes, achievements, accidents, and speeches made.
2. Attributes of the act: Topics coherent with the act, Topics involved in the performance of the act, Adjuncts of the act, Consequences of the act.

Questions of Quintilian

1. Definite questions
2. Indefinite questions

Bases of Quintilian

1. Existence (like fact or conjecture)
2. Definition (like juridical or definition)
3. Quality

Sources of Proof of Quintilian

1. From senses
2. From common belief
3. From laws, contracts, and agreements
4. From admission

Loci of the Act

1. Ante rem
2. In re
3. Circa rem
4. Post rem

in Rome by Longinus. Jane Tompkins writes that "for Longinus, language is a form of power and the purpose of studying texts from the past is to acquire the skills that enable one to wield that power."[84] Longinus' theory of language's potency is organized around a concept he terms "the sublime" or perhaps "sublimity," a measure of the impact that literature combining emotion with great ideas has on readers. Tompkins emphasizes that "Longinus' notion of the sublime is equivalent to a conception of poetry as pure power."[85]

Five Sources of Great Writing

Longinus advises his readers that there are "five sources most productive of great writing (Greek: *hypsos*, also translated 'the sublime'). All five," he adds, "presuppose the power of expression without which there is no good writing at all."[86] Though Longinus mentions writing as his concern, the connection in the ancient world between writing and speaking was more intimate than it is for us. Even written discourse was typically read aloud; silent reading was almost unknown to the Romans.

So, what are the five sources of great writing? The "first and most important," Longinus writes, "is vigor of mental conception," while the "second is strong and inspired emotion." But having great and passionate ideas to inform your writing is not something anyone can teach you. Longinus comments, "Both of these are for the most part innate dispositions." Nevertheless, Longinus spends a long time—six chapters—discussing the qualities of mind that distinguish a great writer. Literary genius and transcendent inspiration of the type exhibited by Sappho, Demosthenes, or Plato are more interesting to Longinus than is technical perfection.

The other qualities of great writing "are benefited also by artistic training." And these other qualities are

> the adequate fashioning of figures (both of speech and of thought), nobility of diction which in turn includes the choice of words and the use of figurative and artistic language; lastly, and including all the others, dignified and distinguished word-arrangement.[87]

The rhetorical art, then, can assist you to become a great writer by teaching you the various devices that enhance expression, the ability to choose words appropriate to your ideas, and the most effective arrangement of those words, that is, composition.

The Use of Examples

Longinus advances numerous examples of these principles from the writers of his own day, as well as from earlier Roman and Greek authors. One of his favorite examples is Sappho, a Greek author of love poetry discussed in Chapter 2. "Sappho, for example, selects on each occasion the emotions which accompany the frenzy of love," writes Longinus. "How does she excel? In her skillful choice of the most important and intense details and in relating them to one another." Longinus then provides his readers with one of Sappho's most famous poems, which illustrates these principles:

Peer of gods he seemeth to me, the blissful
Man who sits and gazes at thee before him,
Close beside thee sits, and in silence hears thee
Silvery speaking,
Laughing Love's low laughter. Oh this, this only
Stirs the troubled heart in my breast to tremble,
For should I but see thee a little moment,
Straight is my voice hushed;
Yea, my tongue is broken, and through and through me
'Neath the flesh, impalpable fire runs tingling;
Nothing see mine eyes, and a noise of roaring
Waves in my ears sounds;
Sweat runs down in rivers, a tremor seizes
All my limbs and paler than grass in autumn,
Caught by pains of menacing death, I falter,
Lost in the love trance.[88]

Figures of Speech

Longinus also advances a great deal of advice about the use of figures of speech or rhetorical devices to enhance writing and speaking. For instance, he writes that "the best use of a figure is when the very fact that it is a figure goes unnoticed."[89] Rhetorical figures can be powerful enhancements to writing and speaking, but the author or an orator must be subtle in their use for audiences are a little suspicious of them:

> The cunning use of figures arouses a peculiar suspicion in the hearer's mind, a feeling of being deliberately trapped and misled. This occurs when addressing a single judge with power of decision, and especially a dictator, a king, or an eminent leader. He is easily angered by the thought that he is being outwitted like a silly child by the expert's use of pretty figures; he sees in the fallacious reasoning a personal insult; sometimes he may altogether give way to savage exasperation, but even if he controls his anger he remains impervious to persuasion.[90]

Longinus spends considerable time discussing rhetorical figures, and his descriptions of various devices attempt to account for their impact on a reader or listener. Regarding the device known as *asyndeton*—leaving out connectives such as *and* in a descriptive list—Longinus writes, "the words burst forth without connective, pour out, as it were, and the speaker himself cannot keep up with them. 'Shield on shield,' says Xenophon, 'they were pushing, fighting, killing, dying.'"[91] However, Longinus' principal concern in his discussion of rhetorical figures—indeed, his central concern in *On the Sublime*—is the capacity of words to evoke powerful emotions in an audience. As Brian Vickers writes, "what sets him apart is his recognition of the functional relationship between figures and feeling: 'they all make style more emotional and excited,' and emotion (*pathos*) is 'an essential part of sublimity.'"[92]

Longinus is careful to add that the emotional impact of writing is always to be governed by a refined concern for decorum, that is, for what is dignified or proper and in keeping with the subject at hand. The true rhetorician should never stoop to simply tricking an audience into reacting emotionally, such debased tactics being a mark of a Sophist. The content of literature or speech should warrant the emotional response aroused by skillfully employed rhetorical figures.

On the Sublime, then, advances the rhetorical tradition in several ways. First, he explored the emotional power of words, a tradition extending back to Gorgias and that was also a concern for Aristotle. Longinus exhibits a consistent concern for the relationship between well-developed subject matter and the audience's emotional response. He thus is closer to Aristotle and his regard for *pathos* as a rhetorical proof than to Gorgias who believed that he was creating the audience's reality through emotional manipulation. Second, *On the Sublime* marks a shift in emphasis from the primarily spoken rhetoric of Cicero to a rising interest in the rhetoric of the written word. Of course, there had long been a connection between writing and rhetoric as is clear from the case of Isocrates in Athens. This emphasis on writing continues to play an important role in the history of rhetoric right up to the present day. Third, Longinus may be viewed as the inventor of literary criticism, the careful analysis of texts and how they achieve their effects on an audience. In this role, Longinus stands as the greatest figure in the Greek and Roman rhetorical tradition.

RHETORIC IN THE LATER ROMAN EMPIRE

Not surprisingly, as the power of the emperors increased over against that of the Senate, the importance of rhetoric as a means of shaping policy declined. However, rhetorical training remained a means of preparing people to serve as administrators in the vast Roman Empire.

The Second Sophistic

The Second Sophistic refers to the period from about AD 50 to 100, during which some of the oratorical elements associated with original Greek Sophists were reintroduced in parts of the Roman Empire. G. M. A. Grube writes that the Second Sophistic "can best be described as the triumph of display oratory, mainly in the Greek part of the empire, especially in the province of Asia."[93] The Second Sophistic followed times of great crisis for the Greek sections of the Empire. In the preceding centuries, Greece had experienced "the wars of Alexander's successors, the Roman wars of conquest, the exactions of Roman proconsuls under the late Republic, and the Roman civil wars."[94] Following this period of war, the cities of the Eastern Empire began to flourish again. In cities such as Smyrna, Ephesus, and Antioch, orators could make a living by entertaining large crowds with speeches that emphasized style over content.

These new Sophists "made speeches of display at games and international festivals," sometimes amazing the crowds with their feats of memory and dramatic delivery. At this time, "any Sophist of repute could be sure of a good audience and a good fee in almost any city of Asia."[95] Dio Cocceianus (CE 40–120), also known as Chrysostomos or "golden tongued," was among the popular orators of this period. He was a wandering Stoic philosopher who spoke on a variety of apolitical topics such as the merits of sculpture and poetry, how to prepare to be a public speaker, and Greek tragedy. Another prominent orator of the Second Sophistic was Aelius Aristides (b. CE 117). He also specialized in topics that avoided political controversy, including a famous series of speeches on medicine. He was reputed to have been helped to health by the god Asclepius who, he claimed, spoke to him through dreams. Aelius also made speeches defending rhetoric against the attacks of Plato.[96]

As the examples of Chrysostomos and Aelius suggest, in spite of the renewed interest in rhetorical practice, the Second Sophistic represents a serious demotion of rhetoric from its former prominence as a means of shaping public policy and influencing judicial decisions. Rhetoric, in effect, had to be restrained because of the nature of empirical government. "It became a capital crime to insult the Emperor." Even the simple act of defacing a coin "could be construed as an offense punishable by death" because the coin bore the Emperor's image. "Roman orators were therefore effectively denied the safe exercise of the first major type of speaking, the deliberative or political speech."[97]

But this is not to say that the Second Sophistic represents rhetoric employed solely as a form of entertainment. It is possible to identify substantial roles performed by the rhetoricians of this period. First, these Greek orators working in a Roman world sought to preserve Greek culture. Historian of rhetoric George Kennedy writes that these later Sophists "differ from the older Greek Sophists in that they were cultural conservatives, intent on preserving the heritage of Hellenism in language, literature, rhetoric and religion."[98]

Thomas Conley suggests a second important role for rhetoricians during the Second Sophistic. As was true of those who preceded them, the rhetoricians of this period were educators. Conley notes that chairs of rhetoric were established and funded at Roman universities in cities such as Antioch, Gaza, Alexandria, Athens, and Constantinople.[99] In fact, as in Athens, rhetorical training remained the principal vehicle for an ambitious young person to enter political life, albeit as a provincial administrator or perhaps as a lawyer. No longer did citizen–orators wield significant power in the Assembly.

Rhetoric's reduction in the late Roman Empire to a method of training administrators and a form of entertainment point up an important connection between rhetoric and democracy. When democracy flourishes, so does rhetoric and its study. When democracy declines, rhetoric also declines as its role as the method of free public discourse is diminished.

Though rhetoric's significance as the art of public discourse dwindled in empirical Rome, the art of rhetoric as it evolved in Rome outlived the civilization that produced it. Ironically, an essentially Roman rhetoric was reborn in a culture that shared relatively little with either the Roman Republic or the Roman Empire. This curious and important phenomenon in the history of rhetoric will be explored in the next chapter.

CONCLUSION

Rhetoric in the Roman world provided a center for a rigorous education that prepared citizens for personal success and advancement, for participation in civic life, and for public service. Rhetoric's connection with power, both personal and political, then, is clearly evident in the Roman tradition. Rhetorical training was a key to influence and personal advancement. Under the guidance of Longinus and other early literary critics, rhetoric came to be viewed as the means of achieving distinction and grace in writing.

Though the Romans learned rhetoric from the Greeks, they lent the art their own particular emphases. Roman theorists such as Cicero and Quintilian developed the *loci* of judicial pleading, for example, to a very high level of sophistication. But writers such as Longinus also employed the insights of Greek rhetoric to transform the Latin language, considered rough and vulgar by the Greeks, into one of the great beauty, power, and subtlety of expression.

The audience was a key component in the rhetoric of Rome. In Cicero, as in other great Roman rhetoricians, a concern for the audience's tastes, sensibilities, and values is consistently evident. In addition, whether in Cicero's desire to unite wisdom and eloquence or Quintilian's definition of rhetoric as the good citizen skilled in speaking, an ethical dimension attends Roman thinking about rhetoric.

Rhetoric, the ability to speak and write clearly and persuasively, was for the Romans the most practical and potent of linguistic abilities. In the best of Roman rhetorical theory, this ability carried with it a moral responsibility to serve the people of Rome well.

QUESTIONS FOR REVIEW

1. What are Cicero's five canons of rhetoric?
2. Into what two general categories did Cicero divide his *loci* of judicial pleading?
3. How were Greek and Roman understandings of the citizen different?
4. According to Cicero, of what must speakers be wary when using humor?
5. Cicero held that eloquence had been separated from some other crucial factor in Roman rhetoric. What is that other factor, and why was he concerned to bring these two qualities together?
6. What were the five parts of a speech that Quintilian taught to his students?
7. What did Quintilian mean by suggesting that an orator must be a good person?
8. What were the qualities and skills that Longinus suggested helped an author to achieve the quality of sublimity?
9. In what three ways did Longinus extend the rhetorical tradition?
10. What factors characterized the Second Sophistic?

QUESTIONS FOR DISCUSSION

1. For Cicero, the complete orator represented Roman civic values. Is such a conception of a single public figure—whether speaker or writer—possible today? Which persons in our society might take on such a role? Who comes closest? Why?
2. Skill in argumentation was crucially important to courtroom pleading and civic life generally in Rome. Is skill in argumentation still highly regarded? Is argumentation widely taught in our schools? If not, is it assumed that skill in this art is either natural, learned through studying other subjects, or just not important?
3. Longinus found in rhetoric an avenue to beautiful and expressive writing. Can studying examples of great writing, particularly the rhetorical figures employed by great writers, help you to improve your writing? Is great writing still valued, or has visual expression overshadowed writing in contemporary society?
4. If rhetorical practices and democratic forms of government tend to flourish together, how would you characterize the present state of rhetoric and democracy in U.S. culture? Are both flourishing? Are both in decline?

TERMS

Ante rem Events preceding the act in one *loci* system.

Arrangement [*dispositio*] The distribution of arguments in the proper order; the second of Cicero's five canons of rhetoric.

Bases In Quintilian's system, the specific issues that would have to be addressed in resolving a case.

Circa rem Circumstances *surrounding the act* in one *loci* system.

Confirmatio A section of a judicial speech offering evidences in support of claims advanced during the statement of the facts, or *narratio*.

Confutatio In a judicial speech, the refutation or section in which counterarguments are answered.

Contio Public gathering of citizens in the Forum to hear from political leaders.

Controversia A mock judicial speech presented by the advanced student of rhetoric.

Definite questions Issues concerning specific individuals, facts, places, and times.

Definition In Quintilian's system, a concern for categorizing an event.

Delectare To delight; one of Cicero's three functions or goals of rhetoric.

Delivery [*pronuntiatio*] The control of voice and body in a manner suitable to the dignity of the subject matter and the style; the fifth of Cicero's five canons of rhetoric.

Docere To teach; one of Cicero's three functions or goals of rhetoric.

Existence A question of what had occurred, a question of fact.

Exordium An introduction designed to dispose the audience to listen to the speech.

Expression [*elocutio*] Fitting proper language to arguments; the third of Cicero's five canons of rhetoric.

Facetiae Wit or humor.

Gens A clan, a group of influential families in Rome.

Hypsos Sublimity or great writing, the theme of Longinus' *On the Sublime*.

Imitatio Imitation or mimicry.

Indefinite questions In Quintilian's system of rhetoric, questions discussed without specific reference to persons, time, place, or other particular limitation.

In re What occurred in the act itself, a locus of argument in one *loci* system.

Invention [*inventio*] The discovery of arguments; the first of Cicero's five canons of rhetoric.

Jurist: In Rome, an attorney or master of the complex Roman legal code.

Ioci Jokes; discussed in Cicero's theory of humor in *De Oratore*.

Issues Hermagoras of Temnos' *topoi*, which included three classifications of judicial arguments. The three types include:

1. Conjectural issues, or a concern for matters of fact.
2. Legal issues, or a concern for the interpretation of a text or document.
3. Juridical issues, or a concern for the rightness or wrongness of an act.

Issues of definition Questions regarding by what name an act should be called.

Issues of fact Questions concerning such questions as "What occurred?" and "When did it occur?"

Issues of quality Questions concerning the severity of an act.

Loci Location systems that began as memory aids and later assisted the invention of arguments.

Memory [*Memoria*] The firm mental grasp of matter and words; the fourth of Cicero's five canons of rhetoric.

Movere To persuade or move an audience's emotions; one of Cicero's three functions or goals of rhetoric.

Narratio In a judicial speech, a statement of essential facts.

Perfectus orator Complete orator, a leader who embodied and articulated the society's values.

Peroratio The conclusion or final section of a judicial speech in which the orator reiterated the full strength of a case.

Post rem The events *following an act* in one *loci* system.

Pronuntiatio The control of voice and body in a manner suitable to the dignity of the subject matter and the style.

Quality In Quintilian's system of bases, a concern for the severity of the act, once defined or categorized.

Res Publica The Roman citizenry.

Sannio Clown or buffoon, a classification the orator must avoid in using humor.

Senatus Senate; Roman governing body. Literally, a council of elders.

Stasis System Method for discovering arguments by identifying points where clash or disagreement was likely to occur in a case or debate.

Suasoria An elementary practice speech for the younger student of rhetoric.

Topical systems [*topica*] Systems for discovering arguments.

NOTES

1   Joy Connolly, *The State of Speech: Rhetoric and Political Though in Ancient Rome* (Princeton, NJ: Princeton University Press, 2007), 1.

2   Manfred Fuhrmann, *Cicero and the Roman Republic*, trans. W. E. Yuill (Oxford: Blackwell, 1992), 18.

3   Erich Gruen, "Codes of Rome," *Times Literary Supplement* (July 3, 2009), 10.

4   The passage is cited by Connolly, 232.

5   James M. May, *Trials of Character: The Eloquence of Ciceronian Ethos* (Chapel Hill, NC: University of North Carolina Press, 1988), 6.

6   Connolly, 31.

7   Quoted in Connolly, 12.

8   Harold C. Gotoff, *Cicero's Caesarian Speeches: A Stylistic Commentary* (Chapel Hill, NC: University of North Carolina Press, 1993), x.

9   Michael Mooney, *Renaissance Thought and Its Sources* (New York: Columbia University Press, 1979), 36.

10 Graham Anderson, *Sage, Saint, and Sophist: Holy Men and Their Associates in the Early Roman Empire* (London: Routledge, 1994).

11 See: Ann Vasaly, *Representations: Images of the World in Ciceronian Oratory* (Berkeley: University of California Press, 1993).

12 George Maximilian Antony Grube, translator's introduction to Longinus, *On the Sublime* (Indianapolis, IN: Library of Liberal Arts, 1957), ix.

13 Calvin Troup, *Temporality, Eternity, and Wisdom: The Rhetoric of Augustine's Confessions* (Columbia, SC: University of South Carolina Press, 1999), 13.

14 Fuhrmann, 19.

15 Longinus, *On the Sublime*, trans. George Maximilian Antony Grube (Indianapolis, IN: Library of Liberal Arts, 1957), x.

16 Connolly, 3.

17 Christian Habicht, *Cicero the Politician* (Baltimore, MD: Johns Hopkins University Press, 1990), 1.

18 Habicht, 2. Habicht provides a brief and readable account of Cicero's political career. For a more detailed account of Cicero's life, see: David R. Shackleton-Bailey, *Cicero* (New York: Charles Scribner's Sons, 1971).

19 See: Christopher P. Craig, *Form as Argument in Cicero's Speeches: A Study of Dilemma*, American Classical Studies, #31 (Atlanta, GA: Scholars Press, 1993).

20 Gotoff, xii.

21 Mooney, 8.

22 On the *Rhetorica ad Herennium*, see: James J. Murphy, "The Age of Codification: Hermagoras and the Pseudo-Ciceronian *Rhetorica ad Herennium*," in *A Synoptic History of Classical Rhetoric*, ed. Richard Katula and James J. Murphy (Davis, CA: Hermagoras Press, 1983), 77–89. For a detailed discussion of *De Inventione* (and Cicero's other works on rhetoric), see: Donovan J. Ochs, "Cicero's Rhetorical Theory," in *A Synoptic History of Classical Rhetoric*, 90–150.

23 Craig, 14.

24 Brian Vickers, *In Defense of Rhetoric* (Oxford: Oxford University Press, 1988), 28.

25 Cicero, *De Inventione*, trans. H. M. Hubbell (Cambridge, MA: Loeb Classical Library, 1976).

26 M. L. Clark, *Rhetoric at Rome* (New York: Barnes and Noble, 1953), 53.

27 Habicht, 2.

28 *De Inventione*, I. 1.

29 *De Inventione*, I. iv. 5.

30 *De Inventione*, I. vi. 9.

31 Connolly, 129.

32 My translation. The passage is also cited by Connolly, 231.

33 *De Inventione*, I. vii. 9 (emphasis added).

34 *De Inventione*, I. 11–19.

35 *De Inventione*, I. viii. 11.

36 *De Inventione*, I. viii. 16.

37 Connolly, 73.

38 A good survey of the complex territory of loci and topical systems is Michael C. Leff's "The Topics of *Argumentative Invention in Latin Rhetorical Theory*," *Rhetorica* (1), 1983, 23–44. Reprinted in *Rethinking Rhetorical Theory, Criticism, and Pedagogy: The Living Art of Michael C. Leff* (East Lansing MI: Michigan State University Press, 2016), 65–86.

39 Donovan J. Ochs, "Cicero's *Topica:* A Process View of Invention," in *Explorations in Rhetoric: Essays in Honor of Douglas Ehninger*, ed. Ray E. McKerrow (Glenview, IL: Scott, Foresman, 1982), 117. Quoted in Kathleen E. Welch, *The Contemporary Reception of Classical Rhetoric: Appropriations of Ancient Discourse* (Hillsdale, NJ: Lawrence Erlbaum, 1990), 60.

40 Edward P. J. Corbett, "The *Topoi* Revisited," in *Rhetoric and Praxis: The Contribution of Classical Rhetoric to Practical Reasoning*, ed. Jean Deitz Moss (Washington, DC: Catholic University of America Press, 1986), 47. Quoted in Welch, 60–61.

41 Cicero discusses these *loci* in *De Inventione*, Book I. xxiv–xxviii.

42 *De Inventione*, I. xxiv. 34.

43 Leff, 27.

44 *De Inventione*, I. xxvi–xxviii.

45 Leff, 28.

46 Cicero, *De Oratore*, trans. E. W. Sutton and H. Rackham (Cambridge, MA: Harvard University Press, 1976), ix ff.

47 On the Aristotelian influences in *De Oratore*, see: May, 3 ff.

48 *De Oratore*, I. ii. 5.

49 *De Oratore*, I. xxviii. 128. Quoted in Mooney, 36.

50l *De Oratore*, I. vii. 30.

51 Connolly, 14.

52 *De Oratore*, III. xvi. 60–61.

53 *De Oratore*, I. iii. 12.

54 *De Oratore*, I. v. 18 (emphasis added).

55 *De Oratore*, II. xliv. 187 ff.

56 *De Oratore*, II. xliv. 188.

57 *De Oratore*, I. v. 20.

58 *De Oratore*, I. viii. 34.

59 *De Oratore*, II. lvi. 228.

60 *De Oratore*, I. vi. 229.

61 *De Oratore*, II. lviii–lix. 338–339.

62 *De Oratore*, lx.

63 *De Oratore*, II. lx. 247.

64 *De Oratore*, II. lxi. 250.

65 *De Oratore*, II. lxi. 251.

66 *De Oratore*, II. lxi. 252.

67 *De Oratore*, II. lxi. 253.

68 *De Oratore*, II. lxiv. 258–259.

69 *De Oratore*, II. lxiv. 260.

70 R. G. M. Nisbet, "The Speeches," in *Cicero*, ed. T. A. Dorey (New York: Basic Books, 1965), 56.

71 Quoted in Prentice A. Meador, Jr., "Quintilian and the *Institutio Oratoria*," in *A Synoptic History of Classical Rhetoric*, 151–176.

72 On Quintilian's teaching, see: James J. Murphy, "Roman Writing Instruction as Described by Quintilian," in *A Short History of Writing Instruction*, ed. James J. Murphy (Davis, CA: Hermagoras Press, 1990), 19–76.

73 Quintilian, *Institutio Oratoria*, 4 vols., trans. H. E. Butler (Cambridge, MA: Harvard University Press, 1959–1963), Loeb Classical Library. See also: James J. Murphy, Quintilian, *On the Early Education of the Citizen Orator*, trans. John S. Watson (Indianapolis, IN: Library of Liberal Arts, 1965).

74 Quintilian, *Institutes of Oratory*, I. 1.

75 A. Wallace-Hadrill, *Rome's Cultural Revolution* (Cambridge: Cambridge University Press, 2008), 47.

76 Quoted in Meador, 155.

77 Quintilian, *Institutes*, II. 11.

78 Leff, 33.

79 Quintilian, *Institutes*, v. 10, 125. Quoted in Leff, 34.

80 For a more detailed discussion of ancient systems for dividing speeches, see: Vickers, 67–72.

81 Longinus, *On the Sublime*, trans. George Maximilian Antony Grube (Indianapolis, IN: Library of Liberal Arts, 1957). All passages from *On the Sublime* are from this translation.

82 Vickers, 307.

83 Grube, x–xi.

84 Jane Tompkins, "The Reader in History: The Changing Shape of Literary Response," in *Reader Response Criticism*, ed. Jane P. Tompkins (Baltimore, MD: Johns Hopkins University Press, 1980), 203.

85 Tompkins, 203.

86 Longinus, 10.

87 Longinus, 10.

88 Longinus, 17. Translation of the love ode of Sappho by J. A. Symonds (1883).

89 Longinus, 29.

90 Longinus, 29.

91 Longinus, 31.

92 Vickers, 310. Longinus quote from *On the Sublime*, 29.2.

93 Grube, 325.

94 Grube, 325.

95 Grube, 325, 326.

96 Grube, 328.

97 Katula and Murphy, 206.

98 George Kennedy, *A Comparative Rhetoric* (New York: Oxford University Press, 1998), 211.

99 Thomas M. Conley, *Rhetoric in the European Tradition* (New York: Longman, 1994), 60.

Chapter 6

Rhetoric in Christian Europe

We've had enough exhortations to be silent. Cry out with a thousand tongues—I see the world is rotten because of silence.

—Catherine of Siena

EMPEROR Constantine legalized Christianity for Romans in 313 CE, suggesting that the religion had gained a considerable foothold in the late Roman Empire. When Rome fell in the fifth century, its successor, European Christendom, was already present within its boundaries. With the barbarian conquest of the Empire, rhetoric initially suffered a significant decline, as did many other disciplines. The tribes of northern and western Europe did not maintain Roman and Greek traditions, and often hastened the passing of classical learning by acts such as destroying libraries.

This is not to say, however, that the classical tradition in rhetoric disappeared entirely. As George Kennedy writes, "classical rhetoric did not die. A few private teachers of grammar and rhetoric could probably be found at most times in cities of Italy and Gaul."[1] As the cities of Italy started to re-establish a recognizable civic life, rhetoric again became an important study. As it had been in the past, rhetoric was central to both legislative and judicial functions in cities such as Venice and Bologna. The art also ascended to a position of great importance in a new theater of power—the Church.

RHETORIC, TENSION, AND FRAGMENTATION

By far the most important cultural phenomenon in the West in the period following the fall of the Roman Empire was the rise of Christianity. The Church came to control virtually every aspect of public and even of private life. The legislative assemblies and courts of law that had characterized Greek and Roman culture, and that had much to do with the development of the classical rhetorical tradition, were largely absent from the medieval European scene. Nevertheless, true to its nature as a public and practical art, rhetoric was adapted to the needs of Christian European society between the fifth and fifteenth centuries. Medieval Europe's adaptation of Greek and Roman rhetoric, however, reflects a severely constricted and fragmented appropriation of the rich classical tradition.

Medieval Europeans were more familiar with Roman than with Greek rhetoric, their familiarity extending to only a small portion of Roman theory at that. In the early middle ages, knowledge of ancient Greek was almost completely lost to Europeans, and much of Greek rhetoric was simply unknown. Barbarian conquests in what had been the Roman Empire brought about social fragmentation, and the destruction of ancient libraries such as the famous one in Alexandria ensured that many texts of classical antiquity were either damaged, unavailable, or completely lost. Quintilian's *Institutio Oratio*, the Roman master's massive multivolume treatment of rhetoric, survived only in incomplete sets of often mutilated copies. Around the tenth century, Spanish scholars began to retrieve, translate, and disseminate some classical texts. The process of reclaiming the classical tradition was, however, a slow one. Aristotle's *Rhetoric* "was not known to the Latin West before Hermannus Alemannus translated it into Latin (from Arabic) in 1256 and William of Moerbeke again translated it (from Greek) in about 1270."[2]

Still, there were exceptions to the rule of lost and damaged classical works on rhetoric in the Middle Ages. Two of these exceptions proved particularly important. Cicero's *De Inventione* and the anonymous *Rhetorica ad Herennium* were widely known and provided a foundation for the vast majority of medieval rhetorical treatises and practices.[3] Commentaries on *De Inventione* by medieval scholars such as Victorinus influenced how Cicero was interpreted and taught.[4] Kathleen Welch writes that "it is interesting to note that *On Invention* was the only text of Cicero available to most of the medieval period and therefore was frequently cited during this period." Thus, two rhetoric texts—*De Inventione* and *Rhetorica ad Herennium*—were "the major works of Latin antiquity for the Middle Ages."[5] The content of these treatises often was preserved and communicated in commentaries, works by later writers intended to explain the rhetorical systems being presented. Some of these commentaries date from as early as the fourth century CE.

Some educated people in the early Middle Ages viewed the classical tradition with suspicion; the Greek and Roman classics were, after all, the products of a pagan past. Rhetoric in particular was suspect, with its manipulation of audiences, its goal of persuasion, and its connection to a powerful empire that persecuted Christians. A "strong hostility . . . marked the attitudes of Christian scholars toward an art which they viewed as reminiscent of all the immorality of pagan Rome."[6] For this reason—and because of the limited availability of many classical sources—a small number of antiseptically technical Roman works formed the basis of much of the medieval rhetorical curriculum.

Acceptance of rhetoric came slowly to an emerging Christian Europe. Cicero's works and a few other sources benefited from the fifth-century Christian leader Augustine's endorsement in his influential work, *On Christian Doctrine*.[7] Nevertheless, because of the Church's discomfort with pagan antiquity, later medieval scholars often lifted useful components from classical works on rhetoric and shaped them to serve the purposes of a Christian culture. In this way the classical rhetorical tradition often was dismantled or fragmented.[8] Moreover, the oratorical art of rhetoric increasingly was identified with written style during this period. Rhetoric's traditional role of developing persuasive speeches through discovering and arranging arguments was gradually lost to view. Dialectic and logic took over these crucial inventional functions. In order to trace the dramatic changes in both rhetoric's scope and social functions in medieval Europe, it will be helpful to consider the place it occupied in a new educational curriculum.

RHETORIC IN THE EARLY MIDDLE AGES

Ciceronian rhetoric in the Middle Ages shaped education, civic administration, commerce, private life, and Church practice in a variety of ways. Several intellectual figures were important to the process of adapting and interpreting classical rhetoric within the context of Christian Europe.

St. Augustine

In the period between 450 and 1000 CE, rhetoric became important to the functioning of the Church. For guidance in their teaching, debates with opponents and evangelism, Church leaders looked to the rhetorical tradition. Cicero occupied the center of that tradition as it was known to them. His influence on medieval thought was great in other academic areas as well. Christian Habicht writes that Cicero "made Greek philosophy accessible" to scholars in the Middle Ages.[9] Cicero's comprehensive influence is evident from the very beginning of the period. As we shall see, however, even where Cicero's influence is great, innovation is still possible.

Augustine's World and Work

St. Augustine of Hippo (353–430 CE) was the greatest of the Early Church Fathers, a group of theologians writing between about 180 and 450 who did much to shape Christian theology. Augustine was born in northern Africa, then part of the waning Roman Empire. His mother, Monica, was a devout Christian. In 370 CE Augustine was sent to Carthage to study rhetoric—he was 17 years old. Excelling at the subject, he remained there as a teacher of rhetoric for a period of years (376–384) before relocating briefly to Rome.[10]

Augustine's world was marked by conflict between a dying Roman culture and an emerging Christian one, a conflict reflected in his own life. For nearly 10 years Augustine followed a secretive religious sect known as the Manichaeans, a pagan group he eventually repudiated. He also became a professor of rhetoric in the imperial city of Milan, a faculty position he later referred to as "a chair of lies."[11]

Augustine was both a well-known orator and a teacher of rhetoric. He taught rhetoric based on Cicero and influenced by the Second Sophistic. Augustine scholar Calvin Troup writes, "the Second Sophistic rewarded delivery, style and ornamentation with little or no attention to substance" and this approach to rhetoric "dominated the fourth-century Roman schools . . ." Troup affirms that for Augustine "rhetoric and the Second Sophistic were synonymous."[12]

While teaching rhetoric in Milan, and serving as imperial rhetor (384–386), Augustine became acquainted with the Christian leader and famed orator Ambrose (340–397). At first Augustine was more interested in Ambrose's rhetorical skill than in his theology, but this soon changed. Through a series of sermons and discussions, Ambrose contributed to Augustine's decision to convert to Christianity. Ambrose baptized Augustine in 387.[13] Ordained a priest in 391, Augustine was later elevated to the office of Bishop of Hippo, a major port city in Roman North Africa.

Over the three decades that he served as bishop, Augustine spent much of his time teaching Christian doctrine to his parishioners and writing against various heretical groups. In 397 he published *Confessions*, a work describing his early life and his conversion to Christianity. The book also contains a scathing attack on the type of rhetoric Augustine had at one time taught. Between 413 and 426, he wrote and published his great *City of God*, which views the Church as a new order replacing the old Roman Empire. The end of Augustine's life marks the end of the Roman Empire in the West, for the Vandals under Genseric laid siege to Hippo in 430, and Augustine died 3 months into the siege.

Augustine's Rhetorical Theory

Augustine's early education was conducted on a classical Roman model, which meant that the core of his curriculum was rhetoric. Like many young men of the day, Augustine saw rhetoric as a path to wealth and fame. Rhetoric would allow him to "succeed in this world and excel in those arts of speech which would serve to bring honor among men and to gain deceitful riches."[14]

Prior to his conversion, Augustine lived, believed, and taught much like a Sophist. Moreover, when he later attacked rhetoric, as he does at points in his *Confessions*, it is a sophistical model of rhetoric he has in mind. "Augustine never abandons rhetoric qua rhetoric in practice," writes Troup, "but rejects only the abuses of the Second Sophistic."[15] Augustine came to accept much in the rhetorical tradition as useful in the Christian church and in Christian society generally.

As a Christian intellectual, Augustine wrestled with the potential uses of Roman rhetoric in the Church.[16] Like Plato in *Phaedrus*, Augustine sought a true art of rhetoric that could aid the pursuit of truth, in his case the truth of the Christian scriptures. Augustine identified two tasks for the Christian teacher: to discover and then to teach the contents of scripture.[17] His voluminous apologetic writings suggest that he also recognized a third task—to defend scriptural truth when it was attacked. Rhetoric, in spite of its pagan origins and frequent misuse, could assist the Christian teacher in fulfilling each of these obligations. But the classical theory of rhetoric had to be adapted to a new Christian understanding of truth.

The Preacher's Dilemma: Expressing the Inexpressible

A perfect God as the source of transcendent truth posed a serious problem for the Christian rhetorician. Language, the medium of rhetoric, is a finite system of symbols, while God is infinite and thus beyond adequate description by means of finite signs.

However, God commands that the preacher must speak of Him. Thus, Augustine faced a dilemma: a rhetoric of God is both impossible and unavoidable. He sought to adapt the resources of the classical rhetoric he had once taught in Roman schools to the Christian purpose of creating a rhetoric capable of expressing eternal truth about an infinite God.

The rhetorical theory Augustine developed in response to his dilemma is at several points Platonic. Augustine held that in order to contemplate God, the mind should be cleansed, and part of this process of preparing the mind for divine thoughts is rhetorical. The preacher corrects through good preaching the errors that have corrupted the mind. This is reminiscent of Plato's conception of "true rhetoric" as a kind of medicine for sick souls that works by refuting error.

But rhetoric also guides the preacher in preparing truthful messages for maintaining the health of souls now put into a receptive attitude. Augustine's Christian rhetoric, then, assisted the work of the preacher by curing the ailments of the human soul through the refutation of error, and by making possible the soul's health through communicating divine truth. Augustine's rhetoric, again, strikes one as Platonic in its orientation toward both correcting error and teaching truth.

Rhetoric assists the preacher to discover divine truth in the scriptures, and to teach this truth to the congregation. But rhetoric is also an aid to the clear, forceful, and stylistically appealing presentation of one's message. Augustine also endorsed the Ciceronian ends of rhetoric—to teach, to delight, and to move—though he gives each goal a Christian significance. The preacher must know his subject matter in order to teach it well. He must also know how to reach his congregation's emotions (to delight) and to persuade them to Christian living (to move).

The Teacher's Dilemma: Roman Rhetoric in Christian Schools?

We have considered the dilemma Augustine faced as a preacher—discovering in finite rhetoric a means of communicating truth about an infinite God. But Augustine faced a second dilemma as a Christian educator. The art of rhetoric was indispensable to his educational work as a Bishop, and yet the rhetorical tradition was often in conflict with Christian principles. Powerful and worldly Romans such as Cicero developed the art, and the Christians of Augustine's day harbored negative associations with pagan Rome. Rhetoric was also an art aimed at a suspicious goal, persuasion, often by means of verbal trickery.

Thus, rhetoric posed Augustine a second dilemma: It was useful, even vital to confuting the heretics and teaching his own congregation, but it was also suspect and potentially dangerous. Augustine resolved his dilemma by reasoning that rhetoric should not be at the disposal only of the unbelieving. Moreover, the Bible itself was a model of eloquence for the Christian.[18] He treats these problems in his most important work on rhetoric, *De Doctrina Christiana*.

De Doctrina Christiana

Augustine's major work on rhetoric is his guide to preaching, *De Doctrina Christiana* (*On Christian Doctrine*), a work with strong connections to Cicero's *De Oratore* and

Orator. W. R. Johnson has referred to the book as "not merely the most influential but perhaps the most precious book in the tradition of humanistic rhetoric."[19] James J. Murphy calls *De Doctrina*, "one of the most significant works of the early middle ages."[20] Murphy's assessment is based on Augustine's ability to redeem rhetoric for the emerging Christian culture. Murphy explains:

> The *De Doctrina* begins by pointing out that the means of finding material for understanding Scripture (the *modus inveniendi*) is different from the means of expressing the ideas found (the *modus proferendi*). Augustine urged the Church to study the human arts of discourse—in particular, rhetoric—either through formal schooling or through study of great models.[21]

Augustine urged the Church to use what was useful in the classical rhetorical treatises. Rhetorical education must not be given over to learning the elaborate topical and ornamental systems so characteristic of Roman rhetoric. Rather, education in Augustine's view should be centered on what John O. Ward has called "the inculcation of appropriate thought and content."[22]

Signs

De Doctrina sets out a sophisticated theory of the relationship between signs and the things they represent. In Book II, Augustine divides the world into two broad categories: things, and signs pointing to things. "A sign is a thing which causes us to think of something beyond the impression the thing makes upon the senses." Words are signs, but Augustine also held that the world of physical objects was a system of signs pointing to God. Human beings also are a kind of sign in that they are created in the image of God. The created order, then, is to be used to return us to God, not taken as an end in itself.

This distinction between the sign and the thing signified helps the Christian preacher discern two different kinds of meanings in objects encountered in scripture. For example, a rock and a tree in a biblical story are physical objects, signified by the words *rock* and *tree*. However, the rock or the tree may also themselves be signs with their own spiritual meaning. The rock may refer to Christ, as St. Paul suggested that a rock in one Mosaic story did. The tree may represent everlasting life.

Augustine and Rhetorical Education

Augustine's commitment to education is everywhere evident in his treatments of rhetoric. Christians needed training in reading the Bible, and in defending it, if the Christian gospel was to be preserved and propagated. Johnson finds the purpose of *De Doctrina* to have been largely educational. "The *De Doctrina* was written for clergy and highly educated members of the laity," writes Johnson, "to help them in their efforts to read the Bible and to give them advice about how to go about sharing what they had learned with fellow Christians who were less educated than themselves."[23] Central to Augustine's approach to education was his own training in rhetoric.

Augustine posed his readers this question: "For since by means of the art of rhetoric both truth and falsehood are urged, who would dare to say that truth should stand in the person of its defenders unarmed against lying?"[24] The implied answer to this question is, of course, that truth needs its rhetorically trained defenders. The happiness of all people can be achieved if all can be brought to understand and accept the truth of the gospel, and the truth of the gospel can be more effectively propagated when Christians understand the principles of rhetoric.[25] In coming to this resolution, Augustine set a trajectory for rhetoric in medieval Europe.

Martianus Capella

Martianus Capella was one of the late Roman rhetoricians responsible for creating the impression among people living in the fifth and sixth centuries CE that the rhetorical tradition was incompatible with Christianity. A lawyer with a strong interest in mysticism and little regard for religion, Capella lived in the North African city of Carthage around the same time that Augustine was presiding over his parish not far away. Carthage at this time was home to "the best school of rhetoric in all of Roman North Africa."[26]

The Marriage of Philology and Mercury

Capella is best known for a single massive work that explored the seven liberal arts. The impact of *The Marriage of Philology and Mercury* (*De Nuptiis Philologiae et Mercurii*) (429), which included his *Book of Rhetoric*, was enormous. One scholar has called Capella's work, "the most successful textbook ever written"; it certainly was one of the most widely used books in medieval schools.[27]

In his strange, vast, and thoroughly pagan book, Capella imagines a wedding in which the god Mercury gives his bride a gift of the seven liberal arts constituting the core of the medieval curriculum. These seven are grammar, dialectic, rhetoric, geometry, arithmetic, astronomy, and harmonics.[28] The liberal arts were divided among the four major or advanced studies of arithmetic, geometry, astronomy, and harmonics called the *quadrivium* (four roads); and the three fundamental studies of grammar, rhetoric, and logic, called the *trivium* (three roads). Each art is personified as a character in a complex allegorical story.

Capella's approach was widely used, and grammar, rhetoric, and logic became important foundational studies for anyone preparing for public service or for service in the Church. Grammar involved the study of significant literary sources such as Homer, as well as the studies of composition, style in writing, and proper syntax. Composition and literary criticism might be the closest parallels in the modern curriculum. Logic presented the rules governing deduction. But it was rhetoric that dominated the curriculum in schools at the time that Capella wrote, and the study of rhetoric was largely Ciceronian in conception.

Rhetoric as Woman

Capella introduced another innovation to the history of rhetoric—he represented rhetoric as a heavily armed woman, a tradition that continued throughout the Middle Ages. Why did this particular metaphor take hold?

Medievalist Joan Ferrante argues that the association between women (or Woman) and the medieval personification of "Rhetoric" is explained by the natural generative capabilities of women's bodies: women, the conceivers and nurturers of human beings, are the figures that enrich human speech, producing its significatory abundance of figures and tropes.[29]

But, rhetoric is also portrayed in medieval art as armored and carrying a sword, perhaps suggesting that the nurturer is also a warrior. Rhetoric had always wielded a two-edged sword, building consensus and destroying opponents.

Boethius

Anicius Manlius Severinus Boethius (475–524 CE) was a late Roman statesman and philosopher who, around 500, became an important figure in the court of the Gothic king Theodoric. Boethius is best known for his *The Consolation of Philosophy*, a work penned while in prison for daring to challenge Theodoric's oppressive tendencies.

Devoted to advancing Greek culture and language, Boethius translated many works of Aristotle from Greek to Latin. He may have been the last of the Roman philosophers to understand Greek. Just as he served as a bridge between Greek and the late Roman culture, he was also a transitional figure in the movement from Roman to Christian culture in Europe. Boethius is said to have begun "an eclecticism that finds a place for all of the great authors of antiquity, from Plato and Aristotle down to Cicero."[30] Boethius was executed on Theodoric's orders in 524.

Master of a wide range of subjects, including mathematics, philosophy, dialectic, and rhetoric, Boethius presented a modified Roman topical system in his work *De Topicis Differentiis* (*On the Different Topics*).[31] He authored a second book dedicated to reviving the Ciceronian topical systems. One medieval scholar has noted that Boethius' book was "the only text which seems to have enjoyed a currency approaching, but not equaling, the *ad Herennium* and *De Inventione*" in schools of the Middle Ages.[32] Some scholars credit Boethius with preserving the study of Greek and Roman topical systems. His translations of Aristotle's books on logic provided Europe with its only works by Aristotle for a period of 500 years.

Boethius' treatment of the topics of argument is heavily influenced by Cicero's *De Inventione* and *Topica*, where Cicero is "a teacher of rules and precepts" rather than the reflective master of the art we find in the later *De Oratore*.[33] Thus, Boethius' work is itself sometimes criticized as excessively prescriptive, system-bound, and impractical.

In Boethius, rhetoric looks like the technical study known in classical times as dialectic. Nevertheless, as we have noted, *De Topicis Differentiis* remained one of the most popular medieval rhetoric manuals. The dry and systematic treatment rhetoric receives at Boethius' hands may reflect the oppressive circumstances under which the book was written. Rhetoric's role under any tyrannical or authoritarian government is always severely circumscribed and limited, rendering rhetoric the technical study of argument, the formal rules of official communication, or a form of entertainment.

RHETORIC AND MEDIEVAL EDUCATION

As educational practices developed over the long course of the Middle Ages, an intellectual movement known as Scholasticism became dominant in parts of Europe. Scholasticism was a closed and authoritarian approach to education centered on highly structured disputation over a fixed body of premises derived largely from the venerated writings of Aristotle and to a lesser extent, Plato. Scholasticism also involved efforts to reconcile Christian teaching with the thought of ancient philosophers. The highest achievement of the Scholastic tradition is Thomas Aquinas' *Summa Theologica*, an extended effort to synthesize Aristotelian thought and Christian doctrine.

Disputatio and Sententiae

Because complete ancient works were not available for much of the Middle Ages, individual sentences and longer fragments, often taken out of context, were employed to prove a point in a scholastic debate. These isolated statements from Aristotle and a few other sources were called *sententiae*. Some authors collected large numbers of *sententiae* into anthologies for educational and disputational purposes. Scholastic disputes—understood as a method of getting at the meaning of a text—centered on debatable points or *quaestiones* suggested by one or more *sententiae*. Education by *disputatio*–debating general topics drawn from authoritative statements–reveals one way in which rhetorical and dialectical practices made their way into the Middle Ages.

As rigid as it was, the scholastic method did afford certain advantages for students trained under it. As Charles G. Nauert writes, "its great virtue was that it probed each issue in an orderly and rational way, collecting the various possible opinions and making a determination of what seemed to be the correct opinion."[34] Unfortunately for students trained by the use of *sententiae*, however, the actual meaning of a statement in its original context often was lost because sentences had been separated from the texts in which they originally appeared. The classical authors disappeared in this process, leaving a fragment of a thought to represent a whole book, theory, or body of work. As Nauert notes, Scholasticism "simplified and distorted the opinions of authorities by reducing each author's opinion to a single statement, totally divorced from its original context."[35]

Women and Education

The picture of medieval women's opportunities for education and expression is changing as light is shed on a wider range of women's literary activities in the period. Indeed, historian Albrecht Classen writes, "It is of prime importance to acknowledge the fact that women since the early Middle Ages possessed a high degree of learnedness and that they knew fairly well how to contribute to the literary production of their age." In addition to convent education, Shirley Kersey writes that women might receive education in "castle schools, court schools, cathedral schools, college church schools, village schools, apprenticeships and universities." Women might also be educated by "parents, other relatives, tutors, governesses and parish priests."[36]

Literacy was actively promoted in many regions, and many women learned to read Latin and French. Between the ninth and twelfth centuries it is likely that more European women than men were literate. This is because large numbers of men and boys were called into military service or sent abroad on crusades, often interrupting their education. Women also learned practical arts, particularly medicine, for the same reason—wounded soldiers needed medical care.

The number of books being produced was also increasing, and these books addressed a wide range of issues. New literary genres such as the published letter and the adventure story became popular, often because of a demand on the part of literate women. Capella's seven liberal arts were widely taught, which meant that a growing number of women had exposure to rhetoric. A class of highly educated nuns and abbesses emerged who "competed successfully with men in classical scholarship," and some of whom "wrote treatises on logic and rhetoric."[37] Universities appeared and grew at a surprising rate.

Upper class women in particular gained access to education, to writing opportunities, and to economic resources. Classen notes,

> We have sufficient historical evidence to argue that noble and bourgeois women at least since the twelfth and thirteenth centuries were primarily in charge of the household and often, particularly in the cities, held important positions within local industry. Moreover, and quite indisputably, women in cloisters and convents enjoyed a high reputation for their intellectual skills and literary abilities.[38]

Access to rhetorical education, and the adaptability of rhetorical forms to changing social demands and contexts, assisted the entrance of women into the literary world during a period often thought of as closed and authoritarian. Highly regarded female scholars of the Middle Ages include the German nun Radegund (520–587), the English abbess Hilda of Whitby (614–680), the German dramatist Hrotsvitha (935–1002), her country-woman the polymathic genius Hildegarde of Bingen (1098–1179), the French writer and lecturer Heloise (1090–1174), and the famed French poet Mari de France (1160–1215).

Rhetorical Continuity

According to Marjory Curry Woods, rhetoric as a component in the medieval curriculum exhibited remarkable consistency over a long period. "For example," she writes, "the techniques of teaching grammar and rhetoric that John of Salisbury, writing in about 1150, describes in his eulogy of his master, Bernard of Chartres, were used consistently throughout the thirteenth, fourteenth, and fifteenth centuries." Some rhetorical texts formed the basis of educational approaches for virtually the entire medieval period. In fact, rhetoric's duration in this regard is astonishing. Woods writes, "the books that formed the basis of rhetorical education in composition at the beginning of the Middle Ages continued to be taught more than a thousand years later."[39]

Such remarkable continuity points up both the significance of rhetorical training to medieval education and the heavy cultural reliance on portions of the classical tradition of rhetoric. As the medieval period progressed in Europe, the rhetorical tradition developed into three distinct but related arts, each closely tied to a distinct cultural setting.

RHETORICAL ARTS IN THE HIGH MIDDLE AGES

Between 1100 and 1300, the high-water mark for medieval European rhetoric, the art came to be codified in manuals on preaching, letter writing, and poetry.[40] Each art had particular uses in a complex social setting, each reflected its classical heritage in a different way, and each appealed to a different medieval audience.

John O. Ward writes regarding the adaptability of rhetoric and the practical orientation of medieval theorists, teachers, and practitioners: "[as] each generation of medieval students of rhetoric succeeded another, our sources pinpoint ways in which contemporaries kept their teaching and study of the classical rhetorical corpus close to the needs of their day."[41] It is interesting to note, however, that the medieval rhetorical writers produced little or no original theory of speech-making outside of church settings. As James J. Murphy has written, "the middle ages did not produce any major original works on secular speaking" because "the political climate which had encouraged such writing in ancient Greece and Rome simply did not exist in medieval Europe."[42] We will look first at the rhetorical art that most nearly approximates the traditional conception of rhetoric as oratory, and then at the adaptation of rhetoric to instruction in writing.

The Art of Preaching

Rhetoric was appropriated to the needs of a vast Church hierarchy that developed its own peculiar forms of government, discourse, education, and art. The art most easily associated with the purposes of the church was preaching (*ars praedicandi*). From the late eleventh century through the fifteenth century, preaching was an important and popular art in Europe. Orders of preachers, such as the Dominicans and Franciscans, emerged in the Church.[43] Numerous preaching manuals were authored during the Christian Middle Ages, particularly during the thirteenth century.[44]

Themes, Sermons, and Moral Persuasion

Typical of the preaching manuals of the late Middle Ages is Robert of Basevorn's *Forma Praedicandi* (*The Form of Preaching*).[45] The preaching instruction one received from such manuals emphasized expanding on the meanings of brief biblical texts, or themes, toward the goal of improving the moral conduct and religious understanding of one's audience. It was recognized that many members of the preacher's audience would be illiterate and generally unfamiliar with the contents of scripture. Thus, thematic preaching emphasized the selection of appropriate and accessible texts, as well as careful audience adaptation.[46] James J. Murphy, a leading expert on medieval rhetoric, suggests that treatments of thematic preaching began making appearances in European university centers such as Paris around 1230. As an approach to preaching, it became "extremely popular" and "extremely influential."[47]

*Rhetoric in
Christian
Europe*

Structure and Content

In *The Form of Preaching*, Robert complains that most preaching is done with no understanding of the structure of a sermon. Such knowledge is, however, essential to the Church. "Since preaching and teaching are necessary for the Church of God," he writes, "that science which presents the form of preaching artistically is equally necessary, or even more so."[48] Just as Aristotle set about to present an art or *techne* of rhetoric, so Robert intended to provide his readers with an art of preaching—a systematic account of the rationale for preaching as well as instruction in preparing a persuasive sermon "Preaching," he writes, "is the persuasion of many, within a moderate length of time, to meritorious conduct."[49] Preaching was not principally theological investigation; it was, rather, moral persuasion. And, like Cicero, Robert holds out that a preacher ought to be a knowledgeable person, one who unites wisdom and eloquence. A preacher's "competent knowledge" included "explicit knowledge of the Articles of Faith, the Ten Commandments, and the distinction between sin and non-sin."[50]

Robert discusses the method of preaching by developing themes. Themes ought to "contain not more than three statements or convertible to three." He is insistent on this point, devoting an entire chapter to the discussion of divisibility by three. "No matter how many statements there may be, as long as I can divide them into three, I have a sufficient proposition."[51] This notion that sermons ought to be divisible into three sections persists in preaching to this day.

Christ as Model of Audience-Centered Preaching

In his search for models of good preaching, Robert turns to Christ himself. "It is not easy to understand all the methods which Christ used in preaching," Robert writes. "He, as I believe, included all praiseworthy methods in His own, as the fount and origin of good."

Robert's list of preaching methods drawn from Christ's example is audience centered, and includes promises, threats, examples, and reason.[52] The audience governs the selection of the appropriate preaching method. For example, "good and agreeable" audiences are drawn to "sweet and beautiful promises," such as the promise of heaven. "Stubborn" listeners require the use of threats, such as the threat of divine judgment. Examples are stories or parables, which Robert notes that Christ used extensively. Moreover, the Apostle Paul is said to have employed "reason with great success" when addressing his audiences.[53]

Robert devotes a lengthy section to "Winning-over the Audience," in which he makes practical suggestions such as "to place at the beginning something subtle and interesting, [such] as some authentic marvel which can be fittingly drawn in for the purpose of the theme." If this doesn't work to get the attention of the audience, the preacher can always "frighten them by some terrifying tale or example."[54] Such adaptive decisions assisted the preacher's Ciceronian goals of illuminating the passage under consideration, enlightening the audience's understanding, and moving them to more virtuous actions.

The Art of Letter Writing

Interest in letter writing was extensive during the later Middle Ages, particularly in Italy. Lawyers, public officials, secretaries, and notaries all had to understand the intricacies of the formal letter, which often doubled as an official document. The number of published *dictamen* or letter-writing treatises is quite remarkable. Paul Kristeller gives us some idea of the extraordinary interest the practice had generated:

> The body of literature that belongs to *dictamen* and its related enterprises . . . exceeds by far in bulk anything comparable that has been preserved from classical antiquity, and anything else remotely rhetorical, such as the rhetorical commentaries on Cicero, produced in the Middle Ages.[55]

The hierarchical nature of ecclesiastical Europe, and the fragmented nature of governments, meant that correspondence among various Church and government officials came to be highly formalized—letter writers had to negotiate a wide and bewildering range of official relationships. Letters thus became important to civic, commercial, and clerical life. "Official letters," write Bizzell and Herzberg, "were often the only record of laws or commercial transactions and hence had legal standing."[56] Teachers and practitioners of *dictamen*—rhetoricians of the day—were referred to as *dictatores* (*dictare*: to dictate), a term that also carried a more general connotation of any person skilled in rhetoric.

Why Letters?

Why such interest in letter writing as a specifically *rhetorical* art? Why not just write a letter, without consideration of predetermined forms hearkening back to Rome? Nadia Margolis provides some insight when she writes, "The Latin *Artes dictandi* or *dictaminis* ("Arts of Composition") were established as a distinctly separate branch of rhetoric during the tenth century. The goal was to standardize and ennoble letter writing as a genre . . ." She adds that letter writing developed to a high level of rhetorical sophistication due to "its immediate usefulness to secular and ecclesiastical officialdom, since such letters served as the most efficient and forceful verbal tools in government and policy-making . . ."[57] Thus, the close connection between rhetoric—here encountered as instructions in composing a letter—and civic life is once again evident as it had been in Greece and Rome.

Among the most popular letter-writing manuals was one by Guido Faba. Here is a statement from Faba himself on why letter writing emerged as an important art:

> The epistle was invented for two reasons. The first was so that secrets of friends might be concealed through it, whence it is named *epistolo*, that is, "I conceal." The second reason was so that it might express better than a messenger what is sent. For a messenger cannot remember everything; for to retain a memory of everything and not to err at all in anything is a quality of divinity rather than of humanity.[58]

So, Faba identifies secrecy and clarity as two specific reasons for interest in letters.

Speaking Letters

We might assume that secrecy was guaranteed because a letter's recipient would read the letter alone and silently. Often, however, this was not the case. The usual practice was for the messenger—someone other than the author—to read the letter aloud to the recipient, often in the presence of several listeners or trusted assistants. Carol Poster and Richard Utz write,

> [T]ypically, the letter would have been read in public, by the bearer if he were literate, or by some other mediator. And in many cases the bearer was expected to elaborate on the letter's contents, to respond to questions about them, or to supplement them with confidential information delivered (orally) in private.[59]

Perhaps contrary to our contemporary practices, the official dictating a letter only suggested the letter's content; it was the rhetorically trained secretary who formed the letter itself into a persuasive document. Martin Camargo explains the process:

> The "author" would first summarize what the letter should say; then the secretary or notary would reshape this oral précis so that the desired message was arranged in the standard sequence of clearly articulated parts, the formulae of greeting and farewell were those befitting the rank and station of sender and recipient, and the prose consisted of artfully constructed periodic sentences, each clause of which ended in one of the rhythmical patterns of the *cursus* [pleasing cadence].[60]

At the other end of the process, the letter's recipient was, as noted, less a reader than a listener. The letter's appeal to the ear—its rhythm and sound—was even more important than was its clarity. Camargo comments, "While the modern letter, especially the personal letter, is typically informal, even conversational in tone, its medieval counterpart is among the most formalized, least spontaneous types of discourse."[61] Thus, what appeared as a written document was translated quickly into an oral communication that drew heavily on an earlier oratorical tradition. Clearly, if secrecy was to be preserved in such a setting, one would have to exercise care about who would be present when a letter was read.

Manuals

Letter-writing manuals reached their peak of popularity around the year 1100. Letters could be composed in a plain style or written almost as poetry, and the extremely popular manuals told interested readers how to achieve such effects. Italian rhetoricians in particular developed letter writing to a high art in the eleventh through the thirteenth centuries. Murphy notes that "a Benedictine monk, Alberic, is generally credited with the first systematic application of Ciceronian rhetoric to the matter of letter writing, which he wrote at the monastery of Monte Casino in central Italy in the year 1087."[62] Thousands of such treatises on *dictamen* would follow in the next two centuries.

Over time, the central focus of letter writing became recording and transmitting legal documents. Nicholas Mann writes that "the study of what in classical times had been the art of public speaking had by the twelfth century become the *ars dictaminis*, the art of letter writing; the *dictatores*, applied their knowledge to the needs of their patrons and the legal profession."[63] Rhetoric again demonstrated its adaptability and utility, now being shaped into a method for communicating legal agreements, commercial contracts, and personal requests by letter.

The Italian city of Bologna became the center for the study of letter writing. Charles Faulhaber writes that Bolognese manuals reached their highest development under "three masters, Boncompagno of Signa (c. 1165–c. 1235), Bene of Florence (fl. 1220), and most especially Guido Faba (c. 1190–c. 1243), whose *Summa Dictaminis* was published around 1228."[64] Faba wrote eight major books, "all of them dealing with *dictamen*," a fact that indicates the importance accorded to the art.[65] For Faba, a professor of *dictamen* in Bologna, letter writing "was an eminently *practical* discipline."[66] Thus, his *Summa Dictaminis* is "a practical handbook with a limited number of short and succinct precepts."[67] Some of Faba's manuals were available in vernacular languages, which increased their readership and influence.

Many letter-writing manuals conveyed what amounted to various form letters to be employed as persons of different social ranks communicated with one another on a variety of clerical, legal, personal, and business matters. As the structure of such letters will reveal, their purpose was usually to make a request.

From Oral to Written Expression

The rise of letter writing reveals European culture "shifting toward the primacy of the written text" over the orally presented speech.[68] The change from oral to written rhetoric takes place in part because, as Renato Barilli points out, "in the late Middle Ages . . . civic life offers little opportunity for public debate." [69]

This significant cultural shift toward the written text intensified with the advent of Gutenberg's printing press in the middle of the fifteenth century. Corresponding to this trend toward written expression, rhetoric's center begins to shift from matters of argument to matters of arrangement and style. This change was encouraged by the entry into Europe of Aristotle's works on logic in the thirteenth century, which fueled interest in oral dialectical disputation. But argumentation was treated as a concern of logic rather than rhetoric, and rhetoricians often were left to codify components of written style. Moreover, as noted above, even letter writing maintained a component of the public speech through the practice of reading letters aloud.

Letter-Writing Skill

Writing a letter may seem to us a simple albeit, in a world of texting and e-mail, antiquated task. However, in the Middle Ages the skills involved in letter writing required substantial training. One authority notes that

> The ability to write—that is, to produce a physical text by means of pen, ink, and parchment or paper (not to mention other skills, such as those involved in preparing the completed letter for sending)—was for the most part restricted to trained professionals.[70]

These were the notaries, the rhetoricians of the medieval world.

The Parts of a Letter

According to the letter-writing handbooks, a letter should be divided into five parts. Classicist George Kennedy explains that the "standard five-part epistolary structure" is reminiscent of typical Roman divisions of a judicial speech:

> The *salutatio*, or greeting; the *captatio benevoluntatiae*, or exordium, which secured the goodwill of the recipient; the *narratio* [the body of the letter setting out the details of the problem to be addressed]; the *petitio*, or specific request, demand, or announcement; and a relatively simple *conclusio*.[71]

The anonymous writer of our treatise also considers other parts of a letter in detail. For instance, securing goodwill—the role of the *captatio benevoluntatiae*—can be achieved in a variety of ways: "Goodwill will be secured by the person sending the letter if he mentions humbly something about his achievements or his duties or his motives."[72]

Other details of letter writing are also considered, such as how to shorten an overlong letter. But, among all these matters, the *salutatio* received a disproportionate amount of attention, as establishing the correct relationship between yourself and the person to whom you were writing. The *salutatio* was crucial to gaining a hearing, and if executed improperly, a letter might be ignored or, worse yet, insult its recipient.

The All-Important Salutation

Typical of the letter-writing manuals is that by an anonymous Bolognese author, entitled *The Principles of Letter Writing*. The author writes that a letter's salutation is "an expression of greeting conveying a friendly sentiment not inconsistent with the social rank of the persons involved."[73] Whereas this may be obvious, how to write a proper salutation apparently is not. Titles such as deacon or bishop or clerk should always be employed. The respective ranks of the writer and the recipient must also be considered, as well as the subject of the letter. The author includes the following as a model of a salutation from the pope:

> Bishop Innocentius, servant of the servants of God (*servus servorum dei*) in his beloved son Christ, to N—, august emperor of the Romans, sends greetings and papal blessings.[74]

Other formal salutations included those of "prelates to their subordinates," "of close friends and associates," and "of subjects to their secular Lords."[75] Close friends, for instance, might open letters according to the formula, "To N—, the closest of friends," or "the most beloved of comrades," or "the dearest of favorites," or

> Guido, already bound by a sincere bond of affection, N—, follower of the profession of logician, wishes to be bound further to him by a mutual chain of affection and to be disturbed by no hostility, wishes him to live forever and to abound in all good

things, to live always honorably and never to cease in his affection, to possess always wisely a happy life, and to hold always more firmly to the rightful ways.[76]

Such an elaborate greeting certainly makes the modern, "Dear Guido," sound a little shallow.

The possible salutations are numerous, and the relationships covered are intriguingly various. For example, the author includes these salutations from a "delinquent son" to his parents:

> To Peter and Mary his parents, N—, once their son but now deprived of filial affection, once dear to them but now without cause become worthless, does whatever he can though he seems to be able to do nothing.[77]

Though florid and formal, a proper salutation established your relationship to the person receiving your letter. Such writing certainly opened the door into the realm of important ecclesiastical, civic, and business concerns.

Letter Writing and Civic Life

Brian Vickers writes that the letter-writing manuals contained "the most elaborate development of techniques for the manipulation of words in human history."[78] He notes by way of example that "of Guido Faba's eight books, four are simply collections of hundreds of *exordia*," or methods of securing a reader's goodwill. Such extraordinarily elaborate treatments were intended to cover every possible purpose and "every possible combination of rank between sender and receiver, in a highly structured society."[79]

Letter writing provided a framework for pursuing the complex social relationships and business arrangements that characterized a hierarchically organized world dominated by the Church and witnessing the rise of a commercial class. In such a setting letters facilitated social interaction and helped to establish and record agreements.

Formal letters conveyed other benefits as well. A carefully written letter brought a measure of grace and decorum to the often harsh and difficult lives of people living in Europe at this time. In addition, letter writing, through its close connection with rhetoric, allowed a link to classical antiquity. Finally, the *ars dictaminis* placed rhetoric at the center of civic life, where it had often been before. As Faulhaber writes, letter writing "formed an indispensable step in the training of all those who made their living running the administrative machinery of church and state." This also meant that "practitioners of *dictamen* were much in demand, and their positions were lucrative."[80] As in the world of classical antiquity, the rhetorically trained individual proved a valuable asset to many.

Women and Letter Writing

Letter writing made participation in literary life a possibility for an increasing number of women. Fewer restrictions were placed on this form of expression than on book authorship or preaching, and it did not require knowledge of classical languages. As already noted, in some important ways males faced a more limited educational outlook than did women in the late Middle Ages. Young men were often conscripted and sent to fight in the numerous wars that marked the era. Moreover, only the oldest sons of nobility were taught to read, and then allowed to read only certain subjects and works. Classen notes that "Women, by contrast, received in general and much less selectively, a more rounded education and had more leisure time to practice reading and writing skills."[81]

Regardless, male writing style dominated even in a era of rising educational opportunities for women. Malcolm Richardson has explored the ways in which a rhetorical form can actually impose gender-related restrictions on an author. In his study of women responsible for small family businesses, Richardson notes that "the rhetoric of medieval business writers was, at the base, the same as that used by all other writers of nonliterary prose: the *dictamen*, or that part of medieval rhetoric that governed letter writing." And, he notes that the rhetorical form of letter writing "was universally accepted for public and private correspondence."[82]

Richardson writes that the "daily lives" of even relatively prosperous people of the Middle Ages "plainly had more to do with buying and selling and dealing with lawyers than with tournaments and troubadours." And, because women often had responsibility for managing a family's business affairs, they were necessarily involved in practicing the art of letter writing.[83]

The Persistence of a Masculine Style

Richardson also notes that, due to a variety of factors peculiar to the age, the letter-writing style of males and females does not vary in any noticeable way. "The great unasked question . . . must be this: 'Does the writing of medieval women in commerce differ from that of men'? On the limited basis of this study, the answer, it should be clear by now, is 'no.' If a sizable number of these letters by both sexes were mixed together and the writers' identities concealed, it would be difficult to detect any difference."[84]

Why is this? The first part of Richardson's answer has to do with how letters were written. As we have already noted, very often a secretary wrote what an employer dictated, adapting the dictation to the accepted form of a letter as described in *dictamen* manuals. And, "the letters were almost always physically written by male secretaries or professional scribes." Richardson comments, "there is little question that we would have a different view of the medieval world had more women's thoughts been written down by women."[85]

The second reason for the absence of any distinctly female style letters has to do with the rigid form imposed by the letter-writing tradition itself. "The notarial form of the dictamen cast its hand over everything," writes Richardson. Authority for a letter was borrowed from the form it assumed, not the author's skill as a writer nor even the merits of her case.

> A letter that did not at least make gestures toward following the dictamenal formulas had no authority. It would have violated the medieval sense of rhetorical decorum and, however serious its purpose, risked being taken lightly, as would a modern attorney appearing in court without a tie.

Thus, a woman's voice, of necessity, became a man's voice in the business letter. "[W]hen women began using correspondence to do business, they (and their secretaries) had no real option but to adopt the patriarchal voice. There was, after all, no feminine dictamen."[86] Because this form carried with it a "universal, authoritative voice," one notably masculine voice became "a constant in commercial rhetoric."[87]

There may have been a hidden benefit in this imposition of one universal rhetorical voice across medieval culture. Richardson adds, "to end on a fairly positive note, however, we can with justice claim that the chief virtue for women of following the standard commercial rhetoric was (and is) that it rendered them rhetorically equal to men."[88]

Catherine of Siena

Despite the undeniable constraints placed on their letter-writing activity, some women of the Middle Ages explored this path to rhetorical influence in unique ways.[89] Kristie Fleckenstein has written recently that St. Catherine of Siena (1347–1380), for example, was able to "transform a conundrum of her age—the contemplative versus the active life— into an opportunity for rhetorical action." Though she had no formal education, Catherine nevertheless "exercised a unique and powerful agency through which she affected secular and ecclesiastical policies." She was deeply immersed in the political scene of her day and traveled widely advocating for clerical reform. Her letters are thought to have influenced the actions of Pope Gregory XI and other ecclesiastical and secular rulers. Catherine was also the author of a book entitled, *The Dialogue of Divine Providence* (1378).

In an age in which the contemplative life of prayer and service was elevated as an ideal for women, Catherine combined the components of that life with standard rhetorical means such as letter writing (nearly 400 of her letters still exist), and extraordinary social action such as caring tirelessly for the poor, to fashion "a unique rhetorical agency." Her letters are considered by some experts to be masterpieces of the art of *dictamen*. Catherine of Siena's persuasive influence was noteworthy, extending even to the popes of her day, who often heeded her advice. Though she "lacked the cultural capital of education, aristocratic family, and patronage," and whereas she "possessed scanty literacy, no spiritual allies, no formal theological training . . . and no political connections," nevertheless this remarkable woman appropriated and adapted available rhetorical means to change the world in which she lived.[90]

The Art of Poetry

In the twelfth century, interest in written style dominated. This attention evolved into new and highly prescriptive approaches to the writing of poetry, or the art of poetry (*ars poetriae*). Treatises on poetry writing included Matthew of Vendome's *Ars Versificatoria* (1175), Geoffrey of Vinsauf's *Poetria Nova* (1213), and Gervais of Melkley's *Ars Poetica* (early thirteenth century). These books exhibit close attention to the aesthetic potential of the rhetorical devices that had long been discussed in rhetorical treatises.

Recall that Aristotle, for example, discusses metaphor and other stylistic devices in Book III of his *Rhetoric*. However, the treatment of style in the medieval poetry manuals has been described as elementary, and one scholar finds the manuals themselves "superficial" and "lacking a deeper logic."[91] Brian Vickers explains that such flaws in the poetry manuals result from the fact that they were "essentially exercise-books for schoolboys learning to write Latin verse."[92] The central concern of the art of poetry appears to have been to arrange words in such a way as to achieve a pleasing effect. Unlike letter-writing manuals, relatively few poetry manuals were written. We will consider the most famous one of these, that by Geoffrey of Vinsauf.

Geoffrey of Vinsauf

Geoffrey of Vinsauf's *Poetria Nova* (*New Poetry*) was the most widely circulated of the medieval poetry manuals, and more than 200 manuscripts of it still exist.[93] Written around 1210, it was "extremely influential on Latin verse writing of the thirteenth century [and] it continued to exercise authority, especially in France and England, until as late as the fifteenth century."[94] Geoffrey apparently intended his new approach to poetry to replace "the 'Old Poetics' of Horace," a famous and widely studied Roman poet of the first century BCE.

The Need for a Plan

Poetria Nova has as "its central concerns," according to James Murphy, "the style and structure considered proper to poetic narrative."[95] As Murphy's statement suggests, many poems of this period related stories.

Geoffrey emphasizes the need for a plan in writing poetry, in much the way that Robert of Basevorn emphasized the need for a form to guide preaching. In a famous opening passage, Geoffrey writes:

> If a man has a house to build, his hand does not rush, hasty, into the very doing: the work is first measured out with his heart's inward plumb line, and the inner man marks out a series of steps beforehand, according to a definite plan; his heart's hand shapes the whole before his body's hand does so, and his building is a plan before it is an actuality.[96]

Geoffrey's building metaphor is intended to point up the need for a mental plan before one sets about writing a poem. Poetry is personified as a woman who comes to dress thoughts in beautiful words:

> When a plan has sorted out the subject in the secret places of your mind, then let Poetry come to clothe your material with words. Inasmuch as she comes to serve, however, let her prepare herself to be apt for the service of her mistress; let her be on her guard, lest either a head of tousled hair, or a body clothed with rags, or any minor details be displeasing.[97]

Despite such stated concern for planned writing, scholars have found little real attention to composition in the poetry manuals. Most of the advice offered a student focuses on minor details such as choosing the right beginning for a sentence or developing a fitting rhetorical figure to make a passage more pleasing.

Developing Poetic Skill

Geoffrey provided his readers advice on various means of creating vivid metaphors as one component in a pleasing poem. While metaphors and their development may be familiar to modern readers, other aspects of Geoffrey's instruction in poetry writing are less so.

For example, *Poetria Nova* discusses a technique called *conversio* (conversion), which Ernest Gallo defines as "a systematic method of varying a given sentence so that one may choose its most pleasing form." Conversion required a student to "take an important noun in a sentence and vary its cases," that is, its grammatical role in a sentence. Thus, "if the basic sentence is *Splendour illuminates his features*," where *splendour* is the subject of the sentence, one possible change is "His face dazzles with the light of splendour," where *splendour* is used in the genitive or possessive case. A second possible conversion is "His face is wed to splendour," where "splendour" is now in the dative case as an indirect object.[98] The utility of such an approach as a teaching device is evident —it stressed the resources available in language. However, its value as a guide to creating great poetry is questionable.

Some teachers of poetry stressed imitation of great Latin masters, particularly Ovid. Woods notes that,

> medieval student compositions that have come down to us illustrate how students reworked material from the literary texts that they read. Most of those that have survived are based on the works of Ovid, especially the *Metamorphoses*, whose interwoven narratives provided medieval teachers with perfect topics for short composition assignments.[99]

More advanced students could move beyond rehearsing various rhetorical devices in their own writing, and begin "to analyse the larger structure of works."[100]

Thus, some medieval poetry instruction provided students with a rigorous introduction to both the rudiments of writing and methods of critical analysis. As a method for teaching writing, Woods concludes that "the medieval approach is pedagogically sound."[101] Perhaps, but, as Brian Vickers concludes, "whatever Dante, or Chaucer, or the *Gawain* poet knew about form, they did not learn from the arts of poetry."[102]

Poetic Argument

Gallo argues that writing style, however, may not always have been the medieval poet's central concern. Using Virgil's *Aeneid* as their prime example, some medieval poetry instructors pointed out that Virgil crafted his great poem not as an aesthetic experience but rather as an argument in support of the heroism of its main character, Aeneas.

The very fact that the poem opens with an act of heroism that actually occurs chronologically in the middle of the story makes Virgil's method similar to that of a great orator who might place the strongest argument first. Virgil is viewed as "a master rhetorician" who "manipulated the facts of the case so as to amplify the good qualities of Aeneas and to diminish the impact of certain facts that seem to detract from the hero's glory. The poet's aim is that of the orator: Each is arguing a case."[103]

Perhaps Geoffrey of Vinsauf is seeking to develop just such a rhetorical sense in aspiring poets reading his manual. If you wish to teach a lesson through a poem, "let the sentiment you begin with not sink to any particular statement, but rather raise its head to a general pronouncement."[104] That is, begin the poem with a proverb or some similar device that makes a general point. Gallo comments that "the poet can control our response to his material by starting in a way that will lead us to see the subject matter in just the way that he wants us to see it."

All of this suggests that the poet is principally a rhetorician, adapting materials to an audience to achieve the greatest possible persuasive, even argumentative, effect. "In short, poetry is essentially rhetorical; the poet is arguing for a certain point of view."[105] If Gallo's interpretation of Geoffrey is correct, then perhaps the criticism of Vickers and others is blunted just a bit. Poetry manuals may not always have been intended principally to teach style following Ovid, which they admittedly did not always do well. Perhaps their goal on occasion was to teach the effective selection and arrangement of the materials in an argumentative case, following Virgil. If this hypothesis has merit it may also explain why so many medieval letters—which are clearly arguments—also contain sections in poetic verse.

Marie de France

One of the major cultural changes occurring during the later Middle Ages was the appearance of a growing number of female readers. For some types of books there was a larger female audience than male audience and, as we have already noted, a higher percentage of women than men were literate. The fact that they could not enter the university "did not necessarily prevent women from participating in the literary discourse of their time."[106] Moreover, an increasing number of published works were appearing in vernacular languages rather than in academic Latin.

Poetry was popular with female readers, and there are also several examples extant of the published work of women poets in the twelfth and thirteenth centuries. Marie de France, for instance, wrote widely read poetry between the years 1160 and 1215. Born in France, she lived part of her life in England and was associated with the court of Henry II. Marie knew Latin, and spoke and wrote in both French and English. In addition to poetry she also wrote popular romantic stories, some with controversial themes that challenged prevailing sexual mores of the day. That Marie saw a connection between poetry and eloquence is clear from her verse, as is her conviction that the poet should "not be silent":

Whoever has received knowledge
and eloquence in speech from God,
Should not be silent or conceal it
but demonstrate it willingly[107]

The idea that "eloquence in speech"—which includes poetry—must be publicly expressed again challenges the notion that writing poetry was simply a matter of finding a pleasing arrangement of words. Marie's statement also suggests that eloquent speech plays an important *social* role, a concept that hearkens back to the *polis*-centered rhetorical theories of Isocrates, Aristotle, and Cicero.

According to Joan M. Ferrante, Marie de France's three known works are the *Lais*, the *Fables*, and *St. Patrick's Purgatory*.[108] So popular were her poems in the later Middle Ages that they were "translated or adapted in many languages," including "Old Norse, Middle English, Middle High German, Italian and Latin."[109] Marie sometimes developed the theme of a complex love relationship gone wrong, occasionally adapting stories she heard in the songs of traveling minstrels. Her poetry was very popular, and influenced later poets.

CONCLUSION

During the Middle Ages, the thousand years between about 400 and 1400 CE, the rhetoric of Cicero's *De Inventione* and a few other classical sources was adapted to a variety of educational, political, and social ends. St. Augustine stands as a vital link between the period of Greco-Roman classical antiquity and Christian European hegemony. A trained rhetorician himself, Augustine both employed rhetoric to defend Christianity and argued for Christian education in the art of rhetoric in order that Christian truths might have effective advocates. Also drawing on the classical rhetorical tradition—and writing at around the same time as Augustine—Martianus Capella outlined the curriculum of the liberal arts that was to influence education right up to the present. The late Roman writer Boethius represents a somewhat different effort to import the insights of classical rhetoric into a new social setting through his revival of classical topical systems.

The three medieval rhetorical arts explored by James J. Murphy—preaching, letter writing, and poetry writing—adapted Greco-Roman rhetoric to the social setting of later Christian Europe. The need for maintaining records and for preserving social hierarchies gave rise to the art of letter writing—a direct application of classical rhetorical categories to a new set of cultural exigencies. The need to teach Christian principles to an often undereducated and almost entirely Christian public called for a rhetoric of preaching. A rising demand for writing instruction, growing interest in the aesthetic potential of written language, as well as the recognition of poetry's potential argumentative uses, contributed to the adaptation of rhetorical insights from antiquity to the writing of poetry.

Scholars have only recently begun to understand the specific ways in which the adaptations of classical rhetoric in medieval Europe represent not just imitation of ancient systems but also practical application of an available set of theories and practices to pressing cultural changes. However, a classical rhetoric developed to address the practical needs of the Athenian democracy or Roman republic did not always fit well with "medieval Christian learning," which was largely "elitist and hierarchical." As John O. Ward points out, medieval rhetoric "could not, therefore, adopt the principal tenets of an art that assumed a more popular focus of learning and was initially designed for theatres other than the schoolroom."[110]

Other realities of medieval life must, however, be accounted for in understanding the medieval tendency to find inspiration in Greek and Roman rhetoric. Perhaps the most significant of these factors is, according to Ward, the individual "confronted with situations that required persuasion at a nontechnical level." Whether that persuasion was pursued from a pulpit or in the office of an Italian civic official, the insights of classical rhetoricians remained critical to its success. [111]

QUESTIONS FOR REVIEW

1. Which classical rhetorician had the greatest influence on the shape of rhetorical theory and practice in the Middle Ages?
2. Why are the Middle Ages considered a period of fragmentation in rhetorical theory?
3. What for St. Augustine were the two major functions of rhetoric within the Church?
4. What dilemmas faced Augustine of Hippo regarding rhetoric? What was Augustine's response to these dilemmas?
5. How can Boethius be seen as perpetuating the classical tradition of writers like Cicero?
6. Which studies made up Martianus Capella's liberal arts?
7. What were the three rhetorical arts that characterized the middle and later portions of the Middle Ages?
8. What was the goal of preaching as a rhetorical art in the Middle Ages?
9. What social functions did the art of letter writing serve in the medieval period?
10. In which ways did letter writing also involve speaking?
11. Which rhetorical form is Catherine of Siena best known for having employed?

QUESTIONS FOR DISCUSSION

1. How does Augustine's approach to rhetoric resemble Plato's? In what ways is Augustine's relationship to sophistic rhetoric similar to Plato's?
2. In what ways were adaptations of classical rhetoric used to maintain the hierarchical structure of medieval Europe? From your study of classical and medieval rhetoric, does it seem to you that rhetorical theory is often used to maintain existing social orders?
3. Excluding preaching itself, which rhetorical practices of our own time seek goals similar to those of medieval preaching?

4. Despite evidence of a shift from speech to writing during the period, rhetoric in the Middle Ages often involved speaking. Does writing play a more important social role today than does speaking? What important changes take place as a culture moves from oral to written expression?

TERMS

Captatio benevoluntatiae Section of letter securing the goodwill of the recipient.

Conclusio The conclusion of a letter.

Conversio A teaching method in which the structure of a sentence was varied so as to discover its most pleasing form.

Dictaminis (ars) The rhetorical art of letter writing; the craft of composing official letters, contracts, and other documents.

Dictatores Teachers and practitioners of dictamen or letter writing; also any persons skilled in rhetoric.

Exordia In letter writing, methods of securing goodwill.

Modus inveniendi In Augustine, the means of understanding scripture.

Modus proferendi The means of expressing the ideas found in scripture.

Narratio Body of the letter setting out the background of the problem to be addressed.

Petitio Specific request, demand, or announcement in a letter.

Poetriae (ars) The art of poetry; one of the three medieval rhetorical arts. Highly prescriptive approaches to writing poetry.

Praedicandi (ars) The art of preaching; one of the three medieval rhetorical arts.

Quadrivium The four major studies in medieval schools, consisting of arithmetic, geometry, music, and astronomy.

Quaestiones Debatable points suggested by sententiae, or passages from ancient authorities.

Salutatio The greeting in a letter.

Scholasticism A closed and authoritarian approach to education centered on a disputation over a fixed body of premises derived largely from Aristotle.

Sententiae Isolated statements from ancient sources.

Theme In medieval preaching theory, a biblical text that provided the basis for developing a sermon, toward the goal of improving the moral conduct and religious understanding of the audience.

Trivium The three minor studies of grammar, rhetoric, and logic in medieval schools.

NOTES

1   George A. Kennedy, *Classical Rhetoric and Its Christian and Secular Tradition from Ancient to Modern Times* (Chapel Hill, NC: University of North Carolina Press, 1980), 174.

2   Karin Margareta Fredborg, "Twelfth-Century Ciceronian Rhetoric: Its Doctrinal Development and Influences," in *Rhetoric Revalued*, ed. Brian Vickers (Binghamton, NY: Center for Medieval and Early Renaissance Studies, 1982), 88.

3   Roger P. Parr writes that "Geoffrey's [of Vinsauf] primary source, particularly for the devices of style, was *Rhetorica ad Herennium*." Translator's introduction to Geoffrey of Vinsauf's *Documentum do Modo et Arte Dictandi et Versificandi* (Milwaukee, WI: Marquette University Press, 1968), 2.

4   Fredborg, 88.

5   John O. Ward, "From Antiquity to the Renaissance: Glosses and Commentaries on Cicero's *Rhetorica*," in *Medieval Eloquence: Studies in the Theory and Practice of Medieval Rhetoric*, ed. James J. Murphy (Berkeley, CA: University of California Press, 1978), 54, 74. Quoted in Vickers, 216.

6   Joseph M. Miller, Michael H. Prosser, and Thomas, Benson, eds., *Readings in Medieval Rhetoric* (Bloomington, IN: Indiana University Press, 1974), xiii.

7   Miller, xiii.

8   See, for example: Vickers, Chapter 4: Medieval Fragmentation, 214–253.

9   Christian Habicht, *Cicero the Politician* (Baltimore, MD: Johns Hopkins University Press, 1990), 2.

10 Eleonore Stump and David Vincent Mecon ed., *The Cambridge Companion to Augustine* (Cambridge UK: Cambridge University Press, 2014), 2–3.

11 Quoted in Calvin Troup, *Temporality, Eternity, and Wisdom: The Rhetoric of Augustine's Confessions* (Columbia, UK: University of South Carolina Press, 1999), 1. Augustine, *Confessions*, 9.2.4.

12 Troup, 4.

13 Kennedy, 149 ff.

14 *Confessions* 1.9.14. Quoted in Troup, 11.

15 Troup, 27.

16 James J. Murphy, "Saint Augustine and the Debate about a Christian Rhetoric," *Quarterly Journal of Speech* 46 (1960): 400–410.

17 Augustine, *On Christian Doctrine*, trans. D. W. Robertson (Indianapolis, IN: Library of Liberal Arts), 7.

18 Renato Barilli, *Rhetoric*, trans. Giuliana Menozzi (Minneapolis, MN: University of Minnesota Press, 1989), 42.

19 W. R. Johnson, "Isocrates Flowering: The Rhetoric of Augustine," *Rhetoric and Philosophy* 9, 4 (1976): 220.

20 James J. Murphy, ed., *Three Medieval Rhetorical Arts* (Berkeley, CA: University of California Press, 1971), xiii.

21 Murphy, *Arts*, xiii (emphasis added).

22 Ward, 27.

23 Johnson, 220.

24 Augustine, *Christian Doctrine*, 118.

25 Johnson, 221.

26 Troup, 13.

27 Percival Cole, *Later Roman Education in Ausonius, Capella, and the Theodosian Code* (New York: Columbia University Press, 1909), 16. Quoted in *Readings in Medieval Rhetoric*, 1.

28 On Capella, see: Kennedy, 175–177.

29 Joan Connolly, *The State of Speech* (Princeton, NJ: Princeton University Press, 2007), 219.

30 Barilli, 42.

31 Boethius, *De Topicis Differentiis*, trans. Eleanor Stump (Ithaca, NY: Cornell Press, 1978). See also: Michael C. Leff, "The Logician's Rhetoric: Boethius' *De Differentiis Topicis*, Book IV," in *Medieval Eloquence*, 3–24; also see: Michael C. Leff "The Topics of Argumentative

Invention in Latin Rhetorical Theory from Cicero to Boethius," *Rhetorica* 1(1) (Spring 1983): 23–44, reprinted in *Rethinking Rhetorical Theory, Criticism, and Pedagogy: The Living Art of Michael C. Leff*, ed. A. de Velasco, J. A. Campbell, and D. Henry (East Lansing MI: Michigan State University Press, 2016), 65–86.

32 Ward, 55.

33 Barilli, 43.

34 Charles G. Nauert, Jr., *Humanism and the Culture of Renaissance Europe* (Cambridge: Cambridge University Press, 1995), 18.

35 Nauert, 18.

36 Albrecht Classen, "Female Explorations of Literacy: Epistolary Challenges to the Literary Canon in the Late Middle Ages," in Disputatio Volume 1: The Late Medieval Epistle, ed. Carol Poster and Richard Utz (Evanston IL: Northwestern University Press, 1996), 89–122, p. 90. Shirley Kersey, "Medieval Education of Girls and Women," *Educational Horizons* 58(4) (1980): 188–192, p. 188.

37 Kersey, 88.

38 Albrecht Classen, "Female Exploration of Literacy: Epistolary Challenges to the Literary Canon in the Late Middle Ages," in Poster and Utz, 90.

39 Marjory Curry Woods, "The Teaching of Writing in Medieval Europe," in *A Short History of Writing Instruction*, ed. James J. Murphy (Davis, CA: Hermagoras Press, 1990), 80–81.

40 In this section I am following Murphy's analysis of later medieval rhetoric as manifested principally in three arts.

41 Ward, 44.

42 Murphy, *Arts*, xxiii. Quoted in Vickers, 225.

43 Kennedy, 190.

44 Ranulf Higden and Margaret Jennings, C. S. J., "The *Ars compendi sermones* of Ranulph Higden," in *Medieval Eloquence: Studies in the Theory and Practice of Medieval Rhetoric*, ed. James J. Murphy, 113.

45 Murphy, *Arts*, 109–216.

46 Murphy, *Arts*, 112.

47 Murphy, *Arts*, 112–113.

48 Murphy, *Arts*, 114.

49 Murphy, *Arts*, 120.

50 Murphy, *Arts*, 124.

51 Murphy, *Arts*, 138.

52 Murphy, *Arts*, 128.

53 Murphy, *Arts*, 129.

54 Murphy, *Arts*, 146.

55 Paul Kristeller, "Philosophy and Rhetoric from Antiquity to the Renaissance," part 5 in *Renaissance Thought and Its Sources*, ed. Michael Mooney (New York: Columbia University Press, 1979), 241. Quoted in James J. Murphy and Martin Camargo, "The Middle Ages," Chapter 2 in *The Present State of Scholarship in Historical and Contemporary Rhetoric*, ed. Winifred Bryan Horner (Columbia, SC: University of Missouri Press, 1990), 59.

56 Patricia Bizzell and Bruce Herzberg, eds., "The Arts of Letter Writing and Preaching," *The Rhetorical Tradition* (Boston, MA: St. Martin's Press, 1990), 377.

57 Nadia Margolis, "'The Cry of the Chameleon': Evolving Voices in the Epistles of Christine de Pisan," in *Disputatio: An International Transdisciplinary Journal of the Late Middle Ages*, ed. C. Poster and R. Utz (Evanston, IL: Northwestern University Press, 1996), 37–70.

58 Martin Camargo, "Where's the Brief?: The Ars Dictaminis and Reading/Writing between the Lines," in *Disputatio: An International Transdisciplinary Journal of the Late Middle Ages*, ed. C. Poster and R. Utz, vol. 1: The Late Medieval Epistle, 1–17, p. 2. Quotation from Guido Faba's *Summa Dictaminis* (1228–1229) (1996).

59 Carol Poster and Richard Utz, eds., *Disputatio: An International Transdisciplinary Journal of the Late Middle Ages* (Evanston, IL: Northwestern University Press), 3.

60 Camargo, 4.

61 Camargo, 7.

62 Murphy, *Arts*, 3.

63 Nicholas Mann, "The Origins of Humanism," in *The Cambridge Companion to Renaissance Humanism*, ed. Jill Kraye (Cambridge: Cambridge University Press, 1996), 5.

64 Charles B. Faulhaber, "The *Summa Dictaminis* of Guido Faba," in Murphy, *Medieval Eloquence*, 85.

65 Faulhaber, 87.

66 Faulhaber, 86.

67 Faulhaber, 86.

68 Barilli, 49.

69 Barilli, 49.

70 Camargo, 3.

71 Kennedy, 186 (emphasis added). See also: Murphy, *Arts*, 7.

72 Murphy, *Arts*, 17.

73 Murphy, *Arts*, 8. This translation of *The Principles of Letter Writing* is by Professor Murphy.

74 Murphy, *Arts*, 11.

75 Murphy, *Arts*, 13–14.

76 Murphy, *Arts*, 13.

77 Murphy, *Arts*, 15.

78 Vickers, 235.

79 Vickers, 235–236.

80 Faulhaber, 108.

81 Classen, 91.

82 Malcolm Richardson, "Women, Commerce, and Rhetoric in Medieval England," in *Listening to Their Voices: The Rhetorical Activities of Historical Women*, ed. Molly Meijer Wertheimer (Columbia, SC: University of South Carolina Press, 1997), 133–149, p. 136.

83 Richardson, 140.

84 Richardson, 145.

85 Richardson, 146.

86 Richardson, 147.

87 Richardson, 146.

88 Richardson, 147.

89 On women and writing in the Middle Ages, see: John Ward, "Women and Latin Rhetoric from Hortsvit to Hildegard," in *The Changing Tradition: Women in the History of Rhetoric*, ed. Christine Mason and Rebecca Sutcliffe Sutherland (Calgary, AB: University of Calgary Press, 1999), 121–132.

90 Kristie S. Fleckenstein, "In the Blood of the Word: Embodied Rhetorical Authority in St. Catherine of Siena's *Dialogue*," in *Sizing up Rhetoric*, ed. David Zarefsky and E. Benacka (Long Grove, IL: Waveland, 2008), 287–295, pp. 287, 294, 289–290.

91 Edmond Faral, *Les Artes Poétique du XIIe et XIIIe Siécle* (Paris: Champion, 1924), xv. Quoted in Vickers, 239.

92 Vickers, 239.

93 Ernest Gallo, "The *Poetria Nova* of Geoffrey of Vinsauf," in *Medieval Eloquence: Studies in the Theory and Practice of Medieval Rhetoric*, ed. James J. Murphy (Berkely, CA: University of California Press, 1978), 68.

94 Murphy, *Arts*, 29.

95 Murphy, *Arts*, 30. Vinsauf's *The New Poetics* in Murphy's collection is translated by Jane Baltzell Kopp.

96 Murphy, *Arts*, 34.

97 Murphy, *Arts*, 35.

98 Gallo, 71.

99 Woods, 84.

100 Woods, 86.

101 Woods, 87.

102 Vickers, 242.

103 Gallo, 76.

104 *Poetria Nova*, lines 126–131. Quoted in Gallo, 77.

105 Gallo, 77.

106 Classen, 91.

107 From: Joan M. Ferrante, "The French Courtly Poet, Marie de France," in *Medieval Women Writers*, ed. Katharina M. Wilson (Athens: University of Georgia Press, 1984), 65.

108 Ferrante, 64.

109 Ferrante, 64.

110 Ward, 64.

111 Ward, 64.

Chapter 7

Rhetoric in the Renaissance

[T]o control the motions of the mind, to turn your hearer where you will and to lead him back again to the place from which you moved him, pleasantly and with love. These, unless I am mistaken, are the powers of eloquence; this is its work.
—Coluccio Salutati (1331–1406)

FROM the fourteenth through the seventeenth centuries enormous intellectual and social changes was taking place in Europe. Assumptions and institutions that had held sway for centuries were radically challenged, including the Christian worldview and the Catholic Church. Johannes Gutenberg (1398–1468) developed the printing press in the early 1450s, thus making possible the wide dissemination of printed material. Exploration revealed a larger world than Europeans had assumed existed, as evidenced in Columbus' famous voyage of 1492. Europe was split by wars, as well as by the sixteenth-century Protestant Reformation.

During this period of cultural upheaval the rhetorical tradition attained extraordinary prominence in European education and social life. While rhetoric was a prominent element in the education and culture of Greece, Rome, and Christian Europe, rhetoric's greatest influence over a civilization was achieved in Europe during the period known as the Renaissance. Historian of rhetoric Brian Vickers has written that "during the European Renaissance—a period which, for convenience, I take as stretching from 1400 to 1700—rhetoric attained its greatest preeminence, both in terms of range of influence and in value."[1]

Rhetoric flourished in the Renaissance as a method of writing and persuasion, an avenue to personal refinement, a platform allowing women to enter the public arena, a means of managing civic and commercial interests, and a critical tool for studying ancient and contemporary literary texts.

Rhetoric played many roles. It was viewed as an aid to contemplation and moral refinement. Through the study of rhetoric one was helped to think deeply and to act decorously. Renaissance rhetoric even provided the basis for prescriptive manuals on how to conduct oneself in social settings. The most famous example of this phenomenon is the Italian writer Baldassare Castiglione's dialogue, *The Book of the Courtier* (1528).[2] Castiglione's standards of personal refinement and oratorical prowess were drawn from the Roman model of the finished orator, in particular Cicero's portrait of the *perfectus orator* in his *De Oratore*. The Courtier's manner and speech are characterized by *sprezzatura*, an easy grace and casual self-confidence. Castiglione's book was translated into six languages and read throughout Europe for several centuries.

Renaissance interest in rhetoric was also closely related to the rise of Italian commercial culture. Cities like Florence were "governed by a process of discussion, debate, and accommodation."[3] Thus, civic officials wanted a means of persuading citizens and other officials, and rhetoric provided that means. The prevailing attitude, as expressed by Vickers, was that "rhetoric is essential to governors and counsellors because it can persuade men to do what you want them to do."[4]

Another distinguishing feature of rhetorical history during the Renaissance was heightened involvement of women as contrasted to earlier periods. Women were more likely to have access to education during the Renaissance than at earlier periods in Western history, and one of the subjects they would have studied was rhetoric. However, women's access to education, and especially the social mobility such education afforded women, should not be overstated.

Katharina Wilson, perhaps the leading authority on women writers of the Renaissance, notes that access to education for Renaissance women came to them principally through the privilege of birth into a high social rank. "Women of the 'middling rank' or of the lower estate, on the other hand, lacked such opportunities, and neither group was free to pursue unidirectionally learning and scholarship."[5] Education did not provide women the same sort of opportunity to rise above their social station as it did men of the period. "Very little, if any, opportunity existed in the power structure of Renaissance courts, principalities, universities, or professional organizations for the woman scholar to rise above her born position through education and intellectual accomplishments," writes Wilson.[6] Some women who had the opportunity to study rhetoric, however, became ardent advocates for women's education.[7]

Among the women who wrote in favor of women's education during the period are Louise Labe (1520–1566), Laura Cereta (1469–1499), and Madeleine des Roches (1520–1587) and her daughter Catherine (1542–1587).[8] In 1487, a woman named Cassandra Fedele "addressed the students and faculty of the University of Padua on the value of humanistic learning."[9] Cereta was the "author of a spirited letter to an imaginary male opponent in defense of liberal education for women."[10] Some male writers of the period, such as Giovanni Boccaccio and Juan Luis Vives, also advocated education for women.

Though there was considerable opposition to women actually speaking in public during the Renaissance, some women gained reputations for their public oratory. Joanna Vaz, for instance, enters the recorded history of the Renaissance based on her reputation for eloquence. Unfortunately, our knowledge of figures such as Vaz is limited at the present time, but a number of scholars are at work retrieving the historical record of female rhetoricians in the Renaissance period. We do know that Vaz could read and write Greek,

Latin, and Hebrew, and that she was appointed a tutor to the daughter of the King and Queen of Portugal and was active in the Lisbon royal court from 1540–1570.[11] Though famous for her speaking ability, no known written record of her speeches survives. Another woman of the seventeenth century renowned for her eloquence was Publia Hortencia de Castro. She is reputed to have argued with theologians of her day, and to have been invited to speak before King Philip of Spain.[12]

This chapter considers some important trends in the study of rhetoric between 1350 and 1700. We will focus attention first on the important role rhetoric played in a major intellectual movement known as Humanism, and will also consider rhetoric's place in Renaissance education, art, civic life, and academic discourse. The closing sections of this chapter consider influential late Renaissance writers who criticized rhetoric's dominance in the sixteenth century, rhetoric's flourishing in England during the same period, and a turn toward a conversational model of rhetoric toward the end of the period.

ITALIAN HUMANISM

A rhetorical revival of unprecedented scale—centered in the Italian peninsula—developed around a group of writers known as Humanists. The Italian Humanists were responsible for much of the resurgence of interest in the classical languages and rhetoric during the Renaissance. Their curriculum—the *studia humanitatis* (humanistic studies)—provided an educational paradigm of studies deemed important to a free and active mind: rhetoric, poetics, ethics, and politics. These disciplines formed the basis of what are often referred to now as the liberal arts, and rhetoric was of central concern. Don Abbott writes that "it is difficult to separate the study of rhetoric from the study of humanism."[13]

Humanism originated in the commercial cities of Northern Italy at the beginning of the fourteenth century. At this time "Italy became a jumble of urban republics" run by councils, committees, and members of influential families.[14] Humanism developed as part of an effort to educate the leading families of Florence and other important cities in the intricacies of civic government. As in ancient Rome, a few wealthy families held power in Florence, and eloquence was an aid to maintaining and exercising that power.

Marks of the *Umanista*

The Italian term from which we get humanist, *umanista*, referred to "a teacher or student of classical literature and the arts associated with it, including rhetoric." These individuals sought to read ancient works for their true meanings, rejecting the limited or speculative meanings attributed to them during the medieval period.[15]

Lauro Martines summarizes the guiding intellectual values of the Humanist movement in Renaissance Italy. First, the Humanists maintained "a supreme emphasis on the importance of getting the texts right." Martines adds that "this meant collating the earliest existing manuscripts and applying the finest philological techniques, with an eye to producing an authentic text." He credits the Humanists with inventing "classical scholarship."[16]

Second, Humanists attempted to place "the text in its historical context, in order to establish the correct value of words and phrases."[17] In this way they contributed to studies such as *hermeneutics*, the discipline of textual interpretation. As noted in Chapter 6, the scholastic practice of splintering classical sources into individual statements or *sententiae* led to the loss of original meaning and even of authorial identity. Charles Nauert writes, "humanists insisted on reading each opinion in its context, abandoning the anthologies [of passages from classical texts, called *florilegia*] and subsequent interpretations and going back to the full original text in search of the author's real meaning."[18] Consequently, classical authors "re-emerged as real human beings, living at a particular moment in history and addressing their remarks to specific issues."[19]

Third, Humanists placed "emphasis on ascertainable facts: on words, documents, dates, events, and historical persons." As a result, in both their critical and historical writings, these scholars moved toward "exposing or challenging historical myths." Along similar lines, Nauert notes that "Humanists successfully claimed that the ancient texts . . . were subject to critical evaluation by the philological method invented by humanists like Lorenzo Valla and Erasmus." He adds that at this very point "the ugliest academic conflicts occurred," because Humanist scholars "insisted that any study of ancient legal or medical or even biblical sources not based on mastery of ancient languages was invalid."[20]

Fourth, the Italian Humanists revived interest in "secular history, with highlights on politics, war, biography." Thus, they "introduced the study of history into schools" while they also "freed historical writing" from its dependence on "the argument from divine intervention." Martines notes finally that "humanism gave rise to a number of new disciplines: archaeology, epigraphy, numismatics, and topography, which were aids to historical study and by-products of a new and unprecedented feeling, antiquarianism."[21]

Notaries

Also important to rhetoric's revival at this time was the rise of an educated class of notaries. These rhetorically trained secretaries were responsible for negotiating, recording, and communicating the many agreements that enabled Italian commercial cities to function. In Italy's powerful principalities, "the needs of the civic administration and commerce" for educated workers "were to prove stronger than those of the Church." As the demand for rhetorically educated professionals increased, they "emerged as a new literate class" with substantial influence.[22]

During the Renaissance, rhetoric became "a skill for contemporary life."[23] Those who attended universities "heard lectures in Latin on rhetoric, dialectics, and the elements of law."[24] Notaries often took courses in "rhetoric emphasiz[ing] correct writing . . . and the art of speech making." Some of the students in these courses went on to "read more Cicero, some Virgil, and even some Seneca, but more especially certain of the late Latin writers."[25]

Roman law, a complementary component of Roman rhetoric, was taken as a model for rising cities like Florence. Once again, rhetorically trained notaries and lawyers were a crucial conduit of Roman culture. "The need for lawyers and notaries to study, ponder, and apply ancient Roman law," writes Nauert, "predisposed them to develop an interest not only in the law but also in the language, literature, institutions and customs of Antiquity."[26] Several key figures are particularly important to Humanism's development, an intellectual movement that eventually influenced all of Europe.

Retrieving the Classical Tradition

A rising interest in classical languages characterized Renaissance Humanist preoccupation with rhetoric. Attention to Greek and Roman authors was intense, and classical works of rhetoric were translated into vernacular languages and widely read. Knowledge of classical rhetoric was thus available to anyone who could read. Reading led to the notion of imitation.

Renaissance scholar Paul Kristeller writes, "It was the novel contribution of the humanists, to add the firm belief that in order to write and to speak well it was necessary to study and to imitate the ancients."[27] Renaissance rhetoricians looked back to Athens and Rome in the hopes of rediscovering every aspect of the classical tradition—languages, texts, ideas, and style. Such "classicism" marked the entire Renaissance humanist project. George of Trebizond (1395–1472), for example, sought to reunify the various genres and methods of rhetoric, dismantled during the Middle Ages, into a systematic whole.[28] A Greek scholar who migrated to Italy, Trebizond worked to retrieve the rhetorical theory of Greek writers. Trebizond tirelessly translated Greek manuscripts—particularly the works of Aristotle—into Latin, an effort that made a much wider range of Greek thought available to Humanist scholars who were unfamiliar with Greek.

George's most important work was the *Five Books of Rhetoric* (1434), which brought together both Greek and Latin rhetorical theories. It has been called "the first new full-scale rhetoric of the Renaissance," and stands as a prime example of the work of Renaissance Humanists to reclaim the entire classical rhetorical tradition of antiquity.[29] Trebizond admired the ancient Greek Sophists such as Gorgias and disparaged Plato's attack on them in the dialogue *Gorgias*. His criticism of Plato earned him the disdain of several distinguished scholars, however, some of whom questioned the accuracy of his translations of Greek sources.

Assisting the rapidly advancing interest in the classical period was the discovery of a large number of ancient Greek and Latin texts during this period of time. Though a Ciceronian influence is evident in medieval rhetoric, that influence was limited to a narrow range of concepts derived from a small number of Cicero's works, especially *De Inventione*. In the Renaissance, however, serious study of a large number of classical sources was closely tied to the theory and practice of rhetoric. James Murphy points out, for instance, that "by the year 1500, only four decades after the advent of printing, the entire Ciceronian corpus was already available in print all over Europe."[30] In addition, one hundred editions of Quintilian's *Institutes of Oratory* had been printed in Europe by the middle of the sixteenth century.[31]

Renaissance fascination with rhetoric gained impetus from the discovery in the early fifteenth century of both Quintilian's *Institutes of Oratory* and the complete text of Cicero's *De Oratore*.[32] With the recovery of these important works, Italian scholars had a vastly richer and more nuanced rhetorical theory available to them than did writers in the Middle Ages. The rhetoric being retrieved was largely Roman, and the ruling elite of Italy's rising cities "consistently looked back to the ancient Roman republic as its model."[33] And, for many humanist writers such as Mario Nizzolio (1498–1576), the very heart of the ancient rhetorical tradition was Cicero.

Other classical sources—including Greek rhetorical sources—were also becoming widely available, however, and translation of ancient works into contemporary European languages was rapidly taking place. Many of these manuscripts had been preserved by Muslim scholars and translated into Arabic centuries earlier by authorities such as Averroes (Ibn Rushd, 1126–1198), who himself became an ardent proponent of rhetoric as the proper means of advancing political and religious ideas and institutions. As Majid Fakhry writes, "Averroes is known to have written commentaries on, or paraphrases of, the whole Aristotelian logical corpus, as well as the *Rhetoric* and the *Poetics*, which formed part of that corpus in the Arab and Syriac traditions."[34] As Muslim culture entered Europe from North Africa through Spain, Greek sources were translated from Arabic into European vernacular languages.

Plato and Aristotle enjoyed popularity among Renaissance scholars, and a vibrant though somewhat misdirected interest in Plato called Neoplatonism developed in sixteenth-century Italy.[35] In spite of the many newly discovered works, the anonymous Roman treatise, *Rhetorica ad Herennium*, remained a great favorite of Renaissance rhetoricians even after its Ciceronian authorship was disproved in the late fifteenth century.

Petrarch

One of the earliest of the Italian Humanist writers, and the one most often associated with the movement's origins, is Francesco Petrarca, better known as Petrarch (1303–1374). He has been called "the outstanding scholar and creative writer of his generation."[36]

Born in Arezzo, Petrarch spent most of his early life in the southern French city of Avignon, where he was educated by a notary from Prato. During Petrarch's youth, Avignon was "the diplomatic and cultural center of the western world" due to the fact that one claimant to the title of Pope made the city his capital.[37] Avignon was home to a papal library containing classical texts and thus became an important center of scholarship which "attracted scholars and men of letters from all over Europe."[38]

Though fond of writing poetry, Petrarch wielded much of his intellectual influence through letters. One biographer writes that "his letters to friends and sympathizers and occasionally to enemies and rivals were widely circulated and they enhanced his reputation."[39] Nicholas Mann maintains that Petrarch paved the way for "the letter . . . to become one of the most favored and versatile literary genres of the Renaissance."[40] Petrarch's extraordinary interest in classical studies was infectious, turning even the great writer Giovanni Boccaccio (1313–1375), author of the *Decameron*, "to a career dominated by classical studies."[41]

Petrarch was more interested in rhetoric's "persuasive power" than in its possibilities for "harmony and beauty of language."[42] However, Petrarch and other early Italian

Humanists, such as Coluccio Salutati, feared that highly persuasive rhetoric "could be perverted if not anchored in true (Christian) wisdom."[43] Petrarch wrote that "speech can have no dignity unless the soul has dignity."[44] Euginio Garin sums up Petrarch's position: "[T]here is an insoluble connection between interior and exterior, between mind and speech."[45] Petrarch's claim can be read as a statement about rhetorical aesthetics—beautiful speech issues from a beautiful soul.

Cicero and the Greatness of Rome

Petrarch studied, as did other privileged Italian boys of his day, "Latin grammar, elementary logic, rhetoric, and arithmetic."[46] Petrarch's father and tutor had rhetorical training and the young Petrarch was particularly interested in Cicero. "I gave myself wholly to Cicero," he wrote late in his life, "whether through natural sympathy or at the suggestion of my father who always held the author in highest veneration."[47] Sent to study law, Petrarch continued reading Cicero and added to his literary education by studying the poetry of Virgil.

Petrarch revived interest in classical, especially Ciceronian, rhetoric. "He definitely accepted Cicero as his model, and set himself the task of recovering the complete works of the master."[48] An expert in Roman history and culture, Petrarch became the leading authority of his day on the Roman historian Livy. Petrarch personally reconstructed much of Livy's *History of Rome*, and traveled widely in search of portions of this and other Latin manuscripts. He gradually assembled the largest private collection of Roman manuscripts in his day.

Much of the impetus for Petrarch's work came from a desire to see Italy return to the greatness of its Roman past, and rhetoric was central to Rome's cultural achievement. As Charles Nauert comments, Petrarch "believed that the melancholy of Italy in his own time could be remedied only if Italians recaptured the moral qualities, especially the devotion to the welfare of the community, that had been the secret of Roman greatness."[49] Mann notes that "the presence of many physical remains of antiquity, helped to give a sense that the civilization of the past was still alive, and this in turn led to curiosity about that civilization."[50]

Re-establishing Rome's greatness meant reviving Cicero's unity of wisdom and eloquence; Cicero's rhetoric was the key to Italy's return to greatness. "The union of moral virtue and eloquent persuasive power was the distinctive excellence of the Rome that [Petrarch] loved." Petrarch translated this nostalgia for Rome into an educational agenda, believing that "Roman greatness could be restored if young Italians were properly educated in wisdom and eloquence." This rhetorical turn in education would make it necessary to remove logic and science from their dominant positions in the universities "and to replace them with the ethical and rhetorical emphasis that had dominated ancient Roman education."[51]

Christine de Pisan

Christine de Pisan (1364–c.1430) was the daughter of Thomas de Pisan, a professor of astrology and councilor in the Republic of Venice. She became "Europe's first professional woman writer."[52] Christine lived for a time in the court of King Charles V of France, a situation that allowed her access to libraries as well as association with learned people. Largely self-educated, she spent a great deal of her time reading and writing. Jenny Redfern, a scholar who has studied the life of Christine de Pisan, writes, "her self-education . . . included history, science, and poetry from Greek and Roman authors as well as from contemporaries such as Dante and Boccaccio."[53] Christine would, then, have been exposed to classical rhetoric in her vast reading. She also studied languages, becoming familiar with French, Italian, and probably Latin as well.

Christine was one of the rare female writers of this period who attracted a wide audience, and she used her prominence to correct the prevailing view of women. As Jenny Redfern writes, Christine urged women "to discover meaning and achieve worthy acts in their lives." Redfern adds, "her objective was to counteract the slander of the female sex so prominent in texts of the time."[54] Christine identified the power of language as a key to women's advancement. "Her most important lesson," writes Redfern, "is that women's success depends on their ability to manage and mediate by speaking and writing effectively."[55]

Christine modeled what she advocated, using the power of language as an active rhetorician over a long career. As Redfern notes, Christine was a prolific writer of poetry and prose, with "forty-one known pieces written over a career of at least thirty years" from 1399 to 1429.[56] One of the factors contributing to the popularity of her work was that she wrote in the vernacular language of French rather than in academic Latin.[57] As Latin was the domain of men, Christine's authorial decision made it possible for any literate woman to become part of her audience.

Polemical Works

Perhaps Christine de Pisan's most popular work was *The Treasure of the City of Ladies*, which originally appeared in 1401 with the title, *Book of the City of Ladies*. This work was extraordinarily popular, went through eighteen manuscript editions, and eventually was translated into French, Dutch, and Portuguese. The book includes an "outspoken defense of women," which was "an anomaly in her time." [58]

As this last comment suggests, Christine often wrote as polemicist, an advocate actively involved in several controversies of her day. She sought in some of her books to answer the harsh criticism of women expressed in popular books such as Jean de Meun's *Romance of the Rose*, which portrayed women as immoral and incapable of genuine accomplishments. What Redfern calls "woman-hating stories" were popular in the late Middle Ages.[59] Christine attacks de Meun "for his defamation of women and his condoning of men's mistreatment of them."[60] Christine defended women against the many false charges leveled against them in these stories. Her other works include *The Changes of Fortune* (1400–1403) and *Vision of Christine* (1405).

Despite Christine's success as a writer she did not formulate a distinctly feminine rhetorical theory. Historian of rhetoric George Kennedy writes that no woman is "known to have written an account of rhetoric" in this period.[61] This is a significant observation, for it is the theory of rhetoric rather than its practice that determines how rhetoric will be understood in a society, and ultimately how rhetoric will be employed.

Pico della Mirandola

Pico della Mirandola (1463–1494) was a Humanist whose early philosophical training was largely scholastic.[62] Pico learned much of his philosophy from Marsilio Ficino (1433–1499), another influential Humanist. Pico's principal interest was Greek philosophy, particularly that of Plato. He shaped a movement known as *Neoplatonism*, a body of philosophic and religious ideas loosely based on Plato's idealism, but also incorporating astrology, magic, and alchemy.[63]

Neoplatonism, Magic, and Rhetoric

Neoplatonism was closely aligned with esoteric works, including the *Cabala*, a work of Jewish mysticism, and the *Corpus Hermeticum*, magical works of Greek and Egyptian origin. The connection between rhetoric and magic, evident in ancient Greece, is again expressed in Pico's famous *Oration on the Dignity of Man*.[64] Pico was as interested in magic as he was in rhetoric, and the two were for him inseparable. Gorgias had noted centuries earlier that rhetoric was a verbal means of altering reality; magic was simply another method for accomplishing the same end. William Covino writes, "Indeed, the magician and the rhetor are similar figures, and often the same figure, throughout western intellectual history."[65]

Historian John G. Burke helps us to understand the somewhat surprising connection between rhetoric and magic. According to an ancient Egyptian legend, the god Thoth, also known as Hermes, invented language. This myth enjoyed renewed currency in the Renaissance because of the astonishing popularity of the *Corpus Hermeticum*, magical works attributed to the legendary Egyptian writer, Hermes Trismegistus. In fact, the Hermetic writings were composed during the first three centuries CE by various unidentified Greek and Egyptian writers.

Burke writes, "Words, then, according to this magical view of language, are not just verbal symbols attached to things by conventional usage; they have a very real connection with things; there is a direct correspondence between a word and the divine idea it expresses." Thus, when wielded by a master of rhetoric, a magician of language, "words could produce extraordinary effects."[66] People and events were brought under the control of the skilled orator, a theme explored in Renaissance works such as Shakespeare's *The Tempest* and Marlowe's *Dr. Faustus*.

Bringing Order through Language

Also important to Pico's philosophy was the conviction that humans employ language to order the chaotic world of nature. We create the civilized world through the humanizing tool of language—an ability possessed only by humans and a freedom granted only by language. Kristeller writes that "Pico stresses especially man's freedom to choose his own way of life."[67] Human beings differ from other animals in their ability to choose their destiny.

Our power to choose, and thus to create civilization, is a direct consequence of our linguistic capacity. This civilizing force of language, specifically of rhetoric, is nothing short of magical. For Pico, the magic of language allows humans to probe "the miracles concealed in the recesses of the world, in the depths of nature, and in the storehouses and mysteries of God."[68] Like Ficino and others, he sought to harness this power in rhetoric for personal as well as civic advancement.

Rhetoric and the Emotions

Motivated by their interest in persuasion, Humanists such as Pico also studied human will and emotions. Humanist speculation on the topic of emotions, according to Vickers, "resulted in a new sub-discipline of rhetorical psychology, *pathologia*." The source of emotion was identified as the *affectus*. The orator possessing a properly attuned *affectus* experienced a particular emotion with regard to a subject and sought to arouse the same emotion in his audience. This theory was derived from Cicero's doctrine, and from Aristotle's treatment of *pathos*.

Concern for the emotive power of language, as for magic, revealed itself in the intense interest of Renaissance rhetoricians in *elocutio*, or rhetorical style. The period between 1540 and 1640 witnessed an "enormous zest" for the rhetorical devices known tropes, schemes, and figures that enhanced *elocutio*.[69]

Lorenzo Valla

Born in Rome, Lorenzo Valla (1407–1457) has been called "not only the most wide-ranging, but also perhaps the most influential of all humanist scholars."[70] His works, *Dialectical Disputations* (1435) and *Elegancies of the Latin Language* (1444)—the latter work referred to as "the Bible of the later humanists"—attacked scholasticism and "suggested a new approach to human understanding based on rhetoric."[71]

Valla specialized in classical Latin written style. Peter Mack writes that his *Elegancies*, which sought "to restore the rich distinctions of classical Latin was much read and greatly valued in the late fifteenth and sixteenth centuries."[72] Valla broadened the conception of proper Latin beyond the Ciceronian model, and was a great advocate of Quintilian's writings. The point of much of Valla's work is that rhetoric, not the dialectic and philosophy of the universities, is the proper basis for education. Rhetoric was more comprehensive than dialectic, and more informative than philosophy.

Trained as a priest, Valla studied classical literature and philosophy in Naples and Milan. He translated Greek classical texts into Latin and developed New Testament studies by comparing the Greek and Latin versions of the Bible. His expertise in classical languages and profound understanding of written Latin style allowed Valla to expose several influential and allegedly ancient documents as forgeries. The most infamous of these forgeries, the *Donation of Constantine*, reputedly recorded that the Roman emperor Constantine I had bequeathed all of Western Europe to the Roman Catholic Church. Valla "built, through his enthusiasm for linguistic study, the foundations of philology and historical criticism."[73] Great Humanists including Erasmus and Vives were "Valla's disciples in one way or another."[74]

Oratory's Superiority to Philosophy

Valla's Christian piety and intense interest in rhetoric guided his study of ancient sources. He wrote to Pope Eugene IV that the goals of his life were "to please God and help men through the study of oratory."[75] Valla argued in his *De Voluptate* that Christian culture was superior to that of earlier pagan Greece.[76] While Humanism in the Renaissance did not imply rejection of Christianity, for Valla it *did* mean the rejection of the monastic idea of contemplative piety.[77] His religion was active, public, and developed around oratory—the master of philosophy. Seigel points out that in Valla's view "orators treated questions of ethics 'much more clearly, weightily, magnificently' than did 'the obscure, squalid, and anemic philosophers.'"[76] Philosophers dealt only with academic questions, which they debated endlessly within the confines of their universities. Rhetoricians, on the other hand, were active in civic life and worked for the good of society.

Valla subordinated the ethical disputations of philosophers to the moral sense of ordinary people. Moral truth was found in "the standards of common sense," and rhetoric helped shape and perpetuate common moral precepts.[79]

Rhetoric's relationship to other disciplines caused intense and occasionally personal debate about which study was the greatest of all. In the fifteenth century, Ermolao Barbaro sent a letter to Pico in which he condemned philosophers as "dull, rude, uncultured barbarians."[80] Others insisted that philosophy be subordinated to rhetoric, an assertion focused on the Renaissance distinction between *res*, or the substance or matter of one's arguments, and *verba*, or the words of an argument. To possess the *res* of the philosophers without possessing the *verba* that came by way of rhetoric rendered philosophy a tedious and almost meaningless study, at least according to the rhetoricians.[81]

Skill in rhetoric—not academic command of philosophy—became the hallmark of the educated person in the Renaissance, much as it had been in Cicero's Rome. As Donald R. Kelley writes,

> the master of rhetoric fulfilled the idea of the *uomo universale* [the universal man] in moral and political as well as in literary and philosophical terms. The Orator, in other words, was the very prototype and paradigm of the Renaissance man.[82]

Wisdom was joined to eloquence in the thought of Renaissance rhetoricians. Bringing wisdom to eloquence implied study of topics such as law, theology, and even medicine.

The Vita Activa

Like Valla, Petrarch and other Renaissance Humanists advocated the *vita activa*—the life of political and civic involvement. Rhetoric was central to this life, particularly as understood on the Ciceronian model. As Brian Vickers points out,

> the active individual was involved in the life of the state, and rhetoric was central to such involvement. It taught one the essential powers of analysis as well as of presentation that assisted toward the solution of the practical problems facing any city or nation.[83]

Humanists questioned the contemplative life of solitary reflection elevated by medieval Christian society and modeled in the monastic life. "All forms of speech" were crucial to the cooperative task of building a civilized society; thus, "to write or think purely for oneself would have been regarded as perverse."[84] The earlier Christian model of solitary contemplation of divine truth, codified in monastic rules, was rejected as antisocial—an illicit private use of the public property of speech (*oratio*) and reason (*ratio*). As Vickers writes, "If speech is the precondition of social exchange then silence and solitude, the *betes noires* of Ciceronian humanism, are its denial."[85]

A new ideal was developing around a conception of rhetoric as an application of reason to the solution of the social problems. The *vita activa* reflected the belief that one owed a debt to one's city or nation, that "the individual's duties should go first to the country that has given him citizenship and a language, then to his fellow-citizens, his family, his friends, and lastly to himself."[86] Rhetoric was the key to living this active life of civic involvement.

When speech is viewed as *the* characteristic human capacity, to deny speech by silence is to deny one's humanity and to deprive one's community of new ideas. Humanists affirmed the humanizing potential of speech for the individual and its civilizing potential for the society. "Human conversation has the power to elevate, for conversation . . . soothes and shapes our minds."[87] The spoken word also shapes cultures and brings into existence human civilizations. Michael Mooney writes that "at the center of this tradition is the concept of language as the bond of society and the instrument of its change."[88]

Speech, then, is the means by which human beings create civilizations, the highest human accomplishment. Thus, to avoid speech as advocates of the *vita contemplativa* recommended was to reject the essence of humanity and to undermine civilization. Rhetoric and eloquence, not prayer and meditation, brought about constructive, cooperative action on the part of the citizenry. Eloquence civilized the human mind and tamed the wilder impulses of the human heart, thus improving the individual's existence and making social life possible. While speech was the distinctive human capacity, the humanizing potential of rhetoric might also be expressed in other symbolic forms, such as painting.

Juan Luis Vives

Another prominent Humanist, Juan Luis Vives (1492–1540), was born in Valencia, Spain, just 2 years before Pico died. His early education occurred in Spain, and, like Pico's, in the Scholastic tradition. At the age of seventeen Vives left Spain "out of fear of the Inquisition."[89] He studied in Paris, where he was captivated by the ideas of Humanism.[90] Vives edited an edition of Augustine's *City of God*. James K. Cameron writes that Vives eventually "became the friend and disciple of Erasmus, from whom he largely assimilated the principles of humanism that formed the background of his 'grand pedagogical system.'"[91] In 1523 Vives was called to England to educate Princess Mary and to teach at Oxford University. He never returned to his homeland of Spain.

Like another famous Spanish rhetorician, Quintilian, Vives was interested in the possibilities of rhetorical education, but he added to his curriculum the study of many other subjects as well. Like Quintilian's *Institutes of Oratory*, Vives' works *De Disciplinis* (1531) and *Rhetoricae* (1533) set out a course of education "beginning with the initial instruction given by the mother right up to that provided for the advanced student."[92]

Vives' reliance on Cicero and Isocrates is clear in his *De Ratione Dicendi* (1532), though he claimed to be breaking with the classical tradition and discovering a rhetoric "appropriate to the needs of the time."[93] In the process, however, Vives separated argument from rhetoric, leaving rhetoric mainly the territory of style. The goal of his curriculum was a highly moral and articulate individual who could speak forcefully, work diligently for peace, and who embodied Christian principles of conduct.

Rhetoric and Renaissance Education

Rhetoric strongly influenced educational practices during the Renaissance. Vickers writes that "the quantity of rhetoric texts known to have been published" during the period "is immense." Astonishingly, more than 2,500 different books on rhetoric appeared in Europe between the late fourteenth and early eighteenth centuries. If each of these books had enjoyed even ordinary usage in schools of the time, it would mean that "several million Europeans had a working knowledge of rhetoric" during this period, an amazing figure that would include persons from many professional groups, and women as well as men.[94]

A single rhetoric book, Erasmus of Rotterdam's *On an Abundant Style*, "went through 150 editions in the sixteenth century," a remarkable record in any century.[95] Renaissance scholar Don Abbott, noting the extensive reach of rhetoric in Renaissance Europe, calls it "*the* Renaissance subject." He adds, "Rhetoric dominated the thoughts of Renaissance intellectuals and the curriculum of Renaissance schools to a degree that is extraordinary."[96]

Rhetorical Ornaments

Rhetoric enjoyed tremendous prestige as a discipline, and entire academic curricula were structured around it. Extensive and occasionally excessive efforts were made to systematize rhetorical knowledge for educational purposes. In the *Thesaurus Rhetoricae* of 1559, Giovani Baptista Bernardi defined over 5,000 rhetorical terms![97] Drilled repeatedly in rhetorical figures, students were expected to memorize large numbers of them.[98]

Thomas O. Sloane has pointed out that classical rhetoric's emphasis on two-sided argument also characterized Renaissance writers such as Valla and Erasmus.[99] For younger students in Renaissance schools "letter-writing manuals, handbooks of tropes and figures, and dictionaries of proverbs" were used for rhetorical training. While "learning the figures of speech and their names may have encouraged students to overuse them," writes historian Peter Mack, "it may also have made students more sensitive to the manner of their use." Similarly, reading the examples of 200 ways of saying "your letter pleased me greatly" from Erasmus' *De copia* may well have encouraged a tendency towards dense and repetitive writing. But it may also have helped students understand that in using any given expression they were choosing among alternatives, since there were 199 other inflections that could be given to the same material. It must also have encouraged students to rewrite their sentences and paragraphs, and shown them how rewriting could bring out different aims and emphases.[100]

Thus, this rigorous and repetitive rhetorical training had practical benefits to students who must themselves have questioned its utility at times. Erasmus also offered students more than 200 ways to say in Latin, "I shall remember you as long as I live."[101] *De Copia* or *On an Abundant Style* was well named.

FIGURES OF SPEECH: A SAMPLING

The following represent a few of the many rhetorical ornaments and figures of speech that Renaissance rhetoricians catalogued, along with more recent examples of their use.

Asyndeton Leaving out conjunctions between parallel words and clauses. *Example:* She returned from the games covered with golden medals, dressed in deserved glory, basking in the praise of her nation.

Metonymy Referring to an object or person by mentioning an associated item or person. *Example:* The Crown denied that the marriage of the Prince and Princess had been dissolved.

Metaphor Comparing an object, person or idea to another apparently different object, person, or idea. *Example:* "O my luve is like a red, red rose, freshly sprung in June/ My luve is like the melody, that's sweetly play'd in tune" (Robert Burns, "A Red, Red Rose").

Paralepsis Raising an issue or question by a cursory or glancing reference to it, or by a conspicuous omission. *Example:* "Let me say, incidentally, that my opponent, my opposite number for the Vice Presidency on the Democratic ticket, does have his wife on the payroll and has had . . . for the past ten years . . . Now just let me say this: That's his business, and I'm not critical of him for doing that" (Richard Nixon, "Checkers Speech," 1952).

Polysyndeton Employing conjunctions between parallel words or clauses. *Example:* "Today marks my final roll call with you, but I want you to know that when I cross the river my last conscious thoughts will be—of The Corps, and The Corps, and The Corps" (General Douglas MacArthur, "Speech to the Cadets," 1962).

Prosopopoeia Addressing or making reference to an individual or group that is not present. *Example:* "But you will not abide the election of a republican President! In that supposed event, you say you will destroy the Union; and then you say, the great crime of having destroyed it will be upon us!" (Abraham Lincoln, 1860, responding to claims leveled by a southern Democratic contingent that was not present during his speech to fellow Republicans.)

Synecdoche Use of the whole to represent a part, or part for whole. *Examples:* (1) The United States invaded Iraq in 2003; (2) lend me a hand.

Rhetoric and the Brain

Renaissance interest in figures of speech raises an important question: Are rhetorical ornaments merely a way of dressing up language, or is there something more to their persistent appearance in the history of rhetoric?

Literary scholar Richard Lanham provides a fascinating account of the human attraction to rhetorical ornaments such as metaphor—the brain's need for economy. Following the famous biologist, Edward O. Wilson, Lanham writes that rhetorical figures may represent "a basic evolutionary strategy for our species." Lanham quotes Wilson to the effect that "the brain depends upon elegance to compensate for its own small size and short lifetime."

Over the course of human development, Wilson speculates that the brain "was forced to rely on tricks to enlarge memory and speed computation." These tricks included developing a facility with "analogy and metaphor" that allowed for a "sweeping together of chaotic sensory experience into workable categories labeled by words and stacked into categories for quick recovery." Lanham concludes that "such a raison d'être" for rhetorical figures of speech would mean that they were "a kind of data compression, an immensely rapid substitute for iterative searching." That is, rhetorical figures saved us time in recalling information, and valuable space in the human cerebral cortex.[102] So, perhaps there is more to metaphor and other rhetorical devices than "mere ornamentation."

Rhetoric and Renaissance Art

Discussions of the Renaissance will almost certainly bring to mind the famous artwork that the period produced, perhaps especially in southern Europe. There were direct connections between Renaissance Humanism's fascination with the fine arts and its preoccupation with rhetoric. "Renaissance humanists theorized and practiced a visual aesthetic that integrated the arts through rhetorical—and especially epideictic— categories," writes Lawrence Prelli.

The rules of rhetoric often were incorporated into painting and other arts such as poetry. Thus, a painter might aim to portray noble character and virtue through the subject represented on a canvas. Through viewing the painting, like an Athenian hearing an epideictic speech, the audience was encouraged to manifest the same virtues as the painting's subject. The painter was engaging in a rhetorical enterprise "comparable to the task Cicero assigned to his ideal orator in *De oratore*"—the propagation of civic virtues.

Prelli notes that Renaissance humanists employed the expression, "Painting is mute poetry and poetry a speaking picture . . ." The painter and the poet—like the great orators of ancient Greece and Rome—sought to make "visible" to their audiences "idealized images or patterns or examples of people and events limned with moral meanings so that audiences could 'gaze upon' and, perhaps, strive to mirror or otherwise emulate them in their own conduct."[103]

THE TURN TOWARD DIALECTIC

Despite its enormous success, however, rhetoric had its critics during the Renaissance period as well. Several influential writers in the fifteenth and sixteenth centuries demoted rhetoric to a set of concerns for style and expression. Logic and dialectic rather than rhetoric were taken to be the proper study of an academician, and argument in the service of disputation belonged to dialectic. As noted in Chapter 6, however, this trend actually began in the twelfth and thirteenth centuries as the result of various social forces, and was brought about as much by rhetoricians as it was by opponents of rhetoric. Two writers are particularly significant in solidifying dialectic's claim on argument during the fifteenth and sixteenth centuries.

Agricola

The first was a Dutch scholar named Roelof Huusman (1444–1485), who is better known to historians by his latinized name, Rudolph Agricola.[104] Like many other rhetorical theorists, Agricola studied law, a study he began in Italy in 1468 and that kept him in that country for 10 years.[105] During his decade in Italy he also steeped himself in the study of Latin and Greek. Agricola was greatly influenced by the Italian Humanist tradition, and his ideas in turn influenced Humanist writers who "eventually succeeded in reforming scholastic education in its most important subject, dialectic."[106]

Agricola admired the work of Petrarch, and even wrote a biography of the great Humanist. Under Humanist influence, Agricola's interests turned toward the classics, and especially toward rhetoric and dialectic. Like many Humanists, including Petrarch, he argued that "speaking and oration" was a gift from God for the advancement of human civilization.[107] "Thus," writes Charles Nauert, "he had a clear conception of the humanist idea of a rebirth of civilization."[108]

In 1479 Agricola completed his famous book, *On Dialectical Invention* (*De Inventione Dialectica*), though it was not published until 1515, 30 years after his death in Rome. Nauert writes that this book was "the most important manual on logic from its publication down to the middle of the sixteenth century."[109] Agricola was drawn more to the argumentative uses of speech than to the ornaments of the rhetoricians. Clear reasoning and effective teaching should be the goals of dialectic, which he made superior to rhetoric as both a study and practice.

Reducing Rhetoric

Though Agricola discussed many types of argument in *On Dialectical Invention*, he is not interested at all in stylistic considerations; these he assigns to rhetoric. A brief quotation from *On Dialectical Invention* captures his opinion of the subject. "Rhetoric," he writes, "provides us with linguistic embellishment and elegance of language, along with all the baits for capturing ears." Dialectic claims the more substantial territory of "speaking convincingly on whatever matter is included in a speech."[110]

Thus, Agricola split the ancient and venerable Ciceronian pair of wisdom and eloquence, while reducing the latter to ornament and handing it over rather unceremoniously to rhetoric. Dialectic emerged the clear winner, walking away with all of the substance, the wisdom, of a speech.

As for the substance of a speech, Agricola distinguishes exposition from argument on the basis of whether one is explaining a point to a receptive audience or arguing a point before an audience that needs to be persuaded. His rhetorical theory stresses the activities of inventing and assessing arguments, and he is particularly interested in reviving the study of *topoi*.[111] Agricola also discusses the emotions more thoroughly than was typical even in the standard rhetoric books.

Agricola influenced prominent writers on rhetoric and dialectic, including Erasmus, Philip Melancthon, Vives, and especially Peter Ramus.[112] In fact, Walter J. Ong writes that "it is difficult to exaggerate [Agricola's] importance." Ong adds that Agricola's logic "became for generations after him, in the absolute sense, logic unqualified."[113]

Peter Ramus

Agricola's importance is underlined by his disciple, French scholar Peter Ramus (1515–1572). Ramus "has to remind his own generation that the 'true dialectic' which he professed had not sprung from nowhere, but was that of Rudolph Agricola."[114]

A professor of rhetoric at the University of Paris in the sixteenth century, Ramus vehemently opposed scholasticism. He proposed an alternative approach to learning that did not make reference to authorities such as Aristotle or Cicero at all. As Peter Mack writes, the iconoclastic Ramus "built his academic career on scandalous attacks on the academic gods of his time: Aristotle, Cicero and Quintilian."[115] He was skeptical about the value of Aristotle's and Cicero's treatment of rhetoric, calling the former "the man chiefly responsible for confusing the arts of rhetoric and dialectic," and the latter "verbose" and "unable to restrain and check himself" when making a speech.[116]

Though he owed much to Quintilian, the great Roman teacher also became Ramus' target in an angry attack entitled *Arguments in Rhetoric against Quintilian* (1549). Ramus rejected Quintilian's conception of the perfect orator as a virtuous as well as an eloquent person, summed up in the Latin phrase *Vir bonus bene dicendi* ("The good man speaking well"). Such a view, which ignored the brute fact that an eloquent speaker could also be an evil person, was for Ramus simply "useless and stupid."[117]

Ramus extended his disregard for the rhetorical tradition to his contemporaries as well. He was leery of the Italian brand of Humanism that was built around the study of rhetoric. Ong writes that "in a very real sense Italian humanism stood for a rhetorically centered culture opposed to the dialectically or logically centered culture of North Europe."[118] Ramus preferred the latter, less rhetorical, model of liberal education.

As part of his reaction against the classical tradition that typified Italian Humanism, Ramus removed invention from the study of rhetoric, and assigned it to dialectic in his *Institutes of Dialectic* (1543). Rhetoric was merely verbal ornamentation, and thus of little consequence. Because of his enormous intellectual influence, rhetoric suffered considerable loss of prestige as a study. But Ramus may have exerted an even more dramatic influence by driving a wedge between reason and language in his effort to demote rhetoric. Lanham writes that Ramus "separated thought from language" by advancing a model of education in which "reason breaks free of speech."[119] Language became a neutral tool for expressing the discoveries of other disciplines, and was no longer viewed as the substance of an art worthy of an educated person.

Rhetorical treatises after Ramus tended toward discussions of style and ornament. Rhetoric's capacity as the art of civic discourse concerned with discovering arguments was largely lost in such works; it became a marginalized study with a limited practical application. Nevertheless, through the force of the Humanistic tradition, rhetoric continued to exert influence in spite of efforts to render it principally an art of dressing the insights discovered by other means, such as dialectic.[120]

RENAISSANCE RHETORIC IN BRITAIN

Whereas rhetoric was suffering under the criticism of Agricola and Ramus on the European Continent in the fifteenth and sixteenth centuries, England was developing into a particularly fertile field for the growth of interest in the art of rhetoric between 1500 and 1600.[121] Manuals for teaching rhetoric proliferated. The rhetorical tradition also had a considerable influence on England's intellectual and artistic life, including marking the thought of the scientist Francis Bacon (1561–1625) and the literary production of the playwright William Shakespeare (1564–1616).[122] Indeed, an intense debate developed over whether the ornate style that characterized Renaissance rhetoric was well suited to a new age in which science would play a larger role.

Teaching Rhetoric

Leonard Cox's *The Art or Craft of Rhetoryke* (c. 1530) was the first actual rhetorical treatise written in English. The book is largely Ciceronian in its presentation of rhetoric, which it treats as consisting principally of Cicero's five canons. Richard Sherry's *A Treatise of Schemes and Tropes* (1550) focuses on the ornamental uses of language. Thomas Wilson's *The Arte of Rhetorique* (1553) was another important early rhetorical textbook in English. This work was used extensively as a text for teaching rhetoric under the Tudors in England, though it was actually written for people who wanted to study rhetoric on their own.

As George Kennedy writes, "That such works were written is an indication that some English schoolmasters for the first time recognized a need to train students in the composition and appreciation of English."[123] Shakespeare, the great English master of classical rhetoric, was a student at around the time these works were being published.

The popularity of rhetoric in England in the sixteenth century is also suggested by the appearance of treatises such as Richard Reinolde's *A Booke Called the Foundacion of Rhetoric* (1563) and Roger Ascham's *The Scholemaster* (1570), which took a Ciceronian approach to rhetoric and presented the art as a means of promoting social refinement. Later in the century, works such as Gabriel Harvey's *Rhetor* (1577) and Henry

Peacham's *The Garden of Eloquence* (1577) appeared. The former was Ramistic in its approach to rhetoric, while the latter focused on the development of English prose style. As we will see in the following sections, English interest in rhetoric's capacity to enhance written and oral style, and in its ability to enhance the social refinement of its students, remained important to British interest in the subject.

Magic, Science, and Style

We noted earlier in the chapter that Humanists, particularly in Italy, had a decided interest in the magical effects of language. The association of rhetorical style and magical effects sparked considerable debate in Renaissance England.

Ryan J. Stark's recent study, *Rhetoric, Science and Magic in Seventeenth-Century England,* explores this controversy over magic and rhetoric in England.[124] During this period, rhetorical style could be taken to indicate one's political preferences and even one's spiritual state. A florid style featuring rhetorical inversions such as irony could suggest a belief in magical powers, while the choice of a plain or "empirical" style was evidence of a scientific mind. Stark writes that a "polite, cool, plain rhetoric" of a "new epoch" was marking a break with the older and more elaborate style of rhetoricians on the European continent.[125]

A rhetorical revolution was taking place in seventeenth-century England, as English rhetorical theorists sought to mark out a new path for rhetoric. Rhetoric was becoming a contested domain. This desire for a new way had to do with the association of rhetoric and magic, especially in Renaissance Italy. A small group of scientists formed the Royal Society in 1660 as part of an effort to advance scientific research by discussing the works of Francis Bacon and others. A scientific model of discourse began to assert itself in England, and this meant writing in a plain and unadorned style.

As he explores late-Renaissance English thought about language, Stark discovers that members of the Royal Society sought to leave the magical past of the Humanists by developing a new and more empirical rhetoric. Language was to be a scholarly tool fitted to the straightforward work of clear expression. The change from ornate (magical) to plain (scientific) prose marked the triumph of a rising Enlightenment way of thinking. Among the advocates of a more direct style was the famous philosopher, John Locke (1632–1704).

This shift to a less elaborate style was not without its liabilities, however. Stark argues that the movement away from ornate rhetoric was a major cause of declining attention to oral discourse. He writes,

> Walter Ong and most other historians of rhetoric point to the mass circulation of the printed word as the principal force in diminishing the significance of the spoken word in Renaissance and Enlightenment rhetoric, but the collapse of magic is probably even more substantial.[126]

THE LATE RENAISSANCE AND CONVERSATIONAL RHETORIC

Madame Madeleine de Scudéry

Madame Madeleine de Scudéry (1607–1701) was a novelist and essayist of the mid-seventeenth century, a late Renaissance woman with a decided interest in the interpersonal and social potential in rhetoric. "In France, in treatises from the 1640s to the 1680s," writes Jane Donawerth, "Madeleine de Scudéry set out the first fully elaborated early modern theory of rhetoric by a woman." In works such as *Les Femmes Illustres* (1642), "de Scudéry encourages women to educate themselves and to seek social status through their writing rather than their beauty."[127] A gifted speaker, she was awarded a prize for eloquence by the Academie Francaise, a prestigious organization which she, as a woman, could not join.

The Rhetoric of Conversation

Donawerth notes that in works such as *Conversations* (1680) and *Conversations Nouvelles* (1684), and in several novels, "de Scudéry lays out a rhetoric of conversation (and also letter writing) for the salon culture of Renaissance France, a theory that includes (or even centers on) women." In what amounted to a new and distinctly social approach to rhetoric, "de Scudéry imagines a world of leisure in which intellectual exploration and construction of community are carried on primarily through conversation." Indeed, conversation becomes her "model for public as well as private discourse." Donawerth adds that "central to her theory, then, is the agreeable, remaining sensitive to one's audience's interests, entertaining and not imposing one's views on the group."[128]

De Scudéry pointed the way to later developments in which "women taught and theorized conversation as an art" and "used conversation as a model for other forms of communication," and, thus, "anticipated modern theories of composition in important ways." Donawerth asks, "What does this emphasis on conversation, collaboration, and dialogue add to our conception of rhetoric?" One answer is that it, like some earlier theories—notably that of Cicero—"celebrate[s] the civilizing power of speech." She adds, "following the Greek sophists, Cicero represents language as the force that led humanity out of the wilderness into civilization, a political force through public speech that allowed peoples to make laws for themselves."[129] This was reiterated throughout the Renaissance.

For de Scudéry, then, language is "the bond that holds society together, not through public speaking but through the conversation that educates and plants morality daily in ordinary people." Donawerth finds this tendency to mark women rhetorical theorists generally. "As a group, then, women theorists bring a model of communication based on conversation, collaboration, and dialogue to our understanding of the history of rhetoric."[130]

CONCLUSION

Rhetoric achieved its greatest prominence as a subject of study during the Renaissance. The number of books devoted to its study, the number of people who took up the subject, and the degree to which education was rhetorically structured are astonishing. Rhetoric was the language of education and the educated during the Renaissance. As we have seen, the movement known as Humanism, and particularly Italian Humanism, had a great deal to do with rhetoric's influence between 1300 and 1700. The attention paid to rhetoric by intellectual luminaries such as Petrarch, Pico, Vives, and Valla, as well as their arguments against philosophy as the foundation of education, enhanced rhetoric's status substantially.

The impulses of Italian Humanism were iconoclastic and conservative. Humanism blended Christian moral principles with an aggressive study of newly retrieved classical sources. A revived class rhetoric—largely Ciceronian—became a tool for inaugurating new ways of thinking about culture and education.

The Renaissance orator represented the ideal of the broadly educated civic leader. The true orator—the *uomo universal*—was grounded in the wisdom of the liberal arts and highly skilled in the art of eloquence. Cicero's wedding of wisdom and eloquence in one individual was diligently pursued. In response to the monastic ideal of a contemplative life centered on the Christian scriptures, Petrarch advocated the *literae humanae* or liberal arts, and the *vita activa*—the active life of civic involvement. Rhetoric was the key to self-discovery, refinement, and effective government. Rhetoric's influence extended even to the rules of fine arts such as poetry and painting. Late in the period new conversational forms of rhetoric were also explored by innovative figures such as Madeleine de Scudery. At around the same time, the highly influential scholar Peter Ramus moved rhetoric's more substantial elements into the discipline of dialectic, an apparent to rhetoric's intellectual status. However, the sixteenth century also finds rhetoric becoming a prominent study in Britain, sparking debate over what constituted the most effective style. Rhetoric's influence in that country in the eighteenth century is the subject of the next chapter.

QUESTIONS FOR REVIEW

1. What was the status of rhetorical studies in Renaissance education?
2. Identify some of the defining characteristics of the Italian Humanist movement.
3. What famous book by Castiglione retrieved for European readers Cicero's notion of the *perfectus orator*?
4. What is Richard Lanham's explanation of the development of rhetorical figures of speech?
5. What was Valla's opinion regarding the relationship between rhetoric and philosophy?
6. What is the significance of the concept of the *vita activa* to Renaissance rhetoric? To which concept was it opposed?

7.   What was the reaction of many Humanists to the Scholastic approach to education?
8.   In what way are Agricola and Ramus significant to the history of rhetoric?
9.   What orientation did Madame de Scudéry bring to rhetoric?

QUESTIONS FOR DISCUSSION

1.   Is it any longer possible to speak of one discipline as somehow providing the basis for all of education? If so, what discipline might play that role? If not, what has changed since the Renaissance?
2.   Respond to the idea advocated by the Italian Humanists that speech is the means by which human beings create civilization. Is this account too simple? Are there factors other than speech that could be said to be the basis for human civilization?
3.   Does the commercial life of modern capitalistic societies still depend on the language skills of a class of highly trained specialists? If so, what professions do these new notaries represent? If not, what has changed?
4.   What argument could be made against Ramus' reduction of rhetoric to a concern solely for style and ornament in language? What argument could be made in favor of this reduction?
5.   What contemporary examples reflect that we there is a connection between style and political or ideological commitments?

TERMS

Affectus For the Italian Humanists, the source of emotions or passions in the human mind.
Classicism A resurgence of interest in the languages and texts of classical antiquity.
Hermeneutics The science of textual interpretation.
Literae humanae The liberal arts.
Neoplatonism   A body of philosophic and religious ideas loosely based not only on Plato's idealism, but also on incorporating ideas from astrology, magic, and alchemy.
Notaries Rhetorically trained secretaries responsible for negotiating, recording, and communicating the many agreements that enabled Italian commercial cities to function.
Pathologia The study of the emotions.
Res The substance matter of one's arguments.
Sprezzatura In Castiglione's *The Book of the Courtier*, the orator's easy grace and casual self-confidence.
Studia humanitatis Humanistic studies, or studies proper to the development of a free and active human mind—rhetoric, poetics, ethics, and politics.
Umanista Scholars advocating the values of the humanistic movement.
Uomo universale The universal man, the ideal type of an educated person in the Renaissance.
Verba The words in which the subject matter of an argument was advanced.
Vita activa The active life, or life of political involvement.
Vita contemplative The contemplative life of prayer and study.

NOTES

1 Brian Vickers, "On the Practicalities of Renaissance Rhetoric," in *Rhetoric Revalued*, ed. Brian Vickers (Binghamton, NY: Center for Medieval and Early Renaissance Studies, 1982), 133.

2 Baldassare Castiglione, *The Courtier* (1528); Gerald P. Mohrmann, "The Civile Conversation: Communication in the Renaissance," *Speech Monographs* 39 (1972): 193–204.

3 Charles Nauert, Jr., *Humanism and the Culture of Renaissance Europe* (Cambridge: Cambridge University Press, 1995), 25.

4 Vickers, "Practicalities," 135.

5 Katharina Wilson, ed., *Women Writers of the Renaissance and Reformation* (Athens: University of Georgia Press, 1987), xxii–xxiii.

6 Wilson, xxiii.

7 See: Patricia Bizzell and Bruce Herzberg, eds., *The Rhetorical Tradition: Readings from Classical Times to the Present* (Boston, MA: St. Martin's Press, 2000), 463–498. Bizzell and Herzberg include in their collection works by Christine de Pisan and Laura Cereta.

8 Wilson, xxiii. See also: in this volume: Anne R. Larsen, "Les Dames des Roches," 232–259.

9 Kennedy, 1999, 231.

10 Kennedy, 1999, 231.

11 Kevin M. Stevens, "Books Fit for a Portuguese Queen: The Lost Library of Catherine of Austria and the Milan Connection (1540)," *Documenting the Early Modern Book World*, ed. Malcolm Walsby and Natasha Constantinidou (Boston MA: Brill, 2013), 85–116, p. 102.

12 A good source on women scholars of the Renaissance is Patricia H. Labalme ed., *Beyond Their Sex: Learned Women of the European Past* (New York: New York University Press, 1984); and Christopher Lund, Department of Spanish and Portuguese, Brigham Young University, brought de Castro to my attention.

13 Don Paul Abbott, "The Renaissance," in *The Present State of Scholarship in Historical and Contemporary Rhetoric*, ed. Winifred Bryan Horner (Columbia, SC: University of Missouri Press, 1990), 89.

14 Nauert, 5.

15 Nicholas Mann, "The Origins of Humanism," in *The Cambridge Companion to Renaissance Humanism*, ed. Jill Kraye (Cambridge: Cambridge University Press, 1996), 1.

16 Lauro Martines, Jr., *Power and Imagination: City States in Renaissance Italy* (New York: Knopf, 1979), 204.

17 Martines, 204.

18 Nauert, 18.

19 Nauert, 18.

20 Nauert, 193.

21 Martines, 204.

22 Martines, 5.

23 Mann, 5.

24 Martines, 204.

25 Martines, 204.

26 Nauert, 5.

27 Paul Oskar Kristeller, *Renaissance Thought: The Classic, Scholastic, and Humanist Strains* (New York: Harper and Row, 1961), 13.

28 See: John Monfasani, *George of Trebizond: A Biography and a Study of His Rhetoric and Logic* (Leiden, the Netherlands: Brill, 1976).

29 George Kennedy, *Classical Rhetoric in Its Secular and Christian Tradition* (Chapel Hill, NC: University of North Carolina Press, 1999), 232.

30 James J. Murphy, ed., *Peter Ramus's Attack on Cicero*, trans. Carole Newlands (Davis, CA: Hermagoras Press, 1992), xv.

31 Murphy, "Introduction" to *Ramus*, xxxii.

32 Izora Scott, *Controversies over the Imitation of Cicero in the Renaissance* (1910; rpt. Davis, CA: Hermagoras Press, 1991), 113.

33 Nauert, 25.

34 Majid Fakhry, *Averroes: His Life, Work and Influence* (Oxford: Oneworld Publications. 2001), 32.

35 Kristeller, 60–63.

36 Mann, 9.

37 Mann, 8.

38 Mann, 8.

39 Gene Brucker, *Florence: The Golden Age 1138– 1737* (Berkeley, CA: University of California Press, 1969), 202.

40 Mann, 5.

41 Nauert, 25.

42 Seigel, 34.

43 Martines, 199.

44 Euginio Garin, *Portraits of the Quattrocentro* (New York: Harper and Row, 1963).

45 Garin, 19.

46 Morris Bishop, *Petrarch and His World* (Bloomington, IN: Indiana University Press, 1963), 21.

47 Bishop, 21.

48 Scott, 7.

49 Nauert, 24.

50 Mann, 6.

51 Nauert, 24.

52 Jenny R. Redfern, "Christine de Pisan and The Treasure of the City of Ladies: A Medieval Rhetorician and Her Rhetoric," in *Reclaiming Rhetorica: Women in the Rhetorical Tradition*, ed. Andrea A. Lunsford (Pittsburgh, PA: University of Pittsburgh Press, 1995), 73–92, p. 74.

53 Redfern, 77.

54 Redfern, 74.

55 Redfern, 74.

56 Redfern, 74.

57 Redfern, 78.

58 Redfern, 75.

59 Redfern, 76.

60 Nadia Margolis, "'The Cry of the Chameleon': Evolving Voices in the Epistles of Christine de Pisan," in Post and Utz, 43.

61 Kennedy, 1999, 230.

62 Walter J. Ong, S. J., *Ramus: Method and the Decay of Dialogue: From the Art of Discourse to the Art of Reason* (Cambridge, MA: Harvard University Press, 1983), 137.

63 Kristeller, 60–63.

64 John G. Burke, "Hermetism as a Renaissance World View," in *The Darker Vision of the Renaissance: Beyond the Fields of Reason*, ed. Robert Kinsman (Berkeley, CA: University of California Press, 1974), 95.

65   William A. Covino, *Magic, Rhetoric and Literacy: An Eccentric History of the Composing Imagination* (Albany, NY: State University of New York Press, 1994), 19.

66   Burke, 102.

67   Kristeller, 129.

68   Pico, *Oration on the Dignity of Man*. Quoted in Anthony Grafton, "Humanism, Magic and Science," in *The Impact of Humanism on Western Europe*, ed. Anthony Goodman and Angus MacKay (London: Longman, 1990), 111.

69   Vickers, "Practicalities," 137.

70   Kelley, 35.

71   Kelley, 35–36; Vickers, "Practicalities," 266.

72   Mack, "Humanist Rhetoric and Dialectic," 86.

73   Seigel, 137.

74   Kelley, 88.

75   Quoted in Seigel, 139.

76   Vickers, "Practicalities," 187.

77   Seigel writes that Valla "was almost certainly a loyal Christian, even though he may have been a somewhat eccentric one" (145).

78   Seigel, 142.

79   Seigel, 251.

80   Quoted in Mooney, 45.

81   Vickers, "Practicalities," 185.

82   Donald R. Kelley, *Renaissance Humanism* (Boston, MA: Twayne, 1991), 82.

83   Brian Vickers, *In Defense of Rhetoric* (Oxford: Oxford University Press, 1988), 182–183.

84   Vickers, *In Defense of Rhetoric*, 273.

85   Vickers, *In Defense of Rhetoric*, 272.

86   Vickers, *In Defense of Rhetoric*, 271.

87   Garin, 19.

88   Michael Mooney, *Vico in the Tradition of Rhetoric* (Princeton, NJ: Princeton University Press, 1985), xii.

89   Kennedy, 1999, 245.

90   James K. Cameron, "Humanism in the Low Countries," in *The Impact of Humanism on Western Europe*, 148.

91   Cameron, 30.

92   Cameron, 148.

93   Kennedy, 1999, 246.

94   Vickers, "Practicalities," 133.

95   Peter Mack, "Humanist Rhetoric and Dialectic," in *The Cambridge Companion to Renaissance Humanism*, ed. Jill Kraye (Cambridge: Cambridge University Press, 1996), 88.

96   Don Paul Abbott, "Rhetoric and Writing in Renaissance Europe and England," in *A Short History of Writing Instruction*, ed. James J. Murphy (Davis, CA: Hermagoras Press, 1990), 95. See also: Wilbur Samuel Howell, *Logic and Rhetoric in England: 1500–1700* (New York: Russell and Russell, 1961).

97   Vickers, "Practicalities," 269.

98   On Renaissance interest in figures of speech, see: Sylvia Adamson, Gavin Alexander, and Katrin Ettenhuber, eds., *Renaissance Figures of Speech* (Cambridge: Cambridge University Press, 2011).

99   Thomas O. Sloane, *On the Contrary: The Protocol of Traditional Rhetoric* (Washington, DC: Catholic University of America Press, 1997), especially Chap. 4, "Disputatiousness."

100 Mack, "Humanist Rhetoric and Dialectic," 91.

101 Kennedy, 1999, 245.

102 Richard Lanham, *A Handbook of Rhetorical Terms*, 2nd ed. (Berkeley, CA: University of California Press, 1991), 80. Lanham quotes Edward O. Wilson, *Biophilia* (Cambridge, MA: Harvard University Press, 1984), 60.

103 Lawrence J. Prelli, ed., *Rhetorics of Display* (Columbia, SC: University of South Carolina, 2006), 5.

104 For an excellent discussion of Agricola and his influence, see: Ong, Chap. V.

105 George Kennedy, *Classical Rhetoric and Its Christian and Secular Tradition from Ancient to Modern Times* (Chapel Hill: University of North Carolina Press, 1980), 208–210.

106 Nauert, 104.

107 Kelley, 89.

108 Nauert, 104.

109 Nauert, 104.

110 Agricola, *De Inventione Dialectica* (Nieuwkoop, The Netherlands, 1967), 192. Quoted in Mack, 86.

111 Ong, 104.

112 See: Peter Mack, *Renaissance Argument: Valla and Agricola in the Tradition of Rhetoric and Dialectic* (Leiden, the Netherlands: E. J. Brill, 1993), Chaps. VII and VIII.

113 Ong, 93.

114 Ong, 93.

115 Mack, "Humanist Rhetoric and Dialectic," 89.

116 Peter Ramus, *The Questions of Brutus* (1549) trans. Carole Newlands (Davis, CA: Hermagoras Press, 1992), 8.

117 Peter Ramus, *Rhetoricae Distinctiones in Quintilianum* (Arguments in Rhetoric against Quintilian), trans. Carole Newlands (1549; DeKalb, IL: Northern Illinois University Press, 1986), 84.

118 Ong, 49.

119 Richard Lanham, *The Electronic Word: Democracy, Technology and the Arts* (Chicago, IL: University of Chicago Press, 1993), 157–158.

120 See: Mack, *Renaissance Argument*, Chap. XVII. For another perspective on rhetoric in this period, see: Mark U. Edwards, Jr., *Printing, Propaganda, and Martin Luther* (Berkeley, CA: University of California Press, 1994).

121 For a detailed discussion of English rhetorical works in the Renaissance, see: Arthur F. Kinney, *Humanist Poetics: Thought, Rhetoric, and Fiction in Sixteenth-Century England* (Amherst, MA: University of Massachusetts Press, 1986).

122 See: Garry Wills, *Rome and Rhetoric: Shakespeare's Julius Caesar* (New Haven, CT: Yale University Press, 2011).

123 Kennedy, 1999, 247.

124 Ryan Stark, *Rhetoric, Science and Magic in Seventeenth-Century England* (Washington, DC: Catholic University Press, 2009).

125 Stark, 83.

126 Stark, 68.

127 Jane Donawerth, ed. Editor's Introduction to *Rhetorical Theory by Women before 1900* (Lanham, MD: Rowen and Littlefield, 2002), xxii–xxiii.

128 Donawerth, xxiii.

129 Donawerth, xl.

130 Donawerth, xl.

Chapter 8

Enlightenment Rhetoric

All the ends of speaking are reducible to four; every speech being intended to enlighten the understanding, to please the imagination, to move the passions, or to influence the will.

—George Campbell

THE modern age begins somewhere in the late seventeenth or early eighteenth century, during a period of profound intellectual change known as the Enlightenment. Modernity involves radical questioning of traditional religious ideas and texts, placing reason above authority, seeking scientific solutions to social problems, and understanding the universe as governed by the laws of physics. When such commitments came fully into place, a major transition occurred in European intellectual life.

Several writers were particularly important in bringing about these changes. Sir Isaac Newton (1642–1727) described physical laws governing the universe in his *Principia Mathematica* (1687). John Locke (1632–1704) set out an empirical basis for thought in his *Essay Concerning Human Understanding* (1690). David Hume's *Enquiry Concerning Human Understanding* (1748) explored how the mind apprehends the world. Jean-Jacques Rousseau (1712–1778) outlined a theory of government centered on the individual citizen in *The Social Contract* (1762). Francois-Marie Arouet, better known as Voltaire (1694–1778), subjected the bases of Christian belief to severe criticism in his *Dictionairre Philosophique* (1764) and several other works.

This chapter explores several developments in rhetorical theory during the seventeenth and eighteenth centuries, first on the European Continent and then in Britain. The legacy of Renaissance Humanism's influence is still evident in transitional writers like Margaret Cavendish in England and Giovanni Battista Vico in Italy. We will consider Vico's innovative theory of the rhetorical evolution of the human mind, as well as his views on the role of narrative in shaping culture. We will also explore developments on the British Isles where various rhetorical theories addressed matters ranging from psychology and argument to preaching and style. Rhetorical writers during this time also explored such issues as the beneficial use of leisure time, and even how to correct a telltale Irish accent.

RHETORIC'S CHANGING ROLES

Enlightenment rhetorical theory turned away from traditional concerns such as memory and invention systems, and toward aesthetic matters such as style and good delivery. One leading expert on the period, Barbara Warnick, suggests that this shift in emphasis reflects the influence of Peter Ramus in the sixteenth century and René Descartes in the seventeenth. As noted in the previous chapter, some late-Renaissance writers moved argument and proof from rhetoric to logic and dialectic. Warnick writes, "by the late seventeenth century, rhetorical logic had been displaced . . . "The result was a "managerial" emphasis in rhetorical studies. "During the Enlightenment, French and Scottish rhetorics turned to a managerial view of rhetoric that distinguished the discovery of knowledge through reasoning from communication of content to others."

In earlier periods, as we have seen, rhetoric both discovered and communicated knowledge. Late seventeenth- and eighteenth-century writers often seem content to allow rhetoric only the latter responsibility, with discovery of new knowledge left to science or philosophy. Warnick identifies a corresponding shift from rhetoric as guiding the production of discourse to rhetoric as enhancing the consumption of discourse. "While concern for invention and the production of discourse receded, intense interest in the problem of receptive competence emerged to take its place."[1]

Though it would be an exaggeration to say that a concern for invention is completely absent from Enlightenment rhetoric, Warnick's observation is borne out in eighteenth- and early nineteenth-century rhetorical theory, particularly in Britain. Note the emphasis in this chapter on style, taste, delivery, and imagination, as contrasted with earlier concerns for arguments, proofs, and memory. We will also see a shift from a concern for rhetoric as public discourse to a more private interest in rhetoric as a window on the human mind, a means of personal refinement, and even as a source of leisure activity.

The range of rhetorical possibilities is not exhausted, however, in the works of the famous rhetorical theorists who will demand most of our attention in this chapter. Our discussion of the seventeenth and eighteenth centuries will consider a highly innovative Italian teacher of rhetoric whose complex theories of the human mind still intrigue scholars. The chapter is also bracketed by the work of two iconoclastic women who also wrote about and practiced rhetoric in this period, but who explored non-traditional approaches to the rhetorical tradition.

MARGARET CAVENDISH

One of the most intriguing and provocative rhetoricians of the mid-seventeenth century was Margaret Cavendish (1623–1673), Duchess of Newcastle, England. The eighth child of Sir Thomas Lucas and his wife Elizabeth, Margaret received instruction in reading and writing, as well as in music and a number of crafts. She took an early interest in writing, and was producing books even as a young woman. Margaret was a member of the court of Queen Henrietta Maria, and was forced into exile in France along with other Royalists in the 1640s. It was there that she met and married William Cavendish, Duke of Newcastle.

While living on the European continent, Margaret studied both science and philosophy informally. She wrote six books on what was then called natural philosophy, but would today be termed science. Cavendish read Renaissance Humanist rhetoricians, and particularly admired Shakespeare and the Roman writer Ovid. She seems also to have been influenced by the philosophy of Thomas Hobbes. Upon her return to England Margaret became acquainted with and occasionally debated some of the leading scientific and philosophical figures of her day.

Writing Career

After her return to England in the early 1650s, Cavendish wrote continuously and under her own name, an unusual practice for women of her day. Her early publications were dismissed by scholars as immature, but undoubtedly some of the criticism resulted from the fact that she dared to write and publish as a woman. In fact, she is reputed to be the first English woman to have written with the sole purpose of seeking publication and thus literary fame.

A determined self-promoter with a keen sense of her audience, Cavendish ignored her critics and planned lavish and well-publicized public events, sometimes featuring herself in outlandish costumes. Her concern for her audience and her desire to not conform to literary norms led Cavendish to adopt a style of writing that she referred to as "natural" or "wild."[2] Cavendish was aware of the obstacles facing women who sought to write for public consumption in her day, especially if their writing was overtly persuasive in intent, that is, rhetorical. "When any of our Sex doth Write, they Write some Devotions, or Romances, or Receits of Medicines, for Cookery or confectioners, or Complemental Letters, or a Copy or two of Verses . . ."[3] A prolific writer, she is credited with publishing fourteen books as well as a number of essays.

But Cavendish was not satisfied to write devotional literature and recipe books. Rather, much of her writing, including her best-known work *The World's Olio*, takes up philosophical issues being debated in her day. Cavendish wrote plays and poems as well as nonfiction, and penned one of the earliest works of science fiction *The Blazing World* in which she imagines a planet run entirely by women. Margaret Cavendish died at the age of fifty in 1673. The extraordinary range of her writing, her participation in philosophical and scientific debates, and her preference for a highly accessible writing style mark her as a transitional figure standing between the Renaissance Humanist tradition and the Enlightenment period that followed.

VICO AND THE RHETORIC OF HUMAN THOUGHT

Giambattista Vico (1668–1774), a professor of rhetoric from Naples, is the most important of the later Italian Humanist writers.[4] Vico's father was a bookseller, and as a young man Vico spent a great deal of time reading. Lawyers held a prominent place in seventeenth-century Naples, and Vico studied originally for a career in law. However, his interests turned toward literature, history, mathematics, philosophy, and rhetoric. Nearly a recluse, Vico spent long hours alone teaching himself philosophy, law, and *vico famous for myth.*

literature. He was particularly drawn to works of logic, political science, and metaphysics by Spanish writers. Vico also studied Plato, and was intrigued with the Neoplatonism of his Renaissance predecessors, Pico and Ficino. In 1697 Vico was appointed professor of rhetoric at Naples, a position he held for 40 years. His highly influential theories reveal his intimate understanding of rhetoric and related undertakings such as poetry and myth.

Vico versus Descartes

Vico's love of rhetoric and literature led him to write passionately in response to the mathematically inclined philosopher, René Descartes (1596–1650). Descartes despised rhetoric and sought to relegate it to an obscure place in the academy. In his book *On the Study Methods of Our Time* (1708), Vico pointed out that mathematical proofs were just as reliant on symbols as were the orations of the rhetoricians. Thus, Descartes' beloved mathematical proofs were not founded on necessary and unchanging truths as the mathematician had suggested.

science becomes fruitless & only about facts. Vico thinks there more to life.

As we noted at the end of the previous chapter, the idea that science would provide a rational basis for future societies was already gaining influence in the seventeenth century. Vico sought to answer what he took to be a dangerous cultural development; rhetoric was the antidote to the deadening effects of scientific rationalism. Vico argued that rhetoric, not logic, provided a reliable foundation for humane culture, and that what he termed *poetic speech* was the foundation of civilized behavior and of civilization itself. Science's sterile method and reverence for individual reason threatened to undermine the *sensus communis*—common beliefs, values, and communal judgment that allowed great societies to flourish.

Vico's fear of the dominance of science cannot be overstated. Descartes was his *bête noire*, and Vico argued strenuously that only the constructive and communal use of rhetoric could overcome the corrosive effects of Descartes' method of systematic doubt.

Rhetoric and Imagination

Working as something of an early anthropologist, Vico sought to discover the foundations of human thinking in two unusual places—ancient poetry and mythology. This approach alienated him from Naples' leading scholars who saw him as an eccentric who was "dismissed as obscure, speculative, and unsound (*stravagante*, as the Italians put it), or even slightly mad."[5]

Unlike some prominent Enlightenment thinkers, Vico did not look down on earlier historical periods as "times of 'darkness' and irrationality."[6] Vico held that "primitive men were necessarily poets because they possessed strong imaginations which compensated for the weakness of their reason."[7] In Vico's view language and thought originated with what in classical works had been labeled rhetorical devices. For Vico, such figures of speech were not human inventions but rather were native to the human imagination. Moreover, it was language shaped by rhetoric that originally allowed human beings to impose order on their existence, to create meaning out of meaninglessness, and thus to develop societies.

Vico's history of human intellectual development, then, was focused on rhetoric and literature rather than logic and metaphysics.[8] He wanted to know how human beings "humanized" the chaotic natural world in which they found themselves. As Ernesto Grassi points out, for Vico "the problems that concern human beings . . . are the ones that urge themselves upon us in the construction of the human world . . ."[9]

Ingenium

Vico argued in his most famous work, *New Science* (1725), that historical method could be as exact as mathematics, another challenge to Descartes.[10] Decisions in public life were not based on certainties but on weighing options guided by prudence (*prudentia*) or practical judgment based on probabilities. Such decision-making wisdom (*sapientia*) was assisted by the eloquence (*eloquentia*) of trained orators. Vico was drawn to Cicero's notion of the broadly educated speaker, "a public servant whose ability with words is informed by a command of the whole cycle of learning."[11] Such a person, uniting wisdom and eloquence, provided practical and moral leadership to a city or nation. The orator was a heroic figure who spoke wisely for the common good.

Rhetoric was essential to all of the arts. Human social life was constructed by means of poetic language, the human mind imposing order rhetorically on a fundamentally disordered nature. The "humanization of nature" takes place, not through logical inference, but rather through an innate capacity Vico called *ingenium*, or the intuitive ability to grasp similarities or relationships. The person of practical judgment discovers "analogies between matters that lie far apart and are apparently unrelated . . ."[12] Grassi writes, "insight into relationships is not possible through a process of inference, but rather only through an original *in*-sight as invention and discovery (*inventio*)."[13] This interest in invention explains Vico's sustained attention to classical systems of *topoi*, the ancient means by which the invention of arguments took place.

Our capacity for grasping similarities among different objects is central to poetic or metaphoric thought. Analogic thinking allows insights crucial to humanizing the world. Discovering "connections, and so advancing the cause of civil life, is the proper work of ingenuity [*ingenium*]."[14] Through the exercise of *ingenium*, "we surpass what lies before us in our sensory awareness."[15]

This concept is similar to Vico's belief in *fantasia*, or a natural power of imagination that allowed early humans, through myth, to make sense of the world. In the act of transcending perception, of ordering the disorder of nature through narrative and our inborn communal judgment (*sensus communis*), we become human. The rhetorical devices that inform poetry provide us with "the language that constitutes humanity."[16] Thus, for Vico, rhetoric, not science or mathematics, is the key to all human achievements. Indeed, he was of the opinion that "the sciences are taught completely stripped of every badge of eloquence."[17] No help will come from that quarter.

Insights gained through *ingenium* are more poetic than logical, more intuitive than rational. Such thinking, therefore, actually produces new knowledge; it does not merely reformulate things already known. Vico found inspiration for this theory in Cicero and the rhetorical tradition rather than in the philosophers and logicians. Descartes, Vico thought, had ignored the vital rhetorical element in human thinking by focusing his attention solely on the method of demonstrable proof.

Rhetoric and the Evolution of Human Thought

For Vico, the first people "proceeded to create their world through the faculty of imagination rather than by pure abstract thought."[18] As Katherine Gilbert and Helmut Kuhn express the concept, "the poet's imagination is the natural expression of humanity's childhood."[19] Vico's theory of the development of thought has been called "incomparably richer and more fully developed" than those advanced by other scholars of his generation.[20] During "the childhood of the world," human thinking developed first by metaphor or comparisons. Early poets, their thought richly imaginative, compared objects to people. They thus anthropomorphized nature, attributing human qualities to inanimate objects. Metaphor was native to the human mind and an imaginative precursor to more rational thought.

Vico called this early metaphorical tendency the "poetic mode of thought."[21] The capacity for discovering metaphors was a consequence of "rhetorical 'wordplay,' or 'wit' [*acutezza*]," acuteness or mental sharpness.[22] The notion of *acutezza* was elevated in sixteenth- and seventeenth-century humanistic writing, and was displayed in clever metaphors. Rhetorical devices "can only come from an alert, imaginative mind, one with a well-honed facility for seeing connections between separate and apparently unrelated things."[23] Facility with rhetorical devices was thus an aid to creative thought.[24]

From metaphor, "the primary operation of our mind," human thought progressed to metonym, the substitution of a part for the whole, an agent for an act, a sign for the thing signified. From metonym, human thought developed a capacity for synecdoche, in which the whole object represents the part. Vico's final stage of linguistic development is irony, in which indirect statement carries direct meaning, or something is taken to stand for its opposite.[25]

The sense-making capacity that allowed human beings to create civilization out of disordered nature was exhibited in the dreams of poets rather than the deductions of logicians. Vico writes of a faculty he called *fantasia*: "fantasy collects from the senses and connects and enlarges to exaggeration the sensory effects of natural appearances and makes luminous images from them."[26] That is, the imagination—guided naturally by rhetorical tropes—expands on the data of sense impressions and makes a distinctly *human* life possible. As the great French historian Paul Hazzard wrote, "If only Italy had listened to Giambattista Vico . . . our eighteenth-century ancestors . . . would not have believed that reason was our first faculty, but on the contrary that imagination was."[27]

Vico on Myth: The Civilization-Shaping Force of Narrative

At a time when Enlightenment scholars were criticizing myth as a primitive form of reasoning, Vico argued that mythic narratives were foundational to the formation of civilization. In his *The New Science* and other works Vico wrote extensively on this topic, bringing his insights as a rhetorician to his study of ancient narrative. Joseph Mali writes,

[handwritten margin note: Is myth or logic more powerful in our world today?]

"Vico's theory of myth has long been recognized by scholars of myth as a major contribution to the modern science of mythology."[28] Nevertheless, Vico's work was largely ignored in his own day and myth was subsequently dismissed by Enlightenment thinkers.

For Vico, myth was "an early, necessary and wholly admirable phase in the development of civilization," and the "creative impulse" animating history.[29] Vico's study of mythic systems suggested that myth was not inferior to argument, but was its foundation and source—*mythos* was the ground and source of *logos*. Narrative, not argument, provided civilization's foundation. Historical events reflect patterns which can be known only "insofar as we can recognize in them the coherent narrative patterns" inherent to myth.[30]

By presenting *mythos* and *logos* "as different, yet compatible, modes of discourse," Vico elevated myth from the realm of ancient origin story to that of another kind of rational discourse. Myth allowed early humans "to make sense of reality" by means of "imaginary tales projected onto reality and the other by empirical theories derived from it." *Logos* reasons from observation; *mythos* introduces "metaphysical significance."[31] Thus, for Vico myths carry crucial clues about history and culture for "all our cultural creations . . . are recreations of myths."[32] Myth was foundational to the formation of the human world itself.

Studying mythology was thus crucial to self-knowledge, to grasping the origins of human civilization, and to shaping the world we presently inhabit. Human experience is "felt and formed by our power of imagination, or *fantasia,*" the power of imagination to "fully and completely to order the world."[33] Vico investigated the human mind and culture employing a "science" of myth, thus paving the way for subsequent scholars of myth such as Claude Levi-Strauss and John James Frazier.

Influence

For a long time Vico's thought was marginalized either as a later report on Renaissance Humanism or as the work of an interesting eccentric. In the twentieth century, however, the originality of his thought began to be recognized by some leading intellectual figures.

The German philosopher Hans-George Gadamer took an interest in Vico in the 1960s, particularly Vico's ideas about *sensus communis* or common sense and his theories of rhetoric. Donald Philip Verene writes that Gadamer "emphasizes how Vico's thought is rooted in the humanist tradition of rhetoric."[34] Vico was also a major influence on the narrative theories of Hayden White, as reflected in his important book *Tropics of Discourse.*[35] White sought to interpret Vico for a new generation of writers interested in the underlying structures of narrative.

BRITISH RHETORIC IN THE EIGHTEENTH CENTURY

According to historian of rhetoric Wilbur Samuel Howell, once rhetoric was established as the "master of the arts of popular discourse" in Britain, it gradually staked a claim to being "the sole art of communication by means of language . . ."[36] As such, rhetoric was

[handwritten margin notes:]
not against science but against it as one's ONLY way of thinking.

sees rhetoricians as heroes - can shape our thinking & our identity.

should use rhetoric to know who we are & understand our culture & stories.

important to influential educational movements. But, rhetorical concerns also were at the heart of philosophical and psychological theories in this period. Though the rhetorical theories that follow are often labeled "British," most of the thinkers described are Scottish, and one Irish. British should not be taken to mean English when applied to eighteenth-century rhetorical theory.

Rhetoric in British Education

British rhetorical education during the eighteenth century was often pursued in response to pressing social changes. Replying to rising skepticism, writers within the Churches of England and Scotland taught rhetoric under the guise of Christian preaching. In addition, English prose began to assume a new prominence as part of the shift from oral to written discourse.[37] Thus, rhetoric as the study of speechmaking and argumentation was challenged in schools as an emphasis on writing instruction emerged.[38]

Other changes encouraged rhetoric's rise to a prominent place in education. English was displacing Latin as the language of scholarship, and thus more people had access to learning and interest in the English language rose. Though not himself a gifted speaker, when famed Scottish economist Adam Smith (1723–1790) gave public lectures on rhetoric in Edinburgh in 1748, "it was largely in response to a growing need for a comprehensive, thoroughly modern treatment of English and its uses . . ."[39] Moreover, women were being admitted to the British universities in larger numbers during this period, which also increased the demand for instruction in writing and proper English usage.[40] Finally, urbanization was bringing people from the English countryside, from Scotland and from Ireland to urban centers such as London. Many of these new city dwellers recognized that their rustic accents limited the possibility for personal advancement. They thus sought education in "proper" diction, an element of rhetorical education. Winifred Horner notes that the potential for upward mobility in English society, a mobility dependent on a command of "good English," created strong demand for language instruction, particularly instruction in writing.[41] Thus, education in rhetoric was sought out by a broad cross section of the British public in the eighteenth century, and for a wide range of reasons.

The Public

The idea of "the public" requires some attention, for during the eighteenth century a modern sense of the public and a public domain were taking shape. Ordinary people could speak and write their opinions in new venues, and they could engage one another's ideas in a variety of settings. Whether in the public square, the meeting hall, the coffeehouse, or the newly popular periodicals of the day, citizen addressed citizen on a range of religious, social, and political issues.

As a result of the expanding public domain and an increasingly expressive public, a new understanding of rhetorical skill gradually took hold. The ancient model of rhetoric as an oratorical competition was losing ground as a new model of rhetoric as participation in public life developed. Kenneth Cmiel writes that the Scottish rhetorical theorists of this period—George Campbell, Adam Smith, and others—"eschewed the manipulative goals of the Ciceronians. They argued that rhetoric should teach how to forcefully communicate one's reasoned arguments."[42]

The Elocutionary Movement

Rhetoric has always been viewed as a means of personal advancement through the trained capacity to express one's views effectively in public settings. The art has also functioned as a path to refinement and an avenue into elite social circles; recall Castiglione's *Book of the Courtier* discussed in Chapter 7, an effort to refurbish Cicero's *perfectus orator* for Renaissance readers. The elocutionary movement in rhetorical education draws our attention specifically to the performance side of rhetoric, and to rhetoric's use as a method for polishing manners, developing poise, and improving the capacity to express oneself—desirable goals in an increasingly urban culture.[43]

Eighteenth-century British society was relatively open for social advancement if we compare it with other European societies of the time. Coffeehouses, lodges, freethinking clubs, and debating societies attracted individuals from a striking mix of social classes. Women often participated in these public settings. Though class distinctions were still rather rigid, social movement was possible, particularly if one applied oneself to personal improvement. No improvement was more important than speech, as speech was a marker of social class. The goal of the aspiring young urbanite, then, was to speak like a gentleman or a lady.

Moreover, a growing number of professions—law, politics, and religion in particular —demanded skill as a public speaker. We might add that famous English essayists of the day, such as Richard Steele, Joseph Addison, and Jonathan Swift had written critically of the quality of both speaking and writing in England. Such criticism lent some urgency to the search for instruction in proper and effective management of language. English education was not preparing students to explore and refine the potential in the English tongue for eloquent expression.

Thomas Sheridan

As is often the case, rhetoric answered a strongly felt social need in the second half of the eighteenth century. Thomas Sheridan (1719–1788), an Irish actor and educator, provided the ready student with a guide to proper and effective public speaking. In fact, he sought nothing less than a general reform of education in Britain so as to correct what he took to be a serious development—the neglect of elocution or rhetorical delivery. In *British Education* (1756), Sheridan wrote that poor preaching was actually threatening the health of British religion, and thus of Britain itself.

So deep was Sheridan's belief in the beneficial effects of skillful public speaking that he maintained the study of elocution would, in the words of G. P. Mohrmann, "improve religion, morality, and constitutional government; would undergird a refining of the language; and would pave the way for ultimate perfection in all the arts."[44] Sheridan wrote that oratory in the pulpit "must either effectually support religion against all opposition, or be the principal means of its destruction."[45]

The Importance of Delivery

Good delivery was crucial to convincing an audience of the urgency and truthfulness of one's message. In order to convince an audience member of an idea, that individual must "first be convinced that you believe it yourself." This will not happen "unless the tones of voice in which you speak come from the heart, accompanied by corresponding looks, and gestures, which naturally result from a man who speaks in earnest."[46]

Sheridan's deep concern about the poor quality of preaching in England is reflected in the following passage from his *A Discourse Introductory to a Course of Lectures* (1759):

> [A] man shall rise up in a public assembly, and, without the least mark of shame, deliver a discourse to many hundred auditors, in such disagreeable tones and unharmonious cadences, as to disgust every ear; and with such improper and false use of emphasis, as to conceal or pervert the sense; and all without fear of any consequential disgrace ... [And] this is done ... in the very service of the Most High![47]

Sheridan's most famous work, *A Course of Lectures on Elocution*, was published in 1762.[48] This book was a compilation of lectures Sheridan had delivered around Great Britain. Sheridan set out the principles of elocution, emphasizing delivery over the other traditional elements such as invention.

Training the speaking voice was crucial to effective public presentations, as was proper pronunciation.[49] Students of elocution were assigned to read passages aloud from well-known plays or books. But, as one might expect from an actor, Sheridan did not view delivery simply as a matter involving the voice; the face and the body also came into play in his discussion of the art of speaking in public. In fact, the instructions offered by elocutionists regarding facial expression, gesture, posture, and movement strike modern readers as something closer to instruction in acting, or even in dance, than in speaking.

Elocution's emphasis on delivery, and its use of teaching techniques such as the dramatic presentation of a memorized speech, contributed to a decline in concern for argument or invention in rhetoric. Thus, rhetoric's esteem fell in academic settings. However, elocution itself became a standard part of public education in England and the United States.

THE SCOTTISH SCHOOL

In *Democratic Eloquence: The Fight over Popular Speech in Nineteenth-Century America*, Kenneth Cmiel notes the significant influence of a group of Scottish rhetorical theorists in the eighteenth century. Members of this Scottish school of rhetoric include George Campbell, Hugh Blair, Adam Smith, and others. Their new rhetorics not only affected British conceptions of eloquence and argument but also shaped the teaching of rhetoric in America.

Cmiel writes with regard to the early United States that "the texts of the Scottish school swept into the nation's classrooms to replace (or at least balance) the Ciceronian rhetoric used earlier. In 1783 Brown University ordered Blair's *Rhetoric* from England; in 1784 the first American edition was published." The following sections explore the new and rather different approaches to rhetoric of three Scottish theorists that were having such an impact on rhetorical education and practice.[50]

The Belletristic Movement

During the eighteenth century, British interest in literature and writing expanded. Novels by writers such as Daniel Defoe (1660–1731) and Samuel Richardson (1689–1761) achieved a high degree of popularity, satisfying an increasing public desire to read for entertainment. Numerous books promised to help the would-be writer achieve clarity, grace, and beauty. Harold Harding has observed that

> in the latter half of the eighteenth century more than fifty textbooks, essays, lectures, and treatises on rhetoric and literary criticism by thirty different writers were published in England, Ireland, and Scotland. Interest in literature and the teaching of writing ran high.[51]

Barbara Warnick has traced the French roots of the Belletristic Movement in Britain, suggesting that this emphasis on rhetorical style is not native to the British Isles.[52] The study of *belles lettres* may, then, represent a delayed eighteenth-century effect of Pierre Ramus' earlier efforts to remove argument and invention from rhetoric. The Belletristic Movement expanded into a study of literature, literary criticism, and writing generally. Warnick writes, "Belletristic rhetoric and studies of belles lettres were particularly concerned with examining the specific qualities of discourse and their effects."[53] This approach to rhetoric "focused on reception, not production."[54] Historian of rhetoric Herman Cohen identifies *belles lettres* as one outworking of a broader intellectual movement that sought to discover "universal principles that could be applied to all verbal discourse."[55] Cohen ties this interest to the rise of scientific thinking in the Enlightenment.

Elevating the Reader

This shift from rhetoric as the study of invention or production of arguments to rhetoric as the study of universal effects of language on readers and listeners marks an important change of emphasis. The Belletristic Movement pushed rhetoric away from the classical emphasis on developing persuasive arguments for oral presentation, and toward the educated reception or appreciation of written and spoken discourse. We might say that rhetoric was taking on a consumerist perspective, with the audience's response to written material now assuming a central role. This emphasis corresponds to the appearance of written productions such as the novel that carried actual commercial value.

Interest in *belles lettres* grew in the 1760s and 1770s and was marked by an increased attention to matters of style. Douglas Ehninger notes that "the rhetoric of belles lettres was given its classic and most influential expression in Hugh Blair's *Lectures on Rhetoric and Belles Lettres*" (1783). Other important writers and works in the movement include

"William Barron's *Lectures on Belles Lettres and Logic* (London, 1806), and Alexander Jameison's *A Grammar of Rhetoric and Polite Literature* (London, 1818)." Ehninger adds that "in Lord Kame's *Elements of Criticism* (Edinburgh, 1762), some 500 pages of a combined 'rhetoric and poetic' were embedded in an inquiry into the nature of beauty and the foundations of taste."[56] We will take a closer look at the work of two of these writers, Lord Kames and Hugh Blair.

Lord Kames

As rhetoric became more closely aligned with aesthetics, questions of taste and decorum became central to rhetorical theorizing. Some rhetorical theorists such as Henry Home (1696–1782), better known by his title Lord Kames, returned to ancient principles like sublimity in their search for an aesthetic theory suited to a new era in British literature.

Kames was a Scottish philosopher and lawyer whose interests also turned to matters of literary style and the beauty of language. Following the Roman writer Longinus, Kames urged in his *The Elements of Criticism* (1762) that the quality of sublimity was conveyed by "grand" or enormous objects such as a large tree, a high cliff, or an ocean. The emotion or state of mind experienced when in the presence of such an object could be approximated in writing. Kames notes that Shakespeare achieved this effect in his play Julius Caesar:

The pleasant emotion raised by large objects has not escaped the poets:

—He doth bestride the narrow world
Like a Colossus; and we petty men
Walk under his huge legs.
Julius Caesar, Act I, Sc. 3.[57]

Kames also devotes a great deal of attention in the second chapter of *The Elements of Criticism* to arousing emotions, particularly through an appeal to the reader's sense of beauty. Like Gorgias in the ancient world, Kames explored the effects that spoken sounds have on hearers. For example, he writes with great specificity about sounds and cadences in particular words and word combinations:

In the first place, syllables in immediate succession, pronounced each of them with the same or nearly the same aperture of the mouth, produce a succession of weak and feeble sounds; witness the French words *dit-il, pathetique*: on the other hand, a syllable of the greatest aperture succeeding one of the smallest, on the contrary, makes a succession which, because of its remarkable disagreeableness, is distinguished by a proper name, *hiatus*. The most agreeable succession is where the cavity is increased and diminished alternately within moderate limits. Examples, *alternative, longevity, pusillanimous*.[58]

Like others in the Belletristic Movement, Kames was intrigued with the notion of taste. Taste, or the ability to recognize and appreciate high quality in literature and other art, was in Kames' view a natural gift of some individuals. One would not search for taste among "those who depend for food on bodily labor," for example. If this sounds like an elitist idea, it is. Kames envisioned a refined society of readers and listeners capable of appreciating the finer artistic achievements in literature and art. Such individuals were born, not made, though inborn capacities could be refined through proper education. As Warnick writes, "in Kames' theory is manifest an elitism that lies just below the surface of Scottish views on taste but is rarely openly articulated."[59]

Hugh Blair

Hugh Blair (1718–1800) was a Scottish preacher, born and educated in Edinburgh, who made important contributions to the Belletristic Movement. A famous Presbyterian preacher, in 1762, Blair was appointed to the Regius Chair of Rhetoric and *Belles Lettres* at the University of Edinburgh. In 1783, he published *Lectures on Rhetoric and Belles Lettres*. Widely read in England and abroad, the book went through numerous editions. Blair was a student of English literature and an editor of Shakespeare's works. Style, taste, beauty, and decorum are central to Blair's rhetorical theory, as they were to that of Kames. And, like Kames, Blair returns to several ancient rhetoricians for ideas—writers like Aristotle, Cicero, Longinus, and Quintilian.

Blair wrote his *Lectures* with the goal of improving the lives of his students and other readers. Much as Cicero's complete orator was a person of eloquence, wisdom, grace, charm and wit, so Blair's students developed the qualities of taste, eloquence, critical acumen, and style. Rhetoric's educational goals, then, are broader than simple preparation for professional success through making effective speeches. Rhetorical training is preparation for a life that combines graceful and effective expression in the public sphere with contemplation and enhanced aesthetic experience in the private. However, Cicero's orator is a dynamic public figure employing rhetorical skill for the greater good of society. Blair's is a more parochial, even private model—the individual citizen pursuing personal grace, leisure enjoyment, and social advancement.

As rhetorical interests grew to include written as well as spoken discourse, a corresponding shift occurred in the domain of rhetoric; no longer seen as an art pertinent only to public affairs, rhetoric was becoming part of private life as well.

Taste

This shift from public to private worlds is evident in Blair's references to the notion of taste, a developed appreciation of aesthetic experiences. Though taste is in part a matter of "natural sensibility to beauty," Blair is convinced that this capacity can be improved through experience and education.[60] Thus, he urges his readers to develop their capacity for taste toward the goal of enhancing their private lives. "The cultivation of taste is farther recommended, by the happy effects which it naturally tends to produce in human life."

A distinctly modern note characterizes Blair's advice; he writes for a rising educated middle class with time for leisure and a need for relaxation. People who live "in the most active sphere" of public life, "cannot be always occupied by business," he argues. Moreover, persons "of serious professions cannot always be on the stretch of serious thought," that is, cannot always devote their mental energies to serious topics and demanding problems. The development of taste enhances the enjoyment of diversions such as literature. Blair's readers are urged to balance the demands of work and the public sphere, with the retreat and enjoyments of private life.

Style

Blair defines style as "the peculiar manner in which a man expresses his conceptions, by means of language."[61] Style, then, is directly related to one's "manner of thinking." Thus, "when we are examining an author's composition, it is, in many cases, extremely difficult to separate the Style from the sentiment."[62] For Blair, then, one's manner of linguistic expression provided evidence of one's thought.

There are only two considerations to which the critic or student of style should attend. Blair calls these "perspicuity and ornament." For, he writes,

> all that can possibly be required of Language, is, to convey our ideas clearly to the minds of others, and, at the same time, in such a dress, as by pleasing and interesting them, shall most effectually strengthen the impressions which we seek to make.[63]

Practical matters, then, are at the heart of the study of style for Blair. Rhetoric seeks to make a point persuasively. Thus, rhetorical style must attract an audience and present a case clearly. Blair spends a good deal of time trying to explain how to make language both attractive and clear.

Of perspicuity, or clarity, Blair writes that there is no concern more central to style. After all, if clarity is lacking in a message all is lost. Claiming that your subject is difficult is no excuse for lack of clarity according to Blair: If you can't explain a difficult subject clearly, you probably don't understand it.[64] Blair's advice on clarity includes selecting precisely the right terms to make your point, avoiding "obsolete or new-coined words," and always speaking in a manner appropriate to your audience and your subject. Much of Blair's counsel to his young readers includes such reminders as "any words, which do not add some importance to the meaning of a Sentence, always spoil it."[65] This is still good advice.

George Campbell

The Scottish writer George Campbell (1719–1796) was among the most important rhetorical theorists of the late eighteenth century.[66] Scotland's university cities—Edinburgh, Glasgow, and Aberdeen—were sites of great intellectual activity in the eighteenth century. Campbell was born in Aberdeen, where he received his early education. Later, he attended Marischal College in Aberdeen, where he studied law and what would today be called psychology. His interests, however, turned toward theology, and he studied to be a minister. In 1748, he was ordained to the clergy of the Church of Scotland, and in 1758 Campbell was appointed principal of Marischal College. In 1771, he was elevated to the important position of professor of divinity at the same school.

Campbell was a preacher and religious polemicist whose famous *Dissertation on Miracles* (1762) was widely read though rather late response to David Hume's controversial argument against miracles that had been published in 1748. Campbell sought to discover a rational basis for Christian preaching in an increasingly skeptical and scientific age. Deeply interested in rhetoric, he recognized that new and more scientific ideas about the mind would likely change how this subject was understood and practiced. His most important work in rhetoric was *The Philosophy of Rhetoric*, published in 1776.[67] Another major work related to rhetoric was his *Lectures on Pulpit Eloquence*. Campbell's interest in preaching and apologetics provides an important frame for interpreting his rhetorical theory.[68]

A Scientific Rhetoric

Campbell's work on rhetoric incorporates British philosophical thought of the seventeenth and eighteenth centuries.[69] His writing reveals the influence both of philosophers with whom he agreed and those with whom he took issue, especially Thomas Hobbes (1588–1679). He studied the works of Francis Bacon (1561–1626) and John Locke (1632–1704), particularly Locke's influential psychological theories. Though Campbell disagreed sharply with David Hume (1711–1776), he admitted a great debt to the philosopher. In fact, the leading authority of Campbell's work, Lloyd Bitzer, writes that "Campbell's philosophy and his theory of human nature, both of which profoundly affect his treatment of rhetoric, are drawn mainly from Hume."[70]

Campbell was open to new ideas, and intended to develop a new rhetoric that incorporated insights of the Enlightenment period. He believed that he was building on the classical tradition in rhetoric by providing scientific support for traditional insights. He also hoped to move beyond those insights, however.

Rhetoric and philosophy were inseparable for Campbell, as the title of his work *The Philosophy of Rhetoric* suggests. Moreover, Campbell often tested his ideas on rhetoric by reading papers before the Aberdeen Philosophical Society, which he had helped to found. This Society also included thinkers such as Thomas Reid, James Beattie, and Alexander Gerard. Bitzer notes, however, that Hume "was the leading figure in the intellectual movement in which Campbell conceived and tested nearly the whole of his *The Philosophy of Rhetoric*."[71]

Campbell advanced a "scientific" rhetoric, but *science* for him meant something like what philosophy means today: an organized and rational account of a subject. "All art is founded on science," he writes in the introduction to *The Philosophy of Rhetoric*, but he counts as "the most sublime of all sciences" the studies of "*theology* and *ethics*."[72] His rhetoric, then, reflects what were taken to be advances in fields such as ethics and psychology.

"It was widely believed in the eighteenth century, even by defenders of the Ancients," writes George Kennedy, "that modern philosophy had made tremendous strides beyond the past."[73] Through new discoveries, Campbell sought to understand how the human mind operates and to provide instruction in eloquence based on that understanding.[74] His interest in applying recently acquired knowledge to the study of rhetoric also meant that classical sources—Aristotle, Cicero, and Quintilian—became less important to rhetorical theory than they had been in the Middle Ages and Renaissance.[75]

Rhetoric and Psychology

Guided by Bacon and Locke, Enlightenment writers tended to divide up the mind into different capacities or "faculties."[76] In the faculty psychology view, the mind was not a unified entity, but consisted of distinct and identifiable capacities or faculties: the understanding, the imagination, the passions, and the will. Each faculty had its own particular responsibility in the processes of thinking and acting. This view is reflected in Bacon's famous definition of rhetoric as "the application of reason to imagination for the better moving of the will." Campbell also seems to have agreed with Vico that rhetorical tropes were the mind's natural language rather than artistic constructions.

For Campbell, eloquence was "that art or talent by which the discourse is adapted to its end."[77] But, how is this goal best achieved? In Campbell's theory, each mental faculty spoke virtually its own language. The understanding spoke the language of logic, while the passion spoke the language of emotion. Each part also performed a distinct function. The understanding gathered information and, when satisfied, responded with conviction. The imagination perceived beauty. The passions motivated and the will moved one to act.

Thus, each faculty has a part to play in the persuasive process, that is, in rhetoric. As Campbell writes, "all the ends of speaking are reducible to four; every speech being intended to enlighten the understanding, to please the imagination, to move the passions, or to influence the will."[78] The audience is central in this formula, as they are the ones whose understanding, imagination, passions, and will are being addressed. "In both *The Philosophy of Rhetoric* and *Lectures on Pulpit Eloquence*," writes Warnick, "Campbell's principal aim was to describe how style and expression contributed to discourse's ability to appeal to the various faculties of its hearers."[79]

A Theory of Persuasion

One of Campbell's more famous contributions to the history of rhetoric is his theory of persuasion. As Howell explains, "[T]wo things must be done, he said, by an author who would persuade others." The first, according to Campbell,

> is to excite some desire or passion in the hearers; the second is, to satisfy their judgment, that there is a connection between the action to which he would persuade them, and the gratification of the desire of passion which he excites.[80]

Persuasion was a matter of addressing both the emotions and the reason, as audiences are not convinced without arguments and do not act except in response to emotions. "When persuasion is the end, passion [emotion] must be engaged," he writes.[81] Campbell explains the relationships between emotion and reason this way: "The former is effected by communicating lively and glowing ideas of the object; the latter . . . by presenting the best and most forcible arguments which the nature of the subject admits."[82] The faculty theory of the mind is clearly in force: an effective speaker must know how to craft lively or "vivacious" images addressed to the passions and forceful arguments for the understanding.

Important to Campbell's thinking about persuasion was the notion of plausibility. A plausible narrative was instantly believable because of its close association with an audience's experience. Warnick writes that plausibility developed "from any description in which what was portrayed conformed to experience and expectation so as to appeal to the audience's imagination."[83] Plausibility in a narrative corresponded directly to the perceived "probability" in the presentation of "sound arguments and the use of facts."[84] Thus, persuasion was a product of the probability of one's arguments complementing the plausibility of one's narratives.

Education in Eloquence

Campbell's students would have learned how to present a message clearly and attractively, as well how to defend a proposition with sound inference and solid evidence. However, the goal they sought exceeded that of earlier rhetoricians. The "Christian orator" had a more demanding task than did the orators of ancient times. Why is this? Because "it is not a momentary but a permanent effect at which he aims . . . a thorough change of heart and disposition."[85] No demand on eloquence could be greater than "to persuade [a multitude] for the love of God, to be wise, and just and good."[86]

Achieving this end meant the preacher—or any successful orator, for that matter—had to be a verbal artist. Much of what we believe comes not through direct experience, but through a clear and convincing appeal to the imagination, appeal to the imagination with descriptive language is crucial to persuasion. Warnick writes that Campbell

> reminds his readers that oratory is, in a sense, painting, and that an orator must exhibit lively and glowing images of his subjects so as to bring his auditor's imaginations to the point where their representations will impress the mind as do the stimulations of sense and memory.[87]

This capacity to affect the imagination is one sign of true eloquence.

Campbell's rhetoric had practical goals, and was tied most directly to the practical concerns of a public figure—the Christian minister. But any effective speaker, in Campbell's analysis, must understand both the human mind and the resources of language that can engage the mind so as to move the listener to action.

Richard Whately Revives Classical Rhetoric

Despite the innovations of the Scottish school, more traditional rhetoric also survived into the nineteenth century. Richard Whately (1787–1863), an English cleric and Bishop of Dublin, eventually sat as a member of the House of Lords. Educated at Oxford, Whately was deeply interested in traditional logic and rhetoric. Like Augustine, Whately was an active preacher and controversialist during much of his later life, and was a witty and even caustic polemicist. In other words, he lived in a world of arguments. Whately rebutted Campbell's rejection of syllogistic logic, contending that Campbell misunderstood the complementary relationship of deductive and moral reasoning. Moral reasoning, Whately held, discovered the premises of arguments, while syllogistic logic provided a method for drawing conclusions from these premises, or evaluating the arguments of others.[88] "For Whately," writes Ray McKerrow, "the proper and sole role for logic was as an instrument for structuring and evaluating discourse."[89]

Argument

Whately was not particularly concerned with the larger philosophical and psychological issues at rhetoric's foundations. Campbell was concerned to understand how the mind works, while Whately does not mention the issue at all. Whately's rhetoric is focused on issues of practical argument. In this respect, he retrieved a key element of the classical tradition: the centrality of invention—discovering persuasive arguments. Whately is best known, not for an abstract theory of persuasion, but for his perceptive discussion of types of argument and formulation of the principles of debate. Such issues arise out of his interest in the public practice of rhetoric as an art of argumentative disputation. His are the concerns of a trained public pleader and advocate.

Analogy

One of Whately's most important contributions to the history of rhetoric is his discussion of analogy. Whately defines an analogy as an argument "in which the instance adduced is somewhat more remote from that to which it is applied." What does he mean by this?

Whately's own example is instructive. If a physician determined that a certain substance was poisonous to human beings, this would have been learned by experience. If, however, the doctor moved to conclude that the same substance was also poisonous to animals, this conclusion would have been drawn by analogy rather than by experience.[90] Whately distinguishes this sort of direct comparison, which he terms analogy, from the more figurative sort of comparison that involves comparing things "that stand in similar relations to other things."[91]

Thus, following Whately's example, an egg stands in a similar relation to a chicken as a seed stands to the plant that produced it. Both things—the seed and the egg—can produce a new member of the species that generated it. Whately finds the analogy between the body and the mind, however, to be of the less direct, more figurative type. That is to say, the body and the mind are not literally alike, so that when we reason that, just as people's bodies are quite different, so must their minds be quite different, we are reasoning from an indirect or figurative analogy.

Presumption and Burden of Proof

Whately systematized traditional concepts such as presumption and burden of proof for debate settings. Presumption means a "pre-occupation of the ground, as implies that it must stand good till some sufficient reason is adduced against it."[92] That is to say, a statement that has presumption is assumed true until it is challenged in such a way as to raise a question about its truthfulness.

The clearest example today is the presumption of innocence employed in our judicial system. What does it mean to say that you are "presumed innocent until proved guilty"? As Whately points out, it "does not, of course, mean that we are to *take for granted* he is innocent; for if that were the case, he would be entitled to immediate liberation." What it does mean is that the "'burden of proof' lies with the accusers."[93] So what is the "burden of proof"?

Whately says that, in the example of the accused individual, being presumed innocent means that "he is not called on to prove his innocence, or to be dealt with as a criminal till he has done so." The burden of proof requires an accuser to create sufficient doubt about the accused individual's innocence that the accused must reply. Not until a reasonable person would find the evidence considerable has the burden of proof been satisfied, however. Satisfying the burden of proof does *not* mean "proving" anything. It does mean advancing evidence that, on its face (*prima facie*), raises a significant question about the accused's innocence.

Whately cautions his readers not to try to prove "negative" propositions such as, "I'm not guilty." Thus, with Christianity under attack, he thought it ill-advised to try to answer every doubt and question raised against it. Rather, Christianity enjoyed presumption, which meant that its opponents were required to raise a substantial doubt about the religion before any defense at all was required.

Christianity *exists*; and those who deny the divine origin attributed to it, are bound to show some reasons for assigning to it a human origin; not indeed to prove that it *did* originate in this or that way, without supernatural aid; but to point out some conceivable way in which it *might* have so arisen.[94]

Of course, presumption may shift over time, and Whately's observations might not hold in the same way today.

Whately moved the concepts of presumption and burden of proof out of the chambers of the Parliament, making them part of public arguments about religion, justice, and politics. They have come to be important terms in both law and competitive debate.

Maria Edgeworth

As we have seen in our discussions of Margaret Cavendish and Giambattista Vico, rhetoricians of the Enlightenment period reflected a variety of interests and approaches to the topic. Rhetoric scholar Jane Donawerth has noted that in "An Essay on the Noble Science of Self-Justification" (1795), a writer named Maria Edgeworth goes so far as to create "a satiric parody of the masculine rhetorical treatise."[95] Edgeworth's strategy is to read masculine rhetorical theory of her day "through a wife's eyes." Donawerth calls Edgeworth "an innovator in education philosophy and a writer of fiction and textbooks at the end of the eighteenth century."[96] Edgeworth worked with her father to create a series of textbooks based on narratives.

Parodying the Men

Edgeworth sets out to parody Enlightenment rhetorical theory, particularly its goal of turning (she says "reducing") what was once an art into a science, stating with clear ironic intent that she will discuss both "defensive and offensive" rhetorical strategies. Donawerth notes that in this way, "Edgeworth questions the purpose of Enlightenment rhetoric," such as that presented in Campbell's supposedly scientific *Philosophy of Rhetoric*. Donawerth writes, "Edgeworth mockingly parodies and transforms the techniques of traditional rhetoric and thus resists not only the repression of women's voices and powers in marriage but also the dangerous potential for manipulation in rhetoric."[97] She also satirizes the elocutionary movement as well as the Belletristic Movement's emphasis on taste which, she suggests, is a criterion incapable of objective proof.

Donawerth concludes that "Edgeworth is not a passive consumer of eighteenth-century rhetorical standards, but a transgressive and ironic reader of them."[98] In constructing her satirical critique of Enlightenment rhetoric, Edgeworth demonstrates her knowledge of earlier rhetorical traditions as well. Her parody of a scientific approach to rhetoric using the tools of rhetoric itself reminds us the Protagorean dictum that each argument invites a counter argument.

CONCLUSION

Rhetorical scholarship in the eighteenth century reflects a wide range of concerns, from Vico's interests in the origins of human thought processes to Thomas Sheridan's search for a renewed sense of eloquence. Rhetoricians explored ancient themes, such as the importance of style to expression, the contributions of rhetorical training to personal refinement, and the standards of proof for arguments. But new territory was also being explored, as the scientific rhetoric of George Campbell illustrates.

The old European classical order was giving way to new orientations in Western rhetorical studies. Vico's theories, for instance, are so novel and profound that scholars are still trying to fathom their implications. Nevertheless, rhetoric scholars of the period also reflect more traditional concerns such as invention and delivery, often with a nationalistic impulse behind their efforts. Thomas Sheridan, for instance, sought to enhance the status of the English language and consequently traditional British institutions. Hugh Blair and Lord Kames intended to heighten appreciation for British literature, Richard Whately to strengthen the English Church, and George Campbell to appropriate the insights of Scottish and English philosophy for understanding persuasion. A concern for the British nation's development and welfare thus marks much of British Enlightenment rhetorical theory. Britain's status as a rising world empire seemed to demand the recognition of its language and institutions as equal in force to those of Europe. Even the advancement of British Protestantism required rhetorically skilled preachers.

This is not to say that the Enlightenment period represents a complete break with earlier rhetorical scholarship. Campbell's "scientific" interest in the rhetoric of the human mind, with each faculty speaking its own language, reminds us of Plato's speculations about a complex *psyche* in which each part employs its own rhetoric. Recall that in *Phaedrus* Plato defines rhetoric as the "art of influencing the soul [*psyche:* mind] through words." Still, Campbell's treatment of rhetoric's relationship to the mind differs from Plato's in some important respects. Whately's treatment of rhetoric as centered on matters of argument is clearly rooted in a much older conception of rhetoric in which inventional concerns and skill in argument dominated, while the Belletristic Movement's interest in the power of beautiful language finds classical parallels in both Gorgias and Longinus.

Thus, the eighteenth century finds rhetoric again moved to the forefront of educational and scholarly concerns, a place it occupied many times during the course of Western history. But, as Warnick argues, in several important instances rhetoric's role shifts from producing public discourse to enhancing its consumption, from discovering knowledge to managing the discoveries of other disciplines, and from an external focus on public problems to an internal focus on the mind and imagination. Nevertheless, the wide range of ways in which rhetoric was discussed—including Edgeworth's satirical treatment—the many concerns it was asked to address, and the energy that was expended in its development and dissemination, all suggest the relevance of an ancient discipline to an age in which discovery and change were hallmarks of intellectual life.

QUESTIONS FOR REVIEW

1. What expectations regarding the writing of women did Margaret Cavendish challenge?
2. By what means did Vico think the mind ordered the world and made civilization possible?
3. What, according to Vico, was the human capacity of ingenium?
4. What were Vico's principal objections to the philosophy of Descartes?
5. What are some of the social forces that compelled British people to seek education in rhetoric during the eighteenth century?
6. What particular social developments in Britain alarmed Thomas Sheridan? What was his proposed solution?
7. What negative effects did Thomas Sheridan associate with the decline in British eloquence?
8. What were the goals of the Belletristic Movement? What effect did it have on the study of argument as a component of rhetoric?
9. Why was Hugh Blair concerned to develop the quality of taste in his students?
10. What theory of psychology influenced George Campbell's theory of rhetoric? How was this influence revealed in Campbell's theory?
11. How may Campbell's interest in religious questions have influenced his theory of rhetoric?
12. What did Richard Whately hope to accomplish through teaching his students rhetoric?
13. How were presumption and burden of proof related for Whately?
14. What was Maria Edgeworth's response to prominent Enlightenment rhetorical theories?

QUESTIONS FOR DISCUSSION

1. The elocutionary movement of the eighteenth century offered training in rhetorical delivery as a means of personal refinement. Even though this particular idea may be foreign to contemporary education, are there ways in which an ability to speak clearly and effectively is still seen as a mark of personal success or social status?
2. Vico argued that myth—in its capacity to organize our experience—was a rational form of discourse and the foundation of logos or argument. What stories told today might have the organizational or ordering status of myth?

3. What, for you, is the significance of style in speaking and writing? Is it important to clear communication? Is it an element in persuasion? If style is important to persuasion, should it be?

4. George Campbell built his rhetorical theory on a particular view of the human mind. We have seen something like this in the suggestions Plato made in *Phaedrus* about the nature of the human soul. Vico speculated about the mind's development in terms of rhetorical devices. What view of the human mind and its workings might a contemporary rhetorical theory reflect?

5. If she were alive today Margaret Cavendish might be a performance artist. What contemporary parallels do you see to her use of a rhetoric of display, and to her challenging of established norms about what can be discussed and by whom?

TERMS

Acutezza In Vico, rhetorical wordplay or wit.

Belletristic Movement Rhetorical movement in the late eighteenth and early nineteenth centuries that emphasized considerations of style in rhetoric, expanding rhetoric into a study of literature, literary criticism, and writing generally.

Burden of proof In Whately, the responsibility to bring a case against the *status quo* sufficient to challenge its enjoyment of presumption.

Faculty psychology The view that the mind consisted of "faculties" or capacities, including the understanding, the imagination, the passions, and the will.

Fantasia For Vico, the power of imagination to order the world; active when humans formulate myths.

Ingenium For Vico, the innate human capacity to grasp similarities or relationships.

Irony When indirect statement carries direct meaning, or something is taken to stand for its opposite.

Metaphor A comparison of things not apparently similar.

Metonym The substitution of a part for the whole.

Perspicuity In Hugh Blair, clarity of expression.

Plausibility In Campbell's theory, discourse that is instantly believable because of its close association with an audience's experience of their social world.

Presumption A "*pre-occupation* of the ground," in Whately's terms. An idea occupies its place as reasonable or acceptable until adequately challenged.

Prudence Practical judgment.

Sensus communis For Vico, common beliefs and values that provide the basis for society.

Synecdoche The whole object represents the part.

Taste In Kames and Blair, a developed appreciation of aesthetic experiences.

Tropes Rhetorical devices.

NOTES

1   Barbara Warnick, *The Sixth Canon: Belletristic Rhetorical Theory and Its French Antecedents* (Columbia, SC: University of South Carolina Press, 1993), 129.

2   Ryan John Stark, "Margaret Cavendish and Composition Style," *Rhetoric Review* 17(2) (Spring 1999), 264–281.

3   Sarah Heller Mendelson, *The Mental World of Stuart Women: Three Studies* (Amherst, MA: University of Massachusetts Press, 1987), 35.

4   On Vico's life and relationship to rhetoric, see: Michael Mooney, *Vico in the Tradition of Rhetoric* (Princeton, NJ: Princeton University Press, 1985).

5   Peter Burke, *Vico* (Oxford: Oxford University Press, 1985), 2.

6   Burke, 55.

7   Burke, 3.

8   Ernesto Grassi, *Rhetoric as Philosophy* (University Park, PA: Pennsylvania State Press, 1980), 5.

9   Grassi, 6.

10 Mooney, 126.

11 Mooney, 8–9.

12 Mooney, 127.

13 Grassi, 7.

14 Mooney, 135.

15 Grassi, 8.

16 Mooney, 29.

17 Giambattista Vico, *On the Study Methods of Our Time*, trans. Elio Gianturco (Ithaca, NY: Cornell University Press, 1990), 87. Quoted in, Donald Philip Verene, "Gadamer and Vico on *Sensus Communis* and the Tradition of Humane Knowledge," in *The Philosophy of Hans-George Gadamer*, ed. Lewis E. Hahn (Chicago IL: Open Court Publishers, 1997), 140.

18 Richard Manson, *The Theory of Knowledge of Giambattista Vico* (n.p.: Archon Books, 1969), 35.

19 Katherine E. Gilbert and Helmut Kuhn, *A History of Esthetics* (Bloomington, IN: University of Indiana Press, 1953), 268. Quoted in Willson Havelock Coates, *The Emergence of Liberal Humanism* (New York: McGraw-Hill, 1966), 219.

20 Burke, 53.

21 Burke, 53.

22 Joseph Mali, *The Rehabilitation of Myth: Vico's "New Science"* (Cambridge: Cambridge University Press, 1992), 183; Mooney, 66.

23 Mooney, 66.

24 Mali, 183.

25 Mali, 167.

26 Vico, "Orazione in Morte di Donna Angela Cimmino Marchesa di Petrella," in *Opere di G. B. Vico*, ed. Fausto Nicolini, 8 vols. in 11 (Rome: Bari Laterza, 1911–1914), 7:170. Quoted in Grassi, 7.

27 Paul Hazzard, *La Pensée Européenne au XVIIIe siècle de Montesquieu k Lessing* (Paris: Arthone Fayard, 1963), 43. Quoted in editor's introduction to Giambattista Vico, *On Humanistic Education: Six Inaugural Orations, 1699–1707*, ed. Donald Phillip Verene, trans. G. A. Pinton and A. W. Shippe (Ithaca, NY: Cornell University Press, 1993), 2–3.

28 Joseph Mali, *The Rehabilitation of Myth: Vico's* New Science (Cambridge: Cambridge University Press, 1992), 7.

29 Laurence Coupe, *Myth* (New York: Routledge, 1997), 119.

30 Mali, 3.

31 Mali, 150. Benjamin Bennett writes that in *The Birth of Tragedy*, Nietzsche asserts that myth is "unconscious metaphysics." "Nietzsche's Idea of Myth: The Birth of Tragedy from the Spirit of Eighteenth-Century Aesthetics," *Proceedings of the Modern Language Association* 91: 3 (May, 1979), 420–422, p. 421.

32 Mali, 9.

33 Verene 83.

34 Verene, 138.

35 Hayden White, *Tropics of Discourse: Essays in Cultural Criticism* (Baltimore, MD: Johns Hopkins University Press, 1986).

36 Wilbur Samuel Howell, *Eighteenth-Century British Logic and Rhetoric* (Princeton, NJ: Princeton University Press, 1971), 6.

37 Winifred Bryan Horner, "Writing Instruction in Great Britain: Eighteenth and Nineteenth Centuries," in *A Short History of Writing Instruction*, ed. James J. Murphy (Davis, CA: Hermagoras Press, 1990), 124–125.

38 Stephen H. Browne, "Shandyean Satire and the Rhetorical Arts in Eighteenth-Century England," *Southern Communication Journal* 55 (Winter 1990): 191–205.

39 Warnick, 66. Warnick cites Richard Sher on this point.

40 Horner, 136–137.

41 Horner, 121–150.

42 Kenneth Cmiel, *Democratic Eloquence: The Fight over Popular Speech in Nineteenth-Century America* (New York: William Morrow, 1990), 36.

43 See: Howell, *Eighteenth-Century*, 145–256.

44 G. P. Mohrmann, introduction to Thomas Sheridan, *A Discourse Being Introductory to His Course of Lectures on Elocution and the English Language* (1759; rpt. Los Angeles: Augustan Reprint Society, 1969), ii.

45 Quoted in Howell, *Eighteenth-Century*, 155.

46 Quoted in Howell, *Eighteenth-Century*, 156.

47 Sheridan, *A Discourse*, 25–26.

48 Thomas Sheridan, *A Course of Lectures on Elocution* (London: W. Strahan, 1762). On Sheridan's work, see: Wallace A. Bacon, "The Elocutionary Career of Thomas Sheridan," *Speech Monographs* 31 (March 1964): 1–53.

49 Thomas Sheridan, *A General Dictionary of the English Language* (London: J. Dodsley, 1780). This work was published to provide a guide to proper pronunciation of English words.

50 Cmiel, 40.

51 Hugh Blair, *Lectures on Rhetoric and Belles Lettres*, ed. Harold Harding, 2 vols. (Carbondale, IL: Southern Illinois University Press, 1965), v. 1, x–xi.

52 Warnick, especially Chap. 1.

53 Warnick, 4.

54 Warnick, 34.

55 Herman Cohen, "Belles-lettres," in *Encyclopedia of Composition and Rhetoric: Communication from Ancient Times to the Information Age*, ed. Theresa Enos (New York: Routledge, 2004), 71.

56 Richard Whately, *Elements of Rhetoric*, ed. Douglas Ehninger (1828, rpt. Carbondale, IL: Southern Illinois University Press, 1963), xxiv.

57 Henry Home, Lord Kames, *The Elements of Criticism* (1761; rpt. New York: Barnes and Burr, 1865), 133.
58 Kames, 270.
59 Warnick, 112.
60 Blair, 21.
61 Blair, 183.
62 Blair, 183–184.
63 Blair, 184.
64 Blair, 185–186.
65 Blair, 226.
66 See: James L. Golden and Edward P. J. Corbett, *The Rhetoric of Blair, Campbell, and Whately* (New York: Holt, Rinehart and Winston, 1968). Other sources include: Douglas Ehninger, "George Campbell and the Revolution in Inventional Theory," *Southern Speech Journal* 15 (1950): 270– 276; "Campbell, Blair, and Whately Revisited," *Southern Speech Journal* 28 (1963), 169–182; "Campbell, Blair, and Whately: Old Friends in a New Light," *Western Speech* 19 (1955): 263–269; Douglas McDermott, "George Campbell and the Classical Tradition," *Quarterly Journal of Speech* 49 (1963): 403–409; Dominic LaRusso, "Root or Branch? A Reexamination of Campbell's 'Rhetoric,'" *Western Speech* 32 (1968): 85–91; Herman Cohen, "William Leechman's Anticipation of Campbell," *Western Speech* 32 (1968), 92–99.
67 George Campbell, *The Philosophy of Rhetoric*, ed. Lloyd F. Bitzer (Carbondale, IL: University of Southern Illinois Press, 1963). On Campbell, see: Bitzer's Introduction to *The Philosophy of Rhetoric*; Howell, *Eighteenth-Century*, 577–612.
68 On Campbell's thought and work, see: Arthur Walzer, *George Campbell: Rhetoric in the Age of Enlightenment* (Albany NY: State University of New York Press, 2003).
69 Gerard Hauser, "Empiricism, Description, and the New Rhetoric," *Philosophy and Rhetoric* 5 (1972): 24–44; Lloyd Bitzer, "Hume's Philosophy in George Campbell's *The Philosophy of Rhetoric*," *Philosophy and Rhetoric* 2 (1969): 136–166; Vincent Bevilaqua, "Philosophical Origins of George Campbell's *Philosophy of Rhetoric*," *Speech Monographs* 32 (1965): 7–8.
70 Bitzer, Introduction to *The Philosophy of Rhetoric*, xiii.
71 Bitzer, Introduction to *The Philosophy of Rhetoric*, xiii.
72 Campbell, xlv.
73 George Kennedy, *Classical Rhetoric and Its Christian and Secular Tradition from Ancient Times*, 1st ed. (Chapel Hill, NC: University of North Carolina Press, 1980), 234; see also: Thomas Conley, *Rhetoric in the European Tradition* (New York: Longman, 1990), 217–220.
74 Douglas Ehninger, Introduction to Richard Whately, *Elements of Rhetoric* (1828; Carbondale, IL: Southern Illinois University Press, 1963), xxv–xxvi.
75 Kennedy, 240.
76 Wilbur Samuel Howell, "John Locke and the New Rhetoric," *Quarterly Journal of Speech* 53 (1967): 319–321.
77 Campbell, 1.
78 Campbell, 1.
79 Warnick, 68.
80 Quoted in Howell, *Eighteenth-Century*, 587.
81 Campbell, 77.
82 Quoted in Howell, *Eighteenth-Century*, 587.
83 Warnick, 67.
84 Warnick, 67.

85 Campbell, 108.
86 Campbell, 108.
87 Warnick, 119.
88 McKerrow, 7 ff.
89 McKerrow, 9.
90 Whately, 90.
91 Whately, 91.
92 Whately, 112.
93 Whately, 112–113.
94 Whately, 116.
95 Jane Donawerth, "Poaching on Men's Philosophy of Rhetoric: Eighteenth- and Nineteenth-Century Rhetorical Theory by Women," *Philosophy and Rhetoric*, 33(3) (2000), 243–258.
96 Donawerth, 244.
97 Donawerth, 245.
98 Donawerth, 246.

Transition to postmodernism : Unit 3
1) Rise & fall of scientific thinking
2) Reaction against modernity (P. 266)
   - revolves around power structure

■ ■ ■ *Chapter 9*

Contemporary Rhetoric I: Arguments, Audiences, and Advocates

Facts will never appear to us as brute and meaningless; they will always organize themselves into some sort of story, some drama.

—Mary Midgley

As noted toward the end of the last chapter, the classical tradition, with its focus on oral presentations, was already in decline by Richard Whately's time. Rhetoric's diminishing status as an academic study continued through the end of the nineteenth century. The twentieth century opened with interest in rhetorical theory at perhaps its lowest point since the discussion of rhetoric began in ancient Greece. Scientific thinking was now ascendant, and methods of reasoning about contingent matters were dismissed as inferior to scientific method. Logical positivism, or the intellectual effort to apply scientific standards to the resolution of all issues, had apparently rendered rhetoric obsolete.

However, as the twentieth century progressed, confidence in scientific thinking as a means of addressing human social and moral problems was severely undermined. The atrocities associated with World War II and "scientific" approaches to social structuring undertaken by fascist regimes in Europe, left the intellectual world reeling. Many intellectuals began to question whether "scientific socialism" was a viable alternative to the inequities of industrial capitalism. For all of its impressive contributions, science had failed to solve persistent human problems like aggression, racism, economic exploitation, and political domination.

A new approach to discussing human values was required, one suited specifically to resolving perennial moral problems such as how to govern justly. Recognizing the importance of everyday reasoning processes to moral deliberations, some thinkers turned their attention to the structures that characterize everyday or "marketplace" arguments. Others looked for a new language of human values, or sought the conditions under which rational discourse could be cultivated. In this search for a new rhetoric and a new rationality, interest revived in such foundational components of the rhetorical tradition as argumentation, the audience, and the conditions under which rational debate occurs.

Not only had science not provided comprehensive solutions to social problems but scientists also were acknowledging that much scientific discourse was not formulary, clinical and syllogistic, but strategic, argumentative, and rhetorical. The theory that "won out" over competing theories in scientific debates was often the theory presented in the most persuasive manner, not the one supported by the greatest weight of evidence. Moreover, human motives played a role in interpreting scientific data, creating the institutions in which science was practiced, allocating funding to research, and even in formulating theories. Science, it turned out after more than a century of intellectual dominance, was in important respects rhetorical. Scholars in fields as varied as economics, astronomy, psychology, literature, biology, and mathematics were acknowledging that rhetoric played a major role in their professional lives.

ARGUMENTATION AND RATIONAL DISCOURSE

One of the important accomplishments of late twentieth-century rhetorical studies was to provide a means of assessing the rationality of everyday argumentation. The works of scholars such as Chaim Perelman and Jürgen Habermas were directed toward revealing the structure of everyday arguments, demonstrating the place of values in such arguments, and providing a theory about the conditions under which such arguments are most equitably and rationally advanced. The goal of this important intellectual work has been to improve the practice of discourse in contemporary society, to improve the quality of human social life, and to cultivate a more rational society.

Perelman and Olbrechts-Tyteca: A New Rhetoric

Chaim Perelman (1912–1985) was a Belgian philosopher and legal theorist who became interested in the question of how moral claims can be established as rational when values are contested. Perelman's rhetorical theory was largely a response to his experiences during World War II, which convinced him that the survival of Western civilization depended on rational public discourse about values.[1] No longer could such debate depend on resort to religion or absolutist ideologies.[2]

Perelman and colleague Madame Lucie Olbrechts-Tyteca (1899–1987) searched for a nonscientific, nontheistic foundation for discourse involving values. This search led them to the ancient discipline of rhetoric and, more specifically, to argumentation and the audience. "What we preserve of the traditional rhetoric," they write in their major work, *The New Rhetoric*, "is the idea of the audience, an idea immediately evoked by the mere thought of a speech."[3] Sounding like rhetoricians from classical Greece or Rome, they write that "knowledge of those one wishes to win over is a condition preliminary to all effectual argumentation."[4]

No claim is self-evidently true, and resort to God or another source of absolute truth will not uphold arguments about contingent issues in a pluralistic social setting. Moreover, formal logic detached from human values is inadequate to guide action. Only through a sustained process of public argumentation can value-based propositions be established as reasonable, or rejected as lacking rational merit. Thus, the arguments that engage and convince audiences are at the center of Perelman and Olbrechts-Tyteca's concerns.[5] Thus, much of their groundbreaking book, *The New Rhetoric: A Treatise on Argumentation*, is a catalog of various types of arguments common to everyday discourse.

Perelman and Olbrechts-Tyteca also emphasized the audience as crucial to grounding rational discourse. "All argumentation," as they see it, "aims at gaining the adherence of minds, and, by this very fact, assumes the existence of intellectual contact." Rhetoric develops out of the contact of audiences with arguments; an argument's quality results, not from its internal structure, but from the quality of the audience it succeeds in persuading. As Perelman and Olbrechts-Tyteca put the point, the audience "will determine to a great extent both the direction the arguments will take, and the character, the significance that will be attributed to them."[6] Thus, the audience's role in testing ideas is as important as the rhetor's. Perelman and Olbrechts-Tyteca's theory of audience is perhaps the best developed analysis of this topic in contemporary rhetorical theory.[7]

The Centrality of Audience

[handwritten margin note: 1) mankind as a whole 2) dialogue between speaker & (1) person 3) inward deliberation]

Three distinct audiences are particularly important in Perelman and Olbrechts-Tyteca's theory of rhetoric. "The first such audience," they write, "consists of the whole of mankind, or at least, of all normal, adult persons; we shall refer to it as the universal audience."[8] The universal audience is advanced as a test of an argument's reasonableness that transcends local and personal biases.[9] The second audience is "the single interlocutor whom a speaker addresses in a dialogue," while the third audience that can test the reasonableness of arguments is "the subject himself when he deliberates or gives himself reasons for his actions."[10]

Particular Audiences, Starting Points, and Values

Perelman and Olbrechts-Tyteca locate values in the particular audience—the actual audience of persons one addresses. This regard for particular audiences and their "opinions and values" is what Perelman and Olbrechts-Tyteca see as distinguishing a rhetorical approach to argument from other possible approaches. The rhetorical perspective "is a fundamental concern with the opinions and values of the audience that the speaker addresses, and more particularly with the intensity of his audience's adherence to each of these invoked by the speaker."[11]

Public values were the starting points of public argument in Greece and Rome as well. Rhetoricians have long recognized that orators must attend to what real audiences believe and value. "Every social circle or milieu is distinguishable in terms of its dominant opinions and unquestioned beliefs, of the premises that it takes for granted without hesitation." Are such beliefs simply the shifting opinions of the public, as Plato believed? Or, are they the very basis of a sound rhetorical appeal, as Aristotle thought? Perelman and Olbrechts-Tyteca side with Aristotle: "These views form an integral part of its culture, and an orator wishing to persuade a particular audience must of necessity adapt himself to it." Perelman and Olbrechts-Tyteca devote considerable time to discussing what they term the "starting points" of argument. These shared values are the starting points

[handwritten note at bottom: why can adapting to particular audiences be a problematic standard for developing just, rational arguments ——> an echo-chamber / pandering ideas]

of argument, the places of agreement between orator and audience that allow for argumentation to develop. "The unfolding as well as the starting point of argumentation," they write, "presupposes indeed the agreement of the audience."[12] The audience in view at this point is the particular audience of individual citizens.

Perelman and Olbrechts-Tyteca divide their starting points into two general classes. The first they term "the real," which includes "facts, truths and presumptions." The other category they term "the preferable," which takes in "values, hierarchies, and lines of argument relating to the preferable." Thus, one source of the agreements needed to begin constructive argumentation—"the real"—is found in what both speaker and audience accept as well-established facts, widely accepted truths, or uncontested commitments called presumptions.

A second source of the starting points or argumentation is discovered in "the preferable"—commonly held values, value hierarchies (e.g., the group's right to safety outweighs the individual's right to free speech), and preferences such as that for group over individual decision-making in an organization.

From such points of agreement, further agreements may be reached through the process of argumentation. The critical point is that argumentation requires points of agreement between disagreeing parties in order to begin and proceed productively. This search for points of agreement is in keeping with these authors' central concern: discovering a rational method for discussing questions involving values in pluralistic society.[13] The idea of starting points of argumentation rooted in the community's common belief and experience is reminiscent of Aristotle's notion of *endoxa*—commonly held views and values—as providing the foundation of public discourse.

Perelman and Olbrechts-Tyteca, however, recognized a serious problem associated with arguments about values before real audiences: Rhetoric based strictly on the beliefs of a particular group may be biased and parochial. Moreover, arguments capable of winning the adherence of only a particular audience often are not acceptable to most reasonable people. To solve this problem associated with arguments addressed to particular audiences, Perelman and Olbrechts-Tyteca introduced what was to become their most famous concept.

The Universal Audience ⟶ JUSTICE!

Who finally decides which ideas are truly rational, if the judgments of different particular audiences clash? In some instances elite audiences of trained specialists assist in "the attempt to formulate norms and values such as could be proposed to every reasonable being."[14] But even the judgments of experts must meet the approval of a particular audience, or we run the risk of "the philosopher-king who would use the political authority and power of the State" to impose one moral standard on everyone.[15]

The universal audience is something of a mental exercise intended to assist in developing arguments for particular audiences without bowing to the local prejudices always at work in such audiences. Looking beyond persuading their immediate audience, conscientious rhetors will consider how an audience of highly rational individuals would respond to their arguments. In his book *Justice*, Perelman writes, "I do not see [reason] as a faculty in contrast to other faculties . . . I conceive of it as a privileged audience, the

[handwritten marginal notes: "think about conspiracy theorists"; "work together as citizens of the world to solve problems rationally & propel justice"]

universal audience."[16] Perelman and Olbrechts-Tyteca imagine an audience of reasonable people available at all times and not subject to the moral and rational limitations of any particular audience.

In the universal audience, Perelman and Olbrechts-Tyteca reveal their conviction that a reasonable advocate possesses a vision of rationality that transcends particular social groups. A reasonable advocate "seeks to conform to principles of action which are acceptable to everyone [and] considers as unreasonable a rule of action which cannot be universalized."[17] The rational rhetor looks past immediate concerns and recognizes that "what is reasonable must be able to be a precedent which can inspire everyone in analogous circumstances."[18] In sum, these authors write that the "highest point" of assurance that an argument is trustworthy "is reached when there is agreement of the universal audience," which is for them "a universality and unanimity imagined by the speaker."[19]

HOW TO ADVOCATE FOR JUSTICE

are all rational people actually rational advocates for justice? or just in theory?

1) is it realistic?
2) is there a way to adapt all things to UA

The Audience of One

How can we know, in a practical sense, if our arguments are ready for appeal to the universal audience? One check is the careful scrutiny that takes place when one person argues directly with another. "Argumentation before a single hearer" can make a special claim to reasonableness, write Perelman and Olbrechts-Tyteca. Plato's *Gorgias* is an example of the rigor that attends arguing before the audience of a single hearer: "Each of Socrates' interlocutors is the spokesman . . . of a particular viewpoint and their objections must first be disposed of in order to facilitate public adherence to the proposed theses."[20]

The single hearer can act like an audience of one's opponents by advancing counterarguments, raising objections, asking for clarifications. The individual listener can in some cases fulfill this role so well that he or she actually represents the universal audience. "The hearer is assumed to have the same reasoning power at his disposal as the other members of the universal audience."[21] Thus, if our arguments succeed before an audience of a single, careful critic, they may be ready for an appeal to the universal audience.

The Self as Audience

Do we typically think of ourselves as an audience for our own arguments? "The self-deliberating subject," write Perelman and Olbrechts-Tyteca, may also at times be "regarded as an incarnation of the universal audience."[22] We can not, for example, fool ourselves with arguments we know to be specious. The individual "endowed with reason" who directs her own arguments privately to herself "is bound to be contemptuous of procedures aimed at winning over other people." Moreover, such an individual "cannot avoid being sincere" in this process, and "is in a better position than anyone else to test the value" of her arguments.[23]

Regardless of the type of argument one advances—scientific, political, judicial, or religious—an audience is being addressed. Argumentation, therefore, cannot be adequately understood apart from a theory of audience; all arguments are adapted to some audience. Here is a fact about rhetoric that has stood as a criticism of the art ever since Plato raised the concern in *Gorgias*: Does the presence of an audience that needs to be persuaded mean that audience-adapted arguments must be unreasonable? Perelman and Olbrechts-Tyteca think not; indeed, as we have seen, they respond with a theory both of audiences and of arguments intended to secure the rationality of discourse about moral issues. Finding a rational approach to moral discourse remains a pressing problem of rhetorical theory in the twentieth-first century.

Presence

In argumentation a rhetor seeks to lead an audience to *see* relevant facts, or to *experience* the truthfulness of an idea. Their concept of presence brings a nearly visual dimension to Perelman and Olbrechts-Tyteca's new rhetoric. They write, "one of the preoccupations of a speaker is to make present, by verbal magic alone, what is actually absent" but what is considered "important to [the] argument."[24] This reference to rhetoric as a kind of magic sounds like something Gorgias or a Renaissance Humanist like Ficino might say. Perelman and Olbrechts-Tyteca share Gorgias' and the Humanists' intrigue with rhetoric's power to direct thought, particularly rhetoric in the control of a skilled rhetorician.

Jürgen Habermas on a Rational Society

German sociologist and philosopher of language Jürgen Habermas was born in 1929. Like Perelman and other European intellectuals who endured the experience, Habermas was deeply changed by World War II. He was particularly concerned about the failure of German intellectuals to provide any meaningful opposition to National Socialism. And, like Perelman, Habermas began to search for the conditions of rational discourse about matters of human value.

Habermas argued that political corruption, criminality, and class warfare were the major problems to be addressed by the humanities. He affirmed that "critical rationality consists in the unflinching examination of our most cherished and comforting assumptions."[25] Centralized control in large modern economies and the power of science left the public with little real role in decision-making. In response, Habermas advanced the theory of an "ideal speech community" with a goal of individual emancipation.[26] Habermas' vision of a functional and just society is rooted in the tradition of Western philosophy and guided by Marxist analysis of social justice.[27] Though suspicious of persuasion, Habermas is concerned with some of the same issues that have occupied many rhetorical theorists.[28]

Though he does not specifically write about rhetoric, Habermas holds that no aspect of human endeavor—whether philosophy, science, art, or politics—is rationally pure or non-tendentious.[29] Consequently, each arena must test its own propositions in debate or dialogue according to standards appropriate to that arena. Habermas was intrigued with the salon tradition in France. In the setting of the salon, free and equal discourse occurred with constructive criticism of views as an accepted practice. The result was discourse exhibiting respect for rationality in a context of equality. In *Structural Transformation of the Public Sphere* (1962), *Toward a Rational Society* (1970), and *The Theory of Communicative Action* (1984), Habermas explored the possibility of rational discourse in a "public sphere" where ideas of concern to all people are discussed and refined.

*Think about
news channels.
$$ determines
a lot about
society*

A rational society is built on the foundation of liberated individuals speaking to one another as equals. Citizens in such a society participate meaningfully in political and economic decision-making. The powerful forces arrayed against the individual in modern, industrialized societies—especially the rule of experts—can only be counteracted by "communicating citizens themselves" who are adequately equipped for the task. "This could be guaranteed only by the ideal conditions of general communication extending to the entire public and free from domination."[30] Transforming society means ensuring a greater degree of choice across a wider range of options. In such a society, "assent secured by custom or tradition is replaced by . . . rational evaluations of claims," a view that places Habermas squarely in the Enlightenment tradition.[31] He continues to develop this line of thought in books like *The Lure of Technocracy* (2016). The "digital revolution" does not change the fact that political decision-making should be marked by a "free formation of a shared will guided by reason" which "finds expression in the combination of inclusion and deliberation."[32] These values are deeply rooted in the classical rhetorical tradition.

*2 questions:
1) is it possible
2) if not, should
we attempt it*

Cultural traditions must also be subjected to scrutiny through argumentative discourse, especially those ideas that lead to economic injustice.[33] Transcendent values serve as a test of those traditions: "The ideas of reason, truth, justice . . . serve as ideals with reference to which we can criticize traditions we inherit."[34] Habermas writes that "dramatic examples" of this ongoing critical process occur when "the validity claims of mythical and religious world-views could be systematically questioned and tested." Such a critical work, according to Habermas, provided the impetus for "philosophy in the Athens of the classical period."[35]

Communicative Action

#1

Habermas found the interactive critical process of argumentation a key to overcoming the ideological domination that obtains when a society is no longer rational. He called such critical discourse communicative action.[36] Susan Wells writes that communicative action is "the interaction of at least two people who establish a relationship," and who "try to come to a common understanding of the situation in which they are acting through interpretation." The goal of such associations is "to act together, which means they must agree on how to act."[37]

*First time someone
talks about
Rhetoric as an
action. It does
something.*

Not one sided but actually engaged in dialogue

Barbara Fultner writes that the "cornerstone" of Habermas' theory of communicative action consists of three commitments, each involving performance of a task: "In performing a speech act, a speaker represents a state of affairs, establishes an intersubjective relation with a hearer, and expresses her intention."[38] Wells adds that such communicative *action* comes about only in the context of "a shared recognition that speech is subject to criteria of truth, appropriateness, and sincerity" emerging from the unhindered process of communication.[39] Interactive communication action guided by such agreements is central, then, to Habermas' theory of rationality.

Disciplined dialogue is the path to a rational public sphere for Habermas. Dialogue allows propositions and their underlying values to be tested. The goal of such argumentative exchanges is intersubjective agreements, that is, agreements among independent participants in dialogue on the basis of open and fairly conducted argument. Thomas McCarthy writes that Habermas views reason as "a healing power of unification and reconciliation." Such unification is not for him discovered in a mystical "Absolute," but rather in "the unforced intersubjectivity of rational agreement." A true statement can "in the end be redeemed only through intersubjective recognition brought about by the unforced force of reason."[40] Rational communication develops around the "'unforced force of the better argument,' with the aim of coming to an agreement about the validity or invalidity of problematic claims."[41]

Communicative Competence and the Public Sphere

Habermas' theory of universal or formal pragmatics suggests rules for using language rationally, toward the goal of open and equitable discourse aimed at freeing citizens from ideological dominance. Such conversation takes place in Habermas' "public sphere," a term that refers to more than simply public spaces where views are expressed. The public sphere is a place of open discussion among emancipated individuals unrestrained by dominant political systems. "In the public sphere," writes Susan Wells, "the problems of politics, society, and culture are represented in general terms and opened to rational discussion."[42] Rather than dominance, a rational public sphere encourages a fair and rational exchange of views.

Rational communication is possible only under the conditions of communicative competence, which involves three elements. First, a truth claim is shared by speaker and hearer, that is, a speaker makes a claim that both speaker and listener understand in a similar fashion. Second, the hearer understands and accepts the speaker's intention. That is, beneath the truth claim, the competent listener understands the operation of a motive. Habermas reflects a traditionally rhetorical orientation with attention to the underlying motives that animate human communication. As a third element in communication competence, the speaker adapts to the hearer's worldview.[43] Habermas' "intersubjective" orientation is again evident; his goal is communication that is "mutual" and "uncoerced."

[Handwritten margin notes:]
1) be honest about what you believe your truth is
2) must be able to understand one another thru dialogue & convers.
3) Must be sincere & truly believe what you're saying.

Critical Theory and the Critique of Ideology

Critical theory is the systematic analysis of discourse which reveals its hidden assumptions and implications. This process assists the project of liberation by exposing ideologies—irrational, unexamined, or coercive systems of thinking. For instance, technological thinking becomes an ideology as it closes off certain possibilities in a society's discourse. When educational reform is considered under technological ideology, as an example, some possibilities are excluded and others are given privilege. Education moves toward the service of technology with emphasis and funding going to studies such as mathematics and science, while disciplines such as philosophy and literature are relegated to the position of inconsequential ornaments to education.

The influence of ideology is not felt only at the level of policy; the problem of ideological dominance is as deep as the human psyche. For Habermas, false ideologies lead to false thinking, which in turn leads to false consciousness or a distorted view of reality, of the world, and of people. Critical theory seeks, through the analysis of ways we talk and think, a new and liberating consciousness. McCarthy writes, "Habermas's argument is, simply, that the goal of critical theory—a form of life free from unnecessary

[Handwritten note at bottom with arrow:]
Do you think its possible to achieve?

domination in all its forms—is inherent in the notion of truth; it is anticipated in every act of communication."[44]

Critics

His critics have alleged that Habermas' theory is naive in its failure to account for the real differences among people as regards access to channels of communication, ability to communicate, and social power.[45] His vision of rational citizens talking as equals, the critics respond, neglects the massive social inequities that prevent just this sort of conversation from taking place. In addition, his theory of communicative action is sometimes seen as favoring "the specific structures of rationality associated with technological cultures of Europe and North America," which opens Habermas to the charge of "paternalistic guidance" when standards employed in "other regions of the world" are taken to represent an underdeveloped rationality.[46]

We have already noted that Habermas was suspicious of persuasion as a goal of discourse. This aversion to persuasion—apparently taken to be an enemy to rationality— has led to another criticism of his work. Joy Connolly writes, "In its attempt to protect modes of rational discourse from rhetorical 'taint,' Habermasian theory remains embedded in the tradition of Western philosophy that tries to 'purify' communication of emotion and prejudice."[47] Ultimately, the project of attempting to formulate a non-rhetorical model of public discourse is destined to fail as people are natural advocates determined to persuade one another.

Feminist critics have pointed out other inadequacies and blind spots in Habermas' theories. Marie Fleming, for example, writes, "While initially promising, Habermas theory is bound to be disappointing to feminists. The problem is more than his general lack of attention to mater of gender." The real issue is that Habermas' basic approach to the public or private divide "appears to be fundamentally at odds with feminist attempts to reconceptualize modern social and political theory." Fleming points out a contradiction: "Why does a theory that aims at inclusion and equality not give immediate and urgent attention to the need to secure gender equality?"[48]

In spite of these criticisms, Habermas argues that as we enter dialogue under the conditions of communicative competence, we afford ourselves a greater opportunity to interact and to act interdependently, free of the constraints of ideology. Habermas' concern for a more rational society led him to advance a theory of rational communication that shares some elements in common with rhetorical theories, such as an account of how assertions are supported in public debate and of the ethical conduct of persuasion.

THE RHETORIC OF SCIENCE

Public debates over such issues, apparently scientific concerns, as the theory of evolution and global warming underline the fact that our discourse about science can be deeply politicized and influenced by personal motives, money, and organizational agendas. Has science itself acquired a rhetorical dimension over its long history? Rhetorical theorist

Herbert Simons wrote in 1990 that "it is generally acknowledged that . . . scholars have no choice but to rely on rhetorical appeals and arguments in the forging of a discipline."[49] This is a remarkable statement, particularly coming at the end of a century in which the natural and social sciences presented themselves as unaffected by human motives and uncontaminated by linguistic strategies, that is, as nonrhetorical. However, as Simons suggests, scholars increasingly have recognized that the methods, procedures and languages of all of the academic disciplines are rhetorical in nature.[50]

This observation has been difficult for some members of the natural and social science communities to accept, for these academic endeavors have promoted themselves as aloof from the irrational realm of persuasion. Even this posture of objectivity may, however, be rhetorical in nature, a strategy intended to persuade the public that science is the one rhetoric-free zone of cooperative human activity. Science thus assumes the status of a protected domain in which critical examination of motives and persuasive tactics is inappropriate. Such an unexamined science would recognize a corresponding increase in its social power.

The usual treatment of science, the story often told, is that science proceeds according to rules that make persuasion unlikely, unnecessary, or easy to expose. For instance, literary scholar Bryan Boyd relates what has become a standard narrative about science: Because science exposes itself to falsifying evidence, in the long run it retains and builds on only the most rigorously selected ideas. This winnowing strategy does not prove all science's ideas to be correct, but it improves on the ratio of tested to untested ideas attainable by any other procedure.[51]

Is Boyd's account correct? Is science's "strategy"—a decidedly rhetorical term—more likely to produce a "tested" result than, say, the strategies pursued by art, history or philosophy? Is scientific method in fact more likely to lead us to reliable conclusions than is "any other procedure"? Such claims would be difficult to prove—or refute—but perhaps this is beside the point. Boyd is rehearsing a popular narrative about science, one by now so well established that it requires no support because it raises no questions. It is also, however, a narrative that ignores the rhetorical qualities of science, perhaps by design. As a result, it is a story about science that may be misleading—perhaps dangerously so—because it is incomplete.

Precursors

The monolithic nature of science began to be seriously challenged in the second half of the twentieth century. Hungarian scientist Michael Polanyi, who lived and taught for many years in England, argued for the role of subjective judgments in *Science, Faith and Society* (1946). Later, in *Personal Knowledge* (1958), Polanyi argued that all knowledge has a personal and emotional quality, that pure objectivity is impossible, and that science does not follow mechanical rules. Thomas Kuhn (1922–1996) also challenged the usual view of science in his landmark book *The Structure of Scientific Revolutions* (1962). Kuhn argued that science does not progress in a linear fashion as models are refined by further research, but that "paradigm shifts" in scientific understanding introduce radically new models in an unpredictable fashion. Moreover, these new models often develop for reasons that have little to do with scientific research as ordinarily understood.

Later, Austrian philosopher of science Paul Feyerabend (1924–1994) opened the door even wider to a rhetorical approach to science with books such as *Against Method* (1975) and *Science in a Free Society* (1978). Feyerabend denied that there was a particular approach to research that could be called "the scientific method," and questioned whether scientists conduct their work according to a particular set of rules. He also referred to science as an ideology, and argued that scientists were inclined to adhere to their own set of myths that were no more and no less rooted in reason than were any other myths.

Feyerabend's views were shaped by his famous mentor, the philosopher Karl Popper (1902–1994). Popper argued that scientific theories are not so much subject to proof as to disproof—what he termed falsifiability. Popper also argued that the practice of science is firmly grounded in our use of language, though he opposed the subjective view of science he attributed to figures such as Kuhn.[52]

More recently, British philosopher of science Mary Midgley has argued that the theory of evolution—a scientific model of unparalleled influence—has been treated like a religion by many scientists; Midgley calls it "the creation myth of our age." She argues that "by telling us our origins [evolution] shapes our views of what we are. It influences not just our thought, but our feelings and actions too, in a way which goes far beyond its official function as a biological theory."[53] To explain origins, to suggest ways of thinking, to orient us to the cosmos—these are characteristics of a myth, according to Midgley; she does not use the term to mean a false story or a primitive narrative.

Midgley argues that modern science has developed a strongly mythological quality.[54] Myths form "our imaginative visions" which in turn become "central to our understanding of the world." Thus, far from being "a distraction from our serious thinking," they are "a necessary part of it."[55] This is as true of myths about science as it is of historical or religious myths.

Midgley has been particularly interested in the strategic role scientific myths play in public disputes. One pervasive rhetorical maneuver involves aligning one's claims with a widely adopted scientific narrative, for example the narrative of evolution. "Many of the visions that now dominate our controversies are ones which look as if they were based on science, but are really fed by fantasy," she writes. In this way "a variety of doctrines on all sorts of subjects have used scientific imagery to gain the authority which rightly belongs to science proper." Midgley adds, "because they sound technical, people receive their symbolic message as literal truth."[56] As a result, many influential modern myths "that actually shape our thoughts and actions owe their force to having appeared in scientific dress."[57] Moreover, myths express imaginative patterns that shape expectations of science and the interpretations of facts.[58] Widely embraced narratives about science provide templates for prioritizing and interpreting data. She adds that while we may choose the myths we employ for understanding the physical world, "we do not have a choice of understanding it without using any myths or visions at all."[59]

These writers—Polanyi, Feyerabend, Popper, Kuhn, Midgley, and others—prepared the way for the rhetorical study of science.

A Rhetorical Approach to Science

In the 1970s, American rhetorical critics started investigating the rhetorical components of science. Rhetorical critic John Lyne writes "I investigate scientific arguments because the discourses of science have substantial impact on thought, action and culture in our time—and that influence will be all the stronger if we accept the opinion that they have little to do with persuasion in the public space."[60]

Historically, scientific discourse has been portrayed as "concerned with things rather than words," and thus "innocent of rhetorical seductions."[61] However, by the late 1980s literary scholar Charles Bazerman would write, "Persuasion is at the heart of science, not at the unrespectable fringe." Bazerman did not mean that science was not a trustworthy method of seeking truth. "An intelligent rhetoric practiced within a serious, knowledge-able, committed research community is a serious method of truth seeking."[62] He was simply underlining the essential role played by persuasion in doing science.

Nevertheless, some members of natural and social science disciplines have shown an interest in rhetoric as a means of understanding how their own disciplines operate.[63] Increasingly, scientists are willing to acknowledge, as Charles Willard has written, that "personal preferences and quirks, conventional wisdom, professional politics, and the need for popularization to secure funding, all play a part in the puzzles scientists find interesting."[64] That is, the conduct of science, if we take a broad view of the enterprise, often is as disorderly, irrational, and contaminated by human biases as is politics.

The Power of Unexamined Science

An understanding of the rhetorical nature of scientific discourse is particularly important when we consider the enormous power of scientific institutions in contemporary culture, a power founded directly on the image of science as immune to the ambiguities that mark other arenas of life. Scholars in the rhetoric of science have revealed the place of persuasion and linguistic strategy in scientific writing of science, and in the decisions that determine which projects scientists will undertake. Some scholars note the risks of failing to identify the assumptions beneath the surface of scientific texts. Susan Wells, for example, argues that the posture of neutrality and objectivity in scientific discourse may itself be a reason for concern. "The scientific text," she writes, "reductively segments nature into connected objects of knowledge, open to manipulation in time and capable of being transformed without affecting the knowing subject."

That is, scientific discourse "objectifies" everything it touches, and in this way insulates the scientist from the very object of scientific study. Historically, this insulation has at crucial junctures had dramatic consequences. As Wells points out, historians Max Horkheimer and T. W. Adorno argued that the "practices of language most closely associated with the physical sciences were those which, when transferred to the social, rationalized domination and the Holocaust: Enlightenment in its moment of triumph emerged as chaos and terror."[65] Others have argued that scientific rationality and objectivity, cut free from the shaping influence of values and beliefs, may dangerously objectify nature and even on human beings themselves.[66]

Our cultural failure to subject scientific discourse to probing rhetorical analysis results from a long tradition of attributing to scientific texts a special status as "purely rational discourse." Scientific discourse's special status has also to do with the fact that "no other discursive formation is so relentlessly inaccessible to the public, so exclusively addressed to practitioners of scientific disciplines."[67] The pristine rationality and methodological reliability of science are, however, now widely challenged.

Advocacy in the Sciences

What are the specific qualities that make science rhetorical? One significant quality is advocacy itself, an activity hardly captured in the more common description of scientific activity as *investigation*. Simons writes that "one common thread in the rhetoric of inquiry movement is its rejection of the conventional split between inquiry and advocacy."[68] Natural and social scientists are investigators, but they also function as advocates for points of view, theories, and differing interpretations of data.

A scientist's political perspective, sources of funding and personal beliefs can influence how data are collected and interpreted. Scientists must also make decisions about which questions they will investigate. Sometimes these decisions are connected to current political controversies that generate funds to support some research projects and deny funding to support others. In addition, the scientist's presentation of data and its interpretations must be persuasive, must gain a hearing among colleagues and, perhaps, eventually the general public.

Science and Communities

John Lyne notes that the rhetoric of science also extends to the fact that science "is a collective enterprise that is sustained only within a highly specialized network of communication."[69] That is, scientists must remain in constant communication with other scientists, and this communication is seldom devoid of the motives and strategies we associate with rhetoric. Lyne writes,

> Participation in that network is the very sine qua non of scientific practice . . . Add to this the presence of interpersonal competition, inflated egos, and the constant need to justify expenditures, and one has an area rife not only with communication but with rhetorical practice.[70]

Moreover, other scholars in the rhetoric of science would remind us that the characteristic form of scientific communication—the scholarly article—reflects "trends in style, presentation, and argument," which are "the traditional components of rhetoric."[71]

Lyne points out that science "is also a part of the very fabric of our public discourse as well." Because we live in an age in which a staggering amount of technical information is available to all of us, "scientific information can be called upon by almost anyone." Thus, scientific talk has become part of our political, religious, educational, and economic talk. In virtually any forum we enter where people are seeking to persuade one another, "one usually finds modern science deployed as a resource of persuasion."[72]

To take seriously the study of the rhetoric of science is to become more aware of "the sort of powers that are unleashed in the very language of science."[73] Ultimately, the language of science—its rhetoric—affects actions and decisions in arenas we do not typically identify as scientific at all. "We who take an interest in public discourse," writes Lyne, "must be concerned with how the discourses of scientific knowledge may mesh with the discourses of value and action, because, one way or another, they will."[74]

Deirdre McCloskey and the Rhetoric of Economics

Some social scientists have found that a rhetorical approach to their disciplines allows them to acknowledge and appreciate the rhetorical dimensions of their work. Economist Deirdre McCloskey, for instance, has written that a rhetorical approach to economics "is not an invitation to irrationality in argument," as some economists might presume. "Quite the contrary," she adds, "it is an invitation to leave the irrationality of an artificially narrowed range of argument and to move to the rationality of arguing like human beings." She comments that a rhetorical approach to her discipline "brings out into the open the arguing that economists do anyway."[75]

What is Professor McCloskey saying about the rhetoric of economics? At least this: that economists argue among themselves about economic theories, and that they seek to persuade one another using arguments and strategies that are not linked directly to the methods of economics. The arguments of economists frequently are, that is, persuasively intended, strategically framed, stylistically shaped, and reflective of individual biases, preferences, and values. Is this surprising? Probably not, but it also is not typically admitted as part of "doing economics." At the point of going public, the economist must adopt the voice of the objective investigator whose "discoveries" are based strictly on an investigation of the best available evidence. McCloskey thinks acknowledging the rhetorical nature of academic inquiry can serve to enhance one's understanding of what it means to be a scientist, and can actually advance the scientific project.

Professor McCloskey continues to track the influence of rhetoric in her historical study of the development of capitalism in Europe. In a series of three books on the topic—*The Bourgeois Virtues* (2007), *Bourgeois Dignity* (2011), and *Bourgeois Equality* (2016)—she develops her case—among other arguments—that in the rising European culture, "words or conversations or rhetoric mattered to the economy, and still do."[76]

Rhetoric in Anthropology

"The narrative and rhetorical conventions assumed by a writer . . . shape ethnography," writes John Van Maanen of the rhetorical nature of ethnographic research. The manner or style in which an ethnographer reports on fieldwork has much to do with that report's acceptance by the scholarly community. Thus, the rhetoric of reporting one's experience is as much a part of anthropology as is careful observation of a culture. Van Maanen explains:

Ways of personal expression, choice of metaphor, figurative allusions, semantics, decorative phrasing or plain speaking, textual organization, and so on all work to structure a cultural portrait in particular ways. Style is just as much a matter of choice when the experimentalist writes in a self-conscious, hyper-realistic, attention grabbing, dots-and-dashes fashion . . . as when the traditionalist falls back on a neutral, pale-beige, just-the-facts fashion of reporting. Some styles are, at any given time, more acceptable in ethnographic circles than others.[77]

Rhetoric scholar Jeanne Fahnestock has explored in detail what Van Maanen alludes to in this quotation: the deployment of rhetorical devices in scientific discourse.[78]

Famed anthropologist Clifford Geertz (1926–2006) also wrote about the role of persuasion in anthropology. "The ability of anthropologists to get us to take what they say seriously," he urges,

has less to do with either a factual look or an air of conceptual elegance than it has with their capacity to convince us that what they say is a result of their having actually penetrated . . . another form of life, of having, one way or another, truly "been there."

Thus, the popular image of the anthropologist-as-scientist reporting "only the facts," of a dispassionate observer unmoved by linguistic and stylistic strategies of persuasion is, for both Van Maanen and Geertz, not an accurate one. To understand the work of the anthropologist, one must understand strategies of presentation, that is, rhetoric. Rhetoric seeking persuasion, according to Geertz, enters the picture explicitly as anthropologists sit down to write about their experiences in the field. "Persuading us that this offstage miracle has occurred, is where the writing comes in."[79]

The successful academic anthropologist must also be a rhetorician, a writer writing to "convince" and to "persuade" an audience of colleagues that her or his work is worthy. Geertz acknowledges the presence of the even larger audience of educated readers. He writes, "the most direct way to bring field work as personal encounter and ethnography as reliable account together is to make the diary form . . . something for the world to read."[80] Thus, even the anthropologist's choice of the diary form, like the letter a subjective and intimate prose genre, can be a strategic and persuasive one. Allowing the reader to peer over my shoulder as I record my private observations with no apparent audience in mind is, according to Geertz, a rhetorical act.

John Campbell on the Rhetoric of Charles Darwin

Rhetorical analysis has also been applied to argumentation in the natural sciences. The degree to which sciences such as biology, chemistry, physics, and astronomy proceed rhetorically often has not been well understood. However, the work of scholars such as John Angus Campbell has helped to illuminate the rhetorical nature of these disciplines. Campbell's studies of the work of Charles Darwin (1809–1882) in advancing his theory of natural selection stand as a good example of the rhetorical analysis of discourse in the natural sciences.[81]

Campbell notes that Darwin faced a practical problem when he believed he had discovered the mechanism by which one species evolves into another. Neither the scientific world of the mid-nineteenth century nor the general public were ready to accept that changes from one species to another take place by means of natural processes. Darwin faced a rhetorical problem: how could he make this idea persuasive to these two very different audiences?

Darwin's answer to his rhetorical conundrum was the language of natural selection. This enormously important metaphor was, Campbell argues, a rhetorical invention designed to accomplish a specific persuasive end. Moreover, Darwin knew that the metaphor of natural selection—which compared domestic animal breeding to evolutionary processes—was an implicitly misleading rhetorical strategy. By crafting this strategic analogy between two fundamentally dissimilar phenomena, Darwin transformed the gloomy doctrine of "survival of the fittest" into a hopeful and thus persuasive prospect.[82]

Why was evolution a "gloomy doctrine"? Answering this question involves some historical understanding of Darwin's theory. "Natural selection," explains Campbell, "is the application to evolution of Malthus's doctrine of population dynamics."[83] Thomas Robert Malthus (1766–1834) had observed that "food supply increases arithmetically while population increases geometrically." The result is that "not as many organisms live as are born."[84] That is, evolution is predicated on the certain premature death from starvation of many members of any given species. One of the Darwin's argumentative moves was to add to "this thoroughly negative doctrine" the notions of "variation and inheritance." Campbell notes that "when one combines variation, inheritance, and the struggle for existence, one is left with differential reproduction. Allow differential reproduction to continue over virtually unlimited time in an unlimited variety of changing environments and the result is organic change or evolution."[85]

Evolution under the Darwin doctrine is random and undirected. Biological life is not headed anywhere in particular, and it is not the work of God. These ideas were unacceptable to most people in Darwin's day, and thus posed a serious rhetorical problem for Darwin. Unless he could persuade the scientific community and general public, evolution would remain merely an intellectual novelty. Darwin's rhetorical problem demanded a rhetorical solution.

Darwin chose to argue on religious grounds to the highly religious audience of the public. He made evolution through "natural selection" appear benevolent by arguing that certain decidedly unpleasant natural states were not finished works of God, but rather steps along the way to more "advanced" life. As Campbell writes, "Darwin takes several of nature's ingenious adaptations and underscores the embarrassment they cause to the customary belief in divine goodness."

For instance, the female cuckoo bird lays her eggs in the nests of other birds. When the chicks hatch, they destroy their host's eggs and allow their adopted mother to nurture them instead. Darwin argues,

> to my imagination it is far more satisfactory to look at such instincts as the young cuckoo ejecting its foster-brothers—ants making slaves—the larvae of the ichneumonidae feeding within the live bodies of caterpillars—not as especially endowed

or created instincts, but as small consequences of one general law, leading to the advancement of all organic beings.[86]

In other words, God did not design cuckoos, some species of ant, and certain wasps to be cruel to other species; God allows such cruelties as are necessary in the vast evolutionary process because they will eventually yield more advanced forms of life.

A second strategy involved encouraging readers to "see" evolution take place. Darwin wrote as a simple eyewitness to objective facts that required no interpretation. Campbell writes, "Darwin's skill in setting forth in colloquial language a case for a mechanism plausibly capable of bringing about evolutionary change successfully persuaded many of his readers." The key "was to present evolution by natural selection as though it could be seen—indeed, to convince the reader that his theory was not an inference from facts but a fact the reader had witnessed." Thus, in his writing Darwin "stresses facts and observations," "minimizes theory," and removes the narrator or interpreter from the story of evolution.

But the master rhetorical strategy behind Darwin's success remained the metaphor of natural selection, an implied comparison of undirected natural processes to the highly intentional work of the animal breeder. In employing this metaphor, Darwin walked a fine line between stratagem and deception.

Campbell writes, "[I]n Darwin's theory, nature is like the breeder in that both in nature and in domestication there is an unstaunchable supply of variation; nature is further like the breeder in that both eliminate certain individuals from their breeding stocks." However, Campbell adds, "nature is not like the breeder in that nature does not consciously choose certain animals or plants to achieve a foreseen end." And yet, as Darwin tells the story of evolution, "Nature"—an entity created strictly for the purposes of his argument—and the breeder are essentially similar.

Darwin convinced many readers that his "observations" led directly and without interpretation to his radical new theory. Campbell's work on Darwin illustrates some of the critical possibilities inherent in a rhetorical approach to scientific discourse. Campbell shows us a famous and highly influential scientist operating as a skilled rhetorician. Moreover, Campbell asks his readers to participate in both the rhetorical dilemma and accompanying ethical conundrum Darwin faced. After reading Campbell's accounts, it is difficult to see Darwin simply as a scientist. Campbell also helps us to see that science itself is an inherently rhetorical undertaking.

Some rhetorical scholars see in the rhetoric of scientific discourse a risky expansion of the term *rhetoric*. For example, historian of rhetoric Dilip Gaonkar affirms that "it is a habit of our time to invoke rhetoric, time and again, to make sense of a wide variety of discursive practices . . ."[87]

Gaonkar holds that "we have extended the range of rhetoric to include discourse types . . . that the ancients would have regarded as falling outside its purview."[88] Recall that Aristotle said that rhetoric was the art we employ to guide decision-making when we *do not* have other arts or sciences to guide us. Gaonkar finds rhetoric's current reach to be unprecedented. "Never before in the history of rhetoric, not even during its glory days of the Italian Renaissance, did its proponents claim for rhetoric so universal a scope."[89]

He notes that "the promiscuous invocation of rhetoric" to account for anything and everything in all symbolic realms runs the risk of "trivializing rhetoric."[90] Thus, Gaonkar expresses concern that "the seemingly careless and ubiquitous uses of rhetoric" and the "sheer multiplicity of its uses" may lead the "overwhelmed reader [to] abandon the hope of ever finding what motivates and steers rhetoric."[91]

Should rhetoric be accepted as an approach to understanding all of the many and varied symbolic worlds in which we live, including science, music, medicine, and penology? Does using the label, "The Rhetoric of X," where X can mean any human undertaking, trivialize rhetoric? Gaonkar and others have prompted a re-evaluation of writing in the rhetoric of science, but certainly have not dampened interest in this growing field of research.

Recently, David J. Depew and John Lyne have surveyed advanced in the rhetoric of science. They identify a "small but proud scholarly field that seeks simultaneously to contribute to rhetorical studies and to secure a place for rhetoric in the conversation of . . . science studies." Regarding the role of audiences and arguments in science, Depew and Lyne write:

> The approach of rhetorical studies to . . . scientific argumentation, recognizes that, no matter how valid their reasoning or how strong their evidence, speakers must command authority with audiences and that audiences bring a lot of baggage with them to the context-dependent rhetorical situations in which they encounter rhetorical activity.

Rhetoricians focusing on the sciences also "take seriously the role of rhetorical choices, including the use of tropes and figures, narrative accounts, genre expectations, and terministic framing to shape conversations about science." Describing what is now a maturing field of study, Depew and Lyne note sixteen separate genres in rhetoric of science research, including rhetorical analyses of major scientists (e.g. Darwin), the rhetoric of science related controversies (e.g. evolution vs. creationism), and the use of tropes and figures in scientific writing.[92] The field of the rhetoric of science now appears to be well established, and its future bright.

CONCLUSION

Following World War II, interest in rhetoric began to revive in Europe and America. The ancient study of rhetoric was seen by some scholars as providing a path to rational discourse about values and moral action. Others began to recognize a rhetorical quality in discourse belonging to wide range of disciplines, including the social and natural sciences.

Standards of public argument was among the interest of late twentieth-century rhetorical theorists seeking a new rhetoric. Chaim Perelman and Lucie Olbrechts-Tyteca linked this interest to a theory of audiences in their search for a new rhetoric. The interaction of arguments and audiences became their solution to one of the central intellectual problems of the twentieth century: discovering a means of testing and verifying value claims without reference to transcendent standards such as belief in God or rational confidence only in science. Perceiving a similar problem in Western culture, Jürgen Habermas suggested the means by which we might equip an entire society to conduct more rational discourse.

Rhetoric's persistent concern for arguments and audiences has also been applied in the twentieth century to the study of various social and natural sciences. Scholars in the rhetoric of science have examined the fundamentally rhetorical ways that scientists pursue their work. For those who have read and been persuaded by the work of Geertz, McCloskey, Campbell, Fahnestock, Alan Gross, and many others writing on the rhetoric of science, the discourse of the sciences can never sound the same. Following a thorough review of the field, Depew and Lyne conclude that science is as rhetorical as are other academic disciplines.

QUESTIONS FOR REVIEW

1. What do Perelman and Olbrechts-Tyteca mean by their concept of the "universal audience," and why is it important to their theory of argument?
2. What, according to Perelman and Olbrechts-Tyteca, are the benefits of argumentation before a single listener?
3. Into what two categories do Perelman and Olbrechts-Tyteca divide the starting points of argumentation? What specific sources of agreement are placed under each heading?
4. What is the ultimate goal of Habermas' theorizing? What is "communicative action"?
5. In what different ways are the natural and social sciences presented as rhetorical by writers discussed in this chapter?
6. What concern does Dilip Gaonkar raise regarding the rhetoric of science movement?
7. What do David J. Depew and John Lyne conclude about the current status of the rhetoric of science as a field of study?

QUESTIONS FOR DISCUSSION

1. Perelman and Olbrechts-Tyteca consider self-deliberation a kind of argumentation. Do you agree that you can "reason with yourself"? Is this, as they claim, a particularly reliable way of testing our reasoning?
2. What is your reaction to Jürgen Habermas' search for universal guidelines of conversational practice that might help assure rational and just discourse? Is such a system possible, or is this a utopian dream that does not have any application to the real world of rhetorical interactions?
3. Are you persuaded by the arguments of scientists like Geertz, McCloskey, and Campbell that the natural and social sciences have a distinctly rhetorical dimension to them? Does such an idea violate your notion of science as objective? Should it?

TERMS

Communicative action In Habermas, the interactive process of critical argumentation; a key to overcoming the problems of ideological domination.

Communicative competence For Habermas, the conditions under which rational communication is possible.

Critical theory The systematic means of analyzing discourse for its hidden assumptions and implications.

Elite audience In Perelman and Olbrechts-Tyteca, an audience of trained specialists in a discipline.

False consciousness In Habermas, a flawed and thus distorting view of reality, of the world, and of people.

Falsifiability Philosopher Karl Popper's idea that scientific claims are not subject to proof, but to being shown to be false.

Intersubjective agreements Agreements forged among independent participants in dialogue on the basis of open and fairly conducted argument.

Ideology Irrational or unexamined system of thinking.

Logical positivism The intellectual effort to bring scientific standards to bear on the resolution of all issues.

Particular audience The actual audience of persons one addresses when advancing an argument publicly.

Presence In Perelman and Olbrechts-Tyteca, the choice to emphasize certain ideas and facts over others, thus encouraging an audience to attend to them.

Public sphere For Habermas, public settings where ideas of concern to all people can be discussed and refined.

Starting points In Perelman and Olbrechts-Tyteca, points of agreement between a rhetor and an audience that allow argumentation to develop.

Universal audience In Perelman and Olbrechts-Tyteca, an imagined audience of highly rational individuals; and audience of all normal, adult persons.

NOTES

1   David A. Frank, "A Traumatic Reading of Twentieth-Century Rhetorical Theory: The Belgian Holocaust, Malines, Perelman, and de Man," *Quarterly Journal of Speech* 93(3) (August 2007): 308–343.

2   For a good collection of essays on Perelman's rhetorical theory, see: Ray D. Dearin, ed., *The New Rhetoric of Chaim Perelman* (Lanham, MD: University Press of America, 1989).

3   Chaim Perelman and L. Olbrechts-Tyteca, *The New Rhetoric: A Treatise on Argumentation*, trans. John Wilkinson and Purcell Weaver (Notre Dame, IN: University of Notre Dame Press), 6.

4   Perelman and Olbrechts-Tyteca, 20.

5   Perelman and Olbrechts-Tyteca, 4.

6   Perelman and Olbrechts-Tyteca, 14.

7   On Perelman and Olbrechts-Tyteca's theory of audience, see: Alan Gross, "A Theory of the Rhetorical Audience: Reflections on Chaim Perelman," *Quarterly Journal of Speech* 85 (May 1999): 202–211.

8   Perelman and Olbrechts-Tyteca, 30.

9   If you would like to read more about the concept of the universal audience, see: John R. Anderson, "The Audience as a Concept in the Philosophic Rhetoric of Perelman, Johnstone, and Natanson," *Southern Speech Communication Journal* 38 (Fall 1972): 39–50; Lisa S. Ede, "Rhetoric vs. Philosophy: The Role of the Universal Audience in Chaim Perelman's *The New Rhetoric*," *Central States Speech Journal* 32 (Summer 1981): 118–125; John W. Ray, "Perelman's Universal Audience," *Quarterly Journal of Speech* 64 (December 1978): 361–375; and Allen Scult, "Perelman's Universal Audience: One Perspective," *Central States Speech Journal* 27 (Fall 1976): 176–180.

10 Perelman and Olbrechts-Tyteca, 30.

11 Chaim Perelman, *The New Rhetoric and the Humanities*, trans. William Kluback (Dordrecht, Holland: D. Reidel, 1979), 46.

12 Perelman and Olbrechts-Tyteca, 20–21.

13 Perelman and Olbrechts-Tyteca, 65.

14 Perelman and Olbrechts-Tyteca, 65.

15 Perelman and Olbrechts-Tyteca, 66.

16 Chaim Perelman, *Justice* (New York: Random House, 1967), 78.

17 Perelman, *Justice*, 78.

18 Perelman, *Justice*, 82.

19 Perelman, *Rhetoric and Humanities*, 118.

20 Perelman and Olbrechts-Tyteca, 31.

21 Perelman and Olbrechts-Tyteca, 36.

22 Perelman and Olbrechts-Tyteca, 36.

23 Perelman and Olbrechts-Tyteca, 37.

24 Perelman and Olbrechts-Tyteca, 116–117.

25 Hubert L. Dreyfus and Paul Rabinow, "What Is Maturity? Habermas and Foucault on 'What Is Enlightenment?'" in *Foucault: A Critical Reader*, ed. David Couzens Hoy (Oxford: Basil Blackwell, 1986), 110.

26 Dreyfus and Rabinow, 110. See also: Jürgen Habermas, *Toward a Rational Society: Student Protest, Science and Politics*, trans. J. Shapiro (Boston, MA: Beacon Press, 1970).

27 Jürgen Habermas, *Communication and the Evolution of Society*, trans. Thomas McCarthy (Boston, MA: Beacon Press, 1979), 7.

28 See: Jürgen Habermas, *Knowledge and Human Interests*, trans. Jeremy J. Shapiro (Boston, MA: Beacon Press, 1971); and *Theory and Practice*, trans. John Viertel (Boston, MA: Beacon Press, 1973).

29 McCarthy in editor's introduction to *Philosophical Discourse*, xii.

30 Habermas, *Toward a Rational Society*, 74–75.

31 Susan Wells, *Sweet Reason: Rhetoric and the Discourses of Modernity* (Chicago, IL: University of Chicago Press, 1996), 114.

32 Jürgen Habermas, *The Lure of Technocracy* (Cambridge: Polity Press, 2016), 48.

33 Jürgen Habermas, *The Philosophical Discourse of Modernity: Twelve Lectures*, trans. Frederick Lawrence (Cambridge, MA: MIT Press, 1987), ed. Thomas McCarthy, x.

34 Thomas McCarthy, introduction to Habermas, *Philosophical Discourse*, x.

35 Jürgen Habermas, *Theory and Practice*, trans. John Viertel (Boston, MA: Beacon Press, 1973), 25.

36 McCarthy in editor's introduction to *Philosophical Discourse*, x.

37 Wells, 115.

38 Translator's introduction to Jürgen Habermas, *Truth and Justification*, trans. Barbara Fultner (Cambridge, MA: MIT Press, 2003), xvii.

39 Wells, 103.

40 McCarthy in editor's introduction to *Philosophical Discourse*, xvi.

41 Thomas McCarthy, *The Critical Theory of Jürgen Habermas* (Cambridge, MA: MIT Press, 1978), 292.

42 Wells, 119.

43 Sonja K. Foss, Karen A. Foss, and Robert Trapp, *Contemporary Perspective on Rhetoric*, 2nd ed. (Prospect Heights, IL: Waveland, 1991), 241–272.

44 McCarthy, *Critical Theory*, 273.

45 See, for example: Dick Howard, "A Politics in Search of the Political," *Theory and Society* 1 (Fall 1974): 271–306.

46 Wells, 116.

47 Joy Connolly, *The State of Speech: Rhetorical and Political Thought in Ancient Rome* (Princeton, NJ: Princeton University Press, 2013), 9.

48 Marie Fleming, *Emancipation, and Illusion: Rationality and Gender in Habermas' Theory of Modernity* (University Park, PA: Penn State University Press, 1999), 86.

49 Herbert Simons, ed., *The Rhetorical Turn: Invention and Persuasion in the Conduct of Inquiry* (Chicago, IL: University of Chicago Press, 1990), 8.

50 See, for example: Thomas Kuhn, *The Structure of Scientific Revolutions*, 3rd ed. (Chicago, IL: University of Chicago Press, 1996); Evelyn Fox Keller, "Secrets of Life, Secrets of Death," in *The Rhetoric of the Human Sciences*, ed. J. Nelson, A. Megill and D. McCloskey (Madison, WI: University of Wisconsin Press, 1987); Charles Bazerrman, *Shaping Written Knowledge: The Genre and Activity of the Experimental Article in Science* (Madison, WI: University of Wisconsin Press, 1988); Lawrence Prelli, *A Rhetoric of Science: Inventing Scientific Discourse* (Columbia, SC: University of South Carolina Press, 1989); Alan Gross, *The Rhetoric of Science* (Cambridge, MA: Harvard University Press, 1990); Randy Alan Harris ed., *Landmark Essays in the Rhetoric of Science* (London: Routledge, 1997).

51 Brian Boyd, *On the Origins of Stories* (Cambridge, MA: Harvard University Press, 2010), 411.

52 See: Karl Popper, *Conjectures and Refutations*: *The Growth of Scientific Knowledge* (London: Routledge, 1963).

53 Mary Midgley, *Evolution as a Religion* (London: Routledge, 1985), 30.

54 Mary Midgley, *Science as Salvation: A Modern Myth and Its Meaning* (London and New York: Routledge, 1992).

55 Mary Midgley, *The Myths We Live By* (New York: Routledge, 2004), xii–xiii.

56 Midgley, *Myths*, xii. Segal notes Karl Popper's related idea: "Popper even maintains that scientific theories *remain* myth-like, for theories, like myths, can never be proved, only disproved, and therefore 'remain essentially uncertain or hypothetical,'" 34.

57 Midgley, *Myths*, xii.

58 Mary Midgley, *Science as Salvation: A Modern Myth and Its Meaning* (London and New York: Routledge, 1992), 57.

59 Midgley, *Salvation*, 13.

60 John Lyne, "Rhetoric and Scientific Communities," in *Rhetoric and Community: Studies in Unity and Fragmentation*, ed. Michael J. Hogan (Columbia, SC: University of South Carolina Press, 1998), 266.

61 Wells, 93.

62 Charles Bazerman, *Shaping Written Knowledge: The Genre and Activity of the Experimental Article in Science* (Madison, WI: University of Wisconsin Press 1988), 321.

63 See: Kenneth Gergen and Mary Gergen, "Narrative Form and the Construction of Psychological Sciences," in *Narrative Psychology*, ed. T. R. Sarbin (New York: Praeger Press, 1986), 22–44; and Lisa J. Disch, "More Truth than Fact: Storytelling as Critical Understanding in the Writings of Hannah Arendt," *Political Theory* (1994): 665–694.

64 Charles Arthur Willard, "Argumentation and Postmodern Critique," in *Perspectives on Argumentation: Essays in Honor of Wayne Brockriede*, ed. Robert Trapp and Janice E. Schuetz (Prospect Heights, IL: Waveland, 1990), 221–231, p. 225.

65 Wells, 56.

66 See, for example: Stephen B. Katz, "The Ethic of Expediency: Classical Rhetoric, Technology, and the Holocaust," *College English* 54 (March 1992): 255–275. Katz argues that the objectification of human beings in Nazi rhetoric, often in the name of expediency and technology, contributed to bringing about the Holocaust.

67 Wells, 56.

68 Simons, 4.

69 Lyne, 268.

70 Lyne, 268–269.

71 Alan Gross, Joseph Harmon, Michael Reidy *Communicating Science: The Scientific Article from the 17th Century to the Present* (Oxford, UK: Oxford University Press, 2002), viii. See also: Alan G. Gross, *Starring the Text: The Place of Rhetoric in Science Studies* (Carbondale, IL: Southern Illinois University Press, 2006).

72 Lyne, 272–273.

73 Lyne, 273.

74 Lyne, 275.

75 Deirdre N. McCloskey, *The Rhetoric of Economics* (Madison, WI: University of Wisconsin Press, 1985; 2nd ed. 1998), 36. Quoted in Herbert W. Simons, "The Rhetoric of Inquiry as an Intellectual Movement," *The Rhetorical Turn*, ed. Herbert W. Simons (Chicago, IL: University of Chicago Press, 1990), 1–31, p. 9.

76 Deirdre N. McCloskey, *Bourgeois Dignity Why Economics Can't Explain the Modern World* (Chicago, IL: University of Chicago Press, 2011), 40.

77 John Van Maanen, *Tales of the Field: On Writing Ethnography* (Chicago, IL: University of Chicago Press, 1988), 5.

78 Jeanne Fahnestock *Rhetorical Figures in Science* (New York: Oxford University Press, 1999).

79 Clifford Geertz, *Works and Lives: The Anthropologist as Author* (Stanford, CA: Stanford University Press, 1988), 4–5.

80 Geertz, 84. For other views of rhetoric's role in anthropology, see: Renato Rosaldo, "Where Objectivity Lies," in *The Rhetoric of the Human Sciences*, 87–110; Christopher Nash and Martin Warner, eds., *Narrative in Culture* (London: Routledge, 1988); and Alessandro Duranti, *From Grammar to Politics: Linguistic Anthropology in a Western Samoan Village* (Berkeley, CA: University of California Press, 1994).

81 See: John Angus Campbell, "Darwin, Thales, and the Milkmaid: Scientific Revolution and Argument from Common Beliefs and Common Sense," in *Perspectives on Argument*, ed. Robert Trapp and Janice Schuetz (Prospect Heights, IL: Waveland, 1990), 207–220; and John Angus Campbell, "Scientific Discovery and Rhetorical Invention: The Path of Darwin's Origin," *The Rhetorical Turn*, 58–90.

82 Campbell, "Darwin, Thales," 209.

83   Campbell, "Darwin, Thales," 209.
84   Campbell, "Darwin, Thales," 210.
85   Campbell, "Darwin, Thales," 213.
86   Campbell, "Darwin, Thales," 214.
87   Dilip Parameshwar Gaonkar, "The Idea of Rhetoric in the Rhetoric of Science," *Southern Communication Journal*, 58(4) (Summer, 1993): 255–327, p. 258–259. Also published in Alan G. Gross and William M. Keith, eds., *Rhetorical Hermeneutics: Invention and Interpretation in the Age of Science* (Albany, NY: State University of New York Press, 1997).
88   Gaonkar, 259.
89   Gaonkar, 266.
90   Gaonkar, 267.
91   Gaonkar, 267.
92   David J. DePew and John Lyne, "The Productivity of Scientific Rhetoric," *POROI: An Interdisciplinary Journal of Rhetorical Analysis and Invention*, 9(1) (2013), 1–21, pp. 1–2.

Chapter 10

Contemporary Rhetoric II: Situation, Story, Display

Rhetoric is rooted in an essential function of language itself, a function that is wholly realistic and continually born anew: the use of language as a symbolic means of inducing cooperation in beings that by nature respond to symbols.

—Kenneth Burke

IN the last chapter we considered rhetorical scholarship focusing on argumentation and audiences as playing major roles in a twentieth-century revival of rhetoric. Writers like Chaim Perelman and Lucie Olbrechts-Tyteca emphasize argument as a means of resolving pressing moral issues. Jürgen Habermas sought the conditions of rational discourse in a set of communication standards hearkening back to Greek and Roman models of argumentation among informed citizens. The rhetoric of science movement situates the social and natural sciences in scholarly communities and emphasizes that scientists, like the rest of us, make arguments before audiences.

Other contemporary rhetorical scholars, however, have focused on rhetoric as a means of understanding and living successfully in a world of symbols. Rather than focusing on a defining element of rhetoric such as argument or audience, these theorists emphasize the cultural contexts and underlying structures of rhetoric. Such an understanding of rhetoric as situated allows us to negotiate the complex symbolic interactions that characterize all of life. This chapter also considers emerging arenas of rhetorical interaction, including visual and digital rhetorics.

RHETORIC IN CONTEXT

Several contemporary rhetorical theorists emphasize the context or situation in which rhetoric occurs. James L. Kinneavy writes that

> certainly one of the most overpowering concepts in contemporary rhetoric . . . is the notion that a piece of discourse must be judged against the cultural and situational contexts in which it was produced and in which it is being interpreted.[1]

Rhetorical scholar Michael C. Leff (1941–2010) has written that the situational approach to rhetoric is a natural extension of the classical oratorical approach to rhetorical pedagogy. "To teach rhetoric within this perspective," writes Leff, "invites attention to the situated character of discourse and to the way that the context of particular situations limit and enable discursive performance."[2] Two of the most prominent representatives of the situational approach to rhetoric are Kenneth Burke and Lloyd Bitzer.

Kenneth Burke and Rhetoric as Symbolic Action

Kenneth Burke (1897–1993) was the most influential of twentieth-century U.S. rhetorical theorists.[3] A writer of wide-ranging interests, Burke was known principally as a literary critic. His writing, however, draws freely on disciplines as diverse as philosophy, drama, religion, political science, history and rhetoric.[4]

Burke's work is vast in scope, his influence pervasive, and his vocabulary idiosyncratic. Sidney Hook has written, "The greatest difficulty that confronts the reader of Burke, is to find out what he means."[5] Even the circumspect classicist George Kennedy calls Burke a "sometimes quirky writer."[6] Yet despite the difficulties associated with Burke's writing, the effort to understand him is repaid with genuine insights into the nature of rhetorical discourse. We will begin with his most foundational ideas: that rhetoric makes human unity possible, that language use is symbolic action, and that rhetoric is symbolic inducement.

Identification

Among Burke's foundational claims is the following: You persuade an individual "only insofar as you can talk [the same] language by speech, gesture, tonality, order, image, attitude, idea," thus "identifying your ways" with those of the other.[7] Burke referred to this notion of persuasion through emphasizing commonality as *identification*. Rhetorical scholar Lloyd Bitzer calls identification "the key term in Burke's theory of rhetoric."[8] For Burke, the human predicament is alienation or separation from others, and rhetoric is alienation's only solution. Burke wrote in *A Rhetoric of Motives* that if people were not alienated from one another, "there would be no need for the rhetorician to proclaim their unity."

Burke's interest in rhetoric was focused on finding symbolic means of overcoming human alienation. Identification, he writes, "is affirmed with earnestness precisely because there is division. Identification is compensatory to division," that is, identification is the antidote to our separation from one another.[9] Bitzer adds, however, that we experience

> a constant condition of both division and community; our efforts to bridge gaps, even when successful, sometimes create others; and some of our most exhausting labor towards cooperation only anticipates division, as when we take great pains to rally ourselves to war.

Rhetoric is needed "to find common meaning, unifying symbols, and ways of acting together, and thus promoting cooperation."[10]

That cooperation is never complete, nor is it ever permanent. Nevertheless, Burke found efforts at identification to be pervasive in human experience. "Identification," he writes, "ranges from the politician who, addressing an audience of farmers, says, 'I was a farm boy myself,' through the mysteries of social status, to the mystic's devout identification with the source of all being."[11] Symbolic interaction is possible precisely because in language we recognize and appropriate hidden sources of commonality that unite us as symbol users.

In seeking identification we strive for a state which Burke labeled as consubstantiality, a term borrowed from theology literally meaning commonality of substance. The rhetorician affirms our common substance—physical embodiment, unifying aspirations, symbol use including language itself. By building identification through rhetorical practices we approach consubstantiality, and thus experience healing from the wound of our separation.

Rhetoric as Symbolic Action

Rhetoric's goal is to bring together individuals separated from one another, alienated and often in competition. Burke sometimes called this condition of human alienation "warfare," and directed his work "toward the elimination of warfare."[12] This process of reconciliation is enhanced when we recognize that language is a form of action— symbolic action. Burke recognized that struggle and separation were inherent to the human condition, and that there was no perfect rhetorical solution to that problem. After all, rhetoric itself often embodies struggle. Thomas Farrell writes, "the very meaning of *symbolic action*" in Burke's thinking "must include notions of identification and *division*, struggle, and tension . . ."

Nevertheless, rhetoric is our most characteristically human activity, and our best hope of avoiding self-destruction. As Farrell writes, for Burke "there is no contradiction ultimately between discourse practice that is always suspect and practice that is the best human embodiment of human civility."[13] We as humans are always seeking something better, always "rotten with perfection," according to Burke. And through symbolic interaction we continuously press on toward unattainable perfection—and always imperfectly.

Rhetoric as Symbolic Inducement

There is at the center of Kenneth Burke's massive project an unyielding interest in the symbolic, and a corresponding interest in symbol use by human agents to change themselves and their communities. Burke's hope was that the power of rhetoric could be harnessed to move human beings toward cooperation and ultimately toward peace. Thus, as noted above, Burke chose the Latin phrase *ad bellum purificandum*—toward the elimination of war—to introduce his rhetorical investigations in *A Grammar of Motives* (1945).

For Burke, rhetoric was the use of symbols to shape and change human beings and their contexts. Rhetoric helps us to understand three fundamental elements of human existence: (1) The symbolic means by which we define ourselves and our communities, (2) the nature of meaning as a matter of interpreting symbols, and (3) human motivation and action.

Burke employed the phrase "symbolic inducement" to sum up the essential nature of rhetoric—the effort to garner cooperation by strategic symbol use. Perhaps his most famous definition of rhetoric occurs in *A Rhetoric of Motives* (1950), a definition that provides insight into Burke's thinking. He writes,

> Rhetoric . . . is rooted in an essential function of *language* itself, a function that is wholly realistic, and is continually born anew; the use of *language* as a symbolic means of inducing cooperation in beings that by nature respond to symbols [emphasis in original].[14]

Burke believed that language was a concrete rather than an abstract aspect of our existence, and that meaning is always being developed anew out of human social interaction. Rhetoric was the key to understanding our symbolic existence.

Being Human

Burke defined human beings in terms of their natural tendency to use symbols; but symbol use reflected our best and worst qualities. To be human was to be "the symbol-using (symbol-making, symbol misusing) animal," and to be the "inventor of the negative." Human beings also are "separated from [our] natural existence by instruments of [our] own making." That is, we manufacture a world that insulates us from the natural world. Finally, human beings are "goaded by a spirit of hierarchy" and "rotten with perfection."

Symbols are the tools we employ to order the world, and this act of ordering reveals our drive to impose perfection on our surroundings. Burke wrote, "the mere desire to name something by its 'proper' name . . . is intrinsically 'perfectionist.'"[15] Language is at the very center of our existence, and through it we exhibit our desire for order, our wish to control the natural world by naming its contents, even our efforts to dominate others. Language that names others as enemies makes their destruction possible. This brings us to Burke's theory of language.

Terministic Screens

For Burke, language is not a neutral tool used to describe an objective existence. Rather, symbols are the essence of our existence, the medium through which we encounter the world, and the means by which we effect change. Language always has a strategic dimension; the linguistic choices we make as we speak shape our perceptions and reveal our intentions.

In *Language as Symbolic Action* (1966) Burke wrote that "even if any given terminology is a *reflection* of reality, by its very nature as a terminology it must be a *selection* of reality; and to this extent it must function also as a *deflection* of reality."[16] Any set of terms used to describe an object, event, or person simultaneously directs attention *toward* some factors and *away from* others. That is, language both *reveals* certain elements in a scene while it simultaneously *conceals* others.

Thus, all language is inherently rhetorical or strategic. For instance, if I describe an individual as a "consumer" rather than as a "citizen," I reveal my preference (at that moment) for economic over political descriptions of people. At the same time, I strategically direct attention *toward* the fact of a person's economic activity and *away from* their political activity. Thus, the choice of consumer over citizen, a choice evident in many media discussions of Americans, is neither neutral nor objective. Rather, it is a significant rhetorical positioning of both a speaker and the subject of the speaker's attention.

Every set of terms or symbols, thus, becomes a kind of screen through which we perceive the world. Burke writes of the origin of his own label for this phenomenon, *terministic screens*, that it was suggested by a photographic exhibit:

> When I speak of "terministic screens," I have particularly in mind some photographs I once saw. They were different photographs of the same objects, the difference being that they were made with different color filters. Here something so "factual" as a photograph revealed notable distinctions in texture, and even in form, depending upon which filter was used for the documentary description of the event being recorded.[17]

Similarly, the terms we employ in thought, and thus in perception, function as filters of our experience. Again, language does not just "reflect" reality, it "selects" reality. Language, then, does not just describe experience. Rather, it directs us to *look at* some things and *overlook* others.

Burke relates an illustrative use of the basic notion of terministic screens from the seventeenth-century French writer, Blaise Pascal. The Catholic Church in France had outlawed dueling. Pascal suggested that persons "intending to take part in a duel" might rather "merely go for a walk to the place where the duel was to be held." Moreover, "they would carry weapons as a precautionary means of self-protection in case they happened to meet an armed enemy." In this way "they could have their duel" without breaking the law.[18] The example satirically reveals how language functions as a perceptual screen.

Burke summarizes the concept of terministic screens in *Language as Symbolic Action* this way: "We *must* use terministic screens, since we can't say anything without the use of terms; whatever terms we use, they necessarily constitute a corresponding kind of screen; and any such screen necessarily directs attention to one field [way of seeing] rather than another."[19]

Burke's Pentad

Burke's best-known contribution to rhetorical theory is his dramatistic pentad, presented in *A Grammar of Motives* (1945).[20] As the name implies, the concept is drawn from the world of drama and divides rhetorical situations into five constituent elements for analysis.

Burke drew an important distinction between simple "motion" and purposeful "action," the principal difference being the presence of a motive in the latter. A motive lies behind an action such as voting for president or leaving a job. Motives make human life and interaction strategic and intentional, that is, rhetorical. Thus, to understand human acts, one must understand human motives; Burke's pentad is an aid to such understanding. Burke proposed the pentad as his "grammar of motives," that is, a means of understanding and evaluating human motivation. He begins with a question: "What is involved, when we say what people are doing and why they are doing it?"

The language of the drama provided a means of assessing why people or organizations choose the actions they do. The five elements of the pentad are the act, the scene, the agent, the agency, and the purpose. Briefly, the act is what was done or is being done—the action performed. The scene is the location of the act, its setting, or context. The agent is the person or organization performing the act, while the agency is the means by which the agent performs the act. Finally, the purpose is the reason or motive for the action, the intended goal.

Burke recognized that individuals and groups are drawn to motivational explanations reflecting a preference for a particular component in the pentad. An example helps to illustrate this point. We have all heard a range of explanations for United States' military involvement in the Middle East. This question, of course, focuses attention on human motives—in this case, the motives of U.S. leaders. One explanation of American involvement in the Middle East emphasized *acts* that catalyzed American presence in the region. For example: We are involved in the Middle East because of actions taken by nations in the region that threatened U.S. security. That is, our military involvement in the Middle East is justified as a response to other *acts*.

A second answer to the same question might emphasize scenic aspects. Thus, someone reasons that the United States is involved in the Middle East because it is a troubled region of the world, that the region combines oil, Islamic countries, and the nation of Israel in a volatile mix. This kind of explanation emphasizes the second element in Burke's pentad, the *scene* or setting.

A third type of explanation for America's military involvement in the Middle East focuses on agents, or the people and organizations making decisions. Thus, those tending to see agents at work in any given situation might argue that American involvement in the region resulted directly from the temperament of an American decision-maker such as a president or military leader, perhaps responding to perceived issues of national security, to ideological commitments, or even to the provocations of a regional leader. A different agent adhering to a different set of beliefs might have responded differently to tensions in the region.

Worldviews

Burke associated each of the five elements of his pentad with a particular worldview, or characteristic theory of why things are the way they are. The worldviews he associated with each element of the pentad are not intuitively obvious, and thus require some explanation

Burke associated an emphasis on the act itself with the worldview he called realism—a commitment to the factual reality of our lived experience. To make actions central in our explanations of motivation is to express a belief in the objective reality of our existence and the consequential nature of our decisions. To act in a real world is to bring about objective changes in the course of events.

A scenic emphasis in our motivational explanations highlights the setting in which an act takes place. Burke related this emphasis to the worldview he called materialistic determinism, a view that diminished the role of free will and rendered conclusive the material conditions in which decisions are made. That is, a preference for the scene suggests that we are compelled to act in a particular way because of the surroundings in which we find ourselves.

Burke associated an emphasis on the agent, the individual, or group performing the act, with the worldview of idealism. This philosophy emphasizes the possibility of altering circumstances according to spiritual or moral convictions embraced by the agent. In this worldview the human decision-maker is placed in the explanatory foreground.

Focusing on agency or the means by which an act is carried out, suggested for Burke a pragmatic worldview—one that sees the world in terms of problems and their practical or cause and effect solutions. In this account of motivation all that is needed is to provide agents with the appropriate tools for resolving a troublesome situation. The equipment available to us—education, money, machinery—determines how we will act.

Finally, an emphasis on purpose, the reason why an act is performed, implied for Burke the worldview he termed mysticism—a spiritual longing for wholeness or cosmic unity. To understand human motivation in terms of purposes is to commit ourselves to a narrative of achievable perfection, the resolution of turmoil by following the patterns of a utopian vision.

Ratios

Burke also suggested that the pentad is most helpful when the elements are combined as ratios to demonstrate the dynamics of a particular rhetorical act. He writes:

> We want to inquire into the purely internal relationships which the five terms bear to one another, considering their . . . range of permutations and combinations—and then to see how these various resources figure in actual statements about human motives.[21]

Two ratios, the ratio of scene to act and that of scene to agent, "are at the very center of motivational assumptions." Burke explained that "both act and agent require scenes that contain them."[22]

For instance, one might emphasize the scene or act ratio to assess a speaker's motives. Thus, in his famous speech at Gettysburg, Abraham Lincoln sought to transform a battleground into a sacred setting in which fallen heroes could be honored. By his act of honoring soldiers through his speech, the scene—the battleground—is transformed into sacred landscape. The motive for Lincoln's speech—his act—is thus best understood in its relationship to the scene in which the act is performed.

Or, alternatively, a rhetorical critic might wish to emphasize the scene or agent ratio. Rev. Martin Luther King speaking before the Lincoln Memorial 100 years after Lincoln spoke at Gettysburg is an instance of an agent interacting with a scene. King stood in front of Lincoln's statue in the Lincoln Memorial in August of 1963. He began by emphasizing his presence in a particular scene: "Five score years ago, a great American in whose symbolic shadow we stand today, signed the Emancipation Proclamation." King's opening line reverberates with the cadence and sound of Lincoln's own familiar opening, "Four score and seven years ago." The agent, Dr. King, speaks in a particular scene, the Lincoln Memorial grounds, and the ratio of these two elements allows us to glimpse King's motives in speaking: to advance the work of justice that Lincoln himself had initiated 100 years earlier.

Richard Lanham summarizes the force of Burke's dramatistic approach in writing that "rhetorical analysis can be used on nonliterary texts and on the conventions of social life is the pivotal insight of Burkean dramatism."[23] Burke's pentad helps us to see the motives and strategies at work in a wide range of human activity.

Form

The Russian playwright, Anton Chekhov (1860–1904), is famous for telling a friend, "If in Act I you have a pistol hanging on the wall, then it must fire in the last act." The quotation suggests that certain dramatic events prepare us for, nearly demand, certain other events. Burke's notion of form is very close to this recognition.[24] In one of his earliest works, *Counter-Statement* (1931), Burke identified several "aspects" of form, which he defines as "*an arousing and fulfillment of desires*."[25] Form, another concept drawn from the world of drama and narrative, helps one to understand an underlying structure of rhetorical appeals in any act of persuasion that has been adapted to an audience.

The first of these formal aspects Burke termed "syllogistic form," which he describes as "the form of a perfectly conducted argument, advancing step by step."[26] An attorney's closing argument, for example, may unfold according to the structure of a logical proof, with reasons set out before an audience in an orderly fashion. However, the plots of some action movies that involve breaking in to a heavily secured building also unfold according to a syllogistic form as the carefully prepared plan is pursued. Each scene represents a step in a reasoning process about how to evade security measures, and each event leads us inexorably to expect the next as we would expect statement to follow statement in a well-constructed argument.

The second form "is subtler" than a syllogism. Burke calls it "qualitative progression," by which he means that "one incident in a plot prepares us for some other incident of plot."[27] Thus, when an innocent victim has been harmed in a novel, we expect a subsequent scene in which the perpetrator is brought to justice. The presence of injury prepares us morally for justice, and the plot is incomplete until justice is done. Similarly, when a politician identifies a particular group—say, drug traffickers—as perpetrating harm on society, we expect a call to arms against that group.

"Repetitive form" is "the consistent maintaining of a principle under new guises."[28] Different images or arguments may be employed to make the same point repeatedly. In his 2008 campaign, Barack Obama emphasized change as a central theme. He and his staffers brought the idea of change before the public in a variety of messages and media —speeches, advertisements, songs, anecdotes, and lines delivered in debates. This repetition of the same principle by different methods is an example of repetitive form.

Some forms are used so often that they achieve the status of a "conventional form." Thus, we expect introductions at the beginning of speeches, emotional stories toward the end of a lengthy appeal, and illustrations following the introduction of a general claim.[29] Finally, "minor or incidental form" occurs any time we encounter such devices as "metaphor, paradox, disclosure, reversal" or any number of other recognizable approaches to securing or illustrating a point.

Burke opened new vistas for rhetorical and literary studies by demonstrating that *all* human symbolic behavior, not just linguistic behavior, exhibits rhetorical qualities. But, he has not escaped criticism for his unusual language and method of presenting his ideas. Brian Vickers, for example, calls Burke's rhetorical theory "free-wheeling, allusive, unhistorical philosophizing that rearranges the components of classical rhetoric so idiosyncratically as to be virtually unusable."[30] Nevertheless, Burke's massive project reveals an appealing fascination with the pervasiveness of human symbolic behavior and the sheer power of language.

Like the Sophist Gorgias and the Renaissance humanists, Burke found rhetoric a kind of verbal magic that created meaning and reality out of the immateriality of the word. Explaining Burke's view of language, William Covino writes, "Language *creates*, and so every utterance is always a magical decree [emphasis added]."[31] Burke himself affirmed in his book *The Philosophy of Literary Form*, "The magical decree is implicit in all language."[32] Thus, Burke retrieves to view in the twentieth century an ancient and venerable orientation to rhetoric that sees language as creating the substance of our lives through "symbolic action."

Lloyd Bitzer and Rhetoric as Situational

Among the most influential proponents of the situational view of rhetoric was Professor Lloyd Bitzer (1931–2016) of the University of Wisconsin. Bitzer's 1968 article "The Rhetorical Situation" marked a turning point in the U.S. study of rhetorical theory.[33] This relatively brief essay defined rhetoric as discourse responsive to a particular kind of situation. "Rhetorical discourse, I shall argue, obtain[s] its character-as-rhetorical from the situation which generates it."[34] That is to say, rhetoric can be defined as language employed to alter—specifically, to improve—a particular kind of situation. Calling rhetoric "a mode of altering reality . . . by the creation of discourse which changes reality through the mediation of thought and action," Bitzer sounded familiar Burkean themes. Bitzer's rhetorical situation is defined by three elements: an exigence, an audience, and constraints.

The Exigence

For Bitzer, rhetoric begins with a problem, a circumstance that is not the way it should be. Bitzer defined an exigence as "an imperfection marked by urgency; it is a defect, an obstacle, something waiting to be done, a thing which is other than it should be."[35]

Not all exigencies, however, constitute rhetorical situations. The particular exigence in question must be one capable of modification by discourse. For instance, the onset of winter cannot be altered by a speech, though the exigence of inadequate snow removal, caused by an inept city government, may be. "An exigence is rhetorical when it is capable of positive modification and when positive modification requires discourse or can be assisted by discourse."[36] The national crisis arising immediately after the assassination of President John F. Kennedy in 1963 stands for Bitzer as an example of a *rhetorical* exigence. A speech could not change the fact of Kennedy's death. However, speeches by Lyndon Johnson and others helped to ameliorate or improve the national and international crisis rhetorically. Today we might point to an exigence such as the national health care crisis, or the failure of public schools. Each situation reflects a problem that seems to call for a rhetorical response.

The Audience

The second element in Bitzer's rhetorical situation is the audience, a constant feature of rhetorical theories. However, it is again important to point out that not all audiences are rhetorical audiences from Bitzer's point of view. A rhetorical audience must be capable of taking action in response to the exigence.

"Properly speaking," Bitzer writes, "a rhetorical audience consists only of those persons who are capable of being influenced by discourse and of being mediators of change."[37] In other words, you are *not* a member of a rhetorical audience merely because you heard a rhetorical appeal. A citizen of Canada listening to a campaign speech by a U.S. presidential candidate is not part of the rhetorical audience because she cannot vote in the United States, and thus can do nothing to alter the exigence facing the candidate or the United States at the time of a presidential election. One must be susceptible to rhetorical influence *and* capable of acting in a manner directly relevant to improving the exigence to qualify as a member of the rhetorical audience.

Constraints

Finally, Bitzer maintains that rhetorical situations exhibit constraints. This is the third and most difficult to understand of the three elements of a rhetorical situation. The word "constraint" conjures up a problem or a restriction on one's actions. But Bitzer also has in mind enabling factors when he writes of constraints.

> Besides exigence and audience, every rhetorical situation contains a set of *constraints* made up of persons, events, objects, and relations which are parts of the situation because they have the power to constrain decision and action needed to modify the exigence.[38]

Bitzer compares constraints to the artistic and inartistic proofs of Aristotle's *Rhetoric*. He apparently has in mind, then, that constraints are any factors that set a practical limit for a rhetorician during the inventional process. Constraints are factors both limiting and enabling the rhetor as arguments and appeals are discovered, arranged, and delivered to the rhetorical audience.

Thus, one's own rhetorical ability is a constraint, as is available evidence, possible arguments, audience beliefs, and a range of other factors. All must be taken into account while composing a rhetorical message. Constraints may be thought of as the boundaries within which rhetoric is both created and advanced.

The Fitting Response

Bitzer argued that the rhetorical situation "dictates" or "prescribes" the response appropriate to it. It is on this point that his theory may be open to the most telling criticism. Nevertheless, he was insistent on the point: "If it makes sense to say that situation invites a 'fitting' response, the situation must somehow *prescribe* the response which fits [emphasis added]."[39]

What did Bitzer mean? He imagines an inventional process by which the rhetor assesses the elements of the rhetorical situation—the audience, the exigence, and the constraints. Having assessed these elements, the astute rhetor discovers the limits of what can properly or effectively be said to improve that particular situation. The rhetor then composes the right rhetorical response by uttering rhetoric that is dictated to her or him by the elements of audience, exigence, and constraints.

Lloyd Bitzer's theory of the rhetorical situation provided an accessible yet powerful tool for assessing a wide variety of rhetorical events. To speak of the rhetorical situation has become an inherent aspect of much U.S. rhetorical theory and criticism. Bitzer's basic insight—that rhetoric is discourse situated in and responsive to particular settings—has been an extraordinarily suggestive one.

RHETORIC AND NARRATION

One important movement in twentieth- and twenty-first-century rhetorical theory developed at the confluence of rhetoric and narrative.[40] The connection between rhetoric and story is an ancient one. It shows up, for instance, in Plato's *Phaedrus*, where Socrates relates stories to argue for a particular view of the human soul (the myth of the charioteer) or to suggest the dangers inherent in moving from oral to written discourse (the myth of the Egyptian god Thoth). Some recent theorists have expanded the concept of narration to the point that it subsumes all of rhetoric, while others have discovered a rhetorical dimension in the writing of all fiction.

Changes

In the age of 140 character messages and social networking, how does one determine what constitutes a rhetorical text? How can interpretive practices accommodate the difficulty of distinguishing a "source" and an "audience" in interactive rhetorical settings? How does rhetorical theory, rooted in classical thinking, come to recognize the multiple meanings evident in discourse created by diverse groups? In a new digital era in which video clips and popular songs compete with campaign speeches and editorials, how are the social functions of rhetorical discourse best explained?

The practice of rhetoric has changed in recent decades, and some rhetoricians have found in narrative theories the flexible structure necessary to account for new rhetorical forms and functions. Susan Wells, for instance, finds narrative to be "central to the discourses of modernity because of its heterogeneity, its complex articulations of time, and its construction of the narrator's fluid subject position."[41] Narrative, according to Wells, is "marked by deep diversity of styles, forms of argument, and rhetorical relations," and offers ways to "organize separate trajectories of knowledge and reflection."[42] Some narrative theories of rhetoric have developed in response to diverse cultural settings demanding a highly adaptable method of analysis.

Mikhail Bakhtin and the Polyphonic Novel

Russian linguist Mikhail Bakhtin (1895–1975) was one of the earliest of the contemporary European thinkers to turn his attention to problems of discourse in cultural contexts.[43] Bakhtin, according to Michael Holquist, "seek[s] to grasp human behavior through the use humans make of language."[44] His particular interest was the novel and what this literary form reveals about the rhetorical nature of language and culture.

Bakhtin was a relatively obscure figure for most of his life, never completing a university degree and publishing only two books—one on Dostoevsky and another on the French writer Rabelais.[45] Several more volumes of his work were published following his death, and his ideas eventually became highly influential. His work reflects a central preoccupation with what Alastair Renfrew has termed "self-other relations."[46] His favorite models of such relations were fictional.

Bakhtin's work, while preserving tenets of Marxist theory, represents a departure from the oppressive Soviet Marxist orthodoxy of his time. He was suspicious of the possibility of "objectivity" in writing, that is, suspicious of the claim that art can convey a monolithic knowledge of the truth. A story may obscure economic relations among various groups by presenting them as matters of fact rather than contingencies. Bakhtin questioned whether any writer or philosopher had access to the "correct view" of the human condition. Marxist analysis, for example, does not present a true picture of social circumstances simply because it has shaken off the ideological trappings of capitalist thinking.

Discourse as Ideology

Bakhtin recognized that all discourse is inherently ideological, and this is for two reasons. First, in a way reminiscent of Kenneth Burke, Bakhtin held that language does not merely reflect an objective world. Rather, words participate in *constructing* the world. To use language is to engage in a construction process, and what is constructed is our view of the world. Speaking and writing are never neutral or value-free activities, but interpretive enterprises.[47]

Second, to speak is to articulate a position, to argue. When we speak or write we give voice to our own system of beliefs, our ideology. To create discourse is to engage in a process of self-disclosure.

[handwritten margin note: Rhetorical value of stories = serve as the "building blocks" for this construction. How you make your world strong. All story is Rhetoric bc it is perception]

Discourse as Dialogue

If language use is inherently ideological, it is also inherently social or dialogic. We fashion speech out of pre-existing, historically bound, linguistic material. Language, the very substance of speech, is a product of social processes. We never invent speech in a vacuum; our words are marked by the meanings and intentions of many people who spoke before we did.

Moreover, every utterance, every word, "is a two-sided act." That is, the word's meaning "is determined equally by *whose* word it is and *for whom* it is meant." This means that by its very nature as a word "it is precisely *the product of the reciprocal relationship between speaker and listener, addresser and addressee . . .*" Consequently, a word is a bridge thrown between myself and another. If one end of the bridge depends on me, then the other depends on my addressee. A word is a territory shared by both addresser and addressee, by the speaker and his interlocutor.[48]

Meanings, therefore, are negotiated territories always involving the participation of more than one person. Thus, discourse always performs a social or relational function; it responds to, or anticipates a response from, another person. *transactional model of communication!*

Discourse as Politics

Language as a dialogic phenomenon is a site of political struggle as each of us "seeks to infuse language with [our] own intentions."[49] Moreover, as we construct meaning corporately, the listener becomes as important to the process as the speaker, the reader as crucial as the author. For these reasons, when describing the basic unit of discourse Bakhtin preferred the term *utterance*, with its implied sense of a personal statement full of potential meanings, to the fixed meaning implied by the word *sentence*.

Bakhtin recognized that the dialogic aspect of language can be subverted by official (governmental) efforts to suppress its inherent possibilities for diversity of expression. He thus elevated a concept he termed *heteroglossia*, the vast variety of language use always evident in any culture. A moment's reflection reveals that each one of us, in fact, employs various "languages" every day depending on our audience, the social setting, and the issues being addressed.

To *heteroglossia*, Bakhtin contrasted *monologia*, or the univocal, fixed meaning of the state or official language. Thus, the "official" language of a nation might be opposed to the innumerable group and individual variations on that language as heard in dialects, slang, or the special vocabulary of an occupational group.

Hearing Voices: The Polyphonic Novel

From Bakhtin's perspective, multiple "voices" or positions constitute the social world. But, while multiple voices are always present, not all voices are valued equally. In the continual process of dialogue, whether friendly or not, the relative value of voices is continually asserted and contested. Bakhtin sought to free discourse from the "constraints" that rendered some voices more valued than others. Consequently, Bakhtin focused on examining dialogues—chains of assertion and response—and on freeing the different voices present in a dialogue, perhaps especially those that may pass unnoticed.

The novel became for Bakhtin a favored means of demonstrating and celebrating the dialogic nature of language, and a model for opposing monologic forms. Josephine Donovan writes that Bakhtin viewed the novel as "an anarchic, insubordinate genre that reflects a kind of popular resistance to centralizing official establishments and unifying disciplines . . ."[50] Of particular interest to Bakhtin were the novels of Dostoevsky.

Novels do not reflect an objective view of reality for, as literary critic Wayne Booth points out, "the author's voice is always present, regardless of how thoroughly it is disguised."[51] Even the forms that discourse takes are infused with meaning and are ideological in their tendency to advocate for a point of view. "The quality pursued by Bakhtin," writes Booth, "is a kind of 'sublimity of freed perspectives' that will always, on all fictional occasions, be superior to every other."[52] Thus, Bakhtin sought the possibility of a full voice for various perspectives in order that, as part of the Great Dialogue that is human existence, we might discover "the best possible avenues to truth."[53]

For these reasons Bakhtin admired the polyphonic nature of Dostoevsky's novels, the quality of each character being fully developed and speaking fully his or her perspective on the world.[54] Bakhtin writes that "a plurality of independent and unmerged voices and consciousness, a genuine polyphony of fully valid voices is in fact the chief characteristic of Dostoevsky's novels."[55] Bakhtin, then, saw the works of Dostoevsky as a model for allowing equal voice to varied perspectives in the continuous dialogue among people about their conditions and the truths by which they live.

Bakhtin's ideas also challenge rhetorical theorists to listen to marginalized voices and to consider how social and political life is transformed as these voices confront those spoken from society's "center." Moreover, Bakhtin's conception of the self as constituted in the dialogic process challenges traditional understandings of "sources" and "audiences."

Wayne Booth and the Rhetoric of Fiction

Wayne Booth (1921–2005), a literary critic with interests in rhetoric and narrative, admired the work of Bakhtin. Booth, who taught at the University of Chicago, was perhaps best known for his rhetorical approach to the study of fiction. In *The Rhetoric of Fiction* (1961), he examined the complex relationship between author and narrator.

Booth notes that some works of fiction affect an "authorial objectivity or impersonality."[56] That is, authors pretend not to be present in the voices of their characters. However, Booth affirms that "the author's judgment is always present, always evident to anyone who knows how to look for it . . ." Though authors can "to some extent" choose their "disguises," they "can never choose to disappear."[57]

Authors as Advocates

Booth sought to answer writers like Sartre who had argued that the author must "give the illusion" of not even existing. If there is an author present "controlling the lives of the characters," the characters "will not seem to be free," argued Sartre.[58] But, responds Booth, not only are authors present in their work, they *should* be in order to provide the reader relief from the "dramatic vividness" of "pure showing." Authors cannot be excised from their writing. "The author's voice is never really silenced. It is, in fact, one of the things that we read fiction for, and we are never troubled by it unless the author makes a great to-do about his own superior naturalness."[59]

Booth, like Bakhtin, questioned whether a writer could adopt a value-neutral stance in writing. Sartre had contended that "a writer . . . must know that dung-heaps play a very respectable part in a landscape, and that evil passions are as inherent in life as good ones."[60] However, Booth counters that even such a claim elevates one set of values over another, and thus advocates the former. Such advocacy is a fundamentally rhetorical activity. Could an author, then, achieve neutrality about values by casting main characters as "everyperson," an ordinary member of the human race? Booth responds to this possibility, "Even among characters of equal moral, intellectual, or aesthetic worth, all authors inevitably take sides."[61]

Wayne Booth has played a major role, then, in sensitizing the literary world to the presence of the author's rhetorical voice in works of fiction. In his interest in discovering motives in the symbolic arena of literature, Booth can be seen as contributing to the larger project of Kenneth Burke and others who would have us attend to the presence of the rhetorical in all symbolic realms.

Reflecting on Narrative

The works of Bakhtin and Booth, and before them of Vico and others, raise a basic question about the role of narrative in the psychological development of human beings. Brian Boyd is a literary scholar with an interest in the psychological evolution of our narrative ability. He writes about narrative as a means of managing time:

> As our brains expanded, we could apply the past to the present and future still more flexibly. But we were still trapped within what we had witnessed and remembered ourselves. With narrative we could, for the first time, share experience with others who could then pass on to still others what they had found most helpful for their reasoning and future actions. We still have to act within our own time, but with narrative we can be partially freed from the limits of the present and the self.

The obvious rhetorical advantages of narrative are clear. An art that has always been concerned to mediate among the past, present, and future will be drawn irresistibly to narrative. Or, perhaps we are drawn to narrative because of an innate story-telling quality within us; this is Vico's view. Though he does seem interested in the rhetorical uses of narrative directly, Boyd writes, "Narrative can provide listeners with clues to the present, hints from the past, examples or analogues for reasoning about future decisions."[62]

Boyd adds, "Stories in particular foster our ability to multiply options and imagine possible actions in the face of any eventuality."[63] Thus, stories have a strategic role to play in testing possible courses of action, a function of deliberative rhetoric. Narrative may also operate something like epideictic discourse, assessing an individual's acts, developing stories around the details of a life, and in this way encouraging audience reflection.

Walter Fisher on the Rhetoric of Narration

An American rhetorical theorist, Walter Fisher (b. 1934), argued that virtually all of human communication is narrative.[64] Important to Fisher's project is how narration provides us with a means of "valuing," or assessing the moral content of ideas. Following Karl Wallace's idea that, just as reason is at the heart logic, so "good reasons" are at the heart of discourse about values. In extending the case for a complete theory of narrative's role in communication, Fisher outlines the "logic of reason." This logic involves the following considerations:

1. What facts are indeed facts?
2. What are the omitted facts?
3. What are the patterns of reasoning?
4. Which reasons are relevant to the issue at hand?
5. Which stock issues are addressed?

In order to "transform the logic of reasons into a logic of *good* reasons," Fisher argues, five components are necessary to bring about this transformation. He begins with the notion of *fact*, what is assumed as true in the narrative. Facts are not neutral data points; what is taken as fact, according to Fisher, reveals the values of a group or individual. Thus, much as Bakhtin found words always to convey a position or ideology, so Fisher finds facts always to reveal values. Second, the concept of *relevance* in the logic of good reasons asks which values are appropriate or germane to resolving the case at hand. Third, the question of *consequence* has to do with the effects of adhering to such a value in the conduct of one's life. *Consistency*, the fourth consideration, asks which values have already been confirmed or validated in individual or group experience. Finally, *transcendent issue* asks us to consider what is the ideal basis for human conduct. Would it be love? Justice?[65]

The Narrative Paradigm

Fisher considers narration as a more revealing metaphor for argument than is law—the traditionally rhetorical metaphor. What Fisher calls the narrative paradigm suggests that arguments are, in fact, a species of narrative, and that all narratives have a rational structure that can be analyzed and evaluated. Fisher writes that "the narrative paradigm advances the idea that good communication is good by virtue of the fact of its satisfying the requirements of narrative rationality, namely, that it offers a reliable, trustworthy, and desirable guide to belief and action."[66] The rationality of stories can be judged on two major criteria, which Fisher calls *coherence* and *fidelity*.

Coherence or probability in a story is a matter of structural, material, and character-ological consistency. That is, when assessing the coherence of a story, we ask if the internal elements hang together in a sensible, believable way. Suppose that during a trial a defendant relates his story of the events in question. Is the structure of the defendant's story plausible? Do the material facts he relates seem to mesh with one another in a reasonable fashion? Do the human agents in his account behave as we would expect them to? These are questions assessing the story's coherence or probability.

Fidelity, Fisher writes, directs us to ask whether the components of a story "represent accurate assertions about social reality . . ."[67] Fisher advances the five criteria detailed above for evaluating narrative fidelity: fact, relevance, consequence, consistency, and transcendent issue. That is, when assessing narrative fidelity we must ask, not simply about a story's internal structure and characterization, but also about its moral consequences in a social context. What values does the narrative advance? What actions would it lead us toward or away from? Fidelity places stories in the larger social situation and asks how a particular narrative would suggest that we live in that context. For Fisher, our thought processes are grounded in the narrative structure of life itself and thus dependent upon "the natural capacity" of people to assess the truthfulness of stories. Thus, to understand stories well is to understand life.[68]

Practical Wisdom

Fisher's emphasis on communication as a guide to moral action brings him to the classical concept of *phronesis* or practical wisdom. Fisher, along with many contemporary theorists of discourse such as Perelman and Olbrechts-Tyteca, and Habermas, asks: How is it possible to solve non-scientific problems in a reliably rational way? Justice is, for Fisher, a universal value that should inform discussions of difficult social issues. He seeks to remove assessments of the rationality of arguments about justice from the domain of privileged or elite audiences such as philosophers and lawyers and return it to ordinary people.

Rationality is, for Walter Fisher, grounded in the narrative structure of life itself and "the natural capacity" of people to identify coherence and fidelity in stories. Thus, the question of justice brings Fisher back to the stories we tell in our social groups. The practical wisdom of a community will be directly related to the stories that prevail in it, and the quality of the community's judgments about justice will result directly from those stories as well.

Ernest Bormann on Stories and Communities

Rhetoric scholar Ernest Bormann (1925–2008) explored the ways stories can be used rhetorically to build communities.[69] Bormann noted how small groups shared stories in their discussions. Starting with the observation of Robert F. Bales (1916–2004) that groups develop corporate fantasies or narrative plots, Bormann noticed that narrative structures such as jokes, stories, tales, and rituals were all significant in creating agreements among people and in establishing mutually accepted meanings.

In his essay, "Fantasy and Rhetorical Vision," Bormann applied Bales' observations about group narratives to public life.[70] Narratives become part of a society's story about itself and thus "sustain the members' sense of community," impelling them "strongly to action" and providing them a social reality "filled with heroes, villains, emotions and attitudes."[71] Bormann argued that a community's identity arises out of the stories that have meaning for the entire group.[72] *Symbolic convergence* occurs when members of a group begin to share the same stories.[73] Groups develop corporate *fantasy themes*—stories or plot lines—and these themes come to define the group and its values.[74]

A group's stories will include what Bormann terms *inside jokes*—encapsulated stories understood only by members of the group. The inside joke is not necessarily humorous; it is simply a narrative which is an abbreviated version of a longer story characterizing the group' life. Bormann also discussed *fantasy types*—basic plots which are repeated in a variety of group or organizational stories. For example, many corporations employ a fantasy type we might title: "Our Founder is also a Decent Human Being." Various stories circulate within the organization about the founder's willingness to forgive an unintended insult by a new member of the group, or the founder's great generosity. Each of these stories is intended to reveal the founder as "a real human being."

This particular fantasy type is part of the corporate narrative of many groups and organizations.

Stories provide the basis for a shared vision that makes sense of the world for a group, thus allowing the group to grow into a community. Over time, a shared vision develops into what Bormann termed an organizational saga. This is a longer story which presents the history of the group in the form of a legend.[75] Bormann's theory reminds us just how important stories are as a group seeks to develop a shared identity. It also suggests that the telling of stories has great significance, for we forge personal and corporate identities out of the stories we tell about ourselves.

THE RHETORIC OF DISPLAY

Among the important recent developments in rhetorical theory is an approach labeled the rhetoric of display—rhetorical analysis focused on visual, representational, or material rather than language-based discourse. Such analyses are present in the works of leading rhetorical scholars such as Carole Blair and Lester Olson.[76] The rhetoric of display approach also recognizes that much traditional, language-based rhetoric was itself designed in such a way as to make audiences "see" something they had not seen before.

Rhetoric of display emphasizes the important fact that, as Lawrence Prelli writes, "Much of what appears or looks to us as reality is constituted rhetorically through the multiple displays that surround us, compete for our attention, and make claims upon us."[77] Perelman's notion of presence and Burke's idea of agents performing acts within a specific scene, suggest that the rhetoric of display was suggested in earlier theories of rhetoric.

Rhetoric of display studies explore how visual rhetoric affects audiences in a variety of ways and through a wide range of rhetorical forms. Prelli writes,

> Displays are manifested rhetorically through the verbally generated "image" in speeches and literature. Displays appear rhetorically in sketches, paintings, maps, statistical graphs, photographs, and television and film images. Displays are manifested rhetorically in the homes we inhabit and in the many places we visit— museums and exhibitions, memorials and statuary, parks and cemeteries, casinos and theme parks, neighborhood street corners and stores. Displays are manifested rhetorically in the "demonstration" of a scientific finding, of a political grievance, of a preferred identity.[78]

This recognition of the visual and material rhetoric all around us is crucial to completing the picture of rhetoric presented in this text. Indeed, Prelli affirms that "rhetorics of display are nearly ubiquitous in contemporary communication and culture and, thus, have become the dominant rhetoric of our time." This may well be the case as we recognize the visual rhetoric of websites, movies, protests, museum displays, stories, architecture, video games, and a host of other persuasively constructed messages that make up our daily lives in the modern urban environment. Thus, understanding the rhetoric of display is crucial to informed citizenship in an increasingly visually oriented society.

The rhetoric of display is now broad enough to include the rhetorical study of material objects generally and the networks of which they form a part. Such studies draw on a set of theories and critical approaches developing around the broad theoretical framework known as materialism.[79] Moving past older models in which a human orator exercised exclusive agency while an audience attended to such a single speaker's words, materialist theorists speak of "circulation," or the patterns and trajectories of an object's (e.g., an image's or a video game's) movement through a culture and across cultures. Scholars refer now to a rhetoric of matter itself or of "things," particularly in networked systems involving human beings. "Things provoke thought, incite feelings, circulate affects, and arouse in us a sense of wonder" write Scot Barnett and Casey Boyle. "But, things are more than what they mean for us. They are vibrant actors, enacting affects that exceed . . . human agency and intentionality. Things are rhetorical, in other words."[80]

Scholars in materialist studies have appropriated theories from various fields of study, such as Actor-Network Theory in which material objects and concepts play important roles in the construction of meaning as they interact with human agents in large social systems or networks. These semiotic theories (theories of meaning), as presented by scholars such as philosopher of science Bruno Latour, challenge traditional distinctions between subject and object, and between nature and culture.[81] Under a principle known as generalized symmetry, an object may assume a kind of social agency once reserved to human symbol users. In Actor-Network Theory, meaning arises out of complex interactions among people, concepts, and objects. Burke would remind us that to show an audience one thing is simultaneously to conceal from that audience something else. To create a television program around the absurdities of work in a modern office setting may involve ignoring the sound creative work and rational decision-making that can also characterize such a work setting. For this reason, "whatever is revealed through display simultaneously conceals alternative possibilities; therein is display's rhetorical dimension."[82]

DIGITAL RHETORICS

Today new rhetorical forms are arising from digital culture and the online experience. Abbreviated forms of communication such as Twitter, networked systems of communication such as Facebook, and hyperlinked pages of text that connect a reader immediately to a new page are innovations that will invite theoretical exploration. These new forms combine display with traditional textual presentations of rhetoric. Such digital formats raise questions about digital rhetorics: Which elements of older rhetorical systems still provide explanatory power in an age of digital communication? Does persuasion remain at the center of these new forms of rhetorical transaction?

The Architecture of the Online Experience

Some investigators of the online world, such as journalist Nicholas Carr, affirm that the structure of our digital experience is teaching us—or coercing us into—new ways of thinking. In other words, the digital world operates on the basis of an implicit rhetoric.

In his book *The Shallows: What the Internet Is Doing to Our Brains*, Carr argues that an "ecology of interruption technology" characterizes the very nature of the online experience. Such a structured environment of distraction is designed into the online experience to ensure that we do not spend too much time on any one page. This assertion is rooted in Carr's observation of the economics of digital experience—the more pages we visit, the more advertising we experience.[83] This point is reminiscent of Richard Lanham's definition of rhetoric itself as the economics of attention—strategic efforts to garner a larger share of the limited resource we call attention. If Carr is right, then classical categories such as disposition or arrangement are being deployed in new digital domains to achieve a particular response from audiences.

Some theorists and critics have speculated that online communication, with its potential for involving hundreds of thousands of people in a discussion, represents a more democratic rhetorical form than did earlier forms such as the speech or the newspaper editorial. However, this new open participation format has not been without its problems. For example, while participating in those discussions we are also generating data about ourselves which is of value to the entities providing the discussion forum, a fact that raises a variety of ethical and rhetorical issues.[84]

Artist and media theorist Clay Shirky is an authority on the structure of the Internet. Shirky has studied, among other phenomena, the architecture of online sites to determine which structures are most conducive to helpful interactions in our new public sphere. He has written that "a rhetorical tragedy of the commons is occurring in many forums. All the participants have an incentive to have good conversations, but each participant also has an incentive to get the most attention."[85] The way some participants seek the attention of other readers in online conversations and Web page comment sections is counterproductive. Shirky wonders if new structures for participating in the online conversation might help solve this problem. The issue of attention—how it is achieved, structured, and even controlled—certainly appears to be one that a new generation of rhetorical theorists will have to address.

Andrea Lunsford's New Literacy

Professor Andrea Lunsford teaches writing and rhetoric at Stanford University. She was recently in charge of the Stanford Study of Writing, which examined nearly 15,000 undergraduate writing samples in forms ranging from blog posts to classroom assignments. Lunsford's conclusion? "I think we're in the midst of a literacy revolution the likes of which we haven't seen since Greek civilization." Lunsford asserts that we are witnessing a "new literacy" emerging as digital formats encourage more writing, not less. The writing that the student generation participates in is active, public, strategic, and persuasive—in other words, traditionally rhetorical.

Reporting on Lunsford's findings in *Wired* magazine, Clive Thompson writes, "Lunsford's team found that the students were remarkably adept at what rhetoricians call *kairos*—assessing their audience and adapting their tone and technique to best get their point across." Student writing today tends to be "conversational and public, which makes it closer to the Greek tradition of argument" than to forms such as the traditional letter.

We are witnessing in digital literacy a return to traditional rhetorical concerns—discourse as audience-adapted, persuasive, responsive, and planned. Thompson writes that Lunsford's students "defined good prose as something that had an effect on the world. For them, writing is about persuading and organizing and debating . . ."[86] These are qualities of discourse that would have been recognized, and taught, in Athens more than 2,400 years ago.

CONCLUSION

Some twentieth and twenty-first century theories focusing on rhetoric as situated, and as adapted to new situations, have opened an avenue of insight into how we now experience rhetoric. Recall that Aristotle's account of the art of rhetoric describes it as an art that allows one to understand and respond well to various real-life settings—the court, the legislature, the public ceremony. This chapter has suggested that rhetoric continues to adapt to an ever-changing environment and to new social demands.

Theories we have considered in this chapter rediscover the relationships between rhetoric and life in the symbolic world. Kenneth Burke has drawn attention to the symbolic nature of our lives and how symbols and human motives interact. Lloyd Bitzer's situational approach also sees rhetoric as revealing a structure in which human agents respond rhetorically to events out of the desire to improve on an imperfect situation. Rhetoric is seen as a response to a particular kind of setting, and as structured by that setting in predictable ways.

Early in this century, linguist Mikhail Bakhtin opened a highly productive discussion about the rhetorical nature of narrative. His interest in the polyphonic—"many voiced"—possibilities in the novel prompted discussion about the relationship between rhetoric and narrative generally. Wayne Booth developed Bakhtin's vision of narrative as rhetoric, exploring the nuanced relationship between author and narrator in fiction. Both contended that the author is always present, despite efforts at concealment.

Writers working in the area of the rhetoric of display have demonstrated that rhetorical concerns extend well beyond the traditional medium of written and spoken language. We now see rhetorical components in art and architecture, as well as in the architecture of the online experience. Materialism has broadened the concept of agency to include even material objects.

We have also taken note of efforts to apply principles of rhetoric and standards of productive public discourse to new digital media. This effort has spawned new understandings of what is meant by a public sphere, and new conceptions of literacy. It is intriguing to observe the remarkable flexibility of the ancient rhetorical tradition, as theorists find themselves returning to such terms and concepts as *kairos* in their efforts to understand and improve these new formats of digital and visual culture.

QUESTIONS FOR REVIEW

1. What are the key terms in Burke's dramatistic pentad? What do the terms describe?
2. What is Wayne Booth's position on the possibility of an author of fiction being "invisible"?

3. What are the three essential components of Bitzer's "rhetorical situation"?
4. What quality did Mikhail Bakhtin find intriguing in the novels of Dostoevsky?
5. Why did Bakhtin consider that discourse is always ideological and social?
6. What did Walter Fisher mean by practical wisdom?
7. What did Walter Fisher mean by coherence and fidelity?
8. What did Ernest Bormann notice about the role of stories in groups?
9. What is meant by the "rhetoric of display"?
10. What is Andrea Lunsford's "new literacy"?
11. What is materialism, and how does this movement redefine agency?

QUESTIONS FOR DISCUSSION

1. After reading this chapter, what argument could be made for broadening the conception of rhetoric beyond public speeches or widely circulated written documents?
2. In your opinion, what kinds of rhetoric would Kenneth Burke's theory be most likely to help one to understand?
3. Identify a novel or movie in which you can identify a rhetorical component. Explain how this novel or movie is rhetorical. Is your example "polyphonic" in Bakhtin's sense of the term?
4. Would classical theories of rhetoric be adequate for explaining and evaluating visual rhetoric, or do we need a new rhetorical theory of the rhetoric of display?
5. What role has narrative played in the life of groups of which you have been a part?
6. What factors might a rhetorical theory for the digital age include that earlier theories of rhetoric have not? How, for example, would such a theory accommodate the social networking phenomenon as contrasted to a traditional speaker–audience model?
7. What changes might be made in how we approach the online experience that would render it more productive of civil discourse that might improve democracy?
8. What is your response to the idea that material objects can exercise rhetorical agency?

TERMS

Actor-Network Theory A theory in which material objects and concepts play important roles as they interact with human agents in large social systems.

Coherence In Fisher, the degree of consistency among elements in a narrative; whether the components of a story appear to hang together.

Constraints In Bitzer, "persons, events, objects, and relations which are parts of the situation because they have the power to constrain decision and action needed to modify the exigence."

Consubstantiality Commonality of substance in Kenneth Burke's rhetorical theory.

Dialogues In Bakhtin, chains of assertion and response that reveal the presence of different voices.

Dramatistic pentad Burke's "grammar of motives," consisting of act, scene, agent, agency, and purpose.

Exigence In Bitzer, "an imperfection marked by urgency; ... a defect, an obstacle, something waiting to be done, a thing which is other than it should be."

Fantasy themes, For Bormann, when stories or plot lines come to define the group and its values.

Fantasy types For Bormann, basic plots which are repeated in group or organizational stories.

Fidelity For Fisher, a concern for whether the components of a story represent accurate assertions about reality.

Fitting response In Bitzer, rhetoric that is dictated to the rhetor by the rhetorical situation.

Form In Burke, arousing and fulfilling desire in an audience.

Generalized symmetry In Actor-Network Theory, the idea that an object may assume a kind of social agency once reserved to human symbol users.

Heteroglossia For Bakhtin, the many languages that proliferate in any culture.

Inside jokes For Bormann, encapsulated stories understood only by members of a group.

Organizational saga For Bormann, a longer story which presents the history of the group in the form of a legend.

Polyphonic Many voiced; Bakhtin's term for quality of narrative in which each character is fully developed and speaks fully about his or her perspective on the world.

Rhetorical audience In Bitzer, an audience capable of being influenced by discourse and of being mediators of change.

Rhetoric of display A critical and theoretical movement emphasizing the visual aspects of rhetoric.

Rhetoric of fiction Booth's insight that, in narrative, "the author's judgment is always present."

Symbolic convergence For Bormann, when members of a group share the same stories.

Symbolic inducement Burke's definition of rhetoric. Garnering cooperation by the strategic use of symbols.

Terministic screens Burke's term to describe the fact that every language or choice of words becomes a filter through which we perceive the world.

Utterance A personal statement full of potential meaning. For Bakhtin, the basic unit of discourse.

NOTES

1 James L. Kinneavy, "Contemporary Rhetoric," in *The Present State of Scholarship in Historical and Contemporary Rhetoric*, ed. Winifred Bryan Horner (Columbia, SC: University of Missouri Press, 1990), 192.

2 Michael C. Leff, "What Is Rhetoric?" *Rethinking Rhetorical Theory, Criticism, and Pedagogy: The Living Art of Michael C. Leff*, eds. A. de Velasco, J. A. Campbell, and D. Henry (East Lansing, MI: Michigan State University Press, 2016), 471–481, p. 476.

3 Kenneth Burke's numerous works include: *Counter-Statement* (Berkeley, CA: University of California Press, 1931); *Language as Symbolic Action* (Berkeley, CA: University of California Press, 1937); *A Grammar of Motives* (Berkeley, CA: University of California Press, 1945); *A Rhetoric of Motives* (Berkeley, CA: University of California Press, 1950); and *The Rhetoric of Religion* (Berkeley, CA: University of California Press, 1961).

4 See, for example: Don Abbott, "Marxist Influences on the Rhetorical Theory of Kenneth Burke," *Philosophy and Rhetoric* 4 (1974): 217–233.

5 Sidney Hook, "The Technique of Mystification," *Critical Responses to Kenneth Burke*, ed. William H. Ruckert (Minneapolis, MN: University of Minnesota Press, 1969), 89. Quoted in Abbott, 217.

6 George Kennedy, *Classical Rhetoric and Its Christian and Secular Tradition* (Chapel Hill, NC: University of North Carolina Press, 1999), 94.

7 Kenneth Burke, *A Rhetoric of Motives* (Berkeley, CA: University of California Press, 1969), 55.

8 Lloyd Bitzer, "Political Rhetoric," in *Landmark Essays on Contemporary Rhetoric*, ed. Thomas Farrell (Mahwah, NJ: Lawrence Earlbaum, 1998), 1–22, p. 9.

9 Burke, *Rhetoric of Motives*, 22.

10 Bitzer, "Political Rhetoric," 9–10.

11 Burke, *Rhetoric of Motives*, xiv.

12 Burke used the Latin phrase, *ad purificandum bellum*.

13 Thomas Farrell, *Norms of Rhetorical Culture* (New Haven, CT: Yale University Press, 1993), 204.

14 Burke, *Rhetoric of Motives*, 43.

15 Burke, *Language as Symbolic Action*, 16.

16 Burke, *Language as Symbolic Action*, 45.

17 Burke, *Language as Symbolic Action*, 45.

18 Burke, *Language as Symbolic Action*, 45.

19 Burke, *Language as Symbolic Action*, 50.

20 Burke, *A Grammar of Motives* (1945; Berkeley, CA: University of California Press, 1969).

21 Burke, *Grammar of Motives*, xvi.

22 Burke, *Grammar of Motives*, 15.

23 Richard Lanham, *The Electronic Word: Democracy, Technology and the Arts* (Chicago: University of Chicago Press, 1993), 56.

24 Burke, *The Philosophy of Literary Form: Studies in Symbolic Action*, 3rd ed. (1941; Berkeley, CA: University of California Press, 1973). Also: *Counter-Statement*.

25 Burke, *Counter-Statement* (1931; Berkeley, CA: University of California Press, 1968), 124.

26 Burke, *Counter-Statement*, 124.

27 Burke, *Counter-Statement*, 124.

28 Burke, *Counter-Statement*, 125.

29 Burke, *Counter-Statement*, 126.

30 Brian Vickers, *In Defense of Rhetoric* (Oxford: Oxford University Press, 1988), 441.

31 William A. Covino, *Magic, Rhetoric and Literacy: An Eccentric History of the Composing Imagination* (Albany, NY: State University of New York Press, 1994), 93.

32 Burke, *The Philosophy of Literary Form*, 4. Quoted in Covino, 91.

33 Lloyd Bitzer, "The Rhetorical Situation," *Philosophy and Rhetoric* 1 (December 1968), 1–14.

34 Bitzer, "The Rhetorical Situation," 3.

35 Bitzer, "The Rhetorical Situation," 6.

36 Bitzer, "The Rhetorical Situation," 7.

37 Bitzer, "The Rhetorical Situation," 8.
38 Bitzer, "The Rhetorical Situation," 8.
39 Bitzer, "The Rhetorical Situation," 10.
40 Sources on rhetoric and narration include: Anne Dipardo, "Narrative Knowers, Expository Knowledge," *Written Communication* 7 (January 1990): 59–95; Doug Hesse, "Aristotle's Poetics and Rhetoric: Narrative as Rhetoric's Fourth Mode," in *Rebirth of Rhetoric: Essays in Language, Culture, and Education*, ed. Richard Andrews (London: Routledge, 1992); Richard Andrews ed., *Narrative and Argument* (Milton Keynes, UK: Open University Press, 1989); and Renato Rosaldo, "Where Objectivity Lies," in *The Rhetoric of the Human Sciences*, ed. John Nelson, Allen Megill and Donald McCloskey (Madison, WI: University of Wisconsin Press, 1987), 87–110.
41 Susan Wells, *Sweet Reason: Rhetoric and the Discourses of Modernity* (Chicago, IL: University of Chicago Press, 1996), 49.
42 Wells, 49.
43 On Bakhtin's thought, see: Michael Holquist, *Dialogism: Bakhtin and His World* (London: Routledge, 1990).
44 Holquist, 15.
45 Alastair Renfrew, *Mikhail Bakhtin* (London: Routledge, 2015), 7–8.
46 Renfrew, 23.
47 Mikhail Bakhtin, *Marxism and the Philosophy of Language*, trans. L. Matejka and I. R. Titunik (New York: Seminar Press, 1973), 9. See also: Liisa Steinby and Tintti Klapuri eds., *Bakhtin and His Others: Intersubject(ivism), Chronotype, Dialogism* (London, UK: Anthem, 2013).
48 Bakhtin, *Marxism*, 86.
49 Charles Schuster, as quoted in editor's introduction to *Landmark Essays on Bakhtin, Rhetoric, and Writing*, ed. Frank Farmer (Mahwah, NJ: Hermagoras Press, 1998), 3.
50 Josephine Donovan in *Feminism, Bakhtin, and the Dialogic*, ed. Dale M. Bauer and S. Jaret McKinstry (Albany, NY: State University of New York, 1991), 86.
51 Mikhail Bakhtin, *Problems of Dostoevsky's Poetics*, ed. and trans. Caryl Emerson (Minneapolis, MN: University of Minnesota Press, 1984), xix.
52 Bakhtin, *Dostoevsky*, xx.
53 Bakhtin, *Dostoevsky*, xxv.
54 Bakhtin, *Dostoevsky*, 3.
55 Bakhtin, *Dostoevsky*, 6.
56 Wayne Booth, *The Rhetoric of Fiction* (Chicago, IL: University of Chicago Press, 1961), 16. See also: *Now Don't Try to Reason with Me* (Chicago, IL: University of Chicago Press, 1970); *Modern Dogma and the Rhetoric of Assent* (Chicago, IL: University of Chicago Press, 1974).
57 Booth, *Fiction*, 20.
58 Booth, *Fiction*, 50.
59 Booth, *Fiction*, 60.
60 Booth, *Fiction*, 69.
61 Booth, *Fiction*, 78.
62 Brian Boyd, *On the Origin of Stories* (Cambridge, MA: Harvard University Press, 2010), 166.
63 Boyd, 411.
64 Walter Fisher, *Human Communication as Narration: Toward a Philosophy of Reason, Value, and Action* (Columbia, SC: University of South Carolina Press, 1987).
65 Fisher, 108–109.
66 Fisher, 95.

67 Fisher, 105.

68 Fisher, 137.

69 See: Ernest Bormann, "Fetching Good Out of Evil: A Rhetorical Use of Calamity," *Quarterly Journal of Speech*, 63 (1977): 130–139; "A Fantasy Theme Analysis of the Television Coverage of the Hostage Release and the Reagan Inauguration," *Quarterly Journal of Speech* 68 (1982): 133–145; *Restoring the American Dream* (Carbondale, IL: Southern Illinois University Press, 1985).

70 Ernest Bormann, "Fantasy and Rhetorical Vision: The Rhetorical Criticism of Social Reality," *Quarterly Journal of Speech* 59 (1972): 398.

71 Bormann, "Fantasy and Rhetorical Vision," 398.

72 Ernest C. Bormann, "Symbolic Convergence: Organizational Communication and Culture," in *Communication and Organizations: An Interpretive Approach*, ed. L. L. Putnam and M. E. Pacanowsky (Newbury Park: Sage, 1983), 99–122.

73 Bormann, "Symbolic Convergence," 102.

74 Bormann, "Symbolic Convergence," 108.

75 Bormann, "Symbolic Convergence," 120.

76 See: Carole Blair, *Places of Public Memory: The Rhetoric of Memorials and Museums* (Tuscaloosa, AL: University of Alabama Press, 2010); and Lester Olson, *Benjamin Franklin's Vision of American Community* (Columbia, SC: University of South Carolina Press, 2004).

77 Lawrence J. Prelli, ed., *Rhetorics of Display* (Columbia, SC: University of South Carolina, 2006), 1.

78 Prelli, 2.

79 See, for example: Laurie E. Gries, *Still Life with Rhetoric: A New Materialist Approach for Visual Rhetorics* (Boulder, CO: University Press of Colorado, 2015).

80 Scot Barnett and Casey Boyle eds., *Rhetoric, through Everyday Things*, (Tuscaloosa, AL: University of Alabama Press, 2016), 1. See also: Mel Y. Chen, *Animacies: Biopolitics, Racial Mattering and Queer Affect* (Durham, NC: Duke University Press, 2012).

81 Bruno Latour, *We Have Never Been Modern* (Cambridge, MA: Harvard University Press, 1991). For a feminist application of Latour's work to questions in science, see: Donna J. Haraway, *Staying with the Trouble: Making Kin in the Chthulucene* (Durham, NC: Duke University Press, 2016).

82 Prelli, 1.

83 Nicholas Carr, *The Shallows: What the Internet Is doing to Our Brains* (New York: Norton, 2011), 104. See also by Carr: *The Glass Cage: How Our Computers Are Changing Us* (New York: W.W. Norton, 2015), and *Utopia Is Creepy: And Other Provocations* (New York: W. W. Norton, 2016).

84 See, for example: Maria Lindh and Jan Nolin, "Information We Collect: Surveillance and Privacy in the Implementation of Google Apps for Education," *European Educational Research Journal* (2016): 1–20.

85 Clay Shirky, "Cleaning up Online Conversation," *Harvard Business Review*: *HBR Agenda 2011* (January 2011), http://hbr.org/web/extras/hbragenda-2011/clay-shirky (accessed June 5, 2011). See also Shirky's books on the online experience: *Here Comes Everybody: The Power of Organizing without Organizations* (New York: Penguin, 2009), and *Cognitive Surplus: Creativity and Generosity in a Connected Age* (New York: Penguin, 2010).

86 Clive Thompson, "Clive Thompson on the New Literacy," *Wired* (August 24, 2009), www.wired.com/techbiz/people/magazine/17-09/st_thompson (accessed June 4, 2011).

Chapter 11

Contemporary Rhetoric III: Texts, Power, Alternatives

Now "everyday language" is not innocent or neutral.

—Jacques Derrida

Men have an ancient and honorable rhetorical tradition.

—Karlyn Kohrs Campbell

A powerful intellectual movement took shape in Europe and the United States in the twentieth century, centered on the relationships among language, culture, and power. Scholars such as Ferdinand de Saussure, Claude Lévi-Strauss, and Jacques Lacan explored language's role in shaping human thinking, human societies, and in the construction of our sense of self. Interest in the inherently rhetorical nature of language has led to renewed interest in persuasive discourse and the strategies by which individuals and groups achieve power.[1] This international discussion by philosophers, linguists, communication theorists, historians, and literary critics placed discourse at the center of academic debate.

This chapter considers alternatives to traditional Western presentations of rhetoric. It opens with an overview of the work of two of the more important European writers on the subject of postmodern approaches to discourse during the closing decades of the twentieth century—Michel Foucault and Jacques Derrida. Resisting simple labels and standard classifications, these theorists have been called radical and conservative, sophisticated and naive, oppressive and liberating, brilliant and confused. Nevertheless, important issues such as the nature of power, the sources of knowledge, the construction of meaning, and the structures of social life animate the debate surrounding their work.

This chapter explores, in addition, a powerful and influential application of the insights provided by Foucault, Derrida, and others into rhetoric's relationship to power— feminist rhetorical theory. We will focus particular attention on feminist responses to the Western rhetorical tradition itself. Feminist scholars have employed the critique of power and language to analyze perhaps the most sustained source of male power ever developed.

The chapter also takes up non-Western alternatives to the European rhetorical tradition, following a development often termed comparative rhetoric. We will consider two examples of distinctly African rhetorical practices. Then, we will explore some fascinating developments in China that occurred at around the same time as the Western tradition of rhetoric was taking shape. The African and Chinese examples suggest that the history and practice of rhetoric is richer and more complex than the Western tradition alone would indicate. Examples of ancient Egyptian and Aztec rhetoric will also be considered, as will medieval Muslim contributions to rhetorical theory. Each discussion reflects the need to broaden our conception of rhetoric in response to cultural developments involving symbols, sources, and audiences.

POSTMODERN RHETORIC

Postmodernism is a reaction to the intellectual values of the European Enlightenment, values that inaugurated the modern age. During the eighteenth century, reason was elevated as our best hope of solving ancient human problems and creating a rational society. Thinkers such as French satirist and playwright Voltaire (1694–1778), British empirical philosopher David Hume (1711–1776), and German philosopher Immanuel Kant (1724–1804) represent the great intellectual luminaries of the period.

In addition to confidence in reason, the hallmarks of modernity include belief in the fixed meanings of symbols, trust in sense perception and direct observation, and the authority of the individual human subject pursuing truth. Under the commitments of modernity, academic disciplines were viewed as moving along a clear line of progress. Enlightenment scholars studied subjects such as history, anthropology, sociology, physics, and literature as they pursued the rational project of delivering humanity from the oppression of what they took to be superstitions and false beliefs, especially those beliefs associated with the Christian tradition and religion generally. Though the Age of Enlightenment is conventionally held to have ended with the French Revolution (1792–1794), modernist confidence in reason and progress as the twin means of solving human problems and resolving moral dilemmas persisted well into the twentieth century.

Questioning the "Taken for Granted"

The nineteenth-century German philosopher Friedrich Nietzsche (1844–1900)—himself a classicist with a thorough understanding of the rhetorical tradition—had already begun to question Enlightenment assumptions, and thus provided the seeds of a new or "post-modern" system of thought. He attacked the grand explanatory narratives of Christianity and Judaism, and strongly opposed all overarching philosophical frameworks. Morality and social principles were relative and only served the "will to power" of those who sought power. Twentieth-century thinkers built on these criticisms of Enlightenment thought.

Jean-Francois Lyotard and Postmodernism

In 1960s Europe developed a view that came to be known formally as postmodernism which began to shake the very foundations of modernity. Postmodernism incorporated insights from philosophy, sociology, history, literature, and the social sciences. As a critical school of thought, postmodern thought questions both reason and progress and rejects what Jean-Francois Lyotard (1924–1998) termed, in his seminal work *The Postmodern Condition* (1979), "metanarratives," grand explanatory schemes such as Christianity, Marxism, or capitalism that claim to account for the entirety of human history and the human condition. Postmodernism rejected even the notion of the autonomous subject or "self" as a sociolinguistic construction. In other words, postmodernism—a general name applied to a host of intellectual, artistic, and cultural trends—challenged the very foundations of Western philosophy.

Claudia Moscovici writes that for Lyotard, "inquiries into the nature of reality," the very goal of modern thinking, are merely "futile pursuits." In fact, "Lyotard advises readers against accepting the concepts of reality, truth, and morality" at all because the sources of each have traditionally been "metanarratives." As an alternative he recommended the *petits recits* or "small narratives" which characterize local human communities and particularly marginalized groups. Armed with such basic assumptions, Lyotard suggested that "to enter the postmodern era . . . we must overcome our enlightenment legacy by abandoning the quest for truth."[2]

Postmodernism set its sights on the Enlightenment project. Lyotard specifically challenged the Enlightenment figure he termed "the hero of knowledge," that careful employer of reason in the pursuit of truth who "works toward a good ethical–political end."[3] It is also the case that Lyotard found language—not fixed and eternal realities—to constitute the worlds we inhabit. Moreover, the possibilities in language for creating realities were numerous. He wrote that "there are many different language games," that is, "ways of creating a reality out of the units of language."[4]

Structuralism

Postmodernism was also, however, a response to an early twentieth-century movement in discourse analysis called Structuralism, forcefully set out in the works of Claude Levi-Strauss (1908–2009). Levi-Strauss, who was building on the pioneering work of earlier writers such as linguist Ferdinand de Saussure (1857–1913), identified striking similarities in mythologies around the world, recurring mythic archetypes that suggested to him a fixed structure shaping various narratives. Levi-Strauss made his case for such structures in his groundbreaking essay, "The Structural Study of Myth." "Throughout the world myths do resemble one another," he wrote.[5] The underlying structure or "grammar" of myths, he argued, revealed the structure of human thought and thus of human experience. "Myth *is* language," he wrote, "it is a part of human speech."[6] A myth's "operative value" derives from a timeless "pattern" embedded within it.[7]

Consequently, the "key" to interpreting a myth is not discovered in its narrative content but in its structure.[8] This pattern or "grammar" originates, not in the myth, but in the human mind itself. Thus, "myths get thought in man unbeknownst to him."[9]

Moreover, the order the mind expresses through myth may reflect a cosmic order. Hence, the properties that define myth are "only to be found *above* the ordinary linguistic level; that is, they exhibit more complex features beside those which are to be found in any kind of linguistic expression."[10] Due to its nature as a response to Structuralism, the work of Lyotard and similar writers is also referred to as Post-structuralism. While Post-modernism describes a "condition" experienced by late-industrial people and societies, Post-structuralism is specifically a philosophy of language that, by questioning stable meanings, contributes to the Postmodern condition.

Michel Foucault

The French scholar Michel Foucault (1926–1984) is probably the most influential European intellectual figure of the last half of the twentieth century. So sweeping has been his influence that one expert concludes that Foucault "changed the basis of the work of all scholars."[11] This writer who changed how so many others did their work is himself difficult to categorize. He was a philosopher, social historian, semiotician, and social critic. Even his biographers sometimes confess "ignorance about what Foucault is really doing."[12] Foucault held various academic positions around Europe between 1955 and 1969, settling eventually at the highly acclaimed College de France, where he occupied the chair of Professor of the History of the Systems of Thought.

Some of Foucault's works, such as *Madness and Civilization* (1961), *The Order of Things* (1966), and *The Archaeology of Knowledge* (1969), are sweeping in scope: the first traces the history of the idea of insanity, the second the development of the human sciences, and the third the relationship between power and knowledge.[13] Others, such as *The Birth of the Clinic* (1963), a work that examines a century in the history of medicine, are focused on single subjects.[14] Toward the end of his life, Foucault wrote the three-volume work *The History of Sexuality* (1976–1984), a pioneering effort to understand how the concept of sexuality has been defined in discourse throughout human history.[15] What concerns render his disparate works part of a common corpus?

Power and Discourse

Foucault's consuming interest in the "central problem of power" is evident in much of his work.[16] Foucault investigated in particular the relationship between power and language, and has been called the "first major writer to pose the question of power in relation to discourse."[17] More specifically, Foucault pondered how power "installs itself and produces real material effects."[18] That is, he wondered about how power comes to be concentrated in certain institutions, and the ways that such concentration of power affects how we live our daily lives. Thus, Foucault "does not approach the question of power in terms of some fundamental principle from which its manifestations may be deduced." Rather, he addresses the phenomenon "in terms of the concrete mechanisms and practices through which power is exercised . . ."[19] How power is demonstrated, how it affects our daily lives, how we ourselves enable power to be concentrated in institutions—these are the questions that preoccupied Michel Foucault.

For Foucault, power is not the result of "conscious or intentional decision," but rather of the complex ways in which language is employed. Thus, "he does not ask: who is in power? He asks how power installs *itself* and produces real material effects."[20] Who is a criminal? What is considered appropriate punishment for a crime? Who is mentally ill, and how are the mentally ill to be treated?[21] These and similar questions intrigued Foucault. Who is president? How are bills passed into law? Questions of this type Foucault considered misleading, for they suggest that power is a fixed, predictable, objective fact.

Discourse and Knowledge

As these examples suggest, power, for Foucault, is not imposed from above through social structures and hierarchies. Rather, power is fluid, flows from discourse, and is inseparable from knowledge. The discourse or systems of talk generated within the limits of disciplines such as psychology or practices such as medicine, establish what we take as known.[22] Thus, modern Western medicine would constitute for Foucault a "discourse," while medicine as practiced in eighteenth-century Europe would constitute a different discourse. Each generated and stood behind a different body of knowledge.

Foucault considered discourse to be more than symbolic representation of real, objective facts in the world of experience. Discourse did not "merely represent 'the real' "but was, in fact, "part of its production."[23] For example, how medical professionals talk about mental illness—what they claim to *know* about mental illness—creates and sustains genuine power over the lives of the mentally ill. This means that power is always in flux, always the result of language competition within a discourse community. Foucault wrote, "although power is an omnipresent dimension in human relations, power in a society is never a fixed and closed regime, but rather an endless and open strategic game."[24] *Game* here should be taken to mean something closer to "contest" than to "amusement."

Power is a matter of which ideas prevail at the moment.[25] Systems of discourse control how we think and what we claim to know. Most people assume that the reverse is true: that what we *know* governs how we *talk*. But for Foucault, the rules of discourse govern knowledge, and these rules are thus the essence of power. The actual material effects of power—for example, how convicted criminals are treated—follow from the rules of discourse in place at a particular time. McHoul and Grace write, "events, no matter how specific, cannot happen just anyhow. They must happen according to certain constraints, rules or conditions of possibility."[26]

Escape and Surveillance

Foucault noted that we are constantly and increasingly under surveillance by those wielding power, a phenomenon Foucault dubbed *panopticism*—to be "watched" everywhere. Thus, the theme of escape or emancipation appears frequently in Foucault's work, and is closely related to the problem of power. Indeed, "Foucault said that he wrote to escape from himself, to become other than he was."[27] Foucault sought to reveal not only how knowledge and power constrain freedom but also to provide his readers the intellectual resources necessary for escaping these constraints.[28] Foucault was also interested in the personally transformative power of confession. Elden writes of Foucault's "long-standing interest in confession, beginning a thousand-year history where the true transformation of the soul must take place through a rhetoric of confession (*aveu*)," a kind of "'telling the truth about oneself'" which in a judicial setting "'will lead to one's transformation from unjust to just.'"[29]

Foucault's interest in captivity and escape may explain why he was drawn to institutions in which people were literally held captive—prisons (*Discipline and Punish*) and mental asylums (*Madness and Civilization*). The prison—especially Jeremy Bentham's circular panopticon design in which prisoners could always be watched by just a few guards—and the mental asylum, symbolized how the uses of power result from systems of discourse. And yet, for all his penetrating analysis, Foucault seldom argued for or against particular social practices. As one commentator notes, even in *Discipline and Punish*, a book that deals with the sometimes horrific treatment of prisoners, Foucault is "hardly polemical, rarely mentions transgression and confines himself to descriptions of the past."[30]

Archaeology of Knowledge

Foucault believed that a culture's collective discourse—its characteristic ways of talking—represented something akin to an archaeological artifact. Thus, he sought to reveal an "archaeology of knowledge" through the study of various discursive texts.[31] "What I am doing is neither a formalization nor an exegesis," he writes, "but an archaeology." As Foucault used the term, archaeology is not the exploration of ancient sites, but "the description of an archive." An archive, for Foucault, was "the set of rules which at a given period and for a given society" define "the limits and forms of the sayable" and "the limits and forms of conversation."[32] As such, an archive is specific to a particular time and location.

An archive reveals what could be said and thus *known* in a particular society at a particular time.[33] Foucault's archaeological study of ways of talking pursued the *episteme* of a culture and an age—its discursive practices over a defined period of time.[34] Karlis Racevskis defines an episteme as "a field of epistemological possibilities structured in a way that will determine the particular mode in which knowledge is to be achieved in a given culture and age."[35] David R. Shumway points out that "each *episteme* is like a stratum of earth in which the artifacts uncovered are the products of a distinct historical period."[36] As Foucault moved through layer upon layer of historical strata, he sought to "show the conditions that allowed the particular ways of dealing with [knowledge and discourse] to come about."[37] He later adopted the term "genealogy" to replace "archaeology." The metaphor of genealogy allowed Foucault to address the influence of one period's ideas on the next.

Was Foucault simply studying intellectual history? It is more accurate to say that he sought the history of rational *possibilities*, the underlying potentialities that made certain thoughts possible—and thus "sayable"—at a given time in human history. What possibilities of human reasoning and talking, for instance, result in contemporary penal institutions in the West in which a prisoner's body is incarcerated, but in which outright physical torture, so common in earlier ages, is uncommon? Or, why did previous ages treat the insane as sources of amusement, while we presently employ clinical metaphors and thus treat the severely mentally ill as hospital patients rather than clowns?

Foucault wished to expose the forces that set the rational boundaries of "the present." In the process he hoped to demonstrate that "the present"—a taken-for-granted and unassailable fact—is not inevitable. That is, Foucault sought to show that how we talk, how we think, and what we say we know (1) are intimately related and (2) might be other than they are.

Foucault, then, studied the discursive practices within a culture that provided the framework for knowledge, meaning, and power. What we term knowledge is a product of *what* can be discussed and *how* it is discussed. As such, knowledge is constantly being reconfigured as the rules governing discourse change over time. But this does not mean simply that people in different historical epochs have known different facts. Foucault saw a direct link between knowledge and power, so differences in knowledge always imply differences in the ways power is distributed in a culture. Thus, all "reorganizations of knowledge also constituted new forms of power and domination."[38]

Excluded Discourse

For Foucault, record of what has been said on a particular topic at a particular time results from a "set of rules (neither grammatical nor logical) to which speakers unwittingly conform."[39] Some of these rules dictate which topics can (or cannot) be discussed and the language that may be used to discuss them. "Excluded discourse" is Foucault's term for discourse that is controlled by being prohibited.[40] And, for Foucault, such prohibitions always govern our knowledge of the world. Of course, only that which can be discussed can be "known," for we cannot "know" something that cannot be expressed symbolically.

Foucault explains that "in every society the production of discourse is at once controlled, selected, organized and redistributed according to a certain number of procedures, whose role is to avert its powers and its dangers."[41] There are, for instance, rules governing who may talk, what can be talked about, and in which settings. Some subjects or views are not recognized as within the realm of legitimate discourse. Sexually transmitted diseases, for example, cannot be discussed among some groups of people within the bounds of acceptable discourse, or may not be discussible in some contexts.

Foucault was intrigued by the connections between rules of discourse and judgments about sanity. "From the depths of the Middle Ages," he writes, "a man was mad if his speech could not be said to form part of the common discourse of men. His words were considered null and void, without truth or significance, worthless as evidence."[42] Thus, by the unspoken rules of discourse, the words of some people carry no weight, are not to be credited as reliable. Prisoners, children, women, and the insane are all groups that have been silenced in some cultural settings. Unspoken rules also govern the qualifications one must have to speak in certain contexts and the places from which discourse may originate.

Queer Theory

Michel Foucault's original insight into the intimate connection between language and power, between symbolic action and social arrangements, has had a profound influence on a variety of important intellectual movements. He was one of the major shaping forces in the development of feminist theory in the 1970s and 1980s. His insight was also foundational to a critical movement known as Queer Theory that began to take shape around 1990. Invention of the actual term *Queer Theory* and of its basic premises is attributed to Teresa de Lauretis and her landmark 1991 essay, "Queer Theory: Lesbian and Gay Sexualities." Interestingly, only a few years after introducing the term, de Lauretis jettisoned it as having taken on its own fixed meaning.

Queer theory is often associated with the advent of academic departments of lesbian and gay studies, but its implications for our uses of language extend beyond issues directly related to homosexuality. This theoretical framework shares with feminist critical theories the notion that gender itself is not so much a fixed fact about individuals as it is a social construct. That is, queer theory sees gender as a product of symbolic interaction and the social negotiation of meaning. Queer theory questions even the idea that there is anything fixed or essential about our conceptions of self, arguing that the "self " is, like gender and sexuality, socially constructed. Thus, discourse in the public arena—one definition of rhetoric—becomes crucial to the construction of gender as to all other components of the self. Queer theory, then, emphasizes the social constructedness of gender, sexual identity, and the self. Each is a matter, not of natural conditions, but rather of symbolically based meanings negotiated in public as well as private settings.

Queer theory began by questioning the allegedly stable meanings associated with sexuality, sexual activity, and gender. But it soon extended this analysis of our social existence to questions regarding everything previously taken as essential and unchanging in personal identity. Linguist Mel Y. Chen has written,

> Queer theory, building upon feminism's critique of gender difference, has been at the forefront of recalibrating many categories of difference, and it has further rewritten how we understand affect, especially with regard to trauma, death, mourning, shame, loss, impossibility and intimacy. . . .[43]

Foucault's explorations of the relationships among language, rules of discourse, and the appropriation of power have informed a variety of critiques of contemporary social practices and much attendant action. His view of power and language can be applied fruitfully to the analysis of political practices, religious discourse, and the uses of the mass media to shape opinion. Foucault provides a wide range of possibilities to those interested in the uses of discourse in shaping culture and distributing power.

Jacques Derrida

The French philosopher Jacques Derrida (1930–2004) was born in Algiers and studied at Harvard in the 1950s. Derrida and his controversial method of reading texts, known as "deconstruction," have greatly influenced literary and philosophical studies.[44] His many books, including *Speech and Phenomena*, *Of Grammatology*, and *Writing and Difference* (all of which originally appeared in 1967), advance a wide-ranging analysis of the hidden operations of language. Contemporary rhetorical theorists and critics have made use of Derrida's insights, as have scholars in a number of other disciplines.[45]

Things aren't always what we think they are, so use discourse to discover truth & power.

Wants us to question the powers at play that cause us to be compliant.
• Netflix, The Push w/ Derren Brown

Derrida held that language—especially *written* language—cannot escape the built-in biases of the cultural history that produced it. "Now 'everyday language' is not innocent or neutral," he commented in an interview in the early 1970s. Derrida explains that language "carries with it . . . a considerable number of presuppositions of all types . . ."[46] Derrida, then, sought to reveal the underlying assumptions of the philosophical and political writing that influences the thinking of all of us.

Deconstruction

Among Derrida's goals in developing the deconstructive approach to written discourse are (1) to reveal the hidden mechanisms at work influencing meaning, (2) to demonstrate the concealed power of symbols to shape thinking, and (3) to underline the fact that no one escapes these elusive qualities of language. Derrida hoped to make fresh reading a possibility, reading that is not merely "handing on ready made results, passing along finished formulas for mechanical repetition and recitation."[47]

Reading a text for what a traditional reading would overlook, dismiss, or omit Derrida referred to as transgression, that is, violating the received interpretation of a text in search of its submerged meanings. Derrida's defenders are quick to assert that he does not promote "saying whatever comes into your head about the text, however absurd and ridiculous," nor discovering by dint of extraordinary cleverness a transcendent and utterly true meaning in a text.[48]

Unstable Meanings

Derrida's principal goal "is to remain acutely sensitive to the deeply historical, social and linguistic 'constructedness' of our beliefs and practices."[49] The discourse of particular concern to Derrida was that produced by Western philosophy. Derrida was determined to show that philosophy, not less than any other enterprise that relies on writing, is not a "privileged, truth-seeking discourse immune from all the vagaries of writing."[50]

Derrida did not see language simply as a system of signifying words, but rather as "a system of relations and oppositions" that must be continually defined.[51] He refused to accept the "reality" of established social structures, unexamined, standardized meanings, and well-worn oppositions such as "mind and body," "form and content," "nature and culture." He sought to "steer clear of the simple opposition of reason and faith" suggested by Enlightenment writers, exposing instead "the extent to which reason is deeply saturated by faith."[52]

Derrida argues that traditional notions like "structure," "opposition," and even "meaning" force stability on concepts that are fundamentally unstable, and obscure the operations through which the *appearance* of stability is created. Meaning is always "the product of a restless play within language that cannot be fixed or pinned down for the purposes of conceptual definition."[53] This may be why Derrida was so reluctant to define the concept "deconstruction," preferring rather to call it simply a "process." One of the goals of the deconstruction of discourse is to reveal "those blind-spots of argument" that result from rigid, unexamined meanings attributed to terms.[54]

Deconstruction examines the "oppositions" embedded in a discourse, to point out how concepts are invested with meaning by contrast. When such oppositions have been brought to light, a text may appear self-contradictory. Thus, "to deconstruct a discourse," writes Jonathan Culler, "is to show how it undermines the . . . oppositions on which it relies, by identifying in the text the rhetorical operations that produce the supposed ground of the argument, the key concept or premise."[55]

In deconstructing the discourse of nuclear deterrence, a particular interest of Derrida's, he shows the "logical incoherence" of the central concept itself. An apparently stable term like *war* is understood or defined only in contrast to the assumed opposite, *peace*. In a curious way, then, an argument for the possibility of war becomes dependent on the opposite concept, peace. Moreover, Derrida sought to demonstrate through deconstructive practices how the entire argument for nuclear deterrence rested on an "elaborate fiction" of nuclear attack and defense.[56] The "rational" and deadly serious rhetoric of nuclear deterrence, then, is built on unstable meanings and irrational assumptions.

Deconstruction and the Rhetorical Tradition

Derrida, then, questions some of the basic components of traditional rhetoric. For Derrida, the foundations of argument—stable meanings, the appeal to reason, the unambiguous nature of principles such as "equality," and the reality of oppositions like "labor" versus "capital"—are the *effects* of rhetorical interactions rather than the objective foundations of arguments. Deconstruction, both as philosophy and as critical method thus involves exposing the fundamental variability, what Derrida calls the "undecidability," of meanings. "What if the meaning of *meaning* 'is infinite implication'" and the "force" of meaning "is a certain pure and infinite equivocalness, which gives signified meaning no respite . . . ?"[57]

If rhetoric teaches us the power of structured discourse, Derrida wants to teach us that no author is in complete, intentional, conscious control of the meanings of any written text. John Caputo puts this point well when he writes:

> A deconstructive reading, Derrida says, always settles into the distance between what the author consciously intends or means to say (*vouloir-dire*), that is, what she "commands" in her text, and what she does not command, what is going on in the text, as it were, behind her back . . .[58]

Derrida adds a dimension to our thinking about rhetoric by calling attention to the fact that each of us is "embedded in various *networks*" of meaning, some of which we are not conscious of as we write.[59]

Thus, even the most skilled rhetorician—one who manages even those hidden persuasive devices operating below the audience's level of conscious awareness—creates a text carrying meanings that resist even *her* conscious control. Derrida finds his approach to texts to move the self out of the way, and thus to make room for "the other," the voice in the text that is not the author's own narcissistic voice. The rhetorical tradition, on the other hand, elevates the self as controlling agent of the text and all of its meanings, and thus as controlling agent of the audience.[60]

Derrida also provides an important counterpoint to the thinking of Jürgen Habermas discussed in Chapter 9, and, on a larger scale, a counterpoint to the entire Western rational tradition in philosophy.[61] Habermas has been said to be completing the modernist project of establishing the supremacy of rationality, while Derrida is *post*modern in his tendency to undermine the foundations of Western rationalism.

While Jürgen Habermas attempted to stabilize discourse by outlining conditions under which it can proceed rationally and with relative freedom from ideological coercion, Derrida wishes to destabilize or "deconstruct" discourse by challenging traditional assumptions concerning language and meaning. But Derrida insisted "that deconstruction was a process, an activity of reading irreducible to a concept or method."[62] Neither does Derrida accept that deconstruction is a method of criticism nor does he accept that it is an interpretation of text. It is only, he claims, a process of reading. Thus, any fixed definition of deconstruction must be held somewhat tentatively.

Responses

Derrida's critics, especially in the discipline of philosophy, have sometimes seen him as exacting "literature's revenge upon philosophy," and as something of a "mischievous latter-day sophist bent upon reducing every discipline of thought to a species of rhetorical play."[63] Moreover, Derrida's ideas have often been misinterpreted as warranting a free-ranging, unrestrained, and undirected dismantling of written texts, a "farewell to rigorous protocols of reading."[64] His defenders adamantly deny these charges, but deconstruction remains an unwelcome guest in the academy to some.

Derrida and deconstruction have been widely criticized, even in the popular media. They "have been blamed for almost everything. For ruining American departments of philosophy, English, French, comparative literature, for ruining the university itself [and] for dimming the lights of the Enlightenment . . ."[65] Deconstruction has been viewed by many as "some sort of intellectual 'computer virus'" that destroys everything with which it comes in contact.[66] And why is this? Because nothing is more crucial to traditional philosophic, political, and literary discourse than the assumption of fixed meanings, unless it is the complementary assumption that authors control those meanings. By violating both sacred ideas at once, Derrida has made himself the *bête noir* of many who cherish these two ancient verities.

Nevertheless, Derrida considered himself a friend of philosophy, if "philosophy is the right to ask any question about all that we hold sacred, even and especially about reason and philosophy itself." Derrida did what he did in the name of "a love for what philosophy loves—knowledge and truth."[67] His iconoclastic approach to reading certainly upset many traditionalists (and others), but it also has been heralded as providing an important corrective to rigid readings that concentrate power in authors and their conscious control of texts. In this respect, deconstruction is a counterpoint to the rhetorical tradition itself, or, perhaps, the cutting edge of a new way in rhetoric.

FEMINISM AND RHETORIC: CRITIQUE AND REFORM

It is quite clear from the history of rhetoric that the vast majority of writers who have shaped this field of study were men. The problems for women that emerge from a male rhetorical history have been pointed out by a number of scholars, and their insight into the largely masculine history of rhetoric has made feminist criticism and theory the most powerful recent developments in rhetoric.[68]

Gesa Kerscher and Jacqueline Royster have observed that "feminist rhetorical inquiry has expanded vastly over the last three decades," and now offers "strong evidence as a specific body of scholarship that knowledge paradigms in the history of rhetoric and writing are shifting." These writers note that "for centuries the world of rhetoric has been anchored by Western patriarchal values, an assertion that is easily documented by a review of rhetorical scholarship over time and that invariably underscores historical patterns of exclusivity." They note several resulting problems in rhetorical scholarship, including "a focus on men as rhetorical subjects" and a geographical emphasis on "the Europeanized/Western world." Moreover, patriarchal approaches have meant that scholarly attention has been "centered on power elites, by class, race, and gender" and "directed toward public domains (political, judicial, religious, academic), that is, arenas in which white elite males have dominated historically . . ." Feminist rhetorical scholarship has reached a point of development that now allows for new methodologies. "The point to be highlighted, then, is that feminist-informed research has opened up our fields of inquiry, taking us well beyond the three Rs: rescue, recovery, and (re)inscrption . . ." These new fields of inquiry will incorporate nuanced and comprehensive approaches these writers term critical imagination, strategic contemplation, and social circulation.[69]

Feminist writers have long argued that women have their own ways of speaking and of knowing, that is, their own rhetoric.[70] Jana Sawicki notes that "the work of Foucault has been of special interest to feminist social and political theorists."[71] His historical work has served to "free [his readers] for new possibilities of self-understanding, new modes of experience, new forms of subjectivity, authority, and political identity."[72]

The Loss of a Woman's Voice

The feminist critique of rhetoric has been sweeping and powerful. Some feminist critics have identified rhetoric as a particularly destructive influence on the fortunes of women in the West. For example, Leslie Di Mare writes, "although other disciplines (history, philosophy, art, film, and so on) have been used by the patriarchy to create the perception that women function best biologically, none has been used so effectively as the discipline of rhetoric."[73]

Sonja Foss writes that "two assumptions that connect gender with rhetoric undergird feminist criticism: (1) women's experiences are different from men's; and (2) women's voices are not heard in language."[74] Foss points out that "much inquiry into rhetorical processes . . . is inquiry into men's experiences," which are in turn assumed to be "universal."[75] But women's experience of the world, she writes, differs from that of men for a number of reasons. Biological differences may be obvious, but less obvious are the socialization processes that both men and women undergo, and that teach women to be quieter than men and to assume positions of service.

More to the point for rhetorical studies, women's "perceptions, experiences, meanings, practices, and values—are not incorporated into language." Thus, women, as Foucault would argue, are denied a voice in culture, because their discourse has been excluded from the public realm.[76] Moreover, they have been denied access to power by being denied access to rhetoric. "Language, then," Foss asserts, "features men's perspectives and silences women's." Moreover, Adrienne Rich asserts that "in a world where language and naming are power, silence is oppression, is violence."[77]

The exclusion of women from the rhetorical mainstream has resulted in the loss of women's meanings, and thus, it is argued, in the loss of women themselves as members of the social world. One critic writes,

[because] women have been unable to give weight to their symbolic meanings they have been unable to pass on a tradition of women's meanings to the world . . . they have been cut off from the mainstream of meaning and therefore have frequently been lost.[78]

Another writes of the "strong voices" of social leadership, that "when these strong voices are feminine, the words are less often recorded and analyzed."[79]

Victoria DeFrancisco and Marvin Jensen point out that speeches by women are infrequently recorded and studied when compared with those by men.[80] Such facts regarding systematic exclusion of women from the history of rhetoric and public address are significant for a variety of reasons, but of perhaps the most immediate concern is the role of women as contributors to a democratic society. "Women will not be equal participants or successful negotiators," writes Sally McConnell-Ginet, "if the language code does not serve them equally."[81]

A society's rhetorical practices are part of a larger language code. Some scholars contend that language itself, by its words and its structures, reflects a male view of the world.[82] Moreover, students of language and culture, including rhetorical critics, often have not viewed women's rhetorical practices as significant. As a result, women have been left out of the history of rhetorical practice. Foss suggests that feminist critics have sought to correct this error:

Rather than assuming, for example, that significant rhetorical artifacts are speeches made in public contexts by famous rhetors . . . the feminist critic seeks out symbolic expressions considered significant in women's lives in the context in which they are likely to occur.[83]

Reconceptualizing Rhetoric

Foss suggests that the feminist perspective on rhetoric seeks nothing less than "the reconceptualization of rhetorical theory." "Feminist criticism," she writes, "does not simply involve the grafting on of women's perspectives to the existing framework of rhetorical theory. Rather, it challenges the theoretical tenets of the rhetorical tradition because they were developed without a consideration of gender."[84] This does not mean that feminist rhetoricians discard the history of rhetoric, though that history "was created largely by men to deal with their interests and concerns." The feminist perspective, however, "encourages us to examine the rhetorical tradition with a new consciousness of its less attractive features and implications, and to create a new body of rhetorical theory that is more satisfying to and reflects the perspectives of all people."[85]

Feminist rhetorical theorists have been interested in the rhetorical practices of early feminist activists, and of groups who have systematically been denied access to rhetorical power.[86] Racial minorities, the illiterate, the poor, the disabled, and children have all been denied rhetorical access. The rhetorical techniques directed to such groups might differ from those used to motivate empowered groups. Campbell comments, "Because oppressed groups tend to develop passive personality traits, consciousness-raising is an attractive communication style to people working for social change."[87] Thus, the feminist perspective reflects a social and intellectual agenda that extends to the interests of persons who may not be women.

Constructing Gender Rhetorically

One rhetorical phenomenon of particular interest to feminist rhetoricians is the construction of gender. "Feminist critics," writes Foss, "examine how masculinity and femininity have been created and ask that these fundamental constructions of gender be changed" when they tend to silence or otherwise degrade women. "Thus," Foss asserts, "feminist rhetorical criticism is activist—it is done not just *about* women but *for* women—it is designed to improve women's lives."[88]

Julia T. Wood has also pointed out the rhetorical nature of gender construction, noting that "social views of gender are passed on to individuals through communication by parents, peers, and teachers."[89] Notions of masculinity and femininity are rhetorical in nature, symbolically constructed through numerous acts of persuasive communication. "For instance, in the early 1800s, masculinity was equated with physical potency, but today masculinity is tied to economic power and success." What accounts for this change? "Changes such as these do not just happen. Instead, they grow out of rhetorical movements that alter cultural understandings of gender and, with that, the rights, privileges, and perceptions of women and men."[90] Thus, Wood concludes, "any effort to understand relationships among gender, communication, and culture must include an awareness of how rhetorical movements sculpt social meanings of men and women."[91]

Rhetoric as Conquest

The history of gender is, then, a rhetorical history that must be studied rhetorically. New methods of rhetorical criticism were needed to do justice to the study of gender. Feminist critics writing during the past 40 years have called in question the standard, male-dominated "history" of rhetoric. In a groundbreaking 1979 essay, Sally Miller Gearhart argued that the history of rhetoric was a history of male rhetorical theory and practice, and as such said little if anything about women's understanding of persuasion and symbol use generally.

"My indictment of our field of rhetoric springs from my belief that any intent to persuade is an act of violence."[92] Gearhart points out that men have "taken as given that it is a proper and even necessary function to attempt to change others."[93] As a result, rhetoric "has spent whole eras examining and analyzing its eloquence, learning how to incite the passions, move the will." She adds, "of all the human disciplines, it has gone about its task of educating others to violence with the most audacity."[94] Gearhart's principal concern was with rhetoric's "*intent* to change people and things, [and] our attempt to educate others in that skill."[95] The rhetoric propounded by male theorists such as Aristotle and Perelman, does not mind its own business, but rather minds the business of other people. In this office as meddler into the affairs of others, rhetoric is aggressive, violent.

In his, *The Art of Persuasion in Greece*, George Kennedy wrote that

> some of the Greek love of speech and argumentation is probably derived from a feeling that oratory is a contest in which man exhibits something of his manliness. Phoenix taught Achilles to be a doer of deeds and a speaker of words. Circumstances of a less heroic age robbed many Greeks of the opportunity to be the former and these made up for it by exercise of the latter.[96]

Thus, oratory was a kind of battle using words rather than swords, one in which one man sought to defeat another by a skill that drew applause rather than blood.

Indeed, rhetoric-as-male-art was built on what Gearhart termed "the *conquest* model of human interaction" which finds its most egregious manifestation in "the *conversion* model of human interaction." The conversion model holds that the goal of rhetoric is to convert others to one's own views. Gearhart takes this activity to be fundamentally an act of violence not unlike rape. When I convert another to my views, this critique affirms, I conquer the other under the justification that the conquest is actually good for the conquered, and is, in fact, what the conquered wanted.[97] The rhetoric of the courtroom, the rhetoric of the legislature, and the rhetoric of the pulpit all "demonstrate precisely a violence not just of conquest but also of conversion." Gearhart finds all such efforts at forceful change to be fundamentally violent.

Gearhart suggested an alternative, "non-persuasive notion of communication," a theory of communication as information for or assistance to others.[98] "Communication can be a deliberate creation or co-creation of an atmosphere in which people or things, if and only if they have the internal basis for change, may change themselves . . ." Encouragement, the recognition of differentness among participants, enhancing the other's feeling of power, and a willingness to yield to others all are important commitments of participants in such communication.[99] Communication must be viewed as a "matrix" in which individuals are nurtured to become whole people. Such communication Gearhart describes as an "essentially . . . womanlike process," and the changes Gearhart calls for would bring about "the womanization of that discipline" of rhetoric.[100] She concluded, "in order to be authentic, in order to be nonviolent communicators, we must all become more like women."[101]

Rhetoric as Invitation

Can there be a non-persuasive practice of rhetoric, or does this question suggest a contradiction? Sonja Foss and Cindy Griffin have outlined what they term an *invitational rhetoric*, one that does not require or assume intent to persuade on the part of a source.[102] "One manifestation of the patriarchal bias that characterizes much of rhetorical theorizing," they write, "is the definition of rhetoric as persuasion."[103] Following Gearhart's analysis, these authors conclude that such a view of rhetoric and communication "disallow[s] . . . the possibility that audience members are content with the belief systems they have developed, function happily with them, and do not perceive a need to change."[104]

Foss and Griffin's proposed solution to the received model centered on persuasion, "is an invitation to understanding as a means to create a relationship rooted in equality, immanent value, and self-determination."[105] Rhetoric, understood in this way, seeks not to persuade, but rather to invite audience members "to enter the rhetor's world, and see it as the rhetor does."[106] Does such rhetoric seek change in the audience? Foss and Griffin suggest that "change may be the result of invitational rhetoric, but change is not its purpose."[107]

"Works," "Texts," and the Work of Reading

Diane Helene Miller has written that feminist scholars have "uncovered the operation of patriarchal systems" that have functioned to exclude women from language-based disciplines such as rhetoric and literature. These same scholars have "chronicled the precise ways in which women's voices were suppressed or omitted from the historical record . . ."[108] The critical task of discovering exactly what challenges women faced opened the way for developing a distinctly feminist theory of rhetoric. Miller adds that in this way "the justification for feminist intervention" in telling rhetoric's story was "abundantly provided by observing that women had been silenced and that, even when they found or created opportunities to speak, their words were largely erased from or hidden by history." She adds that feminist rhetorical criticism has been "excavating and revaluing women's texts."[109]

However, this critical approach can become yet another way of marginalizing women by its tendency to demonstrate how the structures of Western intellectual inquiry left women out of the picture. Assembling the scattered evidences of women's contributions does not affect the patriarchal structures themselves, does not reveal that "[women's] silencing is effected by configurations of gender that are built into the very definition of rhetoric as it has been conceived in Western society from the beginning."[110] Another writer on women and rhetoric, Jane Sutton, arrives at a similar conclusion. She writes,

> . . . I think we should abandon the seventy year old project of finding and recuperating rhetorical women for future posterity. Rather, we need to figure out a way to recuperate women's rhetorical excellences while simultaneously altering the conditions that make her exclusion happen again and again.

New rhetorical structures are needed, ones "allowing the full inclusion of women."[111]

Miller refers to the work of Roland Barthes in suggesting another trajectory for rhetorical investigations by feminist scholars. Barthes famously distinguished a "work" from a "text"—referring by both terms to the same artifact. Finding relatively fixed meanings suggests our approach to a literary "work," while a free or alternate interpretation suggests our approach to a "text." Miller writes that for Barthes "language is viewed as 'polysemic' and unstable, comprised of dominant meanings that can remain privileged only so long as they continually suppress alternate meanings."[112] The work of the feminist rhetorician is to draw out these alternate meanings in such a way as to reveal the structures of male privilege hidden in texts.

Textual deconstruction results in more than one reading of an artifact. Miller writes, "deconstruction thereby introduces the possibility of reading a text *both* in a manner that exposes the workings of the dominant culture *and* for the purpose of generating resistant readings that oppose or modify that dominant meaning."[113] The skilled work of the critic becomes paramount in approaching a "text." Power shifts from the author to the critic. Following this approach, even classic "works" such as Plato's dialogues may be read as "texts" that reveal hidden meanings and assumptions about rhetoric, the Western intellectual tradition, and the treatment women have received from both. Critics find "language as the source of potentially empowering contradictions."[114] "Ultimately," writes Miller, "it is not only the opportunity for critique but the potential for reinvention that provides the impetus for a feminist engagement with the texts of the rhetorical tradition."[115] In proposing this approach, then, Miller advocates an alternative to prior feminist scholarship that aimed at compiling catalogues of women's contributions. Such efforts may inadvertently create a false impression about social structures that worked systematically to exclude women's voices from the rhetorical domain, even as they occasionally allowed women themselves to speak in that domain.

Feminism and the Ancient Tradition

Feminist rhetorical theory represents both a break with and an interrogation of male-dominated rhetorics. Nevertheless, some scholars have argued for connections between contemporary feminist rhetorical theory and rhetorical models originating in Greece and Rome. Antonio de Velasco, for instance, notes that Cicero's vision of the ideal orator, which joins the individual's moral vision with a life lived for the betterment of the community, has endured right down to the present. De Velasco discovers in Cicero a "fulfillment that shuffles between an inwardly personal and outwardly political sense of freedom and possibility." At this juncture, he asserts, there exists a connection between such ancient rhetorical theorists and contemporary feminist rhetoricians such as bell hooks.

hooks and Cicero, writes Velasco, "share a vision of political agency whose fulfillment arises from the rhetorical and ethical exigencies of our experience as individuals." hooks, like Cicero,

> would also be an eloquent transgressor of contexts, one whose highest calling would be to bridge the critical, antihegemonic aims of transgression with the inventive, aesthetic aims of classical eloquence. This explicit attention to the subjectivity of the

rhetorical critic marks a return to rhetoric as a way of being and acting in the world, and not simply as a way of knowing language.

Teachers of rhetoric should emulate both Cicero and hooks, and see themselves "as moved to create a certain kind of person."[116]

COMPARATIVE RHETORIC

Feminist critics have highlighted the specifically male nature of Western rhetoric. This largely male-constructed Western rhetorical tradition predisposes European and American people to consider the argument-based speech as the foundational unit of rhetorical discourse. The traditional speech favors the authority of a single speaker, the individual in possession of knowledge.

In recent years the field of comparative rhetorics has grown and attracted the attention of a number of leading scholars in rhetoric. LuMing Mao and Bo Wang emphasize the fluid and cross-cultural nature of rhetoric in writing, "Rhetorical knowledge, like any other knowledge, is heterogeneous, multidimensional, and always in the process of being created."[117] This section reviews just a few of the numerous efforts to recognize and set in their contexts rhetorics from non-European societies, both ancient and contemporary.

African Rhetorical Forms

Even a brief survey of rhetorical forms from other cultures reveals that the European model is just one of the possibilities for understanding and practicing rhetoric.[118] For instance, scholar of myth Marcel Detienne writes that the Lo Dagaas people of northern Ghana employ a rhetorical form known as the *bagre*, which Detienne describes as simultaneously an "initiation rite" and a speech arranged in the form of a story. Initiates must learn "twelve thousand verses," which are "transmitted from the elderly to the young without being entrusted to specialists."

There is a strong sense that a speech "belongs" to the individual delivering it, thus separating speaker from audience at the level of idea development. But, the *bagre* is a communal property rather than the possession of a politician or teacher; it "belongs to everybody" and "every Lo Dagaa is familiar with its stories." Because it is the property of the group, the content of the *bagre* is not fixed like the content of a traditional speech, but rather is fluid like the lyrics of a folk song. Detienne writes that it "rambles," which "prevents anyone from regulating" content. The *bagre's* persistence in the Lo Dagaas' collective memory is largely due to its narrative form for, as Detienne writes, "memory favors 'stories.'"[119]

Brian Boyd provides another example of a distinctly Africa rhetorical form.[120] "Among the Himba of Namibia," he writes, "the indoctrination of obedience and heroic virtues forms a normal part of everyday life. When men visit, they sit together and start praise-singing, hailing the heroic deeds of their ancestors." Whereas this practice may remind us of Greek epideictic discourse, notice the difference from the Greek rhetorical form: the men sit together rather than one of them standing to speak. Moreover, they sing rather than speak, the songs apparently being known to the group.

George Kennedy on Non-European Rhetorics

George Kennedy, in a groundbreaking study, challenges the specifically Western, especially Greek, nature of the rhetorical tradition.[121] Kennedy accomplishes this goal by comparing the Western world's rhetoric with that of other cultures, and even with the communication behaviors of some animals. The result is a view of rhetoric as universal to human cultures, and perhaps as universal to any sign using biological life. Kennedy's work in this regard, and the work of many scholars he cites, will require the attention of all students of rhetoric as we enter a new millennium of rhetorical study.

Kennedy finds an evolutionary basis for rhetoric, writing that "the probable source of such basic emotions, and thus of rhetoric, is the instinct for self-preservation, which in turn derives from nature's impulse to preserve the genetic line." If this is the case, then

> rhetoric is a natural phenomenon: the potential for it exists in all life forms that can give signals, it is practiced in limited forms by nonhuman animals, and it contributed to the evolution of human speech and language from animal communication.[122]

In fact, Kennedy explores the origins of rhetorical expression in the communication patterns of various species.

Kennedy's project takes him on an excursion into a number of cultures whose rhetorical history is little understood by Western scholars. He examines Native American, Aboriginal Australian, Chinese, Indian, Egyptian, Mesopotamian, Aztec, and other rhetorical traditions. His findings about other rhetorical traditions are fascinating and instructive, especially when contrasted to the Western and largely Greek tradition.

Aztec and Egyptian Rhetorics

In his study of ancient Aztec rhetoric, Kennedy finds a highly developed practice of what the Greeks would have termed *epideictic* oratory. So well-developed is this tradition of speaking that Kennedy writes, "the speeches reveal the great importance of formal speech in Aztec culture, both in public and private life."[123] Though their predominant form of speaking resembles epideictic oratory, their approach to issues such as proof varies dramatically from that of the Greeks. "The predominant means of persuasion in Aztec oratory is ethical and pathetical," writes Kennedy. "Speakers usually proclaim a thought authoritatively and provide no supporting reasons."[124] This is because *ethos* was the basis of rhetorical persuasion. "The primary means of persuasion is the authority of the speaker, who is regularly an older individual of high status, wise in the ways of the culture."[125]

Kennedy collects the findings of scholars working in a variety of disciplines. For example, Michael J. Fox, a scholar in Near Eastern languages, has studied ancient Egyptian rhetorical practices. Fox finds that displays of oratorical skill were not valued in Egypt, but that self-restraint typically won the day. Argument, the centerpiece of Greek rhetoric, was not carefully studied in Egyptian rhetoric. Fox writes, "it does not teach how to formulate arguments because it is not argumentation but rather the ethical stance of the speakers that will maintain harmony in the social order, and that is the ultimate goal of Egyptian rhetoric."[126]

Rhetoric in Ancient China

Kennedy discovers that the very conditions that encouraged a sophistic movement in fifth- and fourth-century BCE Greece were also present in China at that time, and to similar effect. "All these conditions existed in China in the fourth century," leading to a Chinese sophistical movement similar to that in Greece. India also experienced a sophistic movement, though a little later than China and Greece.

Among Chinese writers interested in rhetoric was the sage known as Han Feitzu. His book *Records of the Grand Historian* was written around 280 BCE. Among the observations that Han Feitzu offers is the following. "On the whole, the difficult thing about persuading others is not that one lacks knowledge needed to state his case nor the audacity to exercise his abilities to the full. On the whole, the difficult thing is to know the mind of the person one is trying to persuade and to be able to fit one's words to it."[127] Kennedy notes that "the history of rhetoric in China in the more than two millennia since Han Fei has not yet been written," something that could be said of many other rhetorical traditions.[128]

"Private Speaking"

The practice of rhetoric was certainly known in ancient China, but took rather different forms than in Greece and Rome. From early on there was considerably more interest in writing than in speaking in China. Public oratory of the traditional Greco-Roman variety was virtually unknown, though persuasion was widely practiced and studied. This is largely because there was no conception of a public or of a citizen as there had been in Greece and Rome.

The activity of persuasion often took place in private settings as a professional adviser sought to persuade a highly placed official to take a particular course of action. James Crump, a scholar of Chinese rhetoric, writes that

> there is a vast amount of material ... which demonstrates quite clearly that the Chinese counterpart for Greek public speaking was Chinese "private-speaking" in the form of advice to a patron, remonstrating with a ruler, or persuasion of a prince.[129]

Apparently, however, ancient Chinese scholars were less interested in theorizing about rhetoric than were their Greek and Roman counterparts, for treatises on the theory of rhetoric are lacking despite the survival of a vast literature covering many other topics.

Chinese Sophists and the Intrigues of the Warring States

Based on evidence concerning the practice of rhetoric in China, however, Crump contends that something closely resembling sophistry was not limited to Greece.[130] Conditions that favored the appearance of sophistry were present in China in the fourth and third centuries BCE, including (1) an increasingly diverse social setting, (2) an unstable political situation, (3) the presence of a significant number of foreigners, and (4) radical changes in the moral and religious environment. In fact, some sinologists acknowledge the word *sophist* as "an acceptably accurate and handy term to designate a stage in the growth of Chinese intellectual life."[131]

One important ancient Chinese work in particular was likely a manual for rhetorical training, although it was not presented to readers as such. The *Intrigues of the Warring States* (*Zhanguo Ce*, also *Chan Kuo Ts'e*), attributed to the writer Liu Xiang, ostensibly reports on events that occurred in China during an early period in which a number of principalities contended for control of the nation. As history, *Intrigues* is considered largely unreliable, however, so it must originally have served a different purpose. Crump suggests one "intriguing" possibility: he finds in this work a developed art of rhetoric, something long held not to have existed in ancient China. Crump writes that "every conceivable stylistic device is employed in its stories," and *Intrigues* exhibits a pronounced "attention to polished language" that renders it "completely analogous" to Greek and Roman rhetorical treatises.

Among the rhetorical devices Crump finds displayed in the *Intrigues* are rhythm, antithesis, symmetry, consonance, and, in fact, "all the other devices peculiar to the orator's self-conscious and somewhat fulsome use of language."[132] He concludes that the *Intrigues* must have been intentionally written as a manual or handbook for teaching effective rhetoric, comparing it to the *suasoria* used in Rome, books of example speeches and debates to be memorized and practiced by young students of rhetoric.

More recent scholarship has challenged this interpretation, however. Paul Rakita Goldin, for instance, argues that the *Intrigues* contains a great deal of other kinds of material, and should be considered, collection of anecdotes about a highly competitive political scene in ancient China.[133] Goldin does not discount the rhetorical content of the *Intrigues*, and acknowledges that the rhetorical science for which the book was written differed substantially from that for which Roman rhetorical treatises were written. Speaking was private, not public: "A minister who wanted to press his agenda needed above all to convince the sovereign, whose approval was required for any action. This is why most of the arguments found in the *Intrigues* are tailored to persuade a single personage of absolute authority."[134] Goldin does find in the *Intrigues* a system of *topoi* reflective of the rhetorical purposes of ancient Chinese persuaders operating in such sequestered settings. However, he also finds other types of material that is not clearly rhetorical in nature, but a kind of narrative advice-giving.

Chinese rhetorical practice was codified and transmitted through the creation of teaching narratives—fables or short stories—rather than the textbooks of Greece and Rome. Rhetorical advice was conveyed in brief teaching stories such as those collected in *Intrigues of the Warring States*. Rhetorical devices such as parallelism and rhyme were demonstrated in the stories, and rhetorical instruction was offered by reciting legends in private before prominent leaders. Crump writes,

> we can only theorize, but there is every indication that by 300 BC. Chinese interest in the uses of their own language—in argument, eloquence, and the shaping of opinion—had reached a stage of development comparable in nearly all respects to what we in the West know better in a Mediterranean setting and call the Age of Sophists . . .[135]

Jian, Shui, Pien, and the Traveling Persuaders

Jian is a Chinese word that means advice-giving, and its ancient practitioners were known as *jian shi* or *ke qing*, itinerant advisers or "traveling persuaders." These same rhetoricians were also skilled in *shui*, or persuasion, and *pien*, or disputation. The *jian shi* were essentially political advice-givers who "traveled from state to state attempting to persuade the rulers to adopt their ideas and strategic plans."[136] Crump writes that political advising was "what the entire field of rhetoric was designed for in China."[137]

Rhetorical scholar Xing Lu writes that "*jian*-related activities included alerting the king to wrong or inappropriate actions, and reminding the king of considerations for the future."[138] As Chinese leaders looked to the actions of ancient "sage kings" for direction, the arguments of these professional advisers often relied on analogies to the decisions of such wise rulers of antiquity, especially the legendary Kings of Zhou. Lu writes that

> the goal of *jian* was to give advice in order to correct the past wrongdoings of the king, while the purpose of *shui* was to provide a concrete plan or clever scheme regarding military or foreign affairs for the future benefit of the state."

She adds that "both jobs were highly skillful and professional occupations receiving much respect in ancient Chinese society."[139]

Averroes and the Aristotelian Tradition: Arabic Rhetoric in the Twelfth Century

Ibn Rushd (1126–1198), known to the Western world as Averroes, was a Muslim scholar of the twelfth century who lived in Andalusia (*Al Andalus*), present-day Spain.[140] A famed and highly influential polymath, master of several languages including Greek and Hebrew, Averroes translated into Arabic and wrote commentaries on the works of Aristotle and Plato. Growing up in a politically involved family in Cordoba, he became an advocate for the study of rhetoric, elevating the art to the status of a logical discipline. In this he was following to some degree the earlier work of the great Arabic philosopher Al-Farabi (870–951), who had two centuries earlier commented on the necessity of well-practiced rhetoric to the development of a sound civilization.

Serving for a time as the judge (*Qadi*) of Seville, Averroes found rhetoric to be the most reasonable way to promote religious, legal, and political ideas to a large popular audience. The discipline of rhetoric also comported with his unwavering commitment to reason or in all pursuits, a view which anticipated the European Renaissance by 250 years. His defining rationalism, for which he found support in rhetoric, stood in contrast to the prevailing mysticism of the other Andalusian philosophers. Averroes' commitment to a reason above other sources of knowledge eventually put him at odds with more traditional officials, leading to his exile late in life. Many of his books were also ordered to be burned.

Averroes was drawn to the concept of rhetoric he found set out in Aristotle, though he adapted it in distinct ways to his own cultural context. His treatment of rhetoric was also part of an effort to establish a distinct intellectual tradition for the Western Islamic world as contrasted to the more traditional Islamic homeland to the East. Averroes' work on rhetoric, an effort to accommodate Greek thought to new cultural needs, had impact in both the Christian world of Western Europe and in the Arabic world. Without his work, much of Aristotle's corpus would have been lost to Western civilization. In the centuries following his death his commentaries on Aristotle sparked tremendous interest in Aristotelian studies in Europe. The Andalusian city of Cordoba afforded Averroes and other scholars an open environment for exploring a wide range of ideas. His own studies encompassed religion, law, medicine, politics, mathematics, music, astronomy, philosophy, and psychology. Averroes experimented with adapting Aristotle's Greek rhetoric to a new culture that revered poetry. Among other innovations, he aligned rhetoric more closely with poetics than did Aristotle himself, and both disciplines closely with logic. The poet and the rhetorician were constrained by fewer restrictions than the logician who dealt only with what was true or false.[141] Moreover, poetry itself, with its imaginative premises, could produce syllogistic proofs of its own, and thus be a guide to new knowledge. This idea dates back to Al-Farabi, though what Al-Farabi meant by a poetic syllogism is the subject of some debate.[142]

Averroes considered that poetry "is a form of logical discourse since it is concerned with imitation (*muhakat, mimesis*) . . ." In fact, according to Majid Fakhry, for Averroes, "poetics is a branch of logic, in so far as it is concerned with 'imaginative' and 'imitative' discourse which is liable to truth or falsity."[143] In this respect, Averroes clearly departed from Aristotle's opinion.

Moreover, Averroes expanded the appeals that might be used to persuade a popular audience. According to Charles Butterworth, "even though enthymemes and examples are used in rhetoric, persuasive devices having nothing to do with syllogistic argument may just as easily be used."[144] At the same time he sought to broaden the conception of rhetoric beyond mere displays of eloquence. Rhetoric also involved careful reasoning, proof, and exposing false reasoning.[145]

Averroes adapted the Aristotelian rhetorical tradition to a medieval Arabic context. His work often rankled religious and political authorities who found it too rooted in pagan and rationalistic Greek traditions. Nevertheless, Carol Lea Clark concludes, "What Averroes is teaching to the twelfth-century intellectual elite of Andalusia who were trained in the minutia of Arabic philosophy is not the same rhetoric Aristotle taught at the Lyceum."[146]

Re-visioning the Greek Tradition

For Kennedy, one striking conclusion from the study of comparative rhetoric is that "generally speaking, throughout the non-Western world, rhetoric has been used for purposes of agreement and conciliation, and emotionalism, except in the case of lamentation for the dead, is regarded as in poor taste."[147] This sets many other rhetorical traditions in sharp contrast to the highly competitive Greek approach which informed Western rhetorical practice. Kennedy notes that "contentiousness found an important outlet in athletics, esteemed and organized by the Greeks on a scale not known elsewhere, and in oratorical contests."[148]

In fact, the Greek tradition, which Kennedy himself has done so much to illuminate, does not come in for much praise from the eminent historian of rhetoric when he contrasts it to other rhetorical traditions. "Personal invective and mud-slinging is also a regular feature of Greek deliberative oratory from the beginning," he notes, "and becomes a regular feature of judicial oratory. . ."[149] Moreover, "the Greeks delighted in contentious argument; they often put a relatively low priority on telling the truth if a lie would be more effective; slanderous invective was not out of order in a court of law."[150] The contentious nature of Greek rhetoric likely derived from a broader cultural love of competition that other scholars have noted. "Greek society was characterized by a contentiousness that is expressed in mythology, poetry, athletics, democratic government, and public address. Personal invective was acceptable to a degree not commonly found elsewhere."[151]

Because ancient Greek rhetoric had such a dominant influence on subsequent Western rhetorical theory and practice, we have grown accustomed to some of its peculiarities. For instance, "Western rhetorical practices differ from other traditions in being more tolerant of contention, personal invective, and flattery."[152] Perhaps in other ways Western culture has institutionalized the ancient Greeks' ways. Kennedy writes that "Greek orators were characteristically quarrelsome and emotional, inclined to bitter personal attacks on each other, highly resentful of such attacks on themselves but tolerant of verbal fights by others. Alone among ancient civilizations the Greeks also developed competitive athletics."[153]

But, the picture of a Western rhetoric derived from an unusually contentious Greek rhetoric is not a completely bleak one for Kennedy. Competitiveness brings a certain vigor and energy to Western rhetoric, and Greek competitiveness may actually have led to the development of democratic institutions as a means of avoiding outright violent conflict. "As an answer to sharp political differences the Greeks invented decision-making by majority," Kennedy notes.[154] Further study of the rhetorics of other cultures may suggest rhetorical practices relying less exclusively on a model of competition and seeking the goal of victory over rivals.

CONCLUSION

The writers considered in this chapter have analyzed how rhetoric is implicated in the distribution of power, how gender is rhetorically constructed, and the characteristics of some non-Western rhetorics. Writers like Lyotard, Foucault, Derrida; feminist critics such as Sally Miller Gearhart; and classicist George Kennedy have examined how rhetoric discovers, challenges, or preserve sources of power and knowledge.

Some of the scholars discussed here have sought answers for crucial questions such as: How is power achieved, preserved, and challenged in contemporary society? How do particular discourses or "ways of talking" advance the interests and political fortunes of certain social groups? Where does knowledge come from in a culture? Their work has been widely influential in changing how we think about our uses of persuasive discourse generally.

Feminist rhetoricians have sought, through a rigorous historical and cultural criticism of the rhetorical tradition, to open a way for women to enter public debate on an equal footing with men. They have urged women to engage the public rhetorical sphere, and to do so with confidence of being heard and making a difference. It may be the case that rhetoric itself will be reconfigured as a result of feminist criticism.

Studies of comparative rhetoric suggest a similar direction for the future of rhetorical theory and practice. As more non-Western rhetorics are retrieved to view, Western rhetoric itself may be radically re-evaluated. Are we entering the age of a truly new rhetoric? Through the work of scholars discussed in this chapter we have glimpsed ways in which the rhetorical traditions of earlier eras are being interrogate; explored challenges to the hegemony of Western and masculine rhetorics; and witnessed again the remarkable flexibility of rhetoric as a human practice.

QUESTIONS FOR REVIEW

1. What are the marks of Postmodernism?
2. What tenets characterized the Structuralism of Claude Levi-Strauss?
3. Why, generally, was Foucault interested in language and discourse? What is discourse's relationship to knowledge? To power?
4. What is an "episteme" in Foucault's theory? Why is he interested in discovering the episteme of an age?
5. What did Foucault mean by "an archaeology of knowledge"?
6. What is Derrida's goal in "deconstruction"? How do his goals differ from those of Habermas?
7. What are the basic assumptions of Queer Theory?
8. In your own words, what are the basic feminist criticisms of the Western rhetorical tradition?
9. Why does Sally Gearhart find traditional rhetoric to be a form of violence?
10. What do Foss and Griffin mean by the phrase "invitational rhetoric"?
11. What is unusual in the Greek tradition of rhetoric when compared with other rhetorical traditions?
12. Who were the *jian shi* in ancient China?
13. Who is thought to possess the *bagre* form of discourse among the Lo Dagaa people?
14. What Greek form of speaking does ancient Aztec speaking most closely resemble?
15. Identify the way in which the rhetoric of Averroes departs from that of Aristotle?

QUESTIONS FOR DISCUSSION

1. Is Foucault convincing in his argument that language and power are intimately connected? Explain your answer.
2. What is your response to Foucault's claim that power is not the product of institutions such as a government, but that it is a product of the ways in which we talk?
3. Derrida suggests that the meanings of words are fundamentally unstable. Provide examples of terms you are familiar with that seem to shift meaning with new contexts, or that change meaning depending upon who uses them.
4. Some feminist theorists have called for an "invitational" rather than a competitive rhetoric. Is such a rhetoric possible? Does the nature of rhetoric itself, or of human beings, render this suggestion impracticable?
5. What is your response to George Kennedy's claim that the Western rhetorical tradition is unusually aggressive and competitive when contrasted to other rhetorical traditions?
6. Michael Fox has noted that argument was not central to Egyptian rhetoric. In what ways, if any, is contemporary American rhetoric moving away from argument and toward other discursive forms?
7. In what ways does Michelle Obama's introduction to her September, 2013, speech on food marketing to children reflect the observations and recommendations of feminist rhetorical theorists? Does she exhibit a less competitive and more invitational rhetoric? In what ways, if any, does her introduction reflect the influence of traditional rhetorical models?

Michelle Obama's Speech on Food Marketing: Introduction

Well, welcome to the White House. It is truly a pleasure to be here with all of you today for the first ever White House Convening on Food Marketing to Children. So, we're going to put you to work. Thank you again for being here. . . . I want to thank all of you for joining us today.

All of you in this room, you come to this issue from all different angles. You're experts, advocates, parents. You represent food and beverage companies, media and entertainment companies, and so much more. And we're eager to have a lively and constructive dialogue with you about how we market food to our children.

We're eager to hear more from everyone in this room about what's working, where we're falling short, and how we can keep moving forward together on this complex and challenging but very important issue. And I think it's important to note that we're having this conversation in the midst of what I believe is a cultural shift that is happening in this country—a transformation in how we live and eat that many of us could never have imagined even just a few years ago.

I see it everywhere I go all across this country. I see it in chain restaurants that are serving kale salads, and they're filling kids' menus with not just nuggets and fries, but with broccoli and whole-wheat pasta. I see it in churches where instead of fried chicken and mac and cheese for church supper, they're serving up grilled fish and brown rice. I see it online where parenting, cooking, and health blogs are crammed with healthy recipes and tips about providing better nutrition for our kids. And I see it in schools where students can't wait to tell me about their new salad bar or how they ate a radish or tried cauliflower for the first time, and actually like it.

TERMS

Archive For Foucault, "the set of rules which at a given period and for a given society" define, among other things, "the limits and forms of the sayable" and "the limits and forms of conversation."

Bagre Initiation rite and speech of the Lo Dagaas people of Ghana, arranged as a story.

Conversion model In Gearhart's critique of traditional rhetoric, the model that holds that the goal of rhetoric is to convert others to one's own views.

Deconstruction In Derrida, the work of destabilizing discourse by dissecting its underlying structures of meaning and assumption.

Discourse For Foucault, systems of talk within the limits of particular disciplines or practices.

Episteme The totality of discursive practices of a society over an extended period of time.

Excluded discourse In Foucault, discourse that is controlled by being prohibited.

Invitational rhetoric In Foss and Griffin, a rhetoric that does not require or assume intent to persuade on the part of a source.

Jian shi In ancient China, itinerant political advisors.

Panopticism Foucault's term for the phenomenon of increasing surveillance in modern societies.

Petits recits For Lyotard, the "small narratives" which characterize local human communities and particularly marginalized groups.

Pien In ancient China, the art of disputation.

Queer theory An intellectual movement that sees gender as a product of symbolic interaction and the social negotiation of meaning, and gender, sexuality, and self as socially constructed.

Shui In ancient China, the art of persuasion.

Structuralism An early twentieth-century movement in discourse studies, following the work of Levi-Strauss, that affirmed the presence of underlying structures or "grammars" in myths and other narrative forms.

Transgression To read a text for what a traditional reading would overlook, dismiss, or omit; violating the received interpretation of a text in search of its submerged meanings.

NOTES

1 For a good survey of these developments, see: Ann Gill, *Rhetoric and Human Understanding* (Prospect Heights, IL: Waveland, 1994). See also: Charles C. Lemert and Garth Gillan, *Michel*

Foucault: Social Theory as Transgression (New York: Columbia University Press, 1982), Chap. 1, "Foucault's Field."

2 Claudia Moscovici, *Double Dialectics: Between Universalism and Relativism in Enlightenment and Postmodern Thought* (Lanham, MD: Rowman and Littlefield, 2002), 2.

3 Jean-Francois Lyotard, *The Postmodern Condition: A Report on Knowledge*, trans. Geoff Bennington and Brian Massumi (Minneapolis, MN: University of Minnesota Press, 1988), xxiii.

4 Lyotard, xxiv. Quoted in Moscovici, 3.

5 Claude Levi-Strauss, "The Structural Study of Myth," *The Journal of American Folklore* 68(270), (1955): 428–444, p. 429.

6 Levi-Strauss, 430.

7 Levi-Strauss, 430.

8 Levi-Strauss, 430.

9 Claude Levi-Strauss, *Myth and Meaning* (1978; rpt. Oxford, UK: Routledge), 1.

10 Levi-Strauss, "Study," 431.

11 C. G. Prado, *Starting with Foucault: An Introduction to Genealogy* (Boulder, CO: Westview, 1995), 1.

12 James W. Bernauer, *Michel Foucault's Force of Flight: Toward an Ethics of Thought* (Atlantic Highlands, NJ: Humanities Press, 1990), 2.

13 Michel Foucault, *The Order of Things: An Archaeology of the Human Sciences* (*Les Mots et les Chose*, 1966; New York: Random House, 1970); and *The Archaeology of Knowledge*, trans. A. M. Sheridan Smith (*L'Archaeology du Savoir*, 1969; New York: Random House, 1972).

14 Michel Foucault, *The Birth of the Clinic: An Archaeology of Medical Perception*, trans. A. M. Sheridan Smith (New York: Random House, 1973).

15 See: Stuart Elden, *Foucault's Last Decade* (Cambridge, UK: Polity Press, 2016).

16 Michel Foucault, *Michel Foucault: Power, Truth, Strategy*, ed. Meaghan Morris and Paul Patton (Sydney, Australia: Feral Publications, 1979), 32.

17 Alec McHoul and Wendy Grace, *A Foucault Primer: Discourse, Power and the Subject* (New York: New York University Press, 1997), 22.

18 McHoul and Grace, 22.

19 Michel Foucault, 8.

20 McHoul and Grace, 21.

21 On Foucault's study of madness, see: Gutting, Chap. 2, "Madness and Mental Illness."

22 For a sophisticated discussion of the meaning of *discourse* in Foucault's works, see: Manfred Frank, "On Foucault's Concept of Discourse," in *Michel Foucault: Philosopher*, trans. Timothy J. Armstrong (New York: Routledge, 1992), 99–116.

23 McHoul and Grace, 35.

24 Bernauer, 5.

25 Lemert and Gillan, 6.

26 McHoul and Grace, 39.

27 Edward Craig, ed., *Routledge Encyclopedia of Philosophy* (London: Routledge Press, 1998), 708.

28 Gary Gutting, *Michel Foucault's Archaeology of Scientific Reason* (New York: Cambridge University Press, 1989), 2.

29 Elden, 199.

30 McHoul and Grace, 18.

31 See: Gutting, Chap. 6: "The Archaeology of Knowledge."

32 Graham Burchell, Colin Gordon, and Peter Miller, eds., *The Foucault Effect: Studies in Governmentality* (Chicago, IL: University of Chicago Press, 1991), 59–60.

33 McHoul and Grace, 29.
34 Karlis Racevskis, *Michel Foucault and the Subversion of Intellect* (Ithaca, NY: Cornell University Press, 1983), 58. See also: Lemert and Gillan, Chap. 2, "Historical Archaeology."
35 Racevskis, 59.
36 David R. Shumway, *Michel Foucault* (Charlottesville, VA: University Press of Virginia, 1989), 56.
37 Shumway, 56.
38 Joseph Rouse, "Power/Knowledge," in *The Cambridge Companion to Foucault*, ed. Gary Gutting (Cambridge: Cambridge University Press, 1994), 92.
39 Gutting, 231.
40 Michel Foucault, "Discourse on Language," published with *Archaeology of Knowledge* (New York: Random House, 1972), 215–237, p. 216.
41 Foucault, "Discourse on Language," 216.
42 Foucault, *Archaeology of Knowledge*, 217.
43 Mel Y. Chen, *Animacies: Biopolitics, Racial Mattering and Queer Affect* (Durham, NC: Duke University Press, 2012), 12.
44 See: Gayatri Spivak, translator's preface to: Jacques Derrida, *Of Grammatology* (*De la Grammatologie*, 1967; Baltimore, MD: Johns Hopkins University Press, 1976).
45 John D. Caputo, ed., *Deconstruction in a Nutshell: A Conversation with Jacques Derrida* (New York: Fordham University Press, 1997), 79.
46 Jacques Derrida, *Positions*, trans. and ed. Alan Bass (1972; Chicago, IL: University of Chicago Press, 1981), 19.
47 John Caputo, *Deconstruction*, 205.
48 John Caputo, *Deconstruction*, 79.
49 John Caputo, *Deconstruction*, 52.
50 Christopher Norris, *Derrida* (Cambridge, MA: Harvard University Press, 1987), 22.
51 James A. Aune, "Rhetoric after Deconstruction," in *Rhetoric and Philosophy*, ed. Richard A. Cherwitz (Hillsdale, NJ: Lawrence Erlbaum, 1990), 253–273, p. 256.
52 John Caputo, *Deconstruction*, 55.
53 Norris, 14.
54 Norris, 163.
55 Jonathan Culler, *On Deconstruction* (Ithaca, NY: Cornell University Press, 1982), 86.
56 Norris, 165–166.
57 Jacques Derrida, *Writing and Difference*, trans. Alan Bass (*L'écriture et la Différence*; Chicago, IL: University of Chicago Press, 1978), 42.
58 John Caputo, *Deconstruction*, 78.
59 John Caputo, *Deconstruction*, 78.
60 Jacques Derrida, *Speech and Phenomena*, trans. David Allison (*La Voix et le Phénomène*, 1967; Evanston, IL: Northwestern University Press, 1973).
61 On Derrida's relationship to Habermas, see: Bill Martin, *Matrix and Line* (Albany, NY: State University of New York Press, 1992), Chap. 3, "What Is the Heart of Language? Habermas, Davidson, Derrida."
62 Norris, 27.
63 Norris, 23, 21.
64 Norris, 43.
65 John Caputo, *Deconstruction*, 41.
66 John Caputo, *Deconstruction*, 49.
67 John Caputo, *Deconstruction*, 55.

68 In addition to the other sources discussed in this section, see: Elizabeth A. Fay, *Eminent Rhetoric: Language, Gender, and Cultural Tropes* (Westport, CT: Bergen and Garvey, 1994); and Deborah Tannen, *Gender and Discourse* (Oxford: Oxford University Press, 1994).

69 Gesa E. Kirsch and Jacqueline J. Royster, "Feminist Rhetorical Practices: In Search of Excellence," *College Composition and Communication* 61(4), (2010): 640–672, pp. 641, 647. See also by these authors: *Feminist Rhetorical Practices: New Horizons for Rhetoric, Composition, and Literacy Studies* (Carbondale, IL: Southern Illinois University Press, 2012).

70 General studies of the issue of the differences between men's and women's ways of speaking and knowing can be found in: Carol Gilligan, *In a Different Voice* (Cambridge, MA: Harvard University Press, 1982); Janice Moulton, "A Paradigm of Philosophy: The Adversary Method"; Genevieve Lloyd, "The Man of Reason," and Alison M. Jaggar, "Love and Knowledge" in *Women, Knowledge and Reality: Explorations in Feminist Philosophy*, ed. Ann Gary and Marilyn Pearsall (New York: Routledge, 1989); and Maryann Ayim, "Violence and Domination as Metaphors in Academic Discourse," in *Selected Issues in Logic and Communication*, ed. Trudy Govier (Belmont, CA: Wadsworth, 1988), Chap. 16.

71 Jana Sawicki, "Foucault, Feminism and Questions of Identity," in *The Cambridge Companion to Foucault*, ed. Garry Gutting (Cambridge: Cambridge University Press, 1994), 290.

72 Sawicki, 288. For an example of Foucault's ideas informing feminist critique of discourse see: Judith Butler, *Bodies that Matter* (London: Routledge, 2011).

73 Leslie Di Mare, "Rhetoric and Women: The Private and Public Spheres," in *Constructing and Reconstructing Gender: The Links Among Communication, Language, and Gender*, ed. Linda A. M. Perry, Lynn H. Turner, and Helen M. Sterk (Albany, NY: State University of New York Press, 1992), 47.

74 Sonja Foss, *Rhetorical Criticism* (Prospect Heights, IL: Waveland, 1989), 151–152.

75 Foss, 152.

76 Foss, 152.

77 Dale Spender, *Man Made Language* (Boston, MA: Routledge and Kegan Paul, 1980), 59.

78 Spender, 52.

79 *Women's Voices in Our Time: Statements by American Leaders*, ed. Victoria L. DeFrancisco and Marvin D. Jensen (Prospect Heights, IL: Waveland, 1994), ix.

80 DeFrancisco and Jensen, ix. They cite studies by Karlyn K. Campbell, "Hearing Women's Voices," *Communication Education* 40 (January 1991): 33–48; and K. S. Vonnegut, "Listening for Women's Voices," *Communication Education* 41 (January 1992): 26–39.

81 Sally McConnel-Ginet, et al., *Women and Language in Literature and Society* (New York: Prager, 1980), 66.

82 Barrie Thorne and Nancy Henley, *Language and Sex: Difference and Dominance* (Rowley, MA: Newberry House, 1975).

83 Foss, 153.

84 Foss, 154.

85 Foss, 154.

86 Karlyn Kohrs Campbell, *Man Cannot Speak for Her: A Critical Study of Early Feminist Rhetoric* (New York: Greenwood Press, 1989), 14.

87 Campbell, *Man Cannot Speak for Her*, 14.

88 Foss, 155.

89 Julia T. Wood, *Gendered Lives* (Belmont, CA: 1994), 91.

90 Wood, 91.

91 Wood, 91–92.

92 Sally Gearhart, "The Womanization of Rhetoric," *Women's Studies International Quarterly* 2 (1979): 195–201, p. 195.

93 Gearhart, 195.

94 Gearhart, 195.

95 Gearhart, 196.

96 George Kennedy, *The Art of Persuasion in Ancient Greece* (Princeton, NJ: Princeton University Press, 1963), 189.

97 Gearhart, 196.

98 Gearhart, 198.

99 Gearhart, 199.

100 Gearhart, 200.

101 Gearhart, 201.

102 S. J. Foss and C. L. Griffin, "Beyond Persuasion: A Proposal for an Invitational Rhetoric," *Communication Monographs* 62 (March 1995): 2–18.

103 Foss and Griffin, 2.

104 Foss and Griffin, 3.

105 Foss and Griffin, 5.

106 Foss and Griffin, 5.

107 Foss and Griffin, 6.

108 Diane Helene Miller, "The Future of Feminist Rhetorical Criticism," in M. M. Wertheimer (Ed.), *Listening to Their Voices: The Rhetorical Activities of Historical Women* (Columbia, SC: University of South Carolina Press, 1997), 359–380, pp. 361–362.

109 Miller, 362.

110 Miller, 363.

111 Jane Sutton, *The House of My Sojourn: Rhetoric, Women and the Question of Authority* (Tuscaloosa, AL: University of Alabama Press, 2010), 128–129.

112 Roland Barthes, "From Work to Text," in *Textual Strategies*, ed. Josue V. Harari, 73–81. Quoted in Miller, 366 (London: Methuen, 1980).

113 Miller, 367.

114 Miller, 370.

115 Miller, 371.

116 A. R. deVelasco, "Transgressive Eloquence: Bell hooks, Cicero, and the Aims of Rhetorical Pedagogy," in *Sizing up Rhetoric*, ed. David Zarefsky and Elizabeth Benacka (Long Grove, IL: Waveland, 2008), 393–397, pp. 394, 396.

117 LuMing Mao, Bo Wang, "Manifesting a Future for Comparative Rhetoric," *Rhetoric Review* 34(3), (2015): 239–274, p. 241.

118 For example, see: Jon Sun-Gi, "Toward a Rhetoric of Communication, with Special Reference to the History of Korean Rhetoric," *Rhetorica* 28(3) (Summer 2010) 313–329.

119 Marcel Detienne, *The Creation of Mythology*, trans. Margaret Cook (Chicago, IL: University of Chicago Press, 1986), 37–38.

120 Brian Boyd, *On the Origin of Stories* (Cambridge, MA: Harvard University Press, 2010), 166.

121 George Kennedy, *Comparative Rhetoric: An Historical and Cross-Cultural Introduction* (New York: Oxford University Press, 1998).

122 Kennedy, *Comparative*, 4.

123 Kennedy, *Comparative*, 101.

124 Kennedy, *Comparative*, 103.

125 Kennedy, *Comparative*, 105.

126 Michael J. Fox, "Ancient Egyptian Rhetoric," *Rhetorica* 1 (1983): 21–22. Quoted in Kennedy, *Comparative Rhetoric*, 131.

127 Burton Watson, *Basic Writings of Mo Tzu, Hsun Tzu, and Han Fei-Tzu* (New York: Columbia University Press, 1967), 73. Quoted in Kennedy, *Comparative Rhetoric*, 163–164.

128 Kennedy, *Comparative Rhetoric*, 164.

129 James Crump, *Intrigues: Studies of the Chan-Kuo Tse* (Ann Arbor, MI: University of Michigan Press, 1964), 100.

130 Crump, 93.

131 Crump, 97.

132 Crump, 100.

133 Paul Rakita Goldin, "Miching Mallecho: The Zhanguo Ce and Classical Rhetoric, *Sino-Platonic Papers* 41(October 1993) 1–26.

134 Goldin, 6.

135 Crump, 1.

136 Crump, 117.

137 Crump, 100.

138 Xing Lu, *Rhetoric in Ancient China, Fifth to Third Century, B.C.E.: A Comparison with Classical Greek Rhetoric* (Columbia, SC: University of South Carolina Press, 1998), 79.

139 Lu, 81. On Chinese rhetorical practices, see also: Mary Garrett, "Classical Chinese Conceptions of Argumentation and Persuasion," *Argumentation and Advocacy* 29 (1993): 105–115.

140 See: Carol Lea Clark, "Aristotle and Averroes: The Influences of Aristotle's Arabic Commentator upon Western European and Arabic Rhetoric," *Review of Communication* 7(4), (2007): 369–387.

141 Clark, 375.

142 See: Salim Kemal, *The Philosophical Poetics of Alfarabi, Avicenna and Averroes: The Aristotelian Reception* (London: Routledge, 2003).

143 Majid Fakhry, *Averroes: His Life, Work and Influence* (Oxford, UK: Oneworld Publications: 2001), 41–42.

144 C. Butterworth in Averroes, *Averroes's "Three Short Commentaries on Aristotle's 'Topics,'Rhetoric,'and 'Poetics,'* ed. and trans. C. Butterworth (Albany, NY: State University of New York Press, 1977), 30. Quoted in Clark, 375.

145 Clark, 377.

146 Clark, 378.

147 Kennedy, *Comparative Rhetoric*, 198.

148 Kennedy, *Comparative Rhetoric*, 199.

149 Kennedy, *Comparative Rhetoric*, 199.

150 Kennedy, *Comparative Rhetoric*, 203.

151 Kennedy, *Comparative Rhetoric*, 211. Similarly, Douglas Thomas writes of Nietzsche's observation about Greek competitiveness: "Nietzsche argues that since Homer's time this will to annihilation has been contained by the notion of *contest*." Douglas Thomas, *Reading Nietzsche Rhetorically* (New York: Guilford Press, 1999), 6.

152 Kennedy, *Comparative Rhetoric*, 217.

153 Kennedy, *Comparative Rhetoric*, 221.

154 Kennedy, *Comparative Rhetoric*, 221.

Glossary

Actor-Network Theory: A theory in which material objects and concepts play important roles as they interact with human agents in large social systems.

Acutezza **[Italian]:** In Vico, rhetorical wordplay or wit.

Aesthetics: Study of the persuasive potential in the form, beauty, or force of symbolic expression.

Affectus **[Latin]:** For the Italian Humanists, the source of emotions or passions in the human mind.

Ambigua **[Latin]:** In Cicero's theory of humor, the source of humor inherent in words.

Animorum motus **[Latin]:** The emotions.

Ante rem **[Latin]:** In one Roman topical system, events *preceding an act* in one *loci* system.

Apologia **[Greek]:** Defense. One type of pleading common to forensic oratory, the other being accusation.

Aporia: Placing a claim in doubt by advancing arguments for and against it.

Appeals: Symbolic methods that aim either to elicit an emotion or to engage the audience's loyalties or commitments.

Archive: For Foucault, rules of discourse that define and limit what can be said during a given period in a particular society.

Areté **[Greek]:** An ability to manage one's personal affairs in an intelligent manner and to succeed in public life. Excellence. Natural leadership ability. Virtue. A component of *ethos.*

Argument: Discourse characterized by reasons advanced to support conclusions.

Arrangement [Latin dispositio]: The distribution of arguments in the most effective order. The planned ordering of components in a message to achieve the greatest persuasive effect, whether of persuasion, clarity, or beauty. The second of Cicero's five canons of rhetoric as set out in *De Inventione.*

Artistic proofs [Greek entechnoi pisteis]: Proofs or means of persuasion taught specifically by the art of rhetoric. In Aristotle's rhetorical theory these include *logos, pathos,* and *ethos.*

Audience adaptation: Changes made in a message to tailor it to a particular audience.

Auxesis: Amplification.

Axioms: Unquestioned first principles, the starting points of scientific reasoning.

Bases: In Quintilian's system for teaching argument, the specific issues needing to be addressed in arguing a judicial case.

Belletristic Movement: Rhetorical movement in the late eighteenth and early nineteenth centuries that emphasized considerations of style in rhetoric, expanding rhetoric into a study of literature literacy criticism, and writing generally.

Boule: Representative body of 500 Athenian citizens that met daily to supervise the city.

Burden of proof: In the argument theory of Richard Whately, the responsibility to bring a case against the *status quo* sufficient to challenge its enjoyment of presumption.

Captatio benevoluntatiae **[Latin]:** Section of a letter securing goodwill of the recipient.

Chiasmus: Rhetorical device that takes its name from the reversing of elements in parallel clauses, forming an X (chi) in the sentence.

Circa rem **[Latin]:** In one Roman topical system, the circumstances *surrounding the act.*

Classicism: A resurgence of interest in the languages and texts of classical antiquity that characterized Renaissance Humanism.

Coherence: In Fisher, the degree of consistency among elements in a narrative; whether the components of a story appear to hang together.

Common topics [Greek *koinoi topoi*]: In Aristotle's *Rhetoric*, arguments and strategies useful in a variety of rhetorical settings.

Communicative action: In Jürgen Habermas, the interactive process of critical argumentation crucial to overcoming ideological domination.

Communicative competence: In Habermas, the particular conditions under which rational communication is possible.

Conclusio **[Latin]:** The conclusion of a letter.

Confirmatio **[Latin]:** In Roman rhetorical theory, the section of a judicial speech offering evidence in support of claims advanced during the statement of the facts, or *narratio.*

Confutatio **[Latin]:** In Roman rhetorical theory, the section in a judicial speech that advances counterarguments in response to the opposition's case.

Conjectural issues: In Cicero's stasis system, questions of fact, such as "What occurred?" and "When did it occur?"

Constraints: In Lloyd Bitzer's situation theory of rhetoric, "persons, events, objects, and relations which are parts of the situation because they have the power to constrain decision and action needed to modify the exigence."

Consubstantiality: Commonality of substance.

Contingent matters: Matters in which decisions must be based on probabilities, because absolute certainty is not possible.

Contio: Public gathering of citizens in the Roman Forum to hear from political leaders.

Controversia: A mock judicial speech presented by the advanced Roman student of rhetoric.

Conversio **[Latin]:** A teaching method in which the structure of a sentence was varied so as to discover its most pleasing form.

Conversion model: In Sally Gearhart's critique of traditional rhetoric, the model that holds that the goal of rhetoric is to convert others to one's own views.

Critical theory: The systematic means of analyzing discourse for its hidden assumptions and implications.

Deconstruction: In Derrida, the work of destabilizing discourse by dissecting its underlying structures of meaning and assumption.

Definite questions: In Quintilian's system, issues concerning specific individuals, facts, places, and times.

Definition: In Quintilian's system, a concern for categorizing an event.

Delectare **[Latin]:** To delight. One of Cicero's three functions or goals of rhetoric.

Deliberative oratory: Oratory that occurs in legislative assemblies and that addresses questions concerning the appropriate use of resources.

Delivery [Latin *pronuntiatio*]: The control of voice and body in a manner suitable to the dignity of the subject matter and the style. The fifth of Cicero's five canons of rhetoric.

Demos **[Greek]:** The people.

Dialectic [Greek *dialektike*]: Rigorous, critical questioning. A method of reasoning from common opinions, directed by established principles of reasoning to probable conclusions about general questions. Also, the method of investigating philosophical issues by the give and take of argument. Also, a teaching method involving arguing either side of a case. For Aristotle, a method of debating issues of general interest starting from widely accepted propositions.

Dialogues: In Mikhail Bakhtin, chains of assertion and response that reveal the presence of different voices.

Dictaminis (Ars) **[Latin]:** Medieval art of letter writing.

Dictatores **[Latin]:** In the Middle Ages, teachers of letter writing.

Differentia **[Latin]:** Topics of Boethius divided according to major premises.

Dikanikon **[Greek]:** Courtroom or forensic oratory.

Dikasteria: The Athenian court.

Discourse: Symbols intentionally organized into a message. Also, the systems of talk within the limits of certain disciplines and practices.

Dispositio **[Latin]:** Arrangement. Cicero's term for the effective ordering of arguments and appeals making up the substance of a persuasive case. The second of his five canons of rhetoric.

Dissoi logoi **[Greek]:** Contradictory arguments.

Docere **[Latin]:** To teach. One of Cicero's three functions or goals of rhetoric, the other two being to persuade (*movere*) and to delight (*delectare*).

Doxa **[Greek]:** A belief or opinion. Also, mere opinion.

Dramatistic pentad: Kenneth Burke's "grammar of motives," consisting of act, scene, agent, agency, and purpose.

Dunamis **[Greek]:** Faculty, power, ability, or capacity. Aristotle defined rhetoric as the *dunamis*, or faculty of discovering the available means of persuasion in any given situation.

***Eidei topoi* [Greek]:** The special topics of Aristotle, appropriate to special rhetorical settings such as the courtroom. Contrasted to the *koinoi topoi*, or common topics.

***Eikos*:** Arguing from probability.

***Ekklesia*:** The ruling Athenian Assembly.

Elite audience: In Perelman and Olbrechts-Tyteca's rhetorical theory, an audience of trained specialists in a discipline.

***Elocutio* [Latin]:** Style. Cicero's term to designate the concern for finding the appropriate language or style for a message. One of his five canons of rhetoric.

***Empeiria*:** A knack; a skill learned by experience.

***Endoxa* [Greek]:** The probable premises from which dialectic began—widely held opinions, or the opinions of the wisest people.

***Enthymeme* [Greek *enthymema*]:** A rhetorical syllogism. An argument built from values, beliefs, or knowledge held in common by a speaker and an audience.

***Epainos* [Greek]:** Praise. One of two functions of epideictic oratory, the other being blame (*psogos*).

Epideictic oratory [Greek *epideiktikon*]: The kind of speaking characteristic of public ceremonies such as funerals or events commemorating war heroes.

***Epideixis* [Greek]:** A speech prepared for a formal occasion.

***Episteme* [Greek]:** Plato's term for true knowledge.

***Epoidai*:** Spells or incantations.

***Ergon*:** The goal or outcome of a true art.

***Eristic* [Greek]:** Discourse's power to express, to captivate, to argue, or to injure.

***Ethos* [Greek]:** The study of human character. The persuasive potential of the speaker's character and personal credibility. One of Aristotle's three artistic proofs.

***Eudaimonia* [Greek]:** Human well-being or happiness. The goal of legislation and thus the central concern of deliberative oratory.

***Eunoia* [Greek]:** Goodwill. Along with practical wisdom (*phronesis*) and virtue (*arete*), a component of *ethos,* or good character.

Excluded discourse: In Foucault, discourse that is controlled by being prohibited.

Exigence: In Lloyd Bitzer's situation theory of rhetoric, "an imperfection marked by urgency . . . a defect, an obstacle, something waiting to be done, a thing which is other than it should be."

Existence: In Quintilian, a question of fact.

***Exordia* [Latin]:** Introductions designed to dispose the audience to listen to a speech or to secure a reader's goodwill.

Expression [Latin: *elocutio*]: Fitting proper language to arguments; the third of Cicero's five canons of oratory.

***Facetiae* [Latin]:** Wit or humor.

Faculty psychology: The eighteenth-century view that the mind consisted of "faculties" or capacities including the understanding, the imagination, the passions, and the will.

False consciousness: In Jürgen Habermas' work, a flawed and thus distorting view of reality, of the world, and of people.

Falsifiability: Philosopher Karl Popper's idea that scientific claims are not subject to proof, but to being shown to be false.

Fantasia: For Vico, the power of imagination to order the world; active when humans formulate myths.

Fantasy themes: For Bormann, when stories or plot lines come to define the group and its values.

Fantasy types: For Bormann, basic plots which are repeated in group or organizational stories.

Fidelity: For Fisher, a concern for whether the components of a story represent accurate assertions about reality.

Fitting response: In Lloyd Bitzer's situational theory, a rhetorical response that is dictated by components of the rhetorical situation, including exigence, audience, and constraints.

Forensic oratory (*dikanikon*): Courtroom speaking.

Form: In Kenneth Burke, "an arousing and fulfilling of a desire in an audience."

Generalized symmetry: In Actor-Network Theory, the idea that an object may assume a kind of social agency once reserved to human symbol users.

***Gens* [Latin]:** A clan, a group of influential families in Rome.

Gnorimoi: An elite group enjoying higher social status in Athens than members of the *demos*.

Hataera: Educated female courtesan.

Hermeneutics: The science of textual interpretation.

Heteroglossia: The many languages that proliferate in any culture (Bakhtin).

***Heuristic* [Greek]:** Discourse's capacity for discovery, whether of facts, insights, or even of self-awareness.

Hypothesis: In Hermagoras' system, a conclusion drawn from a thesis or general premise combined with a particular premise that applies the thesis to a given case.

***Hypsos* [Latin]:** Sublimity or great writing, the theme of Longinus' *On the Sublime*.

Ideology: A system of belief, or a framework for interpreting the world. Also, an irrational or unexamined system of thinking.

***Imitatio* [Latin]:** Imitation or mimicry.

***In re* [Latin]:** In one Roman topical system, arguments concerning what occurred in *the act itself*.

Inartistic proofs [Greek *atechnoi pisteis*]: In Aristotle's *Rhetoric,* proofs not belonging to the art of rhetoric.

Indefinite questions: In Quintilian's system of rhetoric, questions discussed without specific reference to persons, time, place, or other particular limitation.

***Ingenium* [Latin]:** In Vico, the innate human capacity to grasp similarities or relationships.

Inside jokes: For Bormann, encapsulated stories understood only by members of a group.

Intersubjective agreements: Agreements forged among independent participants in dialogue on the basis of open and fairly conducted argument.

Invention [Latin *inventio*]: Cicero's term describing the process of coming up with the arguments and appeals in a persuasive case. The first of his five canons of rhetoric.

Invitational rhetoric: In Foss and Griffin, a rhetoric that does not require or assume intent to persuade.

***Ioci* [Latin]:** Jokes. Discussed in Cicero's theory of humor presented in *De Oratore*.

Irony: When indirect statement carries direct meaning, or something is taken to stand for its opposite. In Vico, the final stage in the development of human language and thought.

Isegoria **[Greek]:** In ancient Athens the right of all free male citizens to speak in public settings and assemblies.

Issues: Hermagoras of Temnos' *topoi,* which included three classifications of judicial arguments. The three types include (1) conjectural issues or a concern for matters of fact, (2) legal issues or a concern for the interpretation of a text or document, and (3) juridical issues or a concern for the rightness or wrongness of an act.

Issues of definition: Questions regarding by what name an act should be called.

Issues of fact: Questions concerning such questions as "What occured?" and "When did it occur?"

Issues of quality: Questions concerning the severity of an act.

*Jian shi***:** In ancient China, itinerant political advisors.

Jurist: In Rome, an attorney or master of the complex Roman legal code.

Kairos **[Greek]:** Rhetoric's search for relative truth rather than absolute certainty. A consideration of opposite points of view, as well as attention to such factors as time and circumstances. An opportune moment or situation.

Kategoria **[Greek]:** Accusation. One of the two functions of forensic oratory, the other being defense or *apologia.*

Koinoi topoi **[Greek]:** Aristotle's universal lines of argument. Arguments useful in any setting.

Kolakeia **[Greek]:** Flattery. Promising people what they want without regard for what is best for them. Plato argued that rhetoric succeeded by employing flattery.

*Krites***:** A judge, an audience member.

Literae humanae [Latin]: The liberal arts.

Logical positivism: The intellectual effort to bring scientific standards to bear on the resolution of all issues.

*Logographos***:** A professional speech writer.

Logos, pl. logoi **[Greek]:** The study of arguments. One of Aristotle's three artistic proofs, the other two being *pathos* (the study of emotion) and *ethos* (the study of character). An account, or a clear and logical explanation. Also, a word or an argument.

Memory [Latin *memoria*]: The firm mental grasp of the content of a speech. The fourth of Cicero's five canons of rhetoric.

Meta-narratives: Grand explanatory schemes that claim to account for the entirety of human history and the human condition.

Metaphor: A comparison of things not apparently similar.

Metonym: The substitution of a part for the whole.

Modus inveniendi **[Latin]:** In St. Augustine, material for understanding scripture.

Modus proferendi **[Latin]:** In St. Augustine, the means of expressing the ideas found in scripture.

Motives: Commitments, goals, desires, or purposes when they lead to action.

Movere **[Latin]:** To persuade or move an audience's emotions. One of Cicero's three functions or goals of rhetoric.

Narratio [Latin]: In judicial speech, a statement of essential facts. In a letter, the body setting and details of the problem to be addressed.

Neoplatonism: A body of philosophic and religious ideas loosely based on Plato's idealism, but also incorporating ideas from astrology, magic, and alchemy.

Nomos [Greek]: Social custom or convention. Rule by agreement among the citizenry.

Notaries: Rhetorically trained secretaries responsible for negotiating, recording, and communicating the many agreements that enabled Italian commercial cities to function.

Organizational saga: For Bormann, a longer story which presents the history of the group in the form of a legend.

Panopticism: Foucault's term for the increasing surveillance that characterizes modern life.

Paradeigma [Greek]: Argument from an example or examples to a probable generalization. The inductive argument that complements the deductive enthymeme.

Parasemos [Greek]: Counterfeit.

Particular audience: In Perelman and Olbrechts-Tyteca, the actual audience of persons one addresses when advancing an argument publicly.

Pathos [Greek]: The study of psychology of emotion; one of the three artistic proofs of Aristotle.

Peitho: Greek goddess of persuasion.

Perfectus orator [Latin]: The complete or finished orator. In Roman thought, an eloquent leader embodying and articulating the society's values.

Peroratio [Latin]: The conclusion or final section of a judicial speech in which the orator reiterated the full strength of a case.

Perspicuity: In Hugh Blair, clarity of expression.

Petitio [Latin]: Request, demand, or announcement in a letter.

Petits recits [French]: For Lyotard, the "small narratives" which characterize local human communities and particularly marginalized groups.

Phronesis [Greek]: Practical wisdom. Good sense. In Aristotle, a component of *ethos*.

Physis [Greek]: The law or rule of nature under which the strong dominate the weak.

Pian: In ancient China, the art of disputation.

Pistis [Greek]: Mere belief.

Plausibility: In Campbell's rhetorical theory, discourse that is instantly believable because of its close association with an audience's experience of their social world.

Poetriae, Ars [Latin]: Art of poetry. One of three medieval rhetorical arts. Highly prescriptive approaches to writing poetry.

Polis [Greek]: The city-state, particularly the people making up the state.

Polyphonic: Having many voices. Mikhail Bakhtin's term for quality of narrative in which each character is fully developed and speaks fully his or her perspective on the world.

Post rem [Latin]: In one Roman topical system, *following an act*.

Postmodernism: A twentieth-century intellectual movement that rejected the Enlightenment ideals of progress and reason, and questioned all "meta-narratives."

Praedicandi, ars [Latin]: Preaching. One of three medieval rhetorical arts.

Presence: In Perelman and Olbrechts-Tyteca, the choice to emphasize certain ideas and facts over others, thus encouraging an audience to attend to them.

Presumption: A "*pre-occupation* of the ground," in Richard Whately's terms. The principle that an idea occupies its place as reasonable or acceptable until adequately challenged.

Pronuntiatio **[Latin]:** Delivery. The control of voice and body in a manner suitable to the dignity of the subject matter and the style.

Protreptic **[Greek]:** The potential in language for persuasion.

Prudence: Practical judgment.

Psogos **[Greek]:** Blame. One of two functions of epideictic oratory, the other being praise (*epainos*).

Psychagogos **[Greek]:** A poet. A "leader of souls" through incantation.

Psyche **[Greek]:** Mind or soul.

Public sphere: A place of discussion among individuals unrestrained by the dominating influence of political systems and the interests of the state, and where ideas of interest to everyone are discussed and refined.

Quadrivium **[Latin]:** The four major studies in medieval schools, consisting of arithmetic, geometry, music, and astronomy.

Quaestiones **[Latin]:** Debatable points suggested by passages from ancient authorities.

Quality: In Quintilian's system of bases, a concern for the severity of the act, once defined or categorized.

Queer theory: An intellectual movement that sees gender as a product of symbolic interaction and the social negotiation of meaning, and gender, sexuality and self as socially constructed.

Res **[Latin]:** The substance of one's arguments.

Res *Publica*: The Roman citizenry.

Rhetor: Anyone engaged in preparing or presenting rhetorical discourse.

Rhetores **[Greek]:** Rhetors or orators. Those making their living and wielding power by means of persuasive words. Also, politicians.

Rhetoric: As an art, the study and practice of effective symbolic expression. As a type of discourse, goal-oriented speaking or writing that seeks, by means of the resources of symbols, to adapt ideas to an audience.

Rhetoric of display: Rhetorical theory and criticism focused on visual or representational rather than language-based rhetoric.

Rhetoric of fiction: Wayne Booth's insight that in narrative, "the author's judgment is always present."

Rhetorical audience: In Lloyd Bitzer's situational theory, "those persons who are capable of being influenced by discourse and of being mediators of change."

Rhetorical discourse: Discourse crafted according to the principles of the art of rhetoric.

Rhetorical theory: The systematic presentation of the principles of rhetoric, descriptions of rhetoric's various functions, and explanations of how rhetoric achieves its goals.

Salutatio **[Latin]:** The greeting in a letter.

Sannio **[Latin]:** A clown or buffoon. For Cicero, a classification the orator must avoid in using humor.

Scholasticism: A closed and authoritarian approach to education centered on disputation over a fixed body of premises derived largely from the teachings of Aristotle.

Scientific reasoning: Reasoning that moves from axioms to indubitable conclusions.

***Senatus* [Latin]:** Senate. Roman governing body. Literally, a council of elders.

Sensus *communis* [Latin]: Common beliefs and values that provide the basis for society.

***Sententiae* [Latin]:** Isolated statements from ancient authorities.

***Shui*:** Chinese. In ancient China, the art of persuasion. Also, the formulation of concrete plans of action.

***Sophistes, pl. sophistae* [Greek]:** An authority, an expert, a teacher of rhetoric.

***Sprezzatura* [Italian]:** In Castiglione's *The Book of The Courtier*, the orator's easy grace and casual self-confidence.

Starting points: In Perelman and Olbrechts-Tyteca, points of agreement between a rhetor and an audience that allow for argumentation to develop.

Stasis system: Method for discovering arguments by identifying points at which clash or disagreement was likely to occur in a case or debate.

Structuralism: An early twentieth-century movement in discourse studies, following the work of Levi-Strauss, that affirmed the presence of underlying structures or "grammars" in myths and other narrative forms.

***Studia humanitatis* [Latin]:** Humanistic studies, or studies proper to the development of a free and active human mind—rhetoric, poetics, ethics, politics.

***Suasoria* [Latin]:** An elementary practice speech for the younger Roman student of rhetoric.

Syllogism: A deductive argument moving from a general premise, through a specific application of that premise, to a specific and necessary conclusion.

Symbol: Any mark, sign, sound, or gesture that represents something based on social agreement.

Symbolic convergence: For Bormann, when members of a group share the same stories.

Symbolic inducement: Kenneth Burke's definition of rhetoric. Garnering cooperation by the strategic use of symbols.

***Symboulos* [Greek]:** An advisor; someone offering wise counsel on practical matters.

***Sympheron* [Greek]:** Advantageous course of action and actions.

Synecdoche: The rhetorical device in which the whole object represents one part.

Taste: In Lord Kames and Hugh Blair, a developed appreciation of aesthetic experiences.

***Techne* [Greek]:** A true art or discipline. A scientific or systematic pursuit of a full account and arriving regularly at a good product or outcome.

Terministic screens: Kenneth Burke's term to describe the fact that every language or choice of words becomes a filter through which we perceive the world.

Theme: A biblical text providing the basis for developing a sermon.

***Theoron* [Greek]:** A spectator or observer. An audience member for an epideictic speech.

Thesis: A general premise in an argument under Hermagoras' system.

***Thesmos* [Greek]:** Law derived from the authority of kings.

Topical maxim: In Boethius, rational principle or major premises in arguments.

Topical systems [Latin *topica*]: Systematic methods for discovering arguments.

Topos **[Greek]:** A line of argument.

Transgression: To read a text for what a traditional reading would overlook or omit; violating the received meaning of a text in search of its submerged meanings.

Translative issue: Issues of procedure, objections regarding how a case is being pursued.

Trivium **[Latin]:** Three minor studies of grammar, rhetoric, and logic in medieval schools.

Tropes: Rhetorical devices.

Universal audience: In Perelman and Olbrechts-Tyteca, an imagined audience of highly rational individuals; an audience of all normal, adult persons.

Uomo universale **[Italian]:** The universal man, the ideal type of an educated person in the Renaissance.

Utterance: A personal statement full of potential meaning. For Bakhtin, the basic unit of discourse.

Validity claim: In Jürgen Habermas' works, a claim to having made a true statement.

Verba **[Latin]:** The words in which the subject matter of the argument was advanced.

Vita activa **[Latin]:** The active life, or life of political and civic involvement.

Bibliography

Abbott, Don Paul. "Marxist Influences on the Rhetorical Theory of Kenneth Burke: Theory of Kenneth Burke," *Philosophy and Rhetoric* 4 (1974): 217–233.

Abbott, Don Paul. "The Renaissance," in *The Present State of Scholarship in Historical and Contemporary Rhetoric*, ed. Winifred Bryan Horner. Columbia, MO: University of Missouri Press, 1990.

Abbott, Don Paul. "Rhetoric and Writing in Renaissance Europe and England," in *A Short History of Writing Instruction: From Ancient Greece to Twentieth-Century America*, ed. James J. Murphy. Davis, CA: Hermagoras Press, 1990.

Agricola, Rudolph. *De Inventione Dialectica*. Nieuwkoop, Holland: B. de Graaf, 1967.

Anderson, Graham. *Sage, Saint, and Sophist: Holy Men and Their Associates in the Early Roman Empire*. London: Routledge, 1994.

Anderson, John R. "The Audience as a Concept in the Philosophic Rhetoric of Perelman, Johnstone, and Natanson," *Southern Speech Communication Journal* 38 (1972): 39–50.

Andrews, Richard, ed. *Narrative and Argument*. Milton Keynes, UK: Open University Press, 1989.

Andrews, Richard, ed. *Rebirth of Rhetoric: Essays in Language, Culture, and Education*. London: Routledge, 1992.

Aristotle. *Rhetoric*. Trans. W. Rhys Roberts. New York: Modern Library, 1954.

Aristotle. *Rhetoric*. Trans. Lane Cooper. New York: Appleton-Century-Crofts, 1932.

Arnhart, Larry. *Aristotle on Political Reasoning: A Commentary on the Rhetoric*. DeKalb, IL: Northern Illinois University Press, 1981.

Augustijn, Cornelis. *Erasmus: His Life, Works, and Influence*. Trans. J. C. Grayson. Toronto: University of Toronto Press, 1991.

Augustine. *On Christian Doctrine*. Trans. D. W. Robertson. Indianapolis, IN: Library of Liberal Arts, 1958.

Aune, James A. "Rhetoric after Deconstruction," in *Rhetoric and Philosophy*, ed. Richard A. Cherwitz. Hillsdale, NJ: Lawrence Erlbaum, 1990: 253–273.

Bacon, Wallace A. "The Elocutionary Career of Thomas Sheridan," *Speech Monographs* 31 (1964): 1–53.

Bakhtin, Mikhail. *Marxism and the Philosophy of Language*. Trans. L. Matejka and I. R. Titunik. New York: Seminar Press, 1973.

Bakhtin, Mikhail. *Problems of Dostoevsky's Poetics*. Ed. and trans. Caryl Emerson. Minneapolis, MN: University of Minnesota Press, 1984.

Bakhtin and His Others: Intersubject(ivism), Chronotype, Dialogism, ed. Liisa Steinby and Tintti Klapuri London: Anthem, 2013.

Barilli, Renato. *Rhetoric*. Trans. Giuliana Menozzi. Minneapolis, MN: University of Minnesota Press, 1989.

Barnes, John A. *A Pack of Lies: Towards a Sociology of Lying*. Cambridge: Cambridge University Press, 1994.

Bibliography   Barnes, Jonathan, ed. *The Cambridge Companion to Aristotle.* Cambridge: Cambridge University Press, 1995.

Barrett, Harold. *The Sophists.* Novato, CA: Chandler and Sharp, 1987.

Barthes, Roland. "From Work to Text," in *Textual Strategies*, ed. Josue Harari. Ithaca, NY: Cornell University Press, 1979.

Bauer, Dale M. and S. Jaret McKinstry, eds. *Feminism, Bakhtin, and the Dialogic.* Albany, NY: State University of New York Press, 1991.

Bazerman, Charles. *Shaping Written Knowledge: The Genre and Activity of the Experimental Article in Science.* Madison, WI: University of Wisconsin Press, 1988.

Benardete, Seth. *The Rhetoric of Morality and Philosophy: Plato's Gorgias and Phaedrus.* Chicago: University of Chicago Press, 1991.

Benson, T. and M. Prosser, eds. *Readings in Classical Rhetoric.* Boston, MA: Allyn and Bacon, 1969.

Berlin, James A. "Revisionary Histories of Rhetoric: Politics, Power, and Plurality," in *Writing Histories of Rhetoric*, ed. Victor Vitanza. Carbondale, IL: Southern Illinois University Press, 1994: 112–127.

Bernauer, James W. *Michel Foucault's Force of Flight: Toward an Ethics of Thought.* Atlantic Highlands, NJ: Humanities Press, 1990.

Bevilaqua, Vincent. "Philosophical Origins of George Campbell's *Philosophy of Rhetoric*," *Speech Monographs* 32 (1965): 7–8.

Billig, Michael. *Arguing and Thinking*, 2nd ed. Cambridge: Cambridge University Press, 1996.

Billig, Michael. *Ideology and Opinion.* London: Sage, 1991.

Billig, Michael. "Psychology, Rhetoric, and Cognition," *History of the Human Sciences* 2 (1989): 289–307.

Bishop, Morris. *Petrarch and His World.* Bloomington, IN: Indiana University Press, 1963.

Bitzer, Lloyd. "Aristotle's Enthymeme Revisited," *Quarterly Journal of Speech* 45 (1959): 399–408.

Bitzer, Lloyd. "Hume's Philosophy in George Campbell's *The Philosophy of Rhetoric*," *Philosophy and Rhetoric* 2 (1969): 136–166.

Bitzer, Lloyd. "The Rhetorical Situation," *Philosophy and Rhetoric* 1 (1968): 1–14.

Bitzer, Lloyd. "Rhetoric and Public Knowledge," in *Rhetoric, Philosophy, and Literature: An Exploration*, ed. Don Burks. West Lafayette, IN: Purdue University Press, 1978: 67–93.

Bitzer, Lloyd. "Political Rhetoric," in *Landmark Essays on Contemporary Rhetoric*, ed. Thomas Farrell. Mahwah, NJ: Hermagoras Press, 1998: 1–22.

Bizzell, Patricia and Bruce Herzberg. *The Rhetorical Tradition: Readings from Classical Times to the Present*, 2nd ed. Boston, MA: St. Martin's Press, 2000.

Black, Edwin. "Plato's View of Rhetoric," *Quarterly Journal of Speech* 44 (December 1958): 361–374.

Blair, Hugh. *Lectures on Rhetoric and Belles Lettres.* Ed. Harold Harding. Carbondale, IL: Southern University Press, 1965.

Boethius. *De Topicis Differentiis.* Trans. Eleanor Stump. Ithaca, NY: Cornell University Press, 1978.

Booth, Wayne. *Modern Dogma and the Rhetoric of Assent.* Chicago, IL: University of Chicago Press, 1974.

Booth, Wayne. *Now Don't Try to Reason with Me.* Chicago, IL: University of Chicago Press, 1970.

Booth, Wayne. *The Rhetoric of Fiction.* Chicago, IL: University of Chicago Press, 1961.

Booth, Wayne. *The Vocation of a Teacher.* Chicago, IL: University of Chicago Press, 1988.

Bormann, Ernest. "Fantasy and Rhetorical Vision: The Rhetorical Criticism of Social Reality," *Quarterly Journal of Speech* 59 (1972): 396–407.

Bormann, Ernest. "Symbolic Convergence: Organizational Communication and Culture," in *Communication and Organizations: An Interpretive Approach*, eds L. L. Putnam and M. E. Pacanowsky, Thousand Oaks, CA: Sage, 1983.

Bowersock, G. W. *Greek Sophists in the Roman Empire.* Oxford: Clarendon Press, 1969.

Breitman, George, ed. *Malcolm X Speaks.* New York: Grove Press, 1966.

Browne, Stephen H. "Shandyean Satire and the Rhetorical Arts in Eighteenth-Century England," *Southern Communication Journal* 55 (1990): 191–205.

Brucker, Gene. *Florence: The Golden Age 1138–1737*. Berkeley, CA: University of California Press, 1969.

Brummett, Barry. *Rhetoric in Popular Culture*. New York: St. Martin's Press, 1994.

Burchell, Graham, Colin Gordon, and Peter Miller, eds. *The Foucault Effect*. Chicago, IL: University of Chicago Press, 1991.

Burke, Kenneth. *Counter-Statement*. 1931. Berkeley, CA: University of California Press, 1968.

Burke, Kenneth. *A Grammar of Motives*. 1945. Berkeley, CA: University of California Press, 1969.

Burke, Kenneth. *Language as Symbolic Action*. 1937. Berkeley, CA: University of California Press, 1966.

Burke, Kenneth. *The Philosophy of Literary Form: Studies in Symbolic Action*. 1941. Berkeley, CA: University of California Press, 1973.

Burke, Kenneth. *A Rhetoric of Motives*. Berkeley, CA: University of California Press, 1950.

Burke, Kenneth. *The Rhetoric of Religion*. Berkeley, CA: University of California Press, 1961.

Burke, John G. "Hermetism as a Renaissance World View," in *The Darker Vision of the Renaissance: Beyond the Fields of Reason*, ed. Robert Kinsman, Berkeley, CA: University of California Press, 1974.

Burke, Peter. "The Spread of Humanism," in *The Impact of Humanism in Western Europe*, eds. Anthony Goodman and Angus MacKay. London: Longman, 1990.

Burke, Peter. *Vico*. Oxford: Oxford University Press, 1985.

Butler, Judith. *Bodies that Matter: On the Discursive Limits of Sex*. New York: Routledge, 1994.

Butterworth, Charles. *Averroes's "Three Short Commentaries on Aristotle's 'Topics,' 'Rhetoric,' and 'Poetics.'* Ed. and trans. C. Butterworth. Albany NY: State University of New York Press, 1977.

Cameron, James K. "Humanism in the Low Countries," In ed. Anthony Goodman and Angus MacKay, *The Impact of Humanism on Western Europe*, London: Routledge, 1990

Campbell, George. *The Philosophy of Rhetoric*. 1776. Ed. Lloyd F. Bitzer. Carbondale, IL: University of Southern Illinois Press, 1963.

Campbell, John Angus. "Darwin, Thales, and the Milkmaid: Scientific Revolution and Argument from Common Beliefs and Common Sense," in *Perspectives on Argument: Essays in Honor of Wayne Brockriede*, eds. Robert Trapp and Janice Schuetz. Prospect Heights, IL: Waveland, 1990: 207–220.

Campbell, John Angus. "Scientific Discovery and Rhetorical Invention: The Path of Darwin's Origin," in *The Rhetorical Turn*, ed. Herbert Simon. Chicago, IL: University of Chicago Press, 1990: 58–90.

Campbell, Karlyn K. "Hearing Women's Voices," *Communication Education* 40 (1991): 33–48.

Campbell, Karlyn K. *Man Can Not Speak for Her: A Critical Study of Early Feminist Rhetoric*. New York: Greenwood Press, 1989.

Caputo, John D., ed. *Deconstruction in a Nutshell: A Conversation with Jacques Derrida*. New York: Fordham University Press, 1997.

Caputo, John D. and Mark Yount. *Foucault and the Critique of Institutions*. University Park, PA: Pennsylvania State University Press, 1993.

Carleton, Walter. "What Is Rhetorical Knowledge?" *Quarterly Journal of Speech* 64 (1978): 313–328.

Casson, Lionel. *Selected Satires of Lucian*. New York: Norton, 1968.

Castiglione, Ballasdare. *The Courtier*. n.p.: 1528.

Charles, David. *Aristotle's Philosophy of Action*. Ithaca, NY: Cornell University Press, 1984.

Chen, Mel Y. *Animacies: Biopolitics, Racial Mattering and Queer Affect.* Durham, NC: Duke University Press, 2012.

Cialdini, Robert. *Influence: The Psychology of Persuasion*. New York: William Morrow, 1993.

Cicero. *De Inventione*. Trans. H. M. Hubbell. Cambridge, MA: Loeb Classical Library, 1976.

Cicero. *De Oratore*. Trans. E. W. Sutton and H. Rackham. Cambridge, MA: Loeb Classical Library, 1976.

Cicero. Ed. T. A. Dorey. New York: Basic Books, 1965.

Clark, Carol Lea. "Aristotle and Averroes: The Influences of Aristotle's Arabic Commentator upon Western European and Arabic Rhetoric," *Review of Communication* 7(4) (2007): 369–387.

Clark, Martin L. *Rhetoric at Rome*. New York: Barnes and Noble, 1953.

Bibliography Classen, Albrecht. "Female Explorations of Literacy: Epistolary Challenges to the Literary Canon in the Late Middle Ages," in Disputatio Volume 1: The Late Medieval Epistle, ed. Carol Poster and Richard Utz (Evanston IL: Northwestern University Press, 1996), 89–122, p. 90.

Cmiel, Kenneth. *Democratic Eloquence: The Fight over Popular Speech in Nineteenth-Century America*. New York: William Morrow, 1990.

Coates, Willson Havelock. *The Emergence of Liberal Humanism: An Intellectual History of Western Europe*. New York: McGraw Hill, 1966.

Cohen, Herman. "William Leechman's Anticipation of Campbell." *Western Speech* 32 (1968): 92–99.

Cohen, Herman. "Belles-lettres," in *Encyclopedia of Composition and Rhetoric: Communication from Ancient Times to the Information Age*, ed. Theresa Enos. New York: Routledge, 2004.

Cole, Percival. *Later Roman Education in Ausonius, Capella, and the Theodosian Code*. New York: Columbia University Press, 1909.

Conley, Thomas M. "'Logical Hylomorphism' and Aristotle's *Koinoi Topoi*," *Central States Speech Journal* 29 (1978): 92–97.

Conley, Thomas M. *Rhetoric in the European Tradition*. Chicago, IL: University of Chicago Press, 1994.

Connolly, Joy. *The State of Speech: Rhetorical and Political Thought in Ancient Rome*. Princeton, NJ University Press, 2013.

Corbett, Edward P. J. "The *Topoi* Revisited," in *Rhetoric and Praxis: The Contribution of Classical Rhetoric to Practical Thinking*, ed. Jean Deitz Moss. Washington, DC: Catholic University Press of America, 1986.

Coupe, Laurence. *Myth*. New York: Routledge, 1997.

Covino, William A. *Magic, Rhetoric and Literacy: An Eccentric History of the Composing Imagination*. Albany, NY: State University of New York Press, 1994.

Craig, Christopher P. *Form as Argument in Cicero's Speeches: A Study of Dilemma*, American Classical Studies, 31. Atlanta: Scholars Press, 1993.

Craig, Edward, ed. *Routledge Encyclopedia of Philosophy*. London: Routledge, 1998.

Crombie, I. M. *An Examination of Plato's Doctrines*. London: Routledge and Kegan Paul, 1961.

Crump, James. *Intrigues: Studies of the Chan-Kuo Tse*. Ann Arbor, MI: University of Michigan Press, 1964.

Culler, Jonathan. *On Deconstruction*. Ithaca, NY: Cornell University Press, 1982.

Curran, Jane V. "The Rhetorical Technique of Plato's *Phaedrus*," *Philosophy and Rhetoric* 19 (1986): 66–72.

Dearin, Ray D., ed. *The New Rhetoric of Chaim Perelman: Statement and Response*. Lanham, MD: University Press of America, 1989.

DeFrancisco, Victoria and Marvin Jensen, eds. *Women's Voices in Our Time*. Prospect Heights, IL: Waveland, 1994.

de Lauretis, Teresa. "Habit Changes," *Differences: A Journal of Feminist Cultural Studies* 6 (1994): 296–313.

de Lauretis, Teresa. "Queer Theory: Lesbian and Gay Sexualities," *Differences: A Journal of Feminist Cultural Studies* 3 (1991): iii–xviii.

DePew, David J. and John Lyne. "The Productivity of Scientific Rhetoric," *POROI: An Interdisciplinary Journal of Rhetorical Analysis and Invention* 9(1), (2013).

de Romilly, Jacqueline. *The Great Sophists in Periclean Athens*. Trans. Janet Lloyd. Oxford: Clarendon Press, 1992.

de Romilly, Jacqueline. *Magic and Rhetoric in Ancient Greece*. Cambridge, MA: Harvard University Press, 1975.

Derrida, Jacques. *Of Grammatology* (*De la Grammatologie*). Trans. Gayatri Spivak 1967. Baltimore, MD: Johns Hopkins University Press, 1976.

Derrida, Jacques. *Positions*. Trans. and ed. Alan Bass. 1972. Chicago, IL: University of Chicago Press, 1981.

Derrida, Jacques. *Speech and Phenomena* (*La Voix et le Phénomène*). Trans. David Allison 1967. Evanston, IL: Northwestern University Press, 1973.

Derrida, Jacques. *Writing and Difference* (*L' écriture et la Différence*). Trans. Alan Bass. Chicago, IL: University of Chicago Press, 1978.

Despland, Michael. *The Education of Desire: Plato and the Philosophy of Religion*. Toronto: University of Toronto Press, 1985.

Detienne, Marcel. *The Creation of Mythology*. Trans. Margaret Cook. Chicago, IL: University of Chicago Press, 1986.

deVelasco, A. R. "Transgressive Eloquence: Bell hooks, Cicero, and the Aims of Rhetorical Pedagogy," in *Sizing up Rhetoric*, eds. David Zarefsky and Elizabeth Benacka. Long Grove, IL: Waveland Press, 2008.

Dickinson, Emily. *The Poems of Emily Dickinson*. Ed. Thomas H. Johnson. Cambridge, MA: Belknap Press of Harvard University, 1983.

Dipardo, Anne. "Narrative Knowers, Expository Knowledge," *Written Communication* 7 (1990): 59–95.

Disch, Lisa J. "More Truth than Fact: Storytelling as Critical Understanding in the Writings of Hannah Arendt," *Political Theory* (1994): 665–694.

Donawerth, Jane, ed. *Rhetorical Theory by Women before 1900*. Lanham, MD: Rowman and Littlefield, 2002.

Donovan, Josephine. "Feminism, Bakhtin, and the Dialogic." In *Feminism, Bakhtin, and the Dialogic*, Eds. Dale M. Bauer and S. Jaret McKinstry. Albany, NY: State University of New York Press, 1991.

Duranti, Alessandro. *From Grammar to Politics: Linguistic Anthropology in a Western Samoan Village*. Berkeley, CA: University of California Press, 1994.

Ede, Lisa S. "Rhetoric vs. Philosophy: The Role of the Universal Audience in Chaim Perelman's *The New Rhetoric*," *Central States Speech Journal* 32 (1981): 118–125.

Edwards, Mark U., Jr. *Printing, Propaganda, and Martin Luther*. Berkeley, CA: University of California Press, 1994.

Ehninger, Douglas. "Campbell, Blair, and Whately: Old Friends in a New Light," *Western Speech* 19 (1955): 263–269.

Ehninger, Douglas. "Campbell, Blair and Whately Revisited," *Southern Speech Journal* 28 (1963): 169–182.

Ehninger, Douglas. "George Campbell and the Revolution in Inventional Thinking," *Southern Speech Journal* 15 (1950): 270–276.

Elden, Stuart. *Foucault's Last Decade*. Cambridge: Polity Press, 2016.

Enos, Richard Leo. *Greek Rhetoric before Aristotle*. Prospect Heights, IL: Waveland, 1993.

Erasmus. "The Right Way to Speak," in *Collected Works*, v. 4, ed. J. K. Sowards. Toronto: University of Toronto Press, 1985.

Erickson, Keith V., ed. *Aristotle: The Classical Heritage of Rhetoric*. Metuchen, NJ: The Scarecrow Press, 1974.

Fahnestock, Jeanne. *Rhetorical Figures in Science*. Oxford: Oxford University Press, 1999.

Fakhry, Majid. *Averroes: His Life, Work and Influence*. Oxford: Oneworld Publications: 2001.

Faral, Edmond. "*Les Artes Poetique du XIIe et XIIIe Siècle*." (1924) Paris: n.p., 1971.

Farmer, Frank, ed. *Landmark Essays on Bakhtin, Rhetoric and Writing*. Mahwah, NJ: Hermagoras Press, 1998.

Farrell, Thomas. "Social Knowledge II," *Quarterly Journal of Speech* 64 (1978): 329–334.

Farrell, Thomas. *Norms of Rhetorical Culture*. New Haven, CT: Yale University Press, 1995.

Faulhaber, Charles. "The Origins of Humanism," in *Medieval Eloquence: Studies in the Theory and Practice of Medieval Rhetoric*, ed. James J. Murphy. Berkeley, CA: University of California Press, 1978: 85–111.

Fay, Elizabeth A. *Eminent Rhetoric: Language, Gender, and Cultural Tropes*. Westport, CT: Bergen and Garvey, 1994.

Fisher, Walter. *Human Communication as Narration: Toward a Philosophy of Reason, Value, and Action*. University of South Carolina Press, 1987.

Fleckenstein, Kristie S. "In the Blood of the Word: Embodied Rhetorical Authority in St. Catherine of Siena's *Dialogue*," in *Sizing up Rhetoric*, eds. David Zarefsky and Elizabeth Benacka. Long Grove, IL: Waveland Press, 2008.

Ford, Andrew. "The Price of Art in Isocrates: Formalism and the Escape from Politics," *Rethinking the History of Rhetoric*, ed. Takis Poulakos. Boulder, CO: Westview, 1992.

Fortenbaugh, W. W. *Aristotle on Emotion*. New York: Barnes and Noble, 1975.

Bibliography

Fortenbaugh, W. W. and D. C. Mirhady, eds. *Peripatetic Rhetoric after Aristotle*. New Brunswick, NJ: Transaction, 1994.

Foss, Sonja. *Rhetorical Criticism*. Prospect Heights, IL: Waveland, 1989.

Foss, Sonja. and C. L. Griffin. "Beyond Persuasion: A Proposal for an Invitational Rhetoric," *Communication Monographs* 62 (1995): 2–18.

Foss, Sonja, Karen A. Foss, and Robert Trapp. *Contemporary Perspective on Rhetoric*. 2nd ed. Prospect Heights, IL: Waveland, 1991.

Foucault, Michel. *The Archaeology of Knowledge (L'Archaéologie du Savoir)*. Trans. A. M. Sheridan Smith. 1969. New York: Random House, 1972.

Foucault, Michel. *The Birth of the Clinic: An Archaeology of Medical Perception*. Trans. A. M. Sheridan Smith. New York: Random House, 1973.

Foucault, Michel. *Discipline and Punish: The Birth of the Prison*. London: Allen Lane, 1975.

Foucault, Michel. *The Order of Things: An Archaeology of the Human Sciences (Les Mots et les Chose)*. 1966. New York: Random House, 1970.

Fox, Michael J. "Ancient Egyptian Rhetoric," *Rhetorica* 1 (1983): 21–22.

Frank, David. A. "A Traumatic Reading of Twentieth-Century Rhetorical Theory: The Belgian Holocaust, Malines, Perelman, and de man," *Quarterly Journal of Speech* 93(3): (August 2007) 308–343.

Frank, Manfred. "On Foucault's Concept of Discourse." *Michel Foucault: Philosopher*. Trans. Timothy J. Armstrong. New York: Routledge, 1992: 99–116.

Fredborg, Karin Margareta. "Twelfth-Century Ciceronian Rhetoric: Its Doctrinal Development and Influences," in *Rhetoric Revalued*, ed. Brian Vickers. Binghamton, NY: Center for Medieval and Early Renaissance Studies, 1982: 87–97.

Fuhrmann, Manfred. *Cicero and the Roman Republic*. Trans. W. E. Yuill. Oxford: Blackwell, 1992.

Gadamer, Hans-George. *The Idea of the Good in Platonic-Aristotelian Philosophy*. New Haven, CT: Yale University Press, 1986.

Gagarin, Michael. *Antiphon and the Athenians: Oratory, Law and Justice in the Age of the Sophists*. Austin, TX: University of Texas Press, 2002.

Gagarin, Michael. *The Murder of Herodes: A Study of Antiphon 5*. New York, NY: Verlag Peter Lang, 1989.

Gagarin, Michael. "Telling Stories in Athenian Law," in *Transactions of the American Philological Association* 133(2), (2003): 197–207.

Gallo, Ernest. "The *Poetria Nova* of Geoffrey of Vinsauf," in *Medieval Eloquence: Studies in the Theory and Practice of Medieval Rhetoric*, ed. James J. Murphy. Berkeley, CA: University of California Press, 1978: 68–84.

Gaonkar, Dilip Parameshwar. "The Idea of Rhetoric in the Rhetoric of Science," *Southern Communication Journal* 58 (1993): 255–327.

Garin, Euginio. *Portraits of the Quattrocentro*. New York: Harper and Row, 1963.

Garry, Ann and Marilyn Pearsall, eds. *Women, Knowledge and Reality: Explorations in Feminist Philosophy*. New York: Routledge, 1989.

Gearhart, Sally Miller. "The Womanization of Rhetoric," *Women's Studies International Quarterly* 2 (1979): 195–201.

Geertz, Clifford. *Works and Lives: The Anthropologist as Author*. Stanford, CT: Stanford University Press: 1988.

Geoffrey of Vinsauf. *Documentum do Modo et Arte Dictandi et Versificandi*. Trans. Roger P. Parr. Milwaukee, WI: Marquette University Press, 1968.

Gergen, Kenneth and Mary M. Gergen. "Narrative Form and the Construction of Psychological Sciences," in *Narrative Psychology*, ed. T. R. Sarbin. New York: Praeger Press, 1986: 22–44.

Gilbert, Katherine E. and Helmut Kuhn. *A History of Esthetics*. Bloomington, IN: University of Indiana Press, 1953.

Gill, Ann. *Rhetoric and Human Understanding*. Prospect Heights, IL: Waveland, 1994.

Gilligan, Carol. *In a Different Voice*. Cambridge, MA: Harvard University Press, 1982.

Glenn, Cheryl. "Locating Aspasia on the Rhetorical Map," in *Listening to Their Voices*, ed. Molly Meijer Wertheimer. Columbia, SC: University of South Carolina Press, 1997: 19–41.

Golden, James L. and Edward P. J. Corbett. *The Rhetoric of Blair, Campbell, and Whately*. New York: Holt, Rinehart and Winston, 1968.

Goldin, Paul Rakita. "Miching Mallecho: The Zhanguo Ce and Classical Rhetoric," *Sino-Platonic Papers*, 41 (1993): 1–26.

Goodman, Anthony and Angus MacKay, eds. *The Impact of Humanism on Western Europe*. London: Longman, 1990.

Gorgias. *Encomium on Helen*. Trans. LaRue VanHook. *The Classical Weekly* 6 (1913): 122–123.

Gotoff, Harold C. *Cicero's Caesarian Speeches: A Stylistic Commentary*. Chapel Hill, NC: University of North Carolina Press, 1993.

Govier, Trudy. *Selected Issues in Logic and Communication*. Belmont, CA: Wadsworth, 1988.

Grassi, Ernesto. *Rhetoric as Philosophy*. University Park, PA: Pennsylvania State University Press, 1980.

Gregg, Richard B. *Symbolic Inducement and Knowing: A Study in the Foundations of Rhetoric*. Columbia, SC: University of South Carolina Press, 1984.

Grimaldi, Michael. *Aristotle, Rhetoric I: A Commentary*. New York: Fordham University Press, 1980.

Grimaldi, Michael. "The Aristotelian Topics." *Traditio* 14 (1958): 1–16.

Gronbeck, Bruce E. "Gorgias on Rhetoric and Poetic: A Rehabilitation," *Southern Speech Communication Journal* 38 (1972): 27–38.

Gross, Alan. *The Rhetoric of Science*. Cambridge: Harvard University Press, 1990.

Gross, Alan. "A Theory of the Rhetorical Audience: Reflections on Chaim Perelman," *Quarterly Journal of Speech* 85 (1999): 202–211.

Gross, Alan, Joseph Harmon, and Michael Reidy *Communicating Science: The Scientific Article from the 17th Century to the Present*. Oxford: Oxford University Press, 2002.

Grube, G. M. A. *The Greek and Roman Critics*. Toronto: University of Toronto Press, 1965.

Grube, G. Introduction to Longinus, *On the Sublime*. Indianapolis, IN: Library of Liberal Arts, 1957.

Grube, G. *Plato's Thought*. 1935. Boston, MA: Beacon Press, 1958.

Guthrie, W. K. C. *The Sophists*. Cambridge: Cambridge University Press, 1971.

Gutting, Gary, ed. *The Cambridge Companion to Foucault*. Cambridge: Cambridge University Press, 1994.

Gutting, Gary, ed. *Michel Foucault's Archaeology of Scientific Reason*. New York: Cambridge University Press, 1989.

Habermas, Jürgen. *Communication and the Evolution of Society*. Trans. Thomas McCarthy. Boston, MA: Beacon Press, 1979.

Habermas, Jürgen. *Toward a Rational Society*. Trans. Jeremy J. Shapiro. Boston, MA: Beacon Press, 1970.

Habermas, Jürgen. *Knowledge and Human Interests*. Trans. Jeremy J. Shapiro. Boston, MA: Beacon Press, 1971.

Habermas, Jürgen. *Theory and Practice*. Trans. John Viertel. Boston, MA: Beacon Press, 1973.

Habermas, Jürgen. *The Philosophical Discourse of Modernity: Twelve Lectures*. Ed. Thomas McCarthy. Trans. Frederick Lawrence. Cambridge, MA: MIT Press, 1987.

Habermas, Jürgen. *The Lure of Technocracy*. Cambridge: Polity Press, 2016.

Habicht, Christian. *Cicero the Politician*. Baltimore, MD: Johns Hopkins University Press, 1990.

Halperin, David. *Saint Foucault: Toward a Gay Hagiography*. New York, NY: Oxford University Press, 1995.

Hare, R. M. *Plato*. Oxford: Oxford University Press, 1982.

Haraway, Donna J. *Staying with the Trouble: Making Kin in the Chthulucene*. Durham, NC: Duke University Press, 2016.

Haskins, Ekaterina. *Logos and Power in Isocrates and Aristotle*. Columbia, SC: University of South Carolina Press, 2004.

Hauser, Gerard. "Empiricism, Description and the New Rhetoric," *Philosophy and Rhetoric* 5 (1972): 24–44.

Hauser, Gerard. "The Example in Aristotle's *Rhetoric*: Bifurcation or Contradiction?" *Philosophy and Rhetoric* 1 (1968): 78–90.

Bibliography

Hazzard, Paul. *La Pensée Européenne au XVIIIe Siècle de Montesquieu à Lessing*. Paris: Arthone Fayard, 1963.

Hill, Forbes I. "The Rhetoric of Aristotle." *A Synoptic History of Classical Rhetoric*. Davis, CA: Hermagoras Press, 1983.

Hogan, Michael J., ed. *Rhetoric and Community: Studies in Unity and Fragmentation*. Columbia, SC: University of South Carolina Press, 1998.

Holquist, Michael. *Dialogism: Bakhtin and His World*. London: Routledge, 1990.

Home, Henry: Lord Kames. *The Elements of Criticism*. 1761. New York: Barnes and Burr, 1865.

Horner, Winifred Bryan, ed. *The Present State of Scholarship in Historical and Contemporary Rhetoric*. Columbia, MO: University of Missouri Press, 1990.

Howard, Dick. "A Politics in Search of the Political." *Theory and Society* 1 (1974): 271–306.

Howell, Wilbur Samuel. *Eighteenth-Century British Logic and Rhetoric*. Princeton, NJ: Princeton University Press, 1971.

Howell, Wilbur Samuel. "John Locke and the New Rhetoric," *Quarterly Journal of Speech* 53 (1967): 319–321.

Howell, Wilbur Samuel. *Logic and Rhetoric in England: 1500–1700*. New York: Russell and Russell, 1961.

Hoy, David Couzens. *Foucault: A Critical Reader*. Oxford: Basil Blackwell, 1986.

Hubbard, B. A. F. and E. S. Karnofsky. *Plato's Protagoras: A Socratic Commentary*. Chicago, IL: University of Chicago Press, 1982.

Jarratt, Susan. *Rereading the Sophists: Classical Rhetoric Refigured*. Carbondale, IL: Southern Illinois University Press, 1991.

Jarratt, Susan. and Rory Ong. "Aspasia: Rhetoric, Gender, and Colonial Ideology," in *Reclaiming Rhetorica: Women in the Rhetorical Tradition*, ed. Andrea Lunsford. Pittsburgh, PA: University of Pittsburgh Press, 1995: 9–24.

Jennings, Margaret, C. S. J. "The *Ars Compendi Sermones* of Ranulph Higden," in *Medieval Eloquence: Studies in the Theory and Practice of Medieval Rhetoric*, ed. James J. Murphy. Berkeley, CA: University of California Press, 1978: 112–126.

Johannesen, Richard L., Rennard Strickland and Ralph T. Eubanks, eds. *Language Is Sermonic: Richard M. Weaver on the Nature of Rhetoric*. Baton Rouge, LA: Louisiana State University Press, 1970.

Johnson, W. R. "Isocrates Flowering: The Rhetoric of Augustine," *Philosophy and Rhetoric* 9 (1976): 217–231.

Jonsen, Albert R. and Stephen Toulmin. *The Abuse of Casuistry*. Berkeley, CA: University of California Press, 1988.

Kahn, Victoria. *Rhetoric, Prudence, and Skepticism in the Renaissance*. Ithaca, NY: Cornell University Press, 1985.

Kahn, Victoria. Machiavelian Rhetoric: From the Counter-Reformation to Milton. Princeton, NJ: Princeton University Press, 1994.

Katula, Richard and James J. Murphy, eds. *A Synoptic History of Classical Rhetoric*. Davis, CA: Hermagoras Press, 1995.

Katz, Stephen B. "The Ethic of Expediency: Classical Rhetoric, Technology, and the Holocaust." *College English* 54 (1992): 255–275.

Kraye, Jill, ed. *The Cambridge Companion to Renaissance Humanism*. Cambridge: Cambridge University Press, 1996.

Kelley, Donald R. *Renaissance Humanism*. Boston, MA: Twayne Publishers, 1991.

Kennedy, George, trans. *Aristotle on Rhetoric: A Theory of Civic Discourse*. New York: Oxford University Press, 1991.

Kennedy, George, trans. *The Art of Persuasion in Ancient Greece*. Princeton, NJ: Princeton University Press, 1963.

Kennedy, George, trans. *Classical Rhetoric and Its Secular and Christian Tradition*. Chapel Hill, NC: University of North Carolina Press, 1980.

Kennedy, George, trans. *Classical Rhetoric and Its Secular and Christian Tradition*, 2nd ed. Chapel Hill, NC: University of North Carolina Press, 1999.

Kennedy, George, trans. Comparative Rhetoric: An Historical and Cross-Cultural Introduction. New York: Oxford University Press, 1998.

Kenny, Anthony. *Aristotle on the Perfect Life*. Oxford: Clarendon Press, 1992.

Kerferd, G. B. *The Sophistic Movement*. Cambridge: Cambridge University Press, 1981.

Kersey, Shirley. "Medieval Education of Girls and Women," *Educational Horizons* 58(4) (1980): 188–192.

Kinney, Arthur F. *Humanist Poetics: Thought, Rhetoric, and Fiction in Sixteenth-Century England*. Amherst, MA: University of Massachusetts Press, 1986.

Kinsman, Robert, ed. *The Darker Vision of the Renaissance: Beyond the Fields of Reason*. Berkeley, CA: University of California Press, 1974.

Kirsch, Gesa E. and Jacqueline J. Royster. "Feminist Rhetorical Practices: In Search of Excellence," *College Composition and Communication* 61(4) 2010.

Kitto, H. D. F. *The Greeks*. Baltimore, MD: Penguin Books, 1968.

Kristeller, Paul Oskar. *Renaissance Thought: The Classic, Scholastic, and Humanist Strains*. New York: Harper and Row, 1961.

Kuhn, Thomas. *The Structure of Scientific Revolutions*, 2nd ed. Chicago: University of Chicago Press, 1970.

Labalme, Patricia H. *Beyond Their Sex: Learned Women of the European Past*. New York: New York University Press, 1984.

Landau, Misia. "Paradise Lost: The Theme of Terrestriality in Human Evolution," in *The Rhetoric of the Human Sciences*, eds. John Nelson, Allen Megill, and D. N. McCloskey. Madison, WI: University of Wisconsin Press, 1987: 111–124.

Lanham, Richard. *The Electronic Word: Democracy, Technology and the Arts*. Chicago, IL: University of Chicago Press, 1993.

Lanham, Richard. *The Economics of Attention: Style and Substance in the Age of Information* Chicago, IL: University of Chicago Press, 2007.

Lanham, Richard. *A Handbook of Rhetorical Terms*, 2nd ed. Berkeley, CA: University of California Press, 1991.

LaRusso, Dominic. "Root or Branch? A Reexamination of Campbell's `Rhetoric,'" *Western Speech* 32 (1968): 85–91.

Latour, Bruno. *We Have Never Been Modern*. Cambridge MA: Harvard University Press, 1991.

Leff, Michael. "The Logician's Rhetoric: Boethius' *De Differentiis Topicis*, Book IV," in *Medieval Eloquence: Studies in the Theory and Practice of Medieval Rhetoric*, ed. James J. Murphy. Berkeley, CA: University of California Press, 1978: 3–24.

Leff, Michael. *Rethinking Rhetorical Theory, Criticism, and Pedagogy: The Living Art of Michael C. Leff*, eds. A. de Velasco, J. A. Campbell, and D. Henry. Michigan State University Press, 2016.

Leff, Michael. "The Topics of Argumentative Invention in Latin Rhetorical Theory from Cicero to Boethius," *Rhetorica* 1 (1983): 23–44.

Lemert, Charles C. and Garth Gillan. *Michel Foucault: Social Theory as Transgression*. New York: Columbia University Press, 1982.

Levi-Strauss, Claude. "The Structural Study of Myth," *The Journal of American Folklore* 68(270), (1955): 428–444.

Lincoln, Abraham. "Second Inaugural Address," in *The World's Great Speeches*, ed. Lewis Copeland. New York: Dover, 1958: 316–317.

Lloyd, G. E. R. *Aristotle: The Growth and Structure of His Thought*. Cambridge: Cambridge University Press, 1968.

Locke, John. *Essay on Human Understanding*. London: Edward Mory, 1690.

Lodge, Rupert C. *Plato's Theory of Art*. 1953. New York: Russell and Russell, 1975.

Longinus, *On the Sublime*. Ed. and Trans. G. M. A. Grube. Indianapolis, IN: Library of Liberal Arts, 1957.

Lu, Xing. *Rhetoric in Ancient China, Fifth to Third Century*, B.C.E. Columbia, SC: University of South Carolina Press, 1998.

Lunsford, Andrea A. *Reclaiming Rhetorica: Women in the Rhetorical Tradition*. Pittsburgh, PA: University of Pittsburgh Press, 1995.

Lyotard, Jean-Francois. *The Postmodern Condition: A Report on Knowledge*. Trans. Geoff Bennington and Brian Massumi. Minneapolis, MN: University of Minnesota Press, 1988.

Bibliography Maillonx, Steven. "One Size Doesn't Fit All: The Contingent Universality of Rhetoric," in *Sizing up Rhetoric*, eds. David Zarefsky and Elizabeth Benacka, Long Grove, IL: Waveland Press, 2008.

Mack, Peter. *Renaissance Argument: Valla and Agricola in the Tradition of Rhetoric and Dialectic*. Leiden, Holland: E. J. Brill, 1993.

Mali, Joseph. *The Rehabilitation of Myth: Vico's "New Science."* Cambridge: Cambridge University Press, 1992.

Mann, Nicholas. "The Origins of Humanism," in *The Cambridge Companion to Renaissance Humanism*, ed. Jill Kraye, Cambridge: Cambridge University Press, 1996.

Manson, Richard. *The Theory of Knowledge of Giambattista Vico*. Hamden, CT: Archon Books, 1969.

Mao, LuMing and Bo Wang, "Manifesting a Future for Comparative Rhetoric," *Rhetoric Review* 34(3), (2015).

Margolis, Nadia. "'The Cry of the Chameleon': Evolving Voices in the Epistles of Chris tine de Pisan," in Post and Utz *Disputatio* v. 1, pp. 37–70, 1996

Martin, Bill. *Matrix and Line*. Albany, NY: State University of New York Press, 1992.

Martines, Lauro. *Power and Imagination: City States in Renaissance Italy*. New York: Knopf, 1979.

May, James M. *Trials of Character: The Eloquence of Ciceronian Ethos*. Chapel Hill, NC: University of North Carolina Press, 1988.

McCarthy, Thomas. *The Critical Theory of Jürgen Habermas*. Cambridge, MA: MIT Press, 1978.

McCarthy, Thomas, ed. *The Philosophical Discourse of Modernity: Twelve Lectures*. Trans. Frederick Lawrence. Cambridge, MA: MIT Press, 1987.

McCloskey, D. N. "The Neglected Economics of Talk." *Planning for Higher Education* 22 (1994): 11–16.

McCloskey, D. N. *The Rhetoric of Economics*. Madison, WI: University of Wisconsin Press, 1985.

McCloskey, D. N. *Bourgeois Dignity: Why Economics Can't Explain the Modern World*. University of Chicago Press, 2011.

McConnell-Ginet, Sally, Ruth Borker and Nelly Furman. *Women and Language in Literature and Society*. New York: Praeger, 1980.

McDermott, Douglas. "George Campbell and the Classical Tradition," *Quarterly Journal of Speech* 49 (1963): 403–409.

McHoul, Alec and Wendy Grace. *A Foucault Primer: Discourse, Power and the Subject*. New York: New York University Press, 1997.

McKeon, Richard. *Rhetoric: Essays in Invention and Discovery*. Ed. Mark Backman. Woodbridge, CT: Ox Bow Press, 1987.

McKerrow, Ray E. "Campbell and Whately on the Utility of Syllogistic Logic," *Western Speech Communication Journal* 40 (1976): 3–13.

Meador, Prentice A. "Quintilian and the *Institutio Oratoria*." *A Synoptic History of Classical Rhetoric*. Davis, CA: Hermagoras Press, 1983: 151–176.

Megill, Allan. "Recounting the Past: Description, Explanation, and Narrative in Historiography," *American Historical Review* 94 (1989): 627–653.

Mendelson, Sarah Heller. *The Mental World of Stuart Women: Three Studies*. Amherst, MA: The University of Massachusetts Press, 1987.

Mercier, Hugo and Dan Sperber, "How Do Humans Reason? Arguments for an Argumentative Theory" *Behavioral and Brain Sciences* 34 (2011): 57–111.

Midgley, Mary. *Evolution as a Religion*. London: Routledge, 1985: 30.

Midgley, Mary. *Science as Salvation: A Modern Myth and Its Meaning*. London: Routledge, 1992.

Midgley, Mary. *The Myths We Live By*. New York: Routledge, 2004.

Miller, Diane Helene. "The Future of Feminist Rhetorical Criticism," in *Listening to Their Voices: The Rhetorical Activities of Historical Women*, ed. Molly Meijer Wertheimer. Columbia, SC: University of South Carolina Press, 1997.

Miller, J., M. Prosser, and T. Benson, eds. *Readings in Medieval Rhetoric*. Bloomington, IN: Indiana University Press, 1974.

Mohrmann, G. P. *"The Civile Conversation:* Communication in the Renaissance," *Speech Monographs* 39 (1972): 193–204.

Moline, Jon. *Plato's Theory of Understanding.* Madison, WI: University of Wisconsin Press, 1981.

Monfasani, John. *George of Trebizond: A Biography and a Study of His Rhetoric and Logic.* Leiden, Holland: Brill Publishers, 1976.

Mooney, Michael. *Renaissance Thought and Its Sources.* New York: Columbia University Press, 1979.

Mooney, Michael. *Vico in the Tradition of Rhetoric.* Princeton, NJ: Princeton University Press, 1985.

Morris, Meaghan and Paul Patton, eds. *Michel Foucault: Power, Truth, Strategy.* Sydney: Feral Publications, 1979.

Moscorici, Claudia. *Double Dialectics: Between Universalism and Relativism in Enlightened and Postmodern Thought.* Lanham, MD: Rowman and Littlefield, 2002.

Moss, Jean Deitz, ed. *Rhetoric and Praxis: The Contribution of Classical Rhetoric to Practical Reasoning.* Washington, DC: Catholic University of America Press, 1986.

Murphy, James J., ed. *Medieval Eloquence: Studies in the Theory and Practice of Medieval Rhetoric.* Berkeley, CA: University of California Press, 1978.

Murphy, James J. ed. *Peter Ramus's Attack on Cicero.* Trans. Carole Newlands. Davis, CA: Hermagoras Press, 1992.

Murphy, James J. *A Synoptic History of Classical Rhetoric.* Davis, CA: Hermagoras Press, 1983.

Murphy, James J. ed. *A Short History of Writing Instruction.* Davis, CA: Hermagoras Press, 1990.

Murphy, James J. "Saint Augustine and the Debate about a Christian Rhetoric," *Quarterly Journal of Speech* 46 (1960): 400–410.

Murphy, James J. *Three Medieval Rhetorical Arts.* Berkeley, CA: University of California Press, 1971.

Nash, Christopher and Martin Warner, eds. *Narrative in Culture.* London: Routledge, 1988.

Nauert, Charles G., Jr. *Humanism and the Culture of Renaissance Europe.* Cambridge: Cambridge University Press, 1995.

Nelson, John, Allen McGill and D. N. McCloskey, eds. *The Rhetoric of the Human Sciences.* Madison, WI: University of Wisconsin Press, 1987.

Norris, Christopher. *Derrida.* Cambridge, MA: Harvard University Press, 1987.

Nothstine, William, Carole Blair, and Gary Copeland. *Critical Questions.* New York: St. Martin's Press. 1994.

Ober, Josiah. *Mass and Elite in Democratic Athens: Rhetoric, Ideology, and the Power of the People.* Princeton, NJ: Princeton University Press, 1989.

Ochs, Donovan J. "Aristotle's Concept of Formal Topics," *Speech Monographs* 36 (1969): 419–425.

Ochs, Donovan J. "Cicero's *Topica:* A Process View of Invention," in *Explorations in Rhetoric: Essays in Honor of Douglas Ehninger,* ed. Ray E. McKerrow. Glenview, IL: Scott, Foresman, 1982.

Ong, Walter J., S. J. *Ramus: Method and the Decay of Dialogue.* Cambridge, MA: Harvard University Press, 1983.

Ong, Walter J. *Orality and Literacy: The Technologizing of the Word,* 2nd ed. New York: Routledge, 2002.

Perelman, Chaim. *The Idea of Justice and the Problem of Argument.* New York: Random House, 1963.

Perelman, Chaim. *Justice.* New York: Random House, 1967.

Perelman, Chaim. *The New Rhetoric and the Humanities.* Trans. William Kluback. Dordrecht, Holland: D. Reidel, 1979.

Perelman, Chaim. and Lucy Olbrechts-Tyteca. *The New Rhetoric: A Treatise on Argumentation.* 1958. Trans. John Wilkinson and Purcell Weaver. Notre Dame, IN: University of Notre Dame Press, 1969.

Perry, Linda A. M., Lynn H. Turner, and Helen M. Sterk, eds. *Constructing and Reconstructing Gender: The Links among Communication, Language, and Gender.* Albany, NY: State University of New York Press, 1992.

Philostratus. *Lives of the Sophists.* Trans. W. C. Wright. London: Loeb Classical Library, 1965.

Pico. *Oration on the Dignity of Man.* Quoted in Anthony Grafton, "Humanism, Magic and Science," in *The Impact of Humanism on Western Europe,* ed. Anthony Goodman and Angus MacKay. London: Longman, 1990.

Bibliography   Plato. *Gorgias.* Trans. W. C. Helmbold. Indianapolis, IN: Bobbs-Merrill, 1952.

Plato. *Gorgias.* Trans. T. Irwin. Oxford: Clarendon Press, 1979.

Plato. *Phaedrus.* Trans. W. C. Helmbold and W. G. Rabinowitz. Indianapolis, IN: Liberal Arts Press, 1956.

Plato. *Protagoras.* Trans. C. C. W. Taylor. Oxford: Clarendon Press, 1991.

Plato. *Sophist.* Trans. William S. Cobb. Savage, MD: Rowman and Littlefield, 1990.

Plochmann, George Kimball, and Franklin E. Robinson. *A Friendly Companion to Plato's Gorgias.* Carbondale, IL: Southern Illinois University Press, 1988.

Polanyi, Michael. *Personal Knowledge.* Chicago, IL: University of Chicago Press, 1962.

Poulakos, John. *Sophistical Rhetoric in Classical Greece.* Columbia, SC: University of South Carolina Press, 1995.

Poulakos, John. "Terms for Sophistical Rhetoric," in *Rethinking the History of Rhetoric: Multidisciplinary Essays on the History of Rhetoric,* ed. Takis Poulakos. Boulder, CO: Westview, 1993: 53–74.

Poulakos, John. "Toward a Sophistic Definition of Rhetoric," *Philosophy and Rhetoric* 16 (1983): 35–48.

Prado, C. G. *Starting with Foucault: An Introduction to Genealogy.* Boulder, CO: Westview, 1995.

Prelli, Lawrence. *A Rhetoric of Science: Inventing Scientific Discourse.* Columbia, SC: University of South Carolina Press, 1989.

Prelli, Lawrence, ed. *Rhetorics of Display.* Columbia, SC: University of South Carolina, 2006.

Putnam, L. L. and M. E. Pacanowsky, eds. *Communication and Organizations: An Interpretive Approach.* Newbury Park, CA: Sage, 1983: 99–122.

Quandahl, Ellen. "Aristotle's *Rhetoric:* Reinterpreting Invention," *Rhetoric Review* 4 (1986): 128–137.

Quintilian. *Institutio Oratoria.* 4 vol. Trans. H. E. Butler. Cambridge, MA: Loeb Classical Library, 1959–1963.

Quintilian. *On the Early Education of the Citizen Orator.* Ed. James J. Murphy. Trans. John S. Watson. Indianapolis, IN: Library of Liberal Arts, 1965.

Rabinow, Paul, ed. *The Foucault Reader.* New York: Pantheon Books, 1984.

Racevskis, Karlis. *Michel Foucault and the Subversion of Intellect.* Ithaca, NY: Cornell University Press, 1983.

Ramus, Peter. *The Questions of Brutus.* 1549. Trans. Carole Newlands. Davis, CA: Hermagoras Press, 1992.

Ramus, Peter. *Rhetoricae Distinctiones in Quintilianum* (Arguments in Rhetoric against Quintilian). Trans. Carole Newlands. 1549. DeKalb, IL: Northern University Press, 1986.

Randall, John H. *Aristotle.* New York: Columbia University Press, 1960.

Rankin, H. D. *Sophists, Socratics and Cynics.* London: Croom Helm, 1983.

Ray, John W. "Perelman's Universal Audience," *Quarterly Journal of Speech* 64 (1978): 361–375.

Redfern, Jenny R. "Christine de Pisan and *The Treasure of the City of Ladies*: A Medieval Rhetorician and her Rhetoric," in *Reclaiming Rhetorica: Women in the Rhetorical Tradition,* ed. Andrea A. Lunsford. Pittsburgh, PA: University of Pittsburgh Press, 1995: 73–92.

Renfrew, Alastair. *Mikhail Bakhtin.* London: Routledge, 2015.

Richardson, Malcom. "Women, Commerce, and Rhetoric in Medieval England," in *Listening to Their Voices: The Rhetorical Activities of Historical Women,* ed. Molly Meijer Wertheimer. Columbia, SC: University of South Carolina Press, 1997: 133–149.

Sallis, J. *Being and Logos.* Atlantic Highlands, NJ: Humanities Press, 1986.

Schiappa, Edward. "Did Plato Coin *Rhetorike*?" *American Journal of Philology* 111 (1990): 457–470.

Schiappa, Edward. *Protagoras and Logos.* Columbia, SC: University of South Carolina Press, 1991.

Scot Barnett and Casey Boyle, Ed. *Rhetoric, through Everyday Things.* Tuscaloosa AL: University of Alabama Press, 2016.

Scott, Izora. *Controversies over the Imitation of Cicero in the Renaissance.* 1910. Davis, CA: Hermagoras Press, 1991.

Scott, Robert L. "On Viewing Rhetoric as Epistemic," *Central States Speech Journal* 18 (1967): 9–16.

Scott, Robert L. and Wayne Brockriede. *The Rhetoric of Black Power.* New York: Harper and Row, 1969: 132.

Scult, Allen. "Perelman's Universal Audience: One Perspective," *Central States Speech Journal* 27 (1976): 176–80.

Segal, Charles P. "Gorgias and the Psychology of the *Logos*," *Harvard Studies in Classical Philology* 66 (1962): 99–155.

Seigel, Jerrold E. *Rhetoric and Philosophy in Renaissance Humanism.* Princeton, NJ: Princeton University Press, 1968.

Shackleton-Bailey, D. R. *Cicero.* New York: Charles Scribner's Sons, 1971.

Sher, Richard B. *Church and University in the Scottish Enlightenment.* Edinburgh: Edinburgh University Press, 1985.

Sheridan, Thomas. *A Course of Lectures on Elocution.* London: J. Dodsley, 1762.

Sheridan, Thomas. *A Discourse Being Introductory to His Course of Lectures on Elocution and the English Language.* 1759. Los Angeles: Augustan Reprint Society, 1969.

Sheridan, Thomas. *A General Dictionary of the English Language.* London: 1780.

Shumway, David R. *Michel Foucault.* Charlottesville, VA: University Press of Virginia, 1989.

Simons, Herbert W., ed. *The Rhetorical Turn.* Chicago, IL: University of Chicago Press, 1990.

Simons, Herbert W. *Sizing Up Rhetoric.* Ed. D. Zarefsky and E. Benacka. Long Grove, IL: Waveland Press, 2008.

Sloane, Thomas O. *On the Contrary: The Protocol of Traditional Rhetoric.* Washington, DC: Catholic University of America Press, 1997.

Spender, Dale. *Man Made Language.* Boston, MA: Routledge and Kegan Paul, 1980.

Spitzer, Adele. "The Self-Reference of the *Gorgias*," *Philosophy and Rhetoric* 8 (1975): 1–22.

Stark, Ryan John. "Margaret Cavendish and Composition Style," *Rhetoric Review* 17(2) (Spring 1999): 264–281.

Stevens, Kevin M. "Books Fit for a Portuguese Queen: The Lost Library of Catherine of Austria and the Milan Connection (1540)," in *Documenting the Early Modern Book World*, ed. Malcolm Walsby and Natasha Constantinidou, Boston, MA: Brill, 2013, 85–116.

Stringfellow, Frank. *The Meaning of Irony: A Psychoanalytic Investigation.* Albany, NY: State University of New York Press, 1994.

Strini, Tom. "A Taut Take on Beethoven's Ninth." *The Milwaukee Journal Sentinel.* May 13 (2006).

Sullivan, Dale. "*Kairos* and the Rhetoric of Belief," *Quarterly Journal of Speech* 78 (1992): 317–332.

Sutton, Jane. "The Marginalization of Sophistical Rhetoric and the Loss of History," in *Rethinking the History of Rhetoric*, ed. Takis Poulakos. Boulder, CO: Westview Press, 1993: 75–90.

Sutton, Jane. "The Taming of *Polos/Polis*: Rhetoric as an Achievement without Woman," *Southern Communication Journal* 57(2): 97–119, 1993.

Swearingen, Jan. "A Lover's Discourse: Diotima, Logos, and Desire," in *Reclaiming Rhetorica*, ed. Andrea Lunsford. Pittsburgh, PA: University of Pittsburgh Press, 1995: 25–51.

Swearingen, Jan. *Rhetoric and Irony: Western Literacy and Western Lies.* Oxford: Oxford University Press, 1991.

Tagliacozzo, G. and D. P. Verene, eds. *Giambattista Vico's Science of Humanity.* Baltimore: Johns Hopkins Press, 1976.

Tannen, Deborah. *Gender and Discourse.* Oxford: Oxford University Press, 1994.

Thorne, Barrie and Nancy Henley. *Language and Sex: Difference and Dominance.* Rowley, MA: Newberry House, 1975.

Tompkins, Jane P., ed. *Reader Response Criticism.* Baltimore, MD: Johns Hopkins University Press, 1980.

Trapp, Robert and Janice Schuetz, eds. *Perspectives on Argument: Essays in Honor of Wayne Brockriede.* Prospect Heights, IL: Waveland Press, 1990.

Troup, Calvin. *Temporality, Eternity, and Wisdom: The Rhetoric of Augustine's Confessions.* Columbia, SC: University of South Carolina Press, 1999.

Untersteiner, Mario. *The Sophists.* Oxford: Oxford University Press, 1954.

van Eemeren, Frans H., Rob Grootendorst, and Tjark Kruiger. *Handbook of Argumentation Theory.* Dordrecht, Holland: Foris Publications, 1987.

Van Maanen, John. *Tales of the Field.* Chicago, IL: University of Chicago Press, 1988.

Vasaly, Ann. *Representations: Images of the World in Ciceronian Oratory.* Berkeley, CA: University of California Press, 1993.

Vatz, Richard. "The Myth of the Rhetorical Situation," *Philosophy and Rhetoric* 6, (1973): 154–161.

Bibliography

Verene, Donald Philip, ed. Giambattista Vico, *On Humanistic Education: Six Inaugural Orations, 1699–1707.* Trans. G. A. Pinton and A. W. Shippe. Ithaca, NY: Cornell University Press, 1993.

Vickers, Brian, ed. *Rhetoric Revalued: Papers from the International Society for the History of Rhetoric.* Binghamton, NY: Center for Medieval and Early Renaissance Studies, 1982.

Vickers, Brian. "On the Practicalities of Renaissance Rhetoric," in *Rhetoric Revalued*, ed. Brian Vickers, Binghamton, NY: Center for Medieval and Early Renaissance Studies, 1982.

Vickers, Brian. *In Defense of Rhetoric.* Oxford: Oxford University Press, 1988.

Vico, Giambattista. *On Humanistic Education: Six Inaugural Orations, 1699–1707.* Ed. Donald Phillip Verene. Trans. G. A. Pinton and A. W. Shippe. Ithaca, NY: Cornell University Press, 1993.

Vico, Giambattista. "Oratzione in Morte Donna Angela Cimmino Marchesa Petrella," in *Opere di G. B. Vico*, ed. Fausto Nicolini. Rome: Bari Laterza, 1911–1914.

Vitanza, Victor, ed. *Writing Histories of Rhetoric.* Carbondale, IL: Southern Illinois University Press, 1994.

Vonnegut, K. S. "Listening for Women's Voices," *Communication Education* 41 (1992): 26–39.

Walker, Jeffrey. *Rhetoric and Poetics in Antiquity.* Oxford: Oxford University Press, 2000.

Walzer, Arthur. *George Campbell: Rhetoric in the Age of Enlightenment.* Albany NY: State University of New York Press, 2003.

Ward, John O. "From Antiquity to the Renaissance: Glosses and Commentaries on Cicero's Rhetorica," in *Medieval Eloquence*, ed. J. J. Murphy. Berkeley, CA: University of California Press, 1978: 25–67.

Walzer, Arthur. "Magic and Rhetoric from Antiquity to the Renaissance: Some Ruminations," *Rhetorica* 6 (1988): 57–118.

Warnick, Barbara. *The Sixth Canon: Belletristic Rhetorical Theory and Its French Antecedents.* Columbia, SC: University of South Carolina Press, 1993.

Watson, Burton. *Basic Writings of Mo Tzu, Hsun Tzu, and Han Fei Tzu.* New York: Columbia University Press, 1967.

Watson, Burton. *Visions of Order.* Baton Rouge, LA: Louisiana State University Press, 1964.

Welch, Kathleen E. *The Contemporary Reception of Classical Rhetoric: Appropriations of Ancient Discourse.* Hillsdale, NJ: Lawrence Erlbaum, 1990.

Wells, Susan. *Sweet Reason: Rhetoric and the Discourses of Modernity.* Chicago, IL: University of Chicago Press, 1996.

Wenzel, Joseph. "Three Perspectives on Argument," in *Perspectives on Argumentation: Essays in Honor of Wayne Brockriede*, eds. Robert Trapp and Janice Schuetz. Prospect Heights, IL: Waveland, 1990: 9–26.

Whately, Richard. *Elements of Rhetoric*, ed. Douglas Ehninger. 1828. Carbondale, IL: Southern Illinois University Press, 1963.

Willard, Charles Arthur. "Argumentation and Postmodern Critique," in *Perspectives on Argumentation: Essays in Honor of Wayne Brockriede, Eds. Robert Trapp and Janice Schuetz.* Prospect Heights, IL: Waveland, 1990: 221–231.

Wilson, Katharina, ed. *Women Writers of the Renaissance and Reformation.* Athens: University of Georgia Press, 1987.

Wood, Ellen Meiksins. *Peasant–Citizen and Slave: The Foundations of Athenian Democracy.* London: Verso, 1988.

Wood, Julia T. *Gendered Lives.* Belmont, CA: Wadsworth, 1994.

Woods, Marjorie Currie. "The Teaching of Writing in Medieval Europe," in *A Short History of Writing Instruction*, ed. James J. Murphy. Davis, CA: Hermagoras Press, 1990, 77–94

Index

Abbott, Don 165, 175
Aberdeen Philosophical Society 203
Academie Francaise 182
Academy of Plato 83
acting 7
Actor–Network Theory 257
acutezza 194
Addison, Joseph 197
Adorno, Theodor W. 226
advocacy 18–19, 227
Aelius Aristides 127, 128
Aeneid 154
aesthetics 15–16
affectus 172
African rhetoric 266, 282–283
Against Method 225
Agricola, Rudolph 177
Alberic 147
Alchemy 171
Alexandria 135
Al–Farabi 287
allegoria 47
Ambrose 137
Amyntas 83
analogy 206
Andalusia 286–287
Anderson, Jeffrey 11
ante rem 121
anthropology 228–229
Antidosis 52
antilogos 49
antimetabole 47

Antiphon 37, 44
antistrophos 84
antithesis 48
apologia 92
aporia 48, 58
apostrophe 47
apragmones 49
Arabic rhetoric 286–287
Archaeology of Knowledge 268, 270–271
architecture 7
archive 270
areté 40, 42, 45, 48, 51, 58, 70
argument 13–14, 206
Argumentative Hypothesis 13
argumentation 216, 217
Arguments in Rhetoric against Quintilian 179
Aristophanes 40
Aristotle 16, 43, 45, 83–101, 115, 120, 142, 145, 153, 201, 203, 286–287
Arithmetic 140
Arnhart, Larry 94
arrangement 14–15
ars dictaminis 146–152
ars poetriae 152
ars praedicandi 144
Ars Poetria 152
Ars Versificatoria 152
art 177
Art and Craft of Rhetoryke 180
Arte of Rhetorique 180
artistic proofs 93–95
Ascham, Roger 180

Index

Asia 126
Askēsis 41, 58
Aspasia 54, 56
astronomy 140, 171
asyndeton 111, 125, 176
Athens 1, 35–40, 42–43, 46, 49–50, 52–53, 56, 167, 221
Athenian Assembly 38
attention 11, 258
attributes of the act 113
attributes of the person 113
Atwill, Janet 65
audience 21, 24, 88–89, 94, 145, 217–220, 248
audience adaptation 10–11
Augustine of Hippo 135, 136–142, 205
Averroes 168, 286–287
Avignon 168
Aztec rhetoric 283

Bacon, Francis 180, 181, 203
bagre 282
Bakhtin, Mikhail 250–252, 259
Bales, Robert 255
Barbaro, Ermolao 173
Barilli, Renato 148
Barnett, Scott 257
Barron, William 200
bases 121, 123
Bazerman, Charles 226
beauty 204
belles lettres 199
Belletristic Movement 199–202, 208
Bene of Florence 148
Bernard of Chartres 143
Bernardi, Giovanni Baptista 175
Bible 166, 172
Billig, Michael 5
biography 166
Birth of the Clinic 268
Bitzer, Lloyd F. 16, 89, 203, 240, 247–248
Bizzell, Patricia 78, 146
Blair, Carole 256
Blair, Hugh 198, 199, 201–202
Blazing World 191
Boccaccio, Giovanni 164, 168
Boethius 141
Bologna 148
Boncompagno of Signa 148
Book of the City of the Ladies 170
Booth, Wayne 1, 3, 10, 251, 252–253

Bormann, Ernest 255–256
Brown University 199
boule 38, 58
Bourgeois Dignity 228
Bourgeois Equality 228
Bourgeois Virtues 228
Boyd, Brian 11, 34, 224, 253, 282
Boyle, Casey 257
brain 177
British Education 197
Brutus 111, 116
burden of proof 206–207
Burke, John G. 171
Burke, Kenneth 11, 239, 240–247, 250
Butterworth, Charles 287

Cabala 171
Caesar 118
Callicles 63, 70–72
Camargo, Martin 147
Campbell, George 189, 196, 198, 202–205, 206, 207, 208
Campbell, John A. 229–231
Campbell, Karlyn Kohrs 265, 268
Cameron, James K. 174
canons of rhetoric 110–112, 123, 180
captatio benevoluntatiae 149
Caputo, Jonathan 274
Carr, Nicholas 257–258
Carrey, Jim 7
Carthage 136, 140
Cassandra Fedele 164
Castiglioni 164, 197
Castro, Publia Hortencia de 165
Catherine of Siena 152
Cavendish, Margaret 189, 190–191, 207
cerebral cortex 177
Cereta, Laura 164
Changes of Fortune 170
character 106
Chekhov, Anton 246
Chen, Mel Y. 272
chiasmus 47, 58
Chinese rhetoric 265, 284–286
Christ 145
Christian Orator 205
Christine de Pisan 169–170
Chrysostomos 127, 128
Church of England 196
Church of Scotland 196, 202

Cicero 10, 51, 104, 105, 106, 107, 109–111, 119, 121, 126, 128, 136, 145, 166, 167, 169, 175, 177, 179, 193, 197, 201, 281

circa rem 121

circulation 257

citizen–orator 120

City of God 137, 174

civic life 37

civilization 171

Clark, Carol Lea 287

Classen, Albrecht 142

Classicism 167–168

Cleisthenes 35

Clouds of Aristophanes 40

Cmiel, Kenneth 196, 198–199

Cohen, Herman 199

coherence 254–255

College de France 268

Columbus, Christopher 163

common topics 96

communicative action 221–222

communicative competence 222

community 22–23, 227

comparative rhetoric 282–288

complexity of soul 74–75

conclusion 149

Confessions of St. Augustine 137

Conley, Thomas 127

Connolly, Joy 104, 105, 108, 113, 223

contio 106

controversia 108

conquest model 278–279

consequence 254

consistency 254

Consolation of Philosophy 141

Constantine 134

constraints 248

contingent matters 16

conventional form 246

conversational rhetoric 182

Corax/Tisias 34, 49

Cordoba 286–287

Corpus Hermeticum 171

Counter–Statement 246–247

Course of Lectures in Elocution 198

Courtier 164, 198

Covino, William 247

Cox, Leonard 180

Crassus 107

critical theory 222

Crump, James 284–286

Culler, Jonathan 274

dance 7

Dante 170

Darwin, Charles 229–231

da Vinci, Leonardo 7

Decameron 168

deconstruction 273

De Copia 175, 176

De Differentiis Topicis 141

De Disciplinis 174

De Doctrina Christiana 138

definite questions 120

definition of human 242

Defoe, Daniel 199

De Francisco, Victoria 277

De Inventione 105, 109–114, 122, 141, 167

de Laurentis, Teresa 272

delectare 116

deliberative oratory 90–91

delivery 198

Delphi 38, 45

de Meun, Jean 170

Democratic Eloquence 198

demokratia 35

Democratic National Convention 27–28

Democritus 53

demos 40, 58, 71

Demosthenes 50–52, 64, 124

De Oratore 114–118, 120, 141, 164, 177

Depew, David 232, 233

De Quincy, Thomas 16

De Ratione Dicendi 175

Derrida, Jacques 265, 272–273

de Saussure, Ferdinand 265, 267

Descartes, Rene 192

de Scudery, Madeleine 182

Detienne, Marcel 282

De Topicis Differentiis 141

de Velasco, Antonio 281

De Voluptate 172

dialectic 78, 84–85, 136, 178–180

Dialectical Disputations 172

dialektike 41, 58

dialogue 250–251

Dialogue of Divine Providence 152

Dickinson, Emily 27

dictamen 146, 147, 148

dictators 146, 148

Index

diction 196
Dictionnaire Philosophique 189
digital rhetoric 257–259
dignitas 115
dikaion 92
 dikanikon 90
dikasteria 37, 58
Di Mare, Leslie 276
Discipline and Punish 270
dissoi logoi 41–42, 49, 58
dispositio 111, 142
Dissertation on Miracles 202
docere 116
Dominicans 144
Donation of Constantine 172
Donawerth, Jane 182, 207–208
Donovan, Josephine 251
Dostoevsky, Fyodor 250, 252
doxa 66, 73
dunamis 65, 86

economics 228
economics of attention 11
Edgworth, Maria 207–208, 209
Edinburgh 196, 202
education 36–37, 40, 50–54, 56, 71, 120, 139,
    142–143, 196–197,
Egypt 171
Egyptian rhetoric 284
Ehninger, Douglas 199–200
eikos 44, 58, 72
ekklesia 38, 58
Elegancies of the Latin Language 172
Elements of Criticism 200–201
elocution 111, 172
Elocutionary Movement 198–198
eloquence 205
eloquentia 193
emotions 171
Empedocles 34, 45–46
empeiria 68
Encomium on Helen 46, 47
endoxa 41, 58, 84, 85, 121
England 180–181, 196
English 196
Enlightenment 181, 188–209, 226, 265, 273
Enos, Richard L. 33, 37, 45, 52, 72
Enquiry Concerning Human Understanding
    189
entechnoi pisteis 93

enthymeme 88–89
epoidai 71
Ephialtes 35
epideictic oratory 91–92
epideixis 42, 58, 92
episteme 65, 66
Erasmus 166, 172, 175
ergon 66
eristic 33, 58
escape 269
Essay Concerning Human Understanding 2,
    189
ethics 24, 203
ethos 93, 95, 115
eunoia 95
eudaimonia 91, 96
evolution 230–231
examples 124
excluded discourse 271
exigence 247
existimatio 115
exordium 122, 150

Fables of Marie de France 156
Facebook 257
facetiae 117
fact/ facts 20–21, 254
faculty psychology 204
Fahnestock, Jeanne 229
Fakhri, Majid 168, 287
fallacies 97–98
fantasia 193, 194, 195
"Fantasy and Rhetorical Vision" 255–256
fantasy theme 255
fantasy type 255
Farrell, Thomas 16, 241
Faulhaber, Charles 148, 150
feminism 265, 272, 275–283
Feyerabend, Paul 225
Ficino, Marsilio 171, 192
fiction 252–253
fidelity 254
figures of speech 125, 176
Fisher, Walter 253–254
fitting response 248–249
Five Books of Rhetoric 167
Fleckenstein, Kristie 152
Fleming, Marie 223
Florence 164, 165
florilegia 166

Ford, Andrew 43, 50
forensic oratory 92–93
form 246
Forma Praedicandi 144, 145
Fortenbaugh, W. W. 94
Foss, Sonja 276, 280
Foucault, Michel 265, 268–271
Fox, Michael 289
Franciscans 144
Fuhrmann, Manfred 104
Fultner, Barbara 221

Gadamer, Hans–George 195
Gagarin, Michael 37, 39, 40
Gallo, Ernest 154
game 269
Gaonkar, Dilip 231
Garden of Eloquence 181
Garin, Euginio 169
Gearhart, Sally Miller 278–279
Geertz, Clifford 229
Geoffrey of Vinsauf 152, 153–154, 155
gender 278
generalized symmetry 257
George of Trebizond 167
Gervais of Melkley 152
gesture 198
Gilbert, Katherine 194
Glenn, Cheryl 54
gnorimoi 40, 58
Goldin, Paul Rakita 285
Gorgias 16, 36, 39, 43–51, 64–67, 70, 72, 98,
     208
Gorgias of Plato 2, 41, 43, 63, 64–73, 78, 84, 110,
     115, 219
grammar 140, 267
Grammar of Motives 241, 243
Grammar of Rhetoric and Polite Literature 200
Grassi, Ernesto 154, 193
Gravity 7
Greek/Greeks 33–56, 128, 258, 288
Gregory 152
Griffin, Cindy 280
Gronbeck, Bruce 45
Gross, Alan 233
Groups 255
Grube, G. M. A. 47, 76, 108–109, 122, 126
Guido Faba 146, 148
Gutenberg 148, 163
gymnastics 69

Habermas, Jürgen 216, 220–223, 274–275
Habicht, Christian 136
Han Feitzu 284
Hamer, Mrs. Fannie Lou 27–29
Harmonics 140
Harvey, Gabriel 180
Hasting, Rebecca 19
Hazzard, Paul 194
hedone 70
Heloise 143
Hermannus of Alemannus 135
Hermagoras of Temnos 120
hermeneutics 166
Hermes 171
hero of knowledge 267
Herzberg, Bruce 78, 146
hetaera 54, 56, 58
heteroglossia 252
heuristic 33, 58
Hieron 34
Hilda of Whitby 143
Hildegard of Bingen 143
Himba of Nigeria 282
Hippias 36, 39, 43
Hippo 137
History of Rome 169
History of Sexuality 268
Hobbes, Thomas 191, 203
Holquist, Michael 250
Holocaust 226
Holocaust Museum 15
Homer 33–34, 44
hooks, bell 281–282
Hook, Sidney 240
Horkheimer, Max 226
Horner, Winfred 196
Howell, Wilbur Samuel 195, 204
Hrotsvitha 143
Humanism 165–175, 189
Hume, David 189, 203, 265
humor 116–117
hypallage 47
hypsos 124

Ibn Rushd 168, 286–287
ideal speech community 220
identification 11, 240–241
ideology 222–223, 250
imagination 192–193, 195, 204
imitation 117

Index

indefinite questions 120
ingenium 192
Inquisition 174
in re 121
inside jokes 255
Institutes of Dialectic 179
Institutes of Oratory 119–122, 135, 167
Intrigues of the Warring States 285
inventio/ invention 110, 111
invitational rhetoric 280
*ioci/*jokes 117
Ireland 196
irony 194
isegoria 35, 106
Isocrates 33, 49, 51–52, 54, 78, 175
Italy 146, 165–166, 178

Jameison, Alexander 200
Jarratt, Susan 37, 42–43, 54
Jaws 7
Jensen, Marvin 277
Jesus 47
jian shi 286
John of Salisbury 143
Johnson, W. R. 139
judicial speech 122
justice 69
Justice 218–219

kairos *41–42, 48, 58, 73*
Kames, Lord 200–201, 208
Kant, Immanuel 265
kategoria 92
Katula, Richard 44
Kelley, Donald R. 173
Kennedy, John F. 47, 247
Kennedy, George 6, 45, 46, 127, 134, 149, 170, 180,
        203, 279, 283–284 288
Kerscher, Gesa 276
Kersey, Shirley 142
King, Rev. Martin Luther, Jr. 15, 22–23, 92, 246
Kings of Shou 286
Kinneavy, James L. 239
Kitto, H. D. F 35
knowledge 21–22, 269
koinoi topoi 96–97
Kristeller, Paul Oskar 146, 167, 171
krites 90
Kuhn, Helmut 194
Kuhn, Thomas 224

Labe, Louise 64
Lacan, Jacques 265
Lais of Marie de France 156
Lanham, Richard 3, 11, 177, 180
Latin 128, 170
Latour, Bruno 257
Lectures on Pulpit Eloquence 204
Lectures on Belles Lettres and Logic 200
Lectures on Rhetoric and Belles Lettres 199–201
Lee, Spike 18
Leff, Michael 50, 114, 121, 240
Lesbos 55
Les Femmes Illustres 182
letter writing 144, 146–150
Levi–Strauss, Claude 265, 267
liberal arts 140
Lincoln, Abraham 15, 246
literacy 3, 143
Liu Xiang 285
Livy 106, 169
loci 113–114, 121, 123
Locke, John 2, 3, 181, 189, 202
Lo Dagaa 282
logic 136, 140, 178
logical positivism 215
logic of reason 253
logographer 37
logographos 38, 50, 58
logos/ logoi 44–47, 49, 58, 64, 65, 76, 77,93
logos politikos 50
Longinus 108, 122–126, 128, 201, 208
love 77
Lunsford, Andrea 3, 258–259
Lure of Technology 221
Lu, Xing 286
Lyne, John 226, 227–228, 232
Lyotard, Jean–Francois 267–268
Lysias 74

Mack, Peter 172, 175
Madness and Civilization 268, 269
magic 171–172, 181, 247
Mailloux, Steven 9, 27
Malcolm X 15
Mali, Joseph 194
Malthus, Thomas Robert 230
Manichaeans 136
Mann, Nicholas 147, 168
Mao, LuMing 282
Marie de France 143, 155–156

Marischal College 202
Marlowe, Christopher 171
Marriage of Philology and Mercury 140
Martianus Capella 140, 143
Martines, Lauro 165–166
Marxism 220, 250
Materialism 257
Matthew of Vendome 152
McCarthy, Thomas 221, 222–223
McCloskey, Deirdre 4, 5, 228
McConnell–Ginet, Sally 277
McKeon, Richard 3
McKerrow, Ray 205
meaning 273–274
medicine 5
meletē 41, 58
memoria/ memory 111–112
Menexenus of Plato 54
Mercier, Hugo 13
metanarrative 267
metaphor 98, 176, 194
metoikoi 35, 58
metonym 176, 194
Middle Ages 134–157, 167, 168
Midgley, Mary 215, 225
Milan 136
Miller, Diane Helene 280–281
mimesis 287
Mirandola, Pico della 171, 173, 192
modus inveniendi 139
modus proferendi 139
Mohrmann, G. P. 197
Moline, Jon 77
Monte Casino 147
Mooney, Michael 174
Moscovici, Claudia 267
Moss, Jessica 65
motives 11–12
movere 116
muhakat 287
Munch, Edvard 7
Murphy, James J. 6, 44, 144, 153, 156, 167
music 6–7
myth 194–195, 225, 267–268
mythos/logos 195
myth of charioteer 74, 75

Naples 191
narration 122, 149
narration 249–257

narrative paradigm 254–255
natural selection 230
Nauert, Charles R. 142, 166, 167, 169, 178
Neoplatonism 168, 171–172
New Rhetoric 216–220
New Science 193–194
Newton, Sir Isaac 189
Nietzsche, Friedrich 2, 55, 265
Nizzolio, Mario 168
nomos 44, 58, 70–71
notaries 166–167
Nyad, Diana 8

Obama, Barack 246
Ober, Josiah 35, 64, 67
Of Grammatology 272
Olbrechts–Tyteca, L. 216–220, 232
Olson, Lester 256
On Christian Doctrine 135
On Dialectical Invention 178
Ong, Rory 37, 42, 54
Ong, Walter J. 78
On the Crown 64
On the Study Methods of our Time 192
On the Sublime 122–126
Oration on the Dignity of Man 171
Order of Things 268
organizational sagas 255
ornaments 175
Ovid 154, 155, 191

Padua 164
paideia 40, 59
Panegyricus 51
panopticism 269
paradeigma 88
paralepsis 176
parisosis 47
parody 207
Pascal 243
passions 204
pathologia 172
pathos 93–94, 95, 125
Paul the Apostle 139, 145
pentad 243–244
Peitho 34, 45, 59
Perelman, Chaim 216–220, 232
perfectus orator 114–115, 197
Pericles 35, 49, 54, 56
peroration 122

Personal Knowledge 224
perspicuity 202
persuasion 4–6, 87, 204–205
petitio 149
petits recits 267
Petrarch, Francesco 168–169, 178
Phaedrus 63, 73–79, 137, 208, 249
Philip of Macedon 52
Philosophy of Literary Form 247
Philosophy of Rhetoric 203, 207,
phronesis 95, 255
physis 41, 44, 59, 87
pistis 66
Plataeicus 51
Plato 1, 39, 41–43, 46, 49–51, 54, 55, 63–79, 115,
    124, 127, 137, 168, 208
Plutarch 42, 53, 54
Poetics 85, 98, 168
poetic speech 192
 Poetria Nova 153–154
poetry 144
poets 194
poieses 66
Polanyi, Michael 224
polis 35–37, 39–40, 50, 53, 59, 69, 70, 77, 88, 95, 98
politics 251
Polus 39, 67–70
polyphonic novel 251–252
polysyndeton 111, 176
Pompey 107
Popper, Karl 225
Poster, Carol 147
Postmodern Condition 267
postmodernism 265
post rem 121
posture 198
Poulakos, John 35, 41, 44, 49, 51
power 19–20, 23–24, 67, 105, 122, 268–269, 272
practical wisdom 255
preaching 137–138, 144–145, 198
preferable, the 217
Prelli, Lawrence 177, 256
Presence 220
presumption 206
prima facie case 207
Principles of Letter Writing 149
private speaking 284–285
pronuntiatio 111
proof 123
prosopopoeial 176

Protagoras 36, 39, 41, 43–45, 48–50, 56
Protagoras of Plato 43
protreptic function of language 33, 59
prudence 193
psychagogas/ psychagogia 45, 59, 76
public 196–197
public sphere 222
Pythagoras 46
Pythia 38, 59

quadrivium 140
quaestiones 142
Queer Theory 271
"Queer Theory: Lesbian and Gay Sexualities"
    272
questions, definite and indefinite 123
Quintilian 104, 118–122, 128, 135, 167, 172, 179,
    201, 203

Rabelais 250
Racevskis, Karlis 269
Radigund 143
Ramus, Peter 179–180, 189
Rankin, H. D. 37, 42
ratio/oratio 174
rationalism/mysticism 287
ratios of terms 245
real, the 217
reason 204
Records of the Grand Masters 284
Redfern, Jenny 170
(re)inscription 276
relevance 254
Renaissance 163–181, 287
Renfrew, Alastair 250
repetitive form 24
Republic 74
res gestae 115
res publica 106, 115
res/verba 173
rhetor 9
Rhetor 180
rhetoric: and persuasion 13–16; as responsive
    12–13; as woman 140; defining 6–9, 84–85;
    social functions of 17–23;
rhetorical discourse 9–17
Rhetorica ad Herennium 109, 122, 135, 141, 168
Rhetoricae 174
"The Rhetorical Situation" 247–248
Rhetoric as Narration 253–254

rhetoric as narrative 249–257
Rhetoric of Aristotle 83–101, 135, 248
rhetoric of display 256–257
Rhetoric of Fiction 252–253
Rhetoric of Motives 240
rhetoric of science 223–232
rhetorike 65
Richardson, Malcolm 150
Richardson, Samuel 199
Robert of Basevorn 144, 145, 153
Roche, Madeline and Catherine de 164
Roman education 108
Roman law 111, 166
Roman Senate 106–107
Romance of the Rose 170
Rome 104–131, 167, 169
Romilly, Jacqueline de 36, 46, 47, 56, 73
Rousseau, Jean–Jacques 189
Royal Society 181
Royster, Jacqueline 276

St. Patrick's Purgatory *156*
Salutati, Coluccio 163
salutatio 149
sapientia *193*
Sappho 38, 54–56, 124
Sawicki, Jana 276
Scholasticism 142, 175
Schoolemaster, The 180
science 181, 205
Science in a Free Society 225
Scottish School 198–199
Scotland 196
Second Inaugural Address of Lincoln 15, 26–27
Second Sophistic 126–127, 136
Seigel, Jerrold 173
self 272
self as audience 219–220
senatus 106
Seneca 166
sensus communes 115, 192, 193, 195
sententiae 142, 166
sermons 144–145
Seville 286
Shakespeare, William 47–48, 171, 180, 200
Shallows, The 257
Sheridan, Thomas 197–198, 208
Sherry, Richard 180
Shirky, Clay 258
Shumway, David R. 269

Sicily 34, 49
signs 139
Simons, Herbert 224, 227
situation 247–248
Sloane, Thomas O. 175
Smith, Adam 196, 198
Social Contract 189
society 25
Socrates 1, 39, 40, 49, 54, 56, 63, 64–73, 249
Solon 35, 55
Sophist of Plato 43
Sophists 16, 34–56, 59, 115, 127
sophos 38
Spain 119, 168, 175, 286
Sparta 36, 53, 56
special topics 96
speech 174
Speech and Phenomena 272
Sperber, Dan 13
Spielberg, Steven 18
Spitzer, Adele 67, 70
Sports 8
Sprezzatura 164
Stanford Study of Writing 258
stasis system 112–113, 123
Steele, Richard 197
Strini, Tom 14
Structuralism 267
"Structural Study of Myth" 267
Structural Transformation of the Public Sphere
    220
The Structure of Scientific Revolutions 224
Stark, Ryan J. 181
stravagante 192
studia humanitatis 165
style 98, 122, 181, 191, 202
sublimity 124
suasoria 108, 285
"Success is Counted Sweetest" 27
Summa Dictaminis 148
surveillance 269
Sutton, Jane 44, 90
Swearingen, C. Jan 53
Swift, Jonathan 197
syllogistic form 246
symbolic action 241
symbolic convergence 255
symbolic inducement 241–242
symbouleutikon 90
synecdoche 176, 194

Index

taste 201
technai 68, 86, 108
technē 41, 59, 65, 84, 111, 145
terministic screens 242–243
themes 144
Theodorus 39
theology 203
Theory of Communicative Action 220
Thesaurus Rhetoricae 175
Thesmos 44, 59
Thompson, Clive 258
Thoth 171, 249
thought 193
thymos 89
Tompkins, Jane 122
Toga 119
Topica 113
topical systems 123
Topics of Aristotle 84, 85
topoi 42, 96–97, 113, 179, 193, 285
Toward a Rational Society 220
transcendent issue 254
Treasure of the City of the Ladies 170
Treatise of Schemes and Tropes 180
trivium 140
tropes 194
Tropics of Discourse 195
Troup, Calvin 108, 136, 137
truth 24, 78
typeface 8

umanista *165–166*
universal audience 217, 218–219
University of Utah 11
University of Wisconsin 247
utterance 251
Utz, Richard 147

Valla, Lorenzo 166, 172
Values 221
Vandals 137
Van Maanen, John 228–229
Vaz, Joanna 164
Verene, Donald Philip 195

Vickers, Brian 72, 122, 125, 150, 153, 154, 163, 164, 173
Vico, Giovanni Battista 189, 191–195, 204, 207, 208, 253
Victorinus 135
Vietnam Memorial 7–8
Virgil 154, 166
Vision of Christine 170
vita activa *172–173*
vita contemplativa 173
Vives, Juan Luis 164, 174–175
voice 274
Voltaire 189, 265

Wallace, Karl 253
Wallace–Hadrill, A. 119
Walker, Jeffrey 91–92, 99
Walsh, Lynda 38
Wang, Bo 282
Ward, John O. 139, 144, 157
Warnick, Barbara 189, 204
Welch, Kathleen 135
Wells, Susan 221, 226, 249
Whately, Richard 205–206, 208, 215
White, Hayden 195
will 204
Willard, Charles 226
William of Moerbeke 135
Wilson, E. O. 177
Wilson, Katharina 164
wisdom and eloquence 114–115, 128, 178
wit 194
women and education 142, 164
women and letter writing 150–152
Wood, Ellen 53
Wood, Julia T. 278
Woods, Marjory Curry 143
World's Olio 191
worldviews 244–245
World War II 215, 220
World Wide Web 258
writing 78, 126, 258–259
Writing and Difference 272

Xenophon 42